ADVENTURE GUIDE
TO THE
SOUTH PACIFIC

Thomas H. Booth

ADVENTURE GUIDE TO THE SOUTH PACIFIC

Thomas H. Booth

Hunter Publishing, Inc.
300 Raritan Center Parkway
Edison NJ 08818
(201) 225 1900

ISBN 1-55650–108–0

Second Edition 1990

Printed in Singapore through Palace Press

Cover photograph: "Return to Paradise" Beach, Western Samoa

Published in the UK by:
Moorland Publishing Co. Ltd.
Moor Farm Road, Airfield Estate
Ashbourne, Derbyshire DE6 1HD
England

UK ISBN 0–86190–247–5

Photo Credits

George Climo: 5, 20, 35. Cook Islands Visitor's Bureau: 45, 60, 64.
Tonga Visitor's Bureau: 84, 91. Gary Beckman: 93. Fiji Visitor's Bureau: 171. Vanuatu Visitor's Bureau: 286, 326. Guam Visitor's Bureau: 390, 391, 398, 401, 407, 410, 415. Thomas H. Booth: all others.

Acknowledgements

We hope the following people and organizations realize how much we
value their assistance and encouragement. Our debt to them extends
across the Pacific and back again. We thank them again here.
Stephen Boyle and the Kaimana Beach Hotel in Honolulu; Air Mi-
cronesia of Continental Airlines; Hawaiian Airlines and Elliot
Pulham; John Grey of Pacific Outdoor Adventures in Honolulu; South
Pacific Island Airways; Air Rarotonga and Ewing Smith in the Cook
Islands; Tahiti's Air Polynesie; Western Samoa's Polynesian Airlines;
Aggie Grey, her son Alan and their hospitable Aggie Grey's Hotel;
Mr. and Mrs. Kurt Von Reiche of Western Samoa; Fiji Air in Suva,
Fiji; Air Pacific in Suva, Fiji; Tonga's Friendly Islands Airways and
pilot Bill Johns; Air Caledonie in Nouméa, New Caledonia; Va-
nuatu's Air Melanesia; The Solomon Islands Airline, Solair; Jan and
Peter Barter of New Guinea's *Melanesian Explorer;* New Guinea's Air
Niugini; Gail Norris of Eugene, Oregon's "Adventure in Travel
Agency"; Rick Reed, artist, University of Oregon, Eugene, for the
maps.

CONTENTS

INTRODUCTION

Most atlases concentrate on the large land masses around the Pacific Rim and give short shrift to the thousands of islands scattered across the Pacific. Only the mounted globe on its pedestal gives a clear impression of the enormous size of this area. Even then you've got to have sharp eyes and a good light to find the Cooks, Tonga, Vanuatu, and the Solomons, to say nothing of Kapingamarangi, Mauke, Funafuti, or the Trobriands.

There are, of course, such well-known tourist destinations as Hawaii, Tahiti, Fiji, and perhaps New Caledonia. Most of the other islands, if their names are known at all, are seen as virtually inaccessible to all but the most dedicated adventurer. Even the most experienced independent travelers interested in the rich variety of island cultures have been a little skeptical about setting out for the Solomons, Micronesia, Tonga, or Papua New Guinea.

But this is changing, and we hope this book makes it clear that the islands of the Pacific—Polynesia, Melanesia, and Micronesia—are comfortably accessible. Major airlines go to the administrative centers of nearly all these groups and, once there, domestic sea and air services open up the most remote outer areas.

Facilities range from acceptable to excellent, people are friendly, English is widely spoken and, other than malaria in parts of Melanesia (preventable by prophylactic medication), there are few health problems. Happily too, the US dollar remains reasonably strong against most island currencies and, except for French Polynesia or perhaps New Caledonia, there are surprising travel bargains in the Pacific.

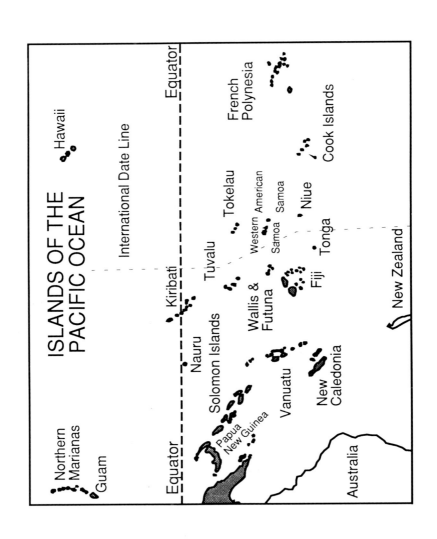

ISLANDS OF THE PACIFIC OCEAN

Equator

International Date Line

Equator

Northern Marianas

Guam

Hawaii

Kiribati

Nauru

Solomon Islands

Tuvalu

Tokelau

French Polynesia

Cook Islands

Western Samoa

American Samoa

Niue

Wallis & Futuna

Fiji

Tonga

Vanuatu

New Caledonia

Papua New Guinea

Australia

New Zealand

Money Matters

The US dollar is the most easily converted currency in the world, whether in cash or traveler's check. And you'll be surprised at how many places off the beaten path will quickly accept credit cards. In reporting prices, we consider the current exchange rate and quote costs in US dollars.

Getting There

By Sea—There is nothing quite like standing on the deck of a ship watching your first Pacific island change from a smudge on the horizon to solid reality. Unfortunately, if cruise ships aren't for you, you'll find that getting passage on a freighter is difficult. Most freight lines would rather load on a few more containers and forget about passengers. The only ships which may still carry passengers into the further reaches of the Pacific are the British Banks Line and a few French cargo vessels that call at East Coast US ports before heading for the South Pacific via Panama. From Japan, Carolineship and Tiger Lines go into Micronesia (see the chapter on Micronesia).

There are travel agencies specializing in this sort of sea venture. Try: Pearl's Freighter Tips, 175 Great Neck Rd., Suite 306F, Great Neck, NY 11021. On the West Coast try: Maggi Horn, 601 California Street, San Francisco, CA 94108.

Then of course there are berths on private yachts and, judging from the number of yachts seen all over the Pacific, a chance to crew is a possibility. You've got to have plenty of time, though, and a modicum of experience to become a share-expense crew member. To further this possibility, read the "classifieds" in yachting magazines, and visit the big yacht clubs on the West Coast—particularly in Hawaii.

By Air—First do some homework on the places you want to go, then choose a travel agent not preoccupied with cruises and collective touring. Find someone patient and tolerant enough to get the best deals on Advance Purchase Tickets, Circle Pacific Tickets (which allow multiple stopovers) or Seasonal Round Trip Economy Fares. A good agent can do all this, plus take advantage of current airline price wars, and can help you with such technical questions as minimum stopover clauses and bargain seats that are rarely available.

Consider starting from Hawaii. Get the first scent of the tropics in Honolulu. Prepare yourself for the deep Pacific by visiting the Polynesian Cultural Center and the Bishop Museum. Then, because Hawaii is the "Gateway to the Pacific," check out the travel options from there.

In Hawaii if you go to Hawaiian Airlines with Tonga and both Samoas in mind, or visit Continental's Air Micronesia for travel to Micronesia, you may pick up the low fare tickets that returning islanders get.

For other destinations, and especially for complicated multiple-stopovers, a well-chosen travel agent at home is best.

World War II and the Navy ship USS Acontius first brought me to the Pacific islands. It was, however, not a time of sloth, languid days at sea, or idly wandering the beaches. But I saw my first coconut palm then, I saw islanders with bones in their noses, and reefs with water clear as gin. It was heady stuff and I was profoundly affected.

Since then Virginia and I have been back 10 times and I'm still deeply affected. I'm a little more discriminating though and some islands, like human beings, are more appealing than others. Still they're all old friends, and we'd like to make some of them yours.

Tom and Virginia Booth

1

FRENCH POLYNESIA

TAHITI

Tahiti is one of the Society Islands which, with the Gambiers, the Tuamotus, the Australs, and the Marquesas, make up French Polynesia. This archipelago spread out over several million miles of the south central Pacific is a mixture of high volcanic islands and low coral atolls.

Tahiti, the biggest island in French Polynesia, has the most magical name in the South Pacific and with good reason. Papeete, her principal port, shares this distinction and for years Tahiti has been considered an island where land and sea are bountiful, the girls sensual, and the French administration casually tolerant.

All sorts of people have been attracted to Tahiti—drifters, yachtsmen, writers, artists, explorers—legions of them whose names span more than 200 years. There were Captains Cook, Bougainville, and Bligh; the artists Gauguin and Matisse; Thor Heyerdahl; and writers Nordhoff and Hall, Frisbie, O'Brien, Stevenson, Loti, Brooke and Maugham. There were scores of sturdy yachtsmen, and they still come. But Tahiti is not what it once was.

The change was inevitable. An island that beautiful becomes a magnet. And when an international airport was constructed in 1959, the tourists poured in by the thousands. Now on Bora Bora, Moorea and Tahiti there are big hotels, condominiums, expensive restaurants, cruise ships, and with all the

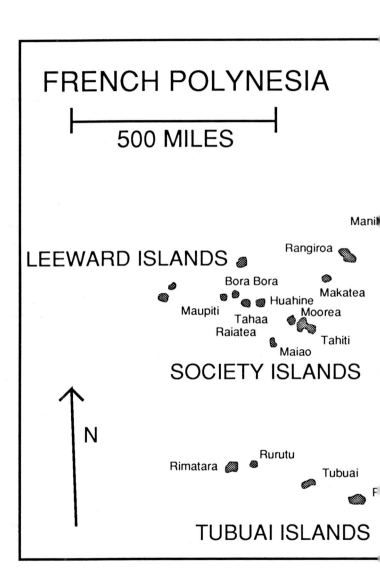

FRENCH POLYNESIA

|————————————————|
500 MILES

Mani

LEEWARD ISLANDS

Rangiroa

Bora Bora

Makatea

Huahine

Maupiti

Moorea

Tahaa

Raiatea

Tahiti

Maiao

SOCIETY ISLANDS

N

Rurutu

Rimatara

Tubuai

TUBUAI ISLANDS

Eiao

Nuku Hiva   Ua Huka

Ua Pou   Hivaoa

Fatu-Hiva

MARQUESAS ISLANDS

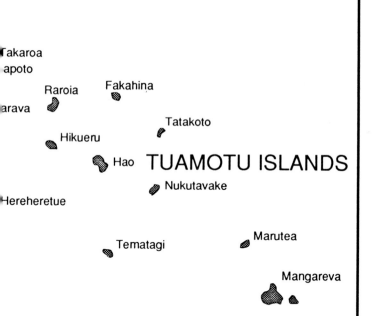

Takaroa

apoto

Raroia   Fakahina

arava

Tatakoto

Hikueru

Hao   TUAMOTU ISLANDS

Nukutavake

Hereheretue

Tematagi   Marutea

Mangareva

GAMBIER ISLANDS

metropolitan implications, Papeete with a population of 80,000 is a city. But Tahiti's burgeoning isn't all born of the tourist industry. There's another reason. The French are conducting nuclear tests on the nearby Tuamotan atoll of Mururoa. To administer such activities 25,000 Frenchmen have arrived, and have brought Parisian style and Parisian economy. Then too, there are the French Navy and elements of the Foreign Legion, to say nothing of their dependents.

Because of the testing, harmony in the Pacific has suffered. New Zealand and Australia aren't enthusiastic, and there are even some French in Tahiti who protest and claim deteriorating health for nearby Polynesians. Greenpeace has been heard of in this area too. Their ship was even sunk in New Zealand, and one of the crew killed by "dirty trick" specialists from France.

The testing continues though. France says it's her territory and of no concern to New Zealand, Australia, the United States, and most certainly not to Greenpeace. The only folks not mentioned are the Polynesians who live there. In spite of all this, the beauty of Tahiti and her adjacent islands is undisputed, and Papeete with its verve is a town to behold.

But, for those of us who cling to the purity of "free and independent travel," French Polynesia poses some problems. Arrival at Faaa International Airport will require a $10 taxi ride into Papeete, four miles away. Hotels will run from "cheapies" of $60 to $375—plus 7% tax. And a cold beer in the sleaziest of bars is at least $4. Expect to pay about $10 for a continental breakfast, $15 for lunch, and $30 for dinner with wine, per person.

Everything is expensive in Tahiti, and there is no way I can think of to remain an individual traveler and not spend a bundle. So I reluctantly defer to the pre-planned, pre-purchased tour. Why bother trying to find adventure on your own when you see ads that promise, "A week in solitary, $798. Escape from crowds and traffic. Escape for a week to Tahiti. Where the world leaves you alone. Catch a UTA flight from Los Angeles and you'll be in Tahiti in 7 1/2 hours. $798 includes round trip airfare, and six nights land arrangements

per person, double occupancy." Or, "9 days, 3 islands—Tahiti, Bora Bora, Moorea in top hotels $1798 per person."

On the other hand, and with high adventure in mind, fire off some letters to shipping agencies in Papeete and ask about trading vessel voyages to the Marquesas and Tuamotus. Then time yourself to a couple of days in Papeete before pushing off to the remote non-tourist areas. More about this under "Outer Islands."

History in Brief

French Polynesia extends over such a large area that it took several explorers many years to chart all 130 of her islands. The English sailor Captain Wallace was first. He landed in 1767. Captain Bougainville, a Frenchman, followed in 1768. Then in 1769 Captain Cook arrived with the express purpose of observing the transit of the planet Venus. The site of that observation, now called Point Venus, is a worthwhile round-island trip destination.

In 1788 Captain Bligh of the *Bounty* appeared. His mission was to gather breadfruit trees for planting in the Caribbean but, because of the well known mutiny, that mission failed.

In the years before and after those early explorers, Tahiti was ruled by a succession of Kings and Queens. In 1880 the last monarch, King Pomare, abdicated, and the archipelago became French Polynesia. Then in 1957 French Polynesia was made a French Overseas Territory and the Polynesians were given all the rights of French citizens.

Perhaps one of the biggest milestones in the island's history was the construction of Faaa International Airport in 1959. That year tourists arrived in force and have increased in number every year since then.

Now, after 144 years of French rule, the old question of independence for French Polynesia is raised. Both Frenchmen and islanders have been predicting it for years. But now advocates for independence refuse to discuss the subject without demanding that France halt nuclear testing. France shows no intentions of stopping, claiming that testing is vital to its security. They insist that it's their business, and that Mururoa atoll is as French as Hawaii is American. Independence for the time being is "on hold."

How to Get There By Air

Tahiti is so remote that a flight from anywhere—Los Angeles, South America, Japan, Australia, or Honolulu—is expensive. But $700 is a realistic round-trip fare from Los Angeles. UTA, the French Airline, makes this run, as does Continental, Air New Zealand, and Qantas. Air France has several flights a week. Check into a "Circle Pacific" ticket. It may be possible to do not only Tahiti, but New Zealand, Australia, Fiji, the Cooks, and Samoa for not much more than $800.

South Pacific Island Airways—This airline has had off-again-on-again services from Honolulu to Tahiti via Rarotonga in the Cook Islands, then direct to Honolulu for about $725. Check with them; they may by flying again.

Coming from Australia—Depending on the season (low, shoulder, or high) you can make a stopover in Tahiti en route to Los Angeles with UTA or Qantas for $800 to $1200 round trip. With an Air New Zealand Circle Pacific ticket you can fly from New Zealand to LA round trip with a Tahiti stopover for about $900.

Coming from South America—LAN the Chilean Airline flies to Tahiti via Easter Island for an excursion fare of $1400 round trip.

Tahiti airfares are seasonal, with the dry season and higher fares from May to October. Visit your travel agent and ask what new and astounding values they're offering.

By Sea

It's the same old story. Freighters hardly exist, and unless you're cruise ship material, forget getting to Tahiti by sea. The only exception is by yacht. Their numbers are impressive, and they've all got to have crew. Check at the big yacht harbors or clubs in San Francisco, Los Angeles, and Honolulu for share-expense possibilities.

Two popular cruise ships, *Majestic Explorer* and *Windsong,* visit the main Society Islands—Huahine, Raiatea, Tahaa, Bora

Bora and Moorea. *Windsong* carries 150 passengers. It sails from Papeete Friday nights and returns seven days later. Fare in twin cabin is $2895 per person. *Majestic Explorer* carries 88 passengers and offers a similar schedule.

Immigration Formalities

French Polynesia's response to recent terrorist activities in Europe was to require non-French to have a visa. This requirement may not last, but don't attempt a trip without inquiring. US citizens can stay for up to 30 days, and extensions are easily obtained. They must also have adequate funds for living, and onward or round-trip tickets.

Currency

The currency used in French Polynesia is the French Pacific franc, the same currency used thousands of miles away in New Caledonia. The franc note comes in denominations of 500,

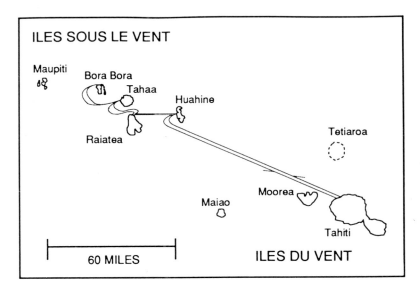

Sea routes in the Society Islands

1000, and 5000. Coins are in 100, 50, 25, 10, 5, 2, and 1 franc denominations.
At this time the American dollar is worth 118 francs.
Travelers checks are easily cashed and Visa and American Express cards are widely accepted. Tipping in French Polynesia is not necessary, but it is cheerfully accepted.

Economy

The key industry is tourism. The prime attraction is the city of Papeete which, with its modern hotels, bars, auditoriums, restaurants and night life, has become a "convention city." Agriculture is second, and the products of the coconut (copra) are the most important. Vanilla, coffee and cultured pearls contribute too.

Then there is the money pumped into the economy by the French Government. A lot of it goes to the military and to nuclear testing, but it filters down nicely, and with it Polynesians are buying TVs, motorcycles, autos, and the latest designer clothes. Thanks to the Chinese, who run most of the shops, the money circulates merrily.

Time Zone

French Polynesia is 10 hours behind Greenwich Mean Time, six hours behind Eastern Standard time, two hours behind Pacific Standard Time.

Power

The electric power is 220 AC. If you're an American accustomed to 110 AC, you should bring a converter and plug adaptor.

Newspapers, Radio, TV and Telephone

There are three daily papers in French and one in English. There is TV, with occasional English broadcasts. Radio Tahiti broadcasts the morning news in English six days a week. Make long-distance calls from the Post Office.

Health

There are no particular problems. Water in most areas is safe but, if there's any question, Hinano beer and bottled water are always available. There's no malaria on any of the islands but, even here in paradise, particularly in Papeete, there is VD.

Treat the sun with respect, carry a good sunscreen and, as anywhere in the tropics, be careful of coral cuts and abrasions. They heal slowly.

Treat buffet-style foods with caution as food left on display in the open spoils quickly.

Medical facilities and pharmacies are of international standard.

Language

If you know a little French, even simple market French, French Polynesia will be a happier place for you. But nearly everyone who serves tourists will speak some English. Tahitian Polynesian is the other official language.

What to Wear

Comfortable informality is in order and, for simplicity, light washable clothes are best. You'll notice that the Tahitians, especially the women, are stylish. They're chic whether they're wearing tight jeans or the wraparound pareu.

Clothing restrictions found on other island groups do not apply in most of French Polynesia. Even topless bathing is permitted in most areas.

Then there's the matter of the Tiare Tahiti flower. This flower, with its six to eight petals, opens up between noon and 2 PM and therefore is called "nature's timepiece." But the way it's worn is more important. A flower behind the right ear means "I am available and looking." Behind the left ear means "I am taken," and behind both ears says "I am taken, but still available."

Holidays

New Year's Day, Good Friday, May Day, Christmas, Armistice Day (November 11) are the usual holidays. But the biggest event of the year is July 14, Bastille Day. This is celebrated for at least five days with music, dancing, and merrymaking. Chinese New Year is an important event too, and there are a number of non-holiday fete days such as "Night of the Guitar," "Ancient Tahiti Ball," and "The Day of the Tiare Flower."

Where to Stay in Papeete and Suburbs

Accommodations range from moderately expensive to ultra-expensive, and there is a 7% tax.

Hotel Pacific—Class B, it's right in town with view of the harbor. Each room has its own balcony. The rooftop restaurant has the best view in town. Its night club, the Laserium, is popular for tourists and locals. Rates are $65 a double.

Ibis Papeete—Class B, and it's even more in the center of town, just around the corner from the market and bus station. Its Terrace Bar is pleasant and there are good shops to left and right. $90 a double.

Sofitel Maeva Beach—Deluxe Class, it's five miles west of town just past the airport. This hotel has everything: fine beach, all water sports, dining rooms, bars, boutiques, and full convention facilities. At seven stories, it apparently violates the old rule that such buildings were to be lower than the tallest palm tree. $170 to $214 a double.

The Tahiti Beachcomber—Deluxe Class, it's in the same area, 4.4 miles west of town and a mile from the airport. This opulent hotel has all amenities including overwater bungalows and convention possibilities. It's in the $200 range for a double.

Te Puna Bel Air—Class B, 4.7 miles west of town, and next door to the Maeva. It has 76 units set in tropical foliage on the sea, with a pool and an excellent dining room. We've stayed there and liked it. $80 a double.

The Tahara'a—Deluxe Class, away from town and six miles to the east. Its dramatic terracing provides ocean views of Matavai Bay. Everything is available: convention facilities, trap shooting, terrace-top swimming and tennis. $200 a double.

Royal Papeete—Class B, and in the center of town. With its colonial facade, this hotel has long been a landmark. It has a good dining room and the La Cave night club, one of the most active after dark spots. We stayed there too and liked it. $60 to $85 a double.

The above listed hotels are approved by the Tahiti Tourist Board. The following establishments are much cheaper and are not endorsed by the Tourist Board.

Hotel Mahina Tea—In town. $30 to $40 a double. Check with them my mail. Write: PO Box 17, Papeete, Tahiti.

Fare Oviri—Rates at this budget inn are about $40 per week. Write: PO Box 3486, Papeete, Tahiti.

The Papeete Youth Hostel—Located at the western end of town near the waterfront. About $12 per person.

Dining

The list of possibilities is a long one, the restaurants are well publicized, and they are not difficult to find. All the hotels have restaurants, most of them coffee shops too. But we list the following for fine dining.

The Maribaude—On a hill overlooking town, Chef Michel Menager turns out fine French cuisine. Lots of butter sauces, vinaigrette, mussels, clams, shrimp, swordfish. About $40 per person with wine.

Le Acajou—This is more bistro than restaurant. It's in the center of town on Boulevard Pomare. Onion soup is $5, Salade Nicoise $6.50, mahi mahi is $13.

La Moana Iti—On the harbor and quite formal. Escargot is $11, marinated raw fish (poisson cru) $9.50, roast lamb $20.

Auberge Landaise—On Blvd. Pomare. Some say it provides the best French cuisine in all Tahiti. About $45 per person with wine.

Le Belvedere—In the hills outside Papeete. They provide transport from town. A fine view and good French food. About $25 per person.

For More Inexpensive Meals

The Polyself—A noisy but good cafeteria downtown, with Chinese and Polynesian food. About $8 per person.

The Food Wagons—On the waterfront across the street from the Royal Papeete Hotel, near the Moorea Ferry there are a number of food trucks with kitchens. Sometimes they're open for breakfast and lunch, but always are open for dinner. They're the most economical places to eat in town and are generally good. Steak with fried potatoes, Chinese food, fried fish, Salade Nicoise. Substantial meals for $6 to $8.

Chinese Restaurants—These are a must in Papeete. There are a lot of them and they're usually good. The best known are: *The Mandarin* (near Town Hall, about $25 per person) and *The Jade Palace* (in the Vaima Center, $30 per person).

There are quite a few smaller family-style restaurants too, but none are cheap.

For traditional food, such as Imaa Tahiti or Himara, try the de luxe hotels, which do them with regularity. But because the dishes are so complex and take a long time to prepare, few restaurants serve them daily. You're better off waiting until you're on an outer island. There you can expect to sit down to roast pig, breadfruit, sweet potatoes, chicken, raw fish marinated in lime and coconut milk, and you'll be entertained by song and dance. Such an event will cost about $35 per person.

Evening Entertainment

Papeete loves uninhibited fun, and everyone's included, the Tahitians, sailors, soldiers, and the tourists. It takes little skill to find evening pleasure, but some night spots show little restraint and are the domain of drunks, B girls, and transvestites. They're fun to visit, but be careful in the raunchy clubs, and keep a good mental count of the drinks they bring.

Several notches up, try La Cave in the Royal Papeete Hotel. They have good music and the place is popular with the locals. The Laserium Bar in the Hotel Pacific is good too, a happy blending of locals and visitors.

We could list 10 more night-out selections, but you won't need them. As you wander about Papeete, they'll become self evident.

When it comes to the matter of sex Tahiti, with its lively acceptance of promiscuity, ranks high. Randy sailors who first saw Tahiti in the 18th century were enthusiastic, the clergy

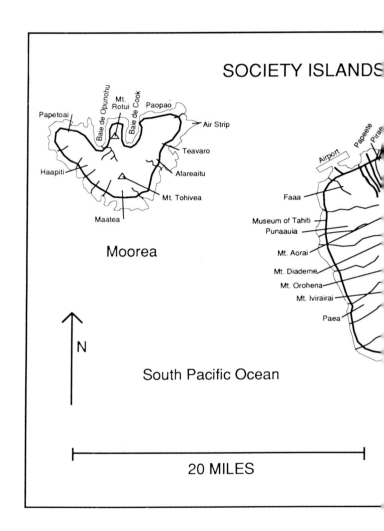

SOCIETY ISLANDS

Papetoai

Baie de Opunohu

Mt. Rotui

Baie de Cook

Paopao

Air Strip

Teavaro

Haapiti

Afareaitu

Mt. Tohivea

Maatea

Moorea

Airport

Papeete

Pirae

Faaa

Museum of Tahiti

Punaauia

Mt. Aorai

Mt. Diademe

Mt. Orohena

Mt. Ivirairai

Paea

N

South Pacific Ocean

20 MILES

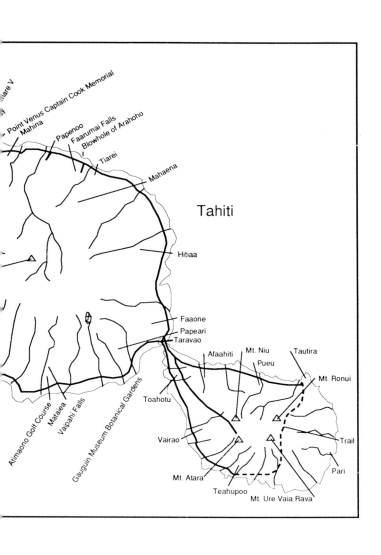

Point Venus Captain Cook Memorial
Mahina
Papenoo
Faarumai Falls
Blowhole of Arahoho
Tiarei
Mahaena

Tahiti

Hitiaa

Faaone
Papeari
Taravao
Afaahiti   Mt. Niu   Tautira
Pueu
Mt. Ronui
Toahotu
Vairao
Trail
Pari
Mt. Atara
Teahupoo
Mt. Ure Vaia Rava

Atimaono Golf Course
Mataiea
Vaipahi Falls
Gauguin Museum Botanical Gardens

dismayed, and over the years the mystique of island magnificence and pliant women has drawn escapists from all over the world.

Some writers describe this mixture of beauty and uncomplicated sex in a sensitive way. Others merely stress the promiscuity. But one author, Somerset Maugham, had another view and chose other parts of the world for sexual settings. He claimed that conflict, repression, guilt, and shame, are necessary ingredients for a book with a sexual theme, and they were missing in Tahiti.

Today that preoccupation with sex remains, but in Papeete it has become tawdry. It's a good place for, as the English put it, "a great dirty turn about town." You'll find it an expensive turn.

Perhaps away from Papeete in Bora Bora, Raiatea, Rurutu, Rapa, or Tahaa, the old attitude towards sex lingers.

What To Do in Papeete and How To Do It

Papeete, with its 75,000 people, is more efficiently structured than its colorful history indicates. It's a city where everything works reasonably well. Telephone and postal service are good, the water is potable, law and order usually prevail and, although traffic lights control activity, accidents happen, and crossing streets requires luck and agility.

With hills rising abruptly behind town, Papeete ranges along the waterfront for about a mile. Tree-shaded Boulevard Pomare which runs the entire distance is lined on one side by new apartments, banks, sidewalk cafes, boutiques, airline offices, hotels and government buildings. On the harbor side at the western end, the yachts are tied up stern first against the seawall. They've all had to sail thousands of miles, but their large numbers tend to make the voyages seem prosaic.

A little further to the east on the harbor side, is the Tahiti Tourist Office. Staffed by courteous people, it's an important destination, the source of quality assistance. Just beyond is the Moorea Ferry dock, and the dock for the car-passenger ferry that goes to Raiatea, Huahine, and Bora Bora. There too are the "food wagons."

Further on, where the land hooks out to form the harbor, are the French Naval docks where there's usually a naval vessel in port. Then come the warehouses and, at the far end of the hook, is the inter-island ship dock where Papeete's soft scent of copra (coconuts) originates.

Inland from Boulevard Pomare are the shops, the parks, government buildings, churches, restaurants, Post Office, the Town Museum and, the center of activity, the Marché (market).

The Marché, which opens at 6 AM, is in a series of old warehouses. Everything is available there—bread, fish, meat, fruit of all sorts, coconut oil soap, tikis of wood, and pareus. As much as anywhere in town, the Marché reflects an earlier Papeete, earthy, vibrant, not entirely sanitary, but filled with amiable confusion. The Tahitians sell the fruit, the Chinese sell almost everything else.

And with the Chinese accounting for about 10% of the population, some explanation of their presence is necessary. The Chinese aren't there because they're great navigators, or because they saw economic possibilities in Tahiti. They came as deportees fleeing the wars of the Manchus in the mid 19th

Papeete

century. Most of them arrived in Tahiti under miserable conditions, being brought to work on cotton, sugar cane, and coffee
plantations. At that time the US Civil War was on and the
world needed such products. But when the war ended and the
South began exporting cotton, the Tahitian plantations failed.
Some of the Chinese went home, but a few remained and, in
spite of some racism, are successful. Now they do the baking,
sell the meats, and run most shops and restaurants.

For transportation, the Marché is important. This is where
"Les Trucks" (buses) depart. As the name implies, these are
enclosed trucks with seats running along the sides. They ac-
commodate about 50 passengers. Except for sliding windows to
keep out the rain, they're completely open. Passengers climb
aboard from the rear and, accompanied by loud rock music, jolt
away. If you're going west, toward Faaa Airport four miles
away, take the bus on the west side of the market. Going east
toward Point Venus, go to the east side of the Marché

For distant areas, Les Trucks leave every half hour, but to
the Airport and the hotels near there (the Beachcomber, The
Maeva Beach Hotel, the Bel Air), they leave every few minutes. To the Airport it's 50¢. A taxi will cost $10.

Other than the distant extension of the harbor at the inter-
island ship dock, you can walk anywhere in town. There are
plenty of places to pause, as in Paris, for refreshments and
none are inexpensive. But you can sit quietly and for free in
the shade of Bougainville Park where stands the statue of
Bougainville himself, the second explorer to arrive in Tahiti.

The shops of Papeete, smart and otherwise, are open from
7:30 to 11 AM, and 2 to 5 PM daily, and half day on Saturday.
If you're looking for something traditional, buy a pareu, either
ready-to-wear or sold by the meter. You need two meters of
material to gracefully drape your body. This is one of the better bargains, about $8. If you have plenty of money for such
things as black pearls or black coral, visit Sanders Pearls in
the Vaima Shopping Center at the west end of town, or Wan
Perles Noires de Tahiti on Boulevard Pomare. However, before
investing in pearls of any kind, visit the Tahiti Pearl Center
on the waterfront and ask for their counsel. For books of all
kinds, particularly on the Pacific, go to La Librairie Archipel
on the Rue Des Remparts near the Moorea Ferry. For Ameri-

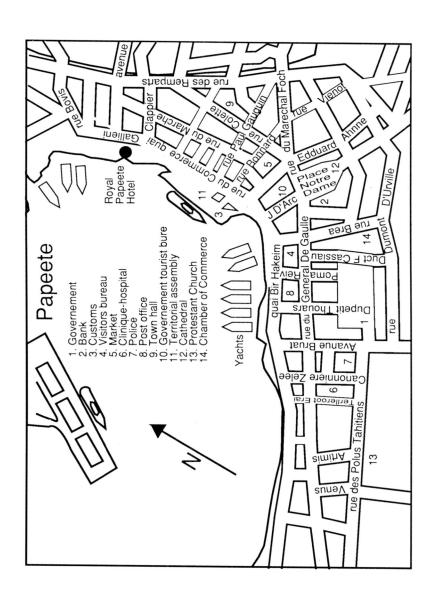

Papeete

1. Governement
2. Bank
3. Customs
4. Visitors bureau
5. Market
6. Clinique-hospital
7. Police
8. Post office
9. Town hall
10. Governement tourist bure
11. Territorial assembly
12. Cathedral
13. Protestant Church
14. Chamber of Commerce

Royal Papeete Hotel

Yachts

N

rue Bovis
Gallieni
Clappier
avenue
rue des Remparts
rue du Marche
Colette
rue Bonnard
rue Paul Gauguin
du Marechal Foch
rue Vienot
Ahnne
rue Edduard
rue du Commerce quai
Place Notre Dame
D'Urville
J D'Arc
rue Brea
Duct F Cassiau
Dumont
quai Bir Hakeim
Pomarev
General De Gaulle
Dupetit Thouars
rue du
Avanue Bruat
Canoniere Zelee
Terlleroot Erai
Artimis
Venus
rue des Polus Tahitiens
rue

6
5
11
3
10
2
12
4
14
8
1
7
9
13

can magazines, some American newspapers, try Bookstore across the street from the Post Office.

To make a long distance phone call or send a telex, go to the Post Office. And if you're a stamp collector, step over to the Philatelic Center at the Post Office and ask for their magnificent "Artists in Polynesia" series.

Beyond Papeete

Mountainous Tahiti, with an area of about 400 square miles, looks from above like a deformed figure eight, a small round island joined to a large round one. A 75-mile road, called La Route de Ceinture (the Belt Road) circles the bigger part of the island, called Tahiti Nui, and a pair of roads extend eight to ten miles along either side of the smaller part of the island, called Tahiti Iti. Beyond, there are only footpaths.

To make a round-island trip, including selected parts of Tahiti Iti, plan on at least two days. Make the run clockwise

Papeete's market and "les trucks"

direction, and do it by Le Truck, rental car, or tour bus.

Le Truck—This is the colorful way but, because no single truck does the entire distance, it's also the difficult way. However, for a start, go to the east side of the market in Papeete and catch a bus going to or near Point Venus, six miles east. The fare will be about $1. From there do the rest of the island in similar catch-as-catch-can increments. It's a matter of finding ongoing trucks in market places along the way.

Rental Car—They have Hertz, Budget, Avis, etc., but cars will be cheaper at some of the smaller local agencies. Check out Robert Rent a Car in Papeete (Tel. 42-97-20). Rates, insurance included, range from $35 to $40 a day. Or try Pacific Rent A Car with similar rates in Papeete (Tel. 42-43-04).

To rent cars, your home driver's license is acceptable, and they drive on the right side. Be aware that Tahitian drivers are not noted for conservative driving habits.

Tour Bus—Tour organizations abound. Most hotels have a tour desk and can arrange any combination of activities. But for unbiased information, contact the Tahiti Tourist Promotion Board in Papeete (Tel. 42-96-26). You'll find that you can do a shorter round-island group tour (omitting Tahiti Iti), lunch included, in one day. Rates will vary with the group size and can be tailored to existing budgets.

Around the Island

Starting from the Post Office in Papeete, every kilometer is marked with a red-topped white stone marked "PK" which states the kilometers to and from Papeete. Using these stones you can always pinpoint your location. In addition to profound beauty, you'll see the following, moving clockwise from Papeete.

PK 5.3—The land of the Royal Family and the tomb of King Pomare. This is the cemetery of Tahiti's Royal Family. King Pomare, the last king, was buried there in 1891. Mounted on top of his tomb is a gigantic brandy bottle. King Pomare in life was enthusiastic about this sort of refreshment.

PK 5.4—If the South Pacific has long had a grip on you, you're sure to have read the stories of Nordhoff and Hall. They were American expatriates who came after World War I and wrote such stirring novels as the *Bounty Trilogy* and *Hurri-*

cane. At Arue on the mountain side of the road you can see Hall's old home.

PK 8.1—After a series of climbing curves you are at "One Tree Hill". From here there's a good view of Matavai Bay where Captain Bligh dropped anchor, as did most of the explorers before him.

PK 10—You turn left off the road and continue a mile or so to the sea at Point Venus, a pretty spot which is fine for picnics, under the trees in the shadow of the old lighthouse. This is where Captain Cook on June 3, 1769 observed the transit of the planet Venus. There's also a museum which displays memorabilia from the Bounty and some wax figures of Bligh, Wallace, Cook, and others.

PK 13.2—Orafara Leper Colony. The Orafara Valley has been a leper colony for 75 years. But now leprosy can be cured, and patients don't spend the rest of their lives here in seclusion.

PK 17.1—Papenoo Village, in a valley on a river of the same name, is an attractive old-style village. For hikers, it's the trail head for the two-day cross-island trek via Lake Vaihiria. The trail ends near Mataiea on the South Coast. For this junket, be in good condition and use a guide.

PK 22—Everyone stops to look and listen at this famous Blowhole. It's formed by a timeworn tunnel in a seacliff which funnels the waves under great pressure into roaring jets of spray. When the weather is bad, it's dangerous to approach.

PK 22.1—Just past the Blowhole, turn inland and proceed up a dirt road a short way to the trail head for Faarumai Waterfalls. It's a short trail, a muddy few minutes' walk to the first of several falls. The walk is hot work, but you can cool off by standing under the cataract. The other falls are a good hard hike away.

PK 37.6—At Hitiaa you can look out to sea and observe two small islands. This is where Bougainville anchored in 1768. It was not a well chosen anchorage and the explorer nearly lost his ship. Just a little further on there are some striking views of Tahiti Iti.

PK 41.8—You'll get a good view of Fa'atautia Waterfall as you cross the bridge, a dramatic tropical sight.

PK 53—Taravao is where Tahiti and little Tahiti (Iti) join. From there a road runs along Tahiti's north coast to Tautira.

Halfway to Tautira at Pueue there is a small hotel run by locals. Food and services are extremely good, it's inexpensive, and is an ideal stopover for a two-day trip.

Tautira, 18 kms. from the turnoff, is where Cook landed in 1773 and 1777. It's also where Robert Louis Stevenson anchored his *Casco* in 1888 and stayed for two months. Stevenson called the area a "Garden of Eden." From there you go by foot and hikers can make their way to Teahupoo on the south coast—a rigorous three-day hike.

There is an easier way to Teahupoo. Just continue on past Taravao and drive 18 kms. along the south coast of Tahiti Iti past Zane Grey's fishing camp to Teahupoo.

PK 52—At this point you're on the way back to Papeete, and at Papeari tradition says Polynesians first settled a thousand years ago. It's also where Paul Gauguin lived and worked in the 1890's. At the nearby Gauguin Museum you can see documents and artifacts from his day. Unfortunately most of his paintings are reproductions.

The Botanical Gardens in the same area are superb and include a wide range of Tahitian flora. There is also the Gauguin Museum Restaurant here.

PK 44—Rupert Brooke's Love Nest is there, where he found and lost his first and only true love. This English poet died at Gallipoli in World War I.

PK 41—Atimaono Golf Course is a fine one—once a cotton plantation, which failed at the end of the American Civil War.

PK 39.2—The Marae Mahaiatea is the site of an ancient temple. All that is left now is a pile of boulders.

PK 20—At Paea there's a craft center for the traditional arts of the island. Much of it is for sale, but the main idea is to encourage the retention of old Polynesian skills.

PK 15.1—The Museum of Tahiti and Other Islands should not be missed. It has everything: natural flora, traditional culture, recent history, paintings, sculpture. The museum is open from 9 AM to 6 PM daily except Monday.

By this time you're nearly back to Papeete. You'll pass the

Beachcomber Hotel at PK 7.2, Faaa Airport at PK 5.5, and then you're in town again.

A Word About Hiking

The mountains in Tahiti's interior are beautiful and challenging, but should be approached with respect, preferably with a guide. In addition to the treks already discussed, the 7,000-foot Mt. Aorai climb is the most rewarding. Allow two days. The trail head for the assault is southeast of Papeete at Fare Rau Ape. This is also where you will find the Belvedere Restaurant.

The trail up the mountain is well marked. Locals say you don't need a guide, but they suggest that you spend the first day getting well up the mountain, then camp, and finish the climb the next day.

MOOREA

Moorea, the land mass you can see in the distance from Papeete, is 12 miles away. It's a lovely 82-square-mile triangular-shaped island of sharp peaks, deep valleys, beaches, and bays.

The 6,000 people who live there are dependent on pineapple, vanilla, and tourists. The town of Afareatu on the southeast coast is their administrative center. Moorea is the second most popular destination in French Polynesia and with good reason.

How to Get to Moorea by Air

From 6:30 AM to 5:30 PM Air Polynesie has flights nearly every half hour from Papeete. Flight time is seven minutes. Round-trip fare is about $40.

Getting There by Sea

Four ships, one of which is a large car ferry, leave from Papeete's downtown waterfront, and most of them go directly across to Vaiare on Moorea's east coast. The big boats, the *Maire, Tamarii II* and the *Moorea Ferry,* take a little over an

Yachts in Papeete. Moorea is in the distance

hour for the crossing. The $9 one way fare includes vehicle transport from the landing to the area of your hotel.

The fast boat, the *Keke III,* takes about 35 minutes and goes either to Cook's Bay or Vaiare. Passengers should make reservations for the *Keke III* at the ship's office on Pomare Blvd., or telephone 42-80-60. One-way fare is about $12.

Where to Stay

Please note that all quoted rates vary with the US dollar exchange. The following rates are estimates.

Bali Hai Moorea—On Cook's Bay close to the airstrip, this deluxe hotel has a restaurant, two bars, fine beach, all water sports, tennis, and spectacular views. Beachfront and over-water bungalows range from $140 to $300 a double.

Kia Ora Moorea—It's just south of the airstrip on a fine east coast beach and has everything a beach resort can offer, plus gourmet dining and a disco. Rates per double start at $125.

Captain Cook Beach Hotel—At the top western end of the island, this resort has rooms and bungalows. They offer nearly all beach activities. Rooms are about $90; bungalows $120.

Moorea Lagoon—On the beach between Opunuho and Cook's Bay, it has a restaurant, bar, pool, all water activities, plus Polynesian dancing on weekends. Bungalows $85 to $130 double.

Moorea Village—This hotel is located near the Captain Cook Beach Hotel, and has bar, pool, and restaurant. The Polynesian-style bungalows come with or without kitchens. Rates without kitchens are about $70 to $90; with kitchens $95 to $100.

Club Mediterranée Moorea—This institution devoted to trendy well-planned fun is situated at the northwestern tip of Moorea on the island's best beach. Rates average $700 per week per person including all meals. But to pay for drinks and other electives you use pre-purchased beads. It's a closed society, but enterprising people can, if inclined, crash Club Med and mingle with the inhabitants.

Club Bali Hai—This is on Cook's Bay and has all beach activities, bar and restaurant. Beach bungalows about $100.

Ibis Kaveka Village—On Cook's Bay with all beach activities, bar and restaurant. Garden bungalows about $90; beach bungalows $100 double.

Climat Moorea—On the beach near Club Med, with nearly everything including bar and restaurant. Rates $120–$170 a double.

Hibiscus—On the beach near Haapiti in the same area as Club Med. There's a restaurant and bar, and rates are about $80 a double.

Residence Les Tipaniers—Near Club Med and known for its fine restaurant. Bungalows with kitchens range from $75 to $100 double.

For More Budget-Minded Accommodations

The Hotel Tiahura—In Haapiti, with a restaurant and pool. Rates $50 to $80 a double.

Chez Albert—At the bottom of Cook's Bay in the village of Pao Pao. A family-run hotel, about $35 for a double.

Where to Eat

Other than the numerous hotel restaurants, there are many which serve Chinese, French, Italian, and American food. A good French restaurant such as *Escargot* near Club Med will cost about $20 per person without wine. For Chinese, try the *Hakka* at Cook's Bay—about $12.

There are plenty of snack bars that offer light meals, but nothing is inexpensive. The cheapest way to eat is to stay at a hotel with your own kitchen and shop at Moorea's grocery stores.

What to Do at Night

There are lots and lots of spirited evening activities but, other than *Pims Club* where the locals go to live it up, most celebrating happens in the hotel bars among visitors.

What to do on Moorea

You'll want to circle the island, a 37-mile run that's best done by rental car. Car rentals are from Rent a Car at Cook's Bay, or at Albert Rentals nearby. Rates are the same as in Papeete.

For more leisurely transport, use a bicycle. Most hotels will provide them. Set off by bike, shop at small local stores, be sure to try the local pamplemousse (grapefruit), and picnic on the beach of your choice.

If you do the round-island trip, you'll see quaint villages, towering mountains, picturesque lagoons, and fine beaches. Don't miss the Catholic Church in Pao Pao where there's a nativity scene painted by Pierre Heyman that portrays a Polynesian Holy Family. You'll see all the above-listed hotels along the way.

A detour from Opunohu Bay up the valley will bring you to a sizeable collection of ancient Marae (temples.)

The most dramatic way to see Moorea is by hiking. The footpaths among the Marae of Opunohu are excellent, but the best walk is the trek from Vaiare west across to Pao Pao at the bottom of Cook's Bay. It's a longish trek, but the abundant flora is delightful and the views magnificent.

HUAHINE

Huahine, 109 miles northwest of Tahiti, is actually two islands totalling 45 square miles within one reef—Huahine Nui (big Huahine) and Huahine Iti (little Huahine.) Four thousand people live on these lush mountainous twin islands, which are connected by a bridge. Fare on Big Huahine is the main settlement and, with its tree-shaded main street, old fashioned frame buildings, Chinese shops, and the Quay, it looks like everyone's image of a South Seas port.

How to Get There by Air

Air Polynesie flies from Papeete to Huahine at least once a day, a 40-minute flight. The one-way fare is about $64.

Air passengers should also note that Air Polynesie will sell you an "Unlimited Use" pass for the islands of Huahine,

Huahine Island

Raiatea, Bora Bora, Moorea, Maupiti, Manihi, and Rangiroa for about $220.

By Sea

The most comfortable vessel sailing to Huahine, then on to Raiatea-Tahaa and Bora Bora, is the big *Raromatai Car Ferry.* It departs Papeete's downtown wharf at 7:30 PM at least twice weekly—schedules change—and arrives Huahine at 7 AM, an 11½-hour voyage. You can sit up in reasonably comfortable reclining chairs or get a pleasant cabin. Fare all the way to Bora Bora with cabin is about $120; without cabin $70. There is an expensive restaurant aboard but the best thing is to bring your own food.

The *Taporo IV* sails from Papeete Mondays and Thursdays in the late afternoon and arrives Huahine in 11 hours. Fares are about the same as the Ferry.

The *Temehani II* does the same trip for about the same fare and, like the other two ships, continues on to Bora Bora.

Where to Stay in Huahine

The Bali Hai Huahine—This is the shiny first cousin to Moorea's Bali Hai. It's got every possible beach-island convenience and is within walking distance of Fare, the main town. Maeva, the site of several old Maraes is just a short distance. A beach-front bungalow will cost about $220 for a double.

For More Economical Accommodations

Hotel Bellevue—Overlooking pretty Maroe Bay on Huahine Iti, this simple hotel has a restaurant-bar, plus good fishing possibilities. Bungalow rates are $65 and a room $35 double.

Chez Line Ah Foussan—This hotel is in the village of Parea on the south end of Huahine Iti. A fully plumbed room is about $25 a double.

Pension Meme—It's another simple inn in the village of *Parea.* Not all rooms have plumbing and the environment is strongly Polynesian. With all meals it's about $80 a double.

Where to Eat

Most restaurants are associated with hotels and most are expensive. But, as in Tahiti, food trucks appear on the quay at Fare every evening. Other than shopping at the Chinese stores for carry-out food, the trucks are the least expensive.

Snack Temarara in Fare is not associated with a hotel. A full meal, seafood or steaks will run about $15 per person.

What to Do on Huahine

To get around, a motor scooter from Kake Rent a Car near Fare will cost about $22 a day. A car will be $50 to $70 a day depending on size. There is a Budget car rental office in Fare with cars for about the same rates.

If you go north of Fare just a few miles to the airport and continue beyond to the ocean side of Lake Fauna there are white sandy beaches. Since the reef is close in, the surfing is excellent here.

In Maeva village on the south side of Lake Fauna on the big island, there are 16 restored marae. Footpaths connect many of these old temples that were the ancestral shrines of local chiefs. Huahine in those ancient days was a center of Polynesian culture.

Go south, cross the bridge onto Huahine Iti and continue on to the village of Parea. Ask around and find someone to take you out to the nearby motus (islets), good places for picnics.

Huahine is beautiful, some say as beautiful as Bora Bora. It's quieter than Bora Bora though, and certainly better for peace and solitude. But, apart from the important archaeological remains and good beaches, Huahine can be seen rather quickly.

RAIATEA AND TAHAA

Twenty-five miles west of Huahine, Raiatea and Tahaa are two separate islands which share a common reef and lagoon. Raiatea's population is 7,400 and it has an area of 105 square miles. Mt. Temehani at 3,000 feet is the highest peak and the main port is Uturoa.

Tahaa to the north is about half the size, 55 square miles, and is much less developed. There are 3,750 locals and, if such a small island can be considered to have a main town, Patio in the north is it.

How to Get There by Air

Air Polynesie flies into Raiatea every day, a 45-minute flight from Papeete. One-way fare is about $74.

By Sea

Refer to the section on sailing to Huahine. The same vessels arrive in Raiatea two hours after their stop in Huahine.

Where to Stay in Raiatea

The Bali Hai—Yet another Bali Hai and, like the others, it offers all amenities. This one is near the town of Uturoa and the airport which is just north of town. Rates for a small over-

Arriving in Raiatea

water bungalow are in the $125-a-double range. A deluxe overwater bungalow is about $240.

The Raiatea Village—This beachside hotel south of Uturoa at Avera has a number of bungalows with kitchenettes. Rates are $65 a double; for $35 more they'll provide meals.

Pension Yolande Roopinia—This small inn in Avera has rooms with kitchens. Rates are reasonable.

The Motu Hotel—We chose this downtown Uturoa hotel only because we could see it when our ship, the *Raromatai,* pulled in. The rooms with baths down the hall were simple but clean. Rates are $50 a double. With its ground floor billiard parlor, and adjacent pinball emporium, the Motu was a mite noisy. On Saturday night, the sounds of hilarity from a nearby disco made sleep difficult.

For dinner at the attached restaurant, we ordered Spanish Chicken and mahi mahi. The mahi mahi in spite of liberal garlic was suspiciously aged and, due to a misprint, the chicken turned out to be Spinach Chicken, not Spanish.

The Motu Hotel and its restaurant may not be the ideal choice for Raiatea but, to sample outer island Polynesian town life, it was excellent. Uturoa with its Chinese shops, its Gendarmerie and Public Market, its school run by teaching nuns, and its noon-time benches laden with prone people, is pure French Polynesia.

Where to Eat

The hotels all provide meals, the grocery stores offer take out possibilities, and in Uturoa there are several small restaurants. Try the *Jade Garden* for Chinese food.

What to Do

As in Papeete, there is a Le Truck service that runs during the day. Catch one at the Market in Uturoa. Taxis, easily available, are somewhat cheaper than on Tahiti. A car rental, insurance included, will cost $65 a day. Contact the Guirourard Agency in Uturoa. Motor scooters are the most economical way to get around, at about $25 a day. Contact the Brotherson Agency in Uturoa.

The archaeological remains of marae are important on

Raiatea too. The best ones, at Taputaputea, are located near the village of Opoa on the south end of the island.

Mt. Temehani, the only home in the world of the Tiare Apetahi flower, can be fairly easily climbed. The trail head is on the western side of the island near the village of Pufau. The views of Raiatea and Tahaa are spectacular.

There are no good beaches on Raiatea, but within the lagoon there is excellent diving. Contact Patrice Philip in Uturoa.

Tahaa Island

This smaller island is completely undeveloped for tourists. It's a tranquil island with no hotels and few other conveniences. Raising chickens and cattle, farming, and copra, are the main activities.

The magnificent lagoon is Tahaa's main attraction. To get there, ask around Uturoa's harbor for boats making the short trip. There is usually one a day. You should try to make it over and back in one day.

BORA BORA

Bora Bora—you can see it like a stage drop in the distance from Raiatea—is 160 miles from Tahiti. The pearl of all islands, it has a beauty borne of lagoon, reef, and green mountains. Nine miles long by eight miles wide, with a population of 2,575, it's understandable that tourists have discovered the island.

During World War II 6,000 American troops were stationed there, and I remember hearing how their Commanding Officer dealt with matters of discipline. "If you cause one more problem," he'd say, "we'll ship you straight back to the States."

Vaitape on the west coast is the principal town, and the airport is on a small islet in the far north. A launch brings arrivals into Vaitape from the airport.

How to Get There by Air

Air Polynesie has daily flights to Bora Bora from Papeete, a 50-minute run. The fare is $90 one way.

By Sea

The same ships that make the trip to Huahine come here as well. One-way cabin-class fares from Papeete are about $120.

Where to Stay on Bora Bora

The Bora Bora—Located in Nunue, four miles south of Vaitape, this is the finest hotel on the island. Conference rooms, boutiques, car rentals, and charter cruises are available. For an overwater bungalow, a double could be $300 but a bedroom suite can be had for $150 or so.

The Club Mediterranée Noa Noa—This Club Med is a little less imposing than the one on Moorea, but it has the full spectrum of Club Med activities. Near Nunue on the west coast, it's the swingiest place on the island, and that's saying a lot. Rates with meals are $600 per person per week.

Sofitel Marara—At the very south end of the island on Matira Beach. All beachside activities plus car rentals, a disco, and glass bottom boat. Rates for an overwater bungalow approach $300 a double.

Bora Bora Marina—This hotel is on the same island as the airport. It's on a good beach with all water sports. A beach bungalow will run about $90 a double.

The Matira—At Vaitape, it has bungalows with kitchenettes. Rates are $80–$95 a double.

Oa Oa—This American-owned hotel in Nunue is on an excellent lagoon beach. Rates are from $90 to $150 a double. It has a good restaurant and plenty of evening activities.

Bloody Mary's—Everybody knows Bloody Mary's. It's the "in" spot to play at night, and not a bad place to stay. Near the Bora Bora Hotel in Nunue, it's on a good beach, with lots of snorkeling and canoeing available. If you can get a reservation, rates will be about $60 a double.

Where to Eat

For good Chinese food, not too expensive, try the *Matira Restaurant* in the Matira Hotel. You can eat well here for $6 to $14 per person.

Bloody Mary's—The fashionable place to go, a dirt floor

Bora Bora

restaurant under a thatched roof. Good lobster, seafood, sandwiches. $12 to $20 per person.

Chez Lulu—Close to Vaitape, this restaurant serves good seafood, steaks, and salads for the same prices as Bloody Mary's.

Hotel Oa Oa—On Friday nights they serve Mexican food, for about $14 per person.

What to Do at Night

There's plenty to do. Drop into almost any of the hotels or follow the sounds of merriment to their source. Try the Oa Oa, certainly Bloody Mary's or Club Med, if you can get in. For such a small island, Bora Bora provides everything a swinger can possibly want.

What to Do

This is no problem, for Bora Bora's attractions are self-evident. To tour the island, you can rent a car at any of the large hotels, but a car really isn't necessary. A bicycle, provided by most hotels, is more practical and more fun. Spend a day riding around the island. Starting from the Hotel Bora Bora at the south end of the island and going clockwise, you'll pass Bloody Mary's, Chez Lulu's Restaurant, and the village of Vaitape, which has more than its share of trendy shops and boutiques.

Nearby, and important to me, is the grave of the French sailor, Alain Gerbault, who wrote about his round-the-world trip in 1923–29. Gerbault's Journals have influenced me deeply, and I recommend his book with enthusiasm.

The Oa Oa Hotel is beyond Vaitape. Then, at Club Med, there's a trail to a pair of World War II American coast artillery pieces. Ask directions locally; it's not far.

To quench your thirst, pause at the Yacht Club. Then continue on to the beginning of Faanui Bay and check out the marae ruins at Marotetini. This is the most important temple on the island.

At Faanui Village there is access to a trail that cuts directly across to the opposite side of the island. It's a difficult, but not impossible, two-mile jungle trek.

As to mountain climbing, if you're experienced, Mt. Pahia's 2,000 feet can be climbed. The trail head is near Vaitape Village. Ask around for a guide or instructions. The other mountain, Mt. Otemanu at 2,200 feet, is for all intents and purposes unclimbable.

You will see the lagoon and its islands in the distance. Bora Bora is the scene of paddling, peddling, snorkeling, walking, climbing, dancing, drinking and eating well. But it is not a source of much consorting with native Polynesians. Unfortunately, these people may not even notice you. They've seen too many "here today, gone tomorrow" visitors to display any marked interested in outsiders.

This however is not true on Maupiti.

MAUPITI

At this writing Maupiti, 29 miles west of Bora Bora, remains off the beaten path and, according to Maupitians, they intend to keep their 25-square mile island just that way. Maupiti, with its 800 inhabitants, is an island of cliffs, tropical vegetation, white beaches, and gem-like off-shore islands. You can walk the island in three hours. It's as close to the real Polynesia as anything we've yet described.

Getting There by Air

Air Polynesie flies in two or three times a week from Papeete via Raiatea. One-way fare is about $100. The airport is on a small reef island, and passengers are transported by launch across the blue lagoon to the village where most of the inns are located.

By Sea

The small *Taporo I* comes in from Raiatea with regularity. The fare is inexpensive. There are other boats too that sail from Papeete. Ask at the Tahitian Visitors Bureau.

Where to Stay and Eat

There are no hotels, only a number of pensions or private homes willing to put you up, but expect to pay $40 per person per day for room and meals. Ask Air Polynesie to arrange housing for you.

TETIAROA

Tetiaroa is a small atoll about 25 miles north of Tahiti, a pretty island owned by Marlon Brando. For folks into rafting, white water sports, riding the tidal bore from the lagoon into the sea or vice versa, Tetiaroa is unusually challenging.

How to Get There and Where to Stay

You can buy an all-inclusive (airfare, hotel, and all-meals) package. For example, a stay from 8:30 AM one day to 4 PM the next will cost about $500 a double. Contact Air Polynesie and the *Tetiaroa Village Hotel* in Tetiaroa.

THE TUAMOTUS

The 69 islands of the Tuamotus, the Dangerous Archipelago, lie to the east of Tahiti's Society Islands and are spread over an area 350 miles wide by 750 miles long. These islands, 42 of which are inhabited, make up the biggest group of coral atolls in the world.

RANGIROA

Rangiroa has a population of 1,430, and is the largest atoll in the group. It's so big that its opposite side is well over the horizon. Most of the people live in the villages of Avatoru and Tiputa on the same islet as the airport. The economy is based on cultured pearls, copra, and tourism.

How to Get There by Air

Air Polynesie flies in six days a week from Papeete, an hour flight. The fare is $165 one way.

By Sea

For traveling to the outer limits of these islands there are a number of trading vessels that carry cargo, pick up copra, carry deck passengers, and provide for two or three cabin passengers. For tourists who are more attuned to cruise ships this is not the way to travel but, to see the Tuamotus as they've always been, this fully qualifies as "adventure travel."

There are several sources of sea travel from Papeete, but for starters write to Compagnie Francaise Maritime de Tahiti, B.P. 368, Papeete, Tahiti.

Their ship *Maire II* makes a 22-day passage touching the islands of Hao, Amanu, Nukutavake, Anuanuraro, Rikitea, Pukarua, and about nine others. They're all elemental atolls a few feet above the sea where life is hard in a beautiful and lonely way. Its departure is normally scheduled from Papeete between the 8th and 10th of each month. The round-trip fare, food included, is about $550.

On arrival in Papeete we made our way to the harbor area of Fare Uto and went aboard the *Maire II*. We found a small trim "coaster" with a pungent odor of copra and room on the fore-deck for numerous deck passengers. The one cabin available was the owner's suite, an ell-shaped, worn but habitable cabin with a table, sofa and two bunks. The dining salon, a compartment made for eating not lingering, was on a deck below. We've got the *Maire II* carefully filed for future use.

The *Aranui,* a cargo-passenger ship, stops at Rangiroa and Takapoto en route to the Marquesas. See section below on getting to the Marquesas.

Where to Stay and Eat

The Kia Ora Village—This is just a short distance from the airport. They've got snorkeling, windsurfing, sailing, fishing, plus the usual Polynesian-inspired evening togetherness. Rates for a beachfront bungalow, with breakfast and dinner included, are $142 per double.

La Bouteille a La Mer—Near the airport, this has all beach activities. Rates are about $120 a double.

Less Expensive Accommodations

Chez James and Henriette—In Tiputo village. Room and bath $40 a couple.

Chez Josephine Maury—Also in Tiputo. Rates are $30 per person including meals.

Another Aspect of Rangiroa

If you're willing to sacrifice hotel life, plan to visit one of the distant motus (islets). Ask Air Polynesie to help, then spend several days living within the discipline of atoll life. Wander among nesting birds, watch sharks patrol a channel to the sea, see manta rays and leaping tuna. Live for a few days under simple shelter, eat what the sea and thin soil provide. It's a sobering experience, but you'll be the better for it.

MANIHI

Manihi Island, with its cultured pearl farming, unsophisticated but friendly people, and lagoon filled with spear fishing possibilities, is 335 miles northeast of Tahiti. It's the only other Tuamotuan island we know of with a major hotel.

Getting There by Air

Air Polynesie flies in from Papeete three times a week. Fare is about $350 round trip.

Where to Stay

The Kaina Village—This place inspired a popular song in the islands, "Kaina Village in Manihi." Their rates are about $120 per person per day, including meals.

With economy in mind, there are several pension-type inns with considerably lower rates. Ask Air Polynesie about them. And for another bit of atoll life, take a boat across to nearby Ahe Island.

THE MARQUESAS

These are the rugged green islands that yachtsmen first see after their 3,900-mile passage from the Galapagos. It almost seems easier for them to get to the Marquesas than for us to get there from Tahiti, which is 750 miles to the southwest.

NUKU HIVA

Nuku Hiva Island with a population of 1,800 is the administrative center for these 12 islands. Nuku Hiva, like most of the others, is majestically mountainous and beautiful. Growing and export of oranges is the main activity.

HIVA OA

Hiva Oa, according to Robert Louis Stevenson, was the loveliest and most ominous spot on earth. And it was there that Paul Gauguin spent his last years.

UA HUKA

On Ua Huka there are some of the oldest archaeological ruins in the group.

FATU HIVA

Fatu Hiva has a population of 400, is lonely, green, and precipitous. The inhabitants there, as on the other islands, live along flowing water in the deep narrow valleys.

Accommodations

There aren't any major hotels in the group, but there are pensions and inns on most islands. The Marquesas are remote, forgotten, strangely beautiful. But changes are coming, and soon the tourists will too.

Getting There by Air

Air Polynesie is usually booked up six months ahead for the seven-hour flight to Hiva Oa. The fare is about $720 round trip.

By Sea

You've got two choices. First contact: Compagnie Francaise Maritime de Tahiti, BP 368, Papeete, Tahiti.

From them you'll find that several ships, such as the *Taporo V,* make a 15-day round-trip passage to Tahuata, Hiva Oa, Nuku Hiva and Ua Pou, all in the Marquesas. Fare, including meals, is about $600. Remember though that the *Taporo V* and others like her are working ships and provide only very minimal comforts.

The other choice is aboard the cargo ship *Aranui.* This 264-foot ship with a fine dining salon has clean, comfortable air conditioned cabins for 40 passengers. The *Aranui* leaves Papeete once a month for an 18-day voyage that includes stops at Rangiroa and Takapoto in the Tuamotus, then Tahuata, Hiva Oa, Ua Pou, Nuku Hiva, and Fatu Hiva in the Marquesas. En route there are many excursions ashore, visits to places made

famous by Herman Melville, Thor Heyerdahl, Robert Louis
Stevenson and Paul Gauguin. Life aboard the *Aranui* is very
good indeed. Round-trip fare is about $1,700 per person.

THE AUSTRALS AND GAMBIERS

These two groups, 900 miles southeast and southwest of
Tahiti, get very few visitors. The volcanic islands of Tubuai,
Rurutu, Rimatara, Raivavae, and Rapa make up the Austral
Group.

The Gambiers are composed of several islands, four of which
are inhabited. Mangareva is the main island. There are inns
on the inhabited islands, but for reasons of nuclear testing,
visitors to the Gambiers must get governmental permission.

Air Polynesie flies to both areas.

Consider these islands only after you've seen everything else
in French Polynesia.

2

THE COOK ISLANDS

The Cook Islands, named after the British Captain who seems to have been everywhere in the Pacific—even up the Oregon Coast where we live—are scattered like tiny jewels over a large stretch of sea between Tahiti and Samoa. Rarotonga, the principal island, is 2,500 miles due south of Honolulu—as far south of the equator as Honolulu is north of it—a similarity that provides both places with ideal climates. But that's as far as the similarity goes, for in spite of her recently built international airport, the Cooks remain off the beaten path. Even Avarua, the port, capital, and mecca to these 15 islands, is little concerned with tourists.

There's no TV on the islands, no buildings taller than the highest palm, no traffic lights, and the people who speak English with a New Zealand accent are friendly and don't regard visitors as walking money. All amenities, all reasonable comforts are available, and everything seems to work. You can drink the water, eat the vegetables, be addressed in English, there's no tipping, and happily for Americans the US dollar goes a fairly long way.

The natural beauty, particularly on Rarotonga with its forest-covered mountains, verdant coastal plain, and fringing reef, is profound. It'll take your breath away when first seen and some writers, with complimentary comparison in mind, insist that Rarotonga is a miniature English-speaking Tahiti.

The population of these islands comes to a mere 18,000. On some of them there are 50 people, on others 700, a few are uninhabited, and, until recently, another had a population of just one. On Rarotonga, the largest island, there are 9,300 people. This independent nation may be small in number, but it is large in area.

Classified politically, the Cooks are called a Self-Governing Free Associated State, which means that the mother country, New Zealand in their case, picks up most of the bills. New Zealand has built the airport, the hospitals, fixed up the roads, the sewers, takes care of all defense, provides at least half of the budget, and has made all Cook Islanders full citizens of New Zealand.

For these reasons, life smiles broadly and paternally for the islanders. But some New Zealanders aren't happy with this arrangement and say they get little in return. They're not allowed to buy land in the Cooks, but the islanders who immigrate can all buy property in New Zealand, and now there are as many Cook Islanders in New Zealand, as in the Islands.

So it goes, but for the visitor, particularly the American with no axe to grind and a strong dollar, the Cooks are very good indeed.

The People

Cook Islanders are Polynesians, handsome light brown Polynesians, who refer to themselves with pride as the original Maoris—the ones who made the ancient voyage of discovery to New Zealand.

They are outgoing people, hospitable and warm, but not nearly as animated as their Tahitian cousins who speak the same language. Animation, or the lack of it, may be a function of church affiliation and, in looking back, the first missionaries to arrive in the Cooks were not known for unbridled humor.

History in Brief

Captain Cook discovered some of these islands, but it was the Bounty mutineers in 1789 who are given credit for discovering Rarotonga. Then in the early 1800's the London Mission-

Gathering plumeria blossoms for leis, Rarotonga

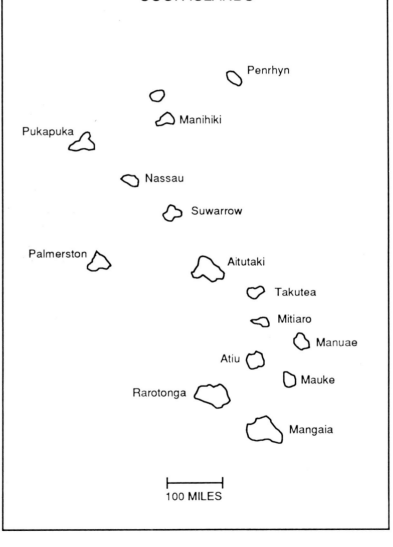

COOK ISLANDS

Penrhyn

Manihiki

Pukapuka

Nassau

Suwarrow

Palmerston

Aitutaki

Takutea

Mitiaro

Manuae

Atiu

Mauke

Rarotonga

Mangaia

100 MILES

ary Society appeared and provided the people with a number of stringent do's and don'ts—some of which still prevail.

In 1888, the Islands, with strong economic ties to New Zealand who later administered them, became a British Protectorate. In 1965 they became independent.

How to Get There by Air

South Pacific Islands Airways recently made their inaugural flight from Honolulu to Rarotonga—a five-hour nonstop which runs every Thursday. We were on that flight, and drawn up at the airport to meet us were a host of dancers, the clergy, officials, and Sir Thomas Davis, the Prime Minister.

A buffet lunch was served, Sir Thomas made a welcoming speech, the clergy blessed the occasion, and Mr. George Wray, president and owner of SPIA responded with gratitude and hopes for continuing good relations between SPIA, the Cook Islands, and the USA.

Coming from Honolulu, this once-a-week flight continues on to Tahiti, and then flies directly back to Honolulu. It's a good triangular flight, one that can be used to provide a week in the Cooks and a week in Tahiti. Write SPIA in Honolulu at 733 Bishop Street, 96813. Ask them about their pre-purchase Honolulu-Rarotonga-Tahiti-Honolulu fares. I hear they've got some good ones developing.

Polynesian Airlines is the flag carrier for Western Samoa and comes in from Apia, Western Samoa on Fridays. Using a combination of SPIA which flies into Apia, and Polynesian Airlines, a very good Western Samoa-Cook Island venture could be worked out. Check with your travel agent, or write to Polynesian Airlines at their US office, 9841 Airport Blvd., Suite 418, Los Angeles, CA.

Air Nauru flies in from Tonga and Western Samoa on Thursdays, but this airline, with some of the cheapest fares in the Pacific and a convoluted route above and below the equator, might better be used leaving Rarotonga than entering.

Air New Zealand has regular flights from New Zealand, Tahiti, and Fiji. There are also connecting services from Australia and the USA.

By Sea

The only way in is by irregular cruise ships. Freighters are a diminishing species, practically a lost cause. Most shipping companies would now rather load on a few more containers and forget about passengers.

Immigration Formalities

All visitors must have a current passport and onward passage booked and paid for. When you enter Rarotonga an official, just to be sure you aren't planning to sleep on the beach, may ask to see a hotel reservation.

A stay of 31 days is allowed in the Cooks, but extensions are easy to come by. And a word for the backpack traveler with a quote from the *Cook Island News* may be appropriate:

"The Immigration Department has received complaints from concerned locals about tourists camping on beaches around Rarotonga. The complainants say that the campers pitch tents at night and like phantoms move out before daybreak. Chief Immigration Officer Tutai Toru said his Department considers this a serious matter. He added that the Cook Islands accept visitors if they stay in licensed housing, but if they cannot afford to meet lodging costs, they will be asked to leave the country."

There is a New Zealand $20-per-person airport exit tax.

Health

There are no health problems whatsoever. There are no poisonous insects or reptiles and, because the Cook Islands are not within the so-called malaria line, that problem does not exist. It has been said that the line between black and brown people in Oceania follows the malaria line, with brown people found only where the disease is absent.

Water in the Cooks is potable. Fruit and vegetables are safe to eat. Well equipped medical and dental services are available.

Currency

The unit of currency is the New Zealand dollar, and at this

writing the US dollar is very strong—good news for Americans, but a little rough on the New Zealanders.

For simplicity, I will quote all prices after exchange in US dollars. And to accomplish the exchange, banks are open in Avarua from 9 AM to 3 PM Monday through Friday. But visitors can change traveler's checks and use most credit cards at nearly all hotels and restaurants.

One matter of interest—when you change currency be sure to ask for a suitable supply of the Cook Island dollar coin. It's called the Tangaroa and, for obvious reasons, is popular with visitors. On one side of the coin stands Tangaroa, the God of Fertility with an immense phallus. In profile on the other side is Queen Elizabeth II. I'm told that Her Majesty was not amused when the coin was first struck in the '70s.

Time Zone

Local time is $10^{1}/_{2}$ hours behind Greenwich Mean Time, $6^{1}/_{2}$ hours behind Eastern Standard Time, $3^{1}/_{2}$ hours behind Pacific Standard Time.

Radio, Newspapers, Telephone

There is no TV, but the government radio station broadcasts in English and the *Cook Island News,* which appears five days a week, is in English as well. Newspapers from New Zealand and Australia are readily available. The Cable and Wireless office is open round the clock for long-distance calls.

Power

220 volts AC.

Climate

I was going to say that it's pleasantly sunny in the Cooks the year around, but this morning's paper carried news of vicious Hurricane Sally hitting Rarotonga. And this is January. Such storms are rare. But to be on the safe side, July and August are considered the best, and the coolest, times for a visit.

Language

Cook Islands Maori, a form of Polynesian, is the local language, but English is used by almost everyone.

Economy

Agriculture is the main activity. Citrus fruit, pineapple, bananas, and copra are processed for export. But tourism, held to a reasonable scale, contributes too.

What to Wear

Informality prevails and, other than going to church on Sunday, I can think of no reason to wear a tie or jacket. The only stricture that comes to mind is that women should avoid wearing brief shorts in public places. Topless, nude, or even bikini bathing is seldom done and will cause offense.

Holidays

Everything closes down on holidays, which are New Year's Day (January 1); Anzac Day (April 25); Good Friday; Easter Monday; Queen's Birthday (June); Constitution Day (August 4); Gospel Day (October 26); Christmas Day (December 25); Boxing Day (December 26).

Tipping

There is none. It causes offense too.

RAROTONGA

How to Get Around

Nothing on Rarotonga is very far away. You literally go in a circle there—a 23-mile circle from and back to the main town, Avarua. Rent a car (about $20 a day) if you must, but the simplest form of transport is the motor or pedal bike. They're available in town and in most of the larger hotels. Motor bikes will cost about $6 a day. A $2 license is necessary and is obtained in town. Pedal bikes cost $3 a day. Traffic here moves on the left hand side of the road.

Local round-the-island buses operate an hourly schedule (fare $1.25) and some of the hotels provide jitney service to town, distant restaurants, and beaches. Taxis are available and can often be hailed at roadside. Expect a fare of about $2 for a 15-minute run. Hitchhiking is not normal practice in the Cooks.

Where to Stay

Only moments before leaving Honolulu we were told that immigration officials may want to see confirmed hotel reservations. Hastily we looked at the list SPIA had on hand and chose the first one on the alphabetized list, the Are Renga.

On arrival we found that our choice, while not the best address on the island, was certainly the cheapest, at about $12 a double. It wasn't on the beach, nor even near the main road, but the island folks in charge were friendly and made us feel welcome.

Each room had its own plumbing, a small refrigerator, a stove, and the place—more apartment than hotel—lay in a beautiful setting under the palms hard by a citrus grove four miles from town. Tired from the trip, we stayed for the night. By morning inertia had settled in, so we continued to stay there, and happily so.

The Rarotongan Resort Hotel is on the other side of the economic spectrum. It's an all-out beach resort with rates of $80 double.

Between the Are Renga at one end of the scale and the Rarotongan at the other, there are plenty of other choices.

The Edgewater—84 units with kitchens, bar and pool on a good beach, two miles from town. $35 a double.

Beach Hotel—Units with kitchens on the beach. Good weekend barbecues. Three miles from town. $35 a double.

Are Renga—As mentioned earlier, four miles from town. $12 a double. Also an *Are Renga Annex* is $12 a double and closer to town (one mile) and the airport.

Arorangi Lodge—In the village of Arorangi. All units have kitchens. Five miles from town and $25 a double.

RAROTONGA

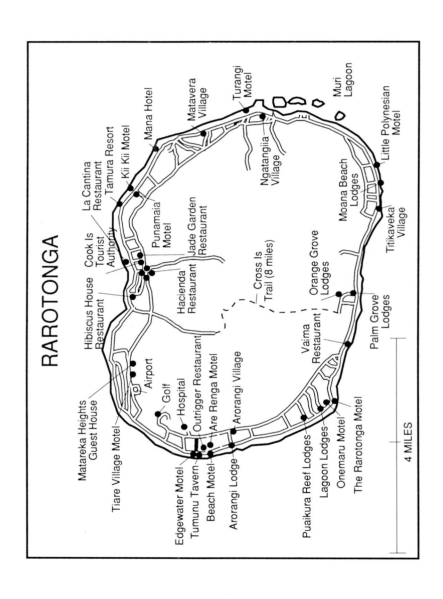

Matareka Heights Guest House
Tiare Village Motel
Hibiscus House Restaurant
Cook Is Tourist Authority
La Cantina Restaurant
Tamura Resort
Kii Kii Motel
Mana Hotel
Matavera Village
Turangi Motel
Muri Lagoon
Ngatangiia Village
Little Polynesian Motel
Moana Beach Lodges
Titikaveka Village
Punamaia Motel
Jade Garden Restaurant
Hacienda Restaurant
Cross Is Trail (8 miles)
Orange Grove Lodges
Airport
Golf
Hospital
Outrigger Restaurant
Are Renga Motel
Arorangi Village
Vaima Restaurant
Palm Grove Lodges
Edgewater Motel
Tumunu Tavern
Beach Motel
Arorangi Lodge
Puaikura Reef Lodges
Lagoon Lodges
Onemaru Motel
The Rarotonga Motel

4 MILES

White Sands Motel—The rooms have kitchens and it's on a sandy beach, six miles from town. $25 a double.

Lagoon Lodge—Bungalows with kitchens, pool, barbecue area near beach. Seven miles from town. $40 a double.

Rarotongan Beach Resort—This is truly a beach resort where the guests, mostly New Zealanders and Aussies, play tennis, snorkel, windsurf, dance, and enjoy barbecues by the pool. In the evening they dine in continental style at *Brandi's*, then fall asleep to the sound of the surf on the nearby reef. Eight miles from town and about $80 a double.

Palm Grove Lodge—Bungalows with kitchens, swimming pool, and on a good beach. Motor scooters for hire, 10 miles from town either direction. $30 a double.

Moana Sands Resort—A motel-type accommodation on a good beach. Extremely comfortable rooms, unusually fine hospitality. Good restaurant, nine miles from town. $35 a double.

Little Polynesian—Bungalows with kitchens on a white sandy beach, with swimming pool. $25 a double.

Raina Motel—On a white sandy beach and with a pool. Seven and a half miles from town, $45 a double.

Muri Beachcomber—Beach and poolside units with kitchens, six miles from town. $30 a double.

Moana Sunrise—On the shore, but on a poor beach, four miles from town. Eight units with kitchens, $25 a double.

Kii Kii Motel—All rooms have kitchen facilities, and there is a pool. Two and a half miles from town, $25 a double.

Tamure Resort Hotel—The rooms all have baths, refrigerators, hot plates. It's on a good beach, has a pool, restaurant, bar, entertainment, and all beach activities. One and a half miles from town, $50 a double.

Food on Rarotonga

Because we approach life slowly in the morning, a room with hot plate and refrigerator is ideal. A chilled papaya, some locally baked rolls, and a pot of coffee taken privately prepares us nicely. For such necessities, mama-papa stores all over the island carry a reasonable range of essentials, but the Public Market in Avarua, open 8 AM until noon daily except Sundays, is filled with the bounty of land and sea. The fresh fruit

Approaching Rarotonga

display is magnificent, and prices for everything are clearly marked. Whether you buy fruit, vegetables, or fish, the marked price applies. There is no bargaining.

By noon, perhaps with cold New Zealand Steinlager beer in hand (90¢ a large bottle), you will start thinking about lunch. In downtown Avarua consider the following:

The Hibiscus—Chinese food under the trees is good and inexpensive.

The Hacienda—Reasonably good and inexpensive hamburgers.

The Portofino—This Italian restaurant is a little more expensive, and perhaps a little too substantial for lunch. Try it for dinner if that's your preference.

Metua's Restaurant and Bar—Local seafood, hamburgers, fish and chips. Economical.

Tere's Bar and Grill—Sandwiches, fish and chips. Inexpensive.

You'll have no trouble finding any of these restaurants, plus a couple of take-out shops. Avarua isn't big enough for confusion. Remember, too, that nearly everywhere on the island is good for picnicking. And, at a distance from town, food is served at all hotels calling themselves resorts.

Evening Dining

All of the above-mentioned restaurants provide evening meals as well as lunch, and all of them are "licensed" which means they have a reasonable range of beer, wine, and spirits. Some of them like Tere's Bar and Grill and Metua's in Avarua are informal, small and inexpensive. Those listed below are somewhat more formal.

Brandi's Restaurant—In the Rarotongan Hotel, this is probably the most elegant international restaurant on the island. Most choices are à la carte and good. It's the sort of place you'd go to in San Francisco, London, or Sydney. Dinner with wine for two will come to about $24.

The Outrigger—Steaks here are good, especially the pepper steak, but the seafood plate, a thing of beauty, features locally gathered oysters, mussels, mahi mahi, and a diced raw fish marinated in coconut sauce called ika-mata. With either selection, forego the salad and order the vegetable plate. Dinner for two with wine will be about $24. Reservations are recommended.

The Vaima—This restaurant, overlooking the lagoon and near the Rarotongan Hotel, is good too. Much like The Outrigger with similar prices.

The Tumumu Bar and Restaurant—Housed in an untidy looking thatched building, it features mediocre food served in a noisy environment. It's best to go there later in the evening for dancing and bar activities.

Portofino's—In downtown Avarua, a cheerful place with lots of food—lasagna, pizza, pasta, seafood, steaks. Not great, but satisfying. About $20 for two with wine.

Tangaroa's Bar and Grill—This friendly, casual place in Avarua serves non-exotic Chinese food. It's good, inexpensive, and take-aways are available.

The Moana Sands—We heartily endorse this inn and restaurant. It's small, reservations are necessary, and the food is a happy blending of good Australian "tucker" and island cooking. Dinner for two with wine will come to about $18.

The Beach Motel—On weekdays, the Beach has only a thatch-roofed outside bar, the scene of friendly and congenial Happy Hours. But on Sunday they do an ample barbecue buffet complete with island music and dancing. The buffet for two is $13.

The Tamure Hotel Restaurant—An older resort hotel, next in rank to the Rarotongan, also provides island music with meals, which are good but rather institutional.

A little exploring will turn up other places, often smaller, often good. Word of mouth is the best source.

Rarotonga and What to do There

The main town, Avarua, is an orderly tree-shaded town set along the seafront. For outer islanders, with its harbor, banks, shipping offices, public market, and restaurants, Avarua is where it all happens.

Behind town, verdant mountains ascend and the 23-mile round-island road running along the coast is fully paved. Everywhere there's beauty. Groves of palms, immense breadfruit and flamboyant trees shade clusters of houses in villages. All around are gardens, taro patches, citrus groves, bananas and, looming over all, are the jungle-clad mountains.

The best way to see Rarotonga is by foot—across the island, or around its perimeter. Both adventures will show you far more than you could ever see by car.

The Cross-Island Trail—The map on page 52 shows the trail. It begins in town behind Tere's Bar and Grill, and is a scrambling trek through rich tropical forest to the "needle"—a stone spire at an elevation of about 1000 feet. The view is spectacular in all directions, the pause welcome. Then it's downhill all the way through coconut plantations and past a dramatic waterfall to the coast, not far from the Vaima Restaurant. Allow four hours for this seven-to-eight-mile hike. A guide arranged for in town is important since there are a couple of confusing forks that need attention. A guide is also useful for pointing out flora and fauna along the way. Please note that the trail is closed on weekends.

Walking Around the Island—This 23-mile hike is more a matter of strolling than walking. The coastal plain is flat and never are you far from cold beer, a sandwich, a swim, dinner, and a bed. All you need to carry is camera, personal impedimenta, and perhaps a bottle of something to be used at sundown.

We set off one morning in a counter-clockwise direction from the Are Renga and, at a many-paused three-mile-per-hour clip, did the circumnavigation in two days. As much as possible we followed the beach but, when that became impassable or private, we took to the road. In this way, and with halts for lunch at the Rarotongan Hotel, dinner and bed at the Moana Sands Hotel, lunch the next day at the Tamure Hotel, we completed the circuit. At sunset we stepped back onto the modest grounds of the Are Renga.

We discovered that on Rarotonga you're never far from the scenes of life or death. And there's always someone about—a clutch of ample Cook Island women under a parasol, children going to school, people working in fields, motorbikes, buses. Considerable waving and hellos are required.

But what you won't see are stereotypical South Sea village scenes. Instead of thatched houses, there are painted cottages with galvanized iron roofs, perhaps a lawn, and a car or motorbike parked alongside. Everywhere there are churches— Catholic, Seventh-Day Adventist, Mormon, Bahai and, in the center of each village, always a CICC, a Cook Islands Christian Church. If you're walking or riding about on a Sunday when everything except churches and hotels are firmly closed, the sound of choirs will be everywhere.

You'll not see big plots of ground under cultivation or signs of industry. Everything here is on a small scale. Cook Island law and a benevolent form of socialism keep anything from getting too large. No one here can buy land, not even Cook Islanders. Land is inherited, and then only in small pieces. So, instead of someone putting together several hundred acres to grow citrus fruit, several hundred farmers do the job.

No foreigners, including New Zealanders, can own land. The best they can do is to get short-term leases on small parcels. With arrangements like this, the Cooks aren't apt to change much very soon.

Fishing—Check with the Cook Islands Game Fishing Club near the Tamure Hotel, practically in town. They've got eight boats for charter and, although rates when we were there were changing, it's said to be the cheapest in the South Pacific. And easy too, since fishing starts as soon as you leave the harbor. Bonita, dolphin, barracuda, marlin and wahoo are what they go after.

Diving—Contact Dive Rarotonga in Arorangi near the Beach Hotel. They have a full range of snorkel and dive gear available. I'm told that if you're going to learn to dive, the teaching, equipment, and certainly the location are excellent. Again, rates are said to be the lowest in the Pacific.

Water Sports—The Sailing Club in beautiful Muri Lagoon has canoes, sailboats, and windsurfers. It is a fine place to swim and snorkel. Off-shore on the reef side there are four tiny palm-clad islands. You can almost swim to them, and they're perfect for a day's lolling, or at least for a picnic. We paused at Muri on our epic round-the-island walk.

Golf—There's a nine-hole course near the airport. It didn't look as if there'd be much trouble getting onto it.

Entertainment

One of the pleasures of unstructured travel is meeting people of similar stripe. Sometimes, and fortunately, the encounter is brief. But usually you meet compatible folks. Comparing notes, a little laughter, and a leisurely dinner, is not only pleasant but mutually informative.

On Rarotonga, however, we know of two places that can provide a wilder evening if that's what you're looking for. One is an institution in Avarua called the *Banana Court,* referred to by the local clergy as the "Infamous Banana Court" where, with live music, dance floor, and extensive bar, locals, visitors, and singles gather with enthusiasm. I'm told that, for matters of the flesh, the BC can be rewarding. Some people who remember that far back say that the BC is much like Quinn's of Tahiti was years ago.

The other place, near the airport, where similar activities occur is called the *Rising Sun.* Both spots are open Monday through Saturday.

All the resort hotels plus the small bars in town are congenial and have reasonable Happy Hour prices.

OUTLYING COOK ISLANDS: THE SOUTHERN GROUP

AITUTAKI

Of the 14 outer islands, the most popular destination is Aitutaki, a raised-reef low island in the Southern or Lower Cooks. Aitutaki, population 2,400, is 142 miles north of Rarotonga. It has been referred to as a "palm-fringed, all-lagoon, all-beach" island where snorkeling and diving in the turquoise lagoon is excellent. So too are the resort accommodations. There are also a couple of spartan and inexpensive guest houses.

The most exotic place to stay is the *Aitutaki Resort Hotel,* a 25-room establishment on one of the motus (islands) that form the lagoon. Rates there by Cook Island standards are moderately expensive.

On the beach too is the older *Rapae Cottage Hotel.* It's close to both the public wharf and the small village of Amuri. Rates are about $30 a double.

The Tiare Maori is a simpler but comfortable bed and breakfast place—rates $23 a double.

The Aitutaki Guest House is also comfortable, a bed and breakfast, about $23 a double.

Getting to Aitutaki from Rarotonga is a simple matter. Cook Island Air with its 10-seat Britton Normander and Air Rarotonga with its 6-seat Cessna make the hour trip daily. Round trip with either airline is about $70.

There's sea transport too. The *Mataoro* and the *Manuvai* of the Silk and Boyd Lines make this run, but the seas in this area can be rough and the trip uncomfortable.

Aitutaki is a place of beauty, perfect for a rest, some fishing, snorkeling, a little golf, and to see the dancing on "Island Nights." But it's neither remote nor unchanged. The tourists are finding Aitutaki.

Cook Island fishermen

ATIU

Atiu, Mauke, Mitiaro, Mangaia, and uninhabited Manuae and Takutea are classified as remote—not in distance, but because visitors come seldom and accommodations are few.

Atiu, 120 miles from Rarotonga, is a raised reef low island measuring three by four miles. It's a verdant place with a few small hills, a lake, a dramatic cave, and numerous fields of coffee and pineapple. There are some good beaches, one called Taungaroa is very good, but most people don't come to Atiu for water activities alone. They come for human reasons, to be part of a quiet Polynesian environment.

The people here, 1,300 mostly protestant Polynesians, live in five center-of-the-island villages where, other than evening choir practice and the Tumunu (about which more later), there is no night life. There's a post office, a radio-telegraphic office, several small shops specializing in canned goods, ships biscuits, ice cream cones, and kerosene. You'll also find a pair of pristine white churches, a 10-bed hospital, a bakery, a pine-apple and coffee packing house, and the Atiu Motel with its three comfortable chalet-style bungalows. There are no restaurants.

We stayed at the Motel—I can't get used to the term motel in places where the entire road system is only a few miles long—run by Roger and Kura Malcolm. Roger is a New Zealand Doctor of Physics.

Each of these attractive units has a refrigerator, cooking facilities, and is stocked with an ample range of food and drink. Guests keep track of what they use on the honor system. A carton of cheddar cheese costs $1.25; a can of tuna, $1; a can of baked beans, 75¢; a package of noodles, 50¢; a large beer, 80¢; New Zealand white wine, $4; a Chinese-made mosquito coil, $1.

There are mosquitos which are unpleasant at night. What you do is light the coil at bedtime and you'll sleep well.

Fresh fruit—pineapples, papaya, bananas, coconuts—are provided free. Rates are about $22 a double, without food.

What to do

You'll enjoy Atiu. But realize that, from the moment of your arrival, the Atiuans will have you under observation. You're the curiosity—and friendly, good-natured behavior will be rewarded in kind.

Probably the first thing to do is take one of the Motel motor bikes, $6 a day, and wander about town where you'll almost immediately be on a first-name basis with the locals. Then, perhaps explore the beaches and, if shells are of interest, walk the shallow lagoon between reef and shore. Remember though to wear tennis shoes; the coral is sharp and irregular. And, for gathering shells from the crystal-clear tidal pools, always wear gloves.

We know little about shells, can only recognize cowries and a few cone shells, but on Atiu our collecting was successful. Don't forget that, if shells are alive, they have to be cleaned out before being put in a suitcase.

Anatakitaki Cave—Visiting this cave is a must. But it's an adventure that requires a guide, preferably Tangi Jimmy.

Make arrangements at the Motel. Then you board motor bikes and follow Tangi down a rough road to the trail leading to the cave. On foot you enter the jungle and scramble through dense vegetation for at least a mile—you'd never manage this on your own. Fortunately there are no snakes, no malevolent animals. The coconut crab, delicious to eat, is the most vicious creature they've got.

At the cave there's a precipitous climb down to the entry. Then, using flashlight and staying close to Tangi Jimmy, you walk deep into the cave among glittering stalagmites and stalactites. It's eerie there, made even stranger by the presence of the rare kopeka bird of the swift family. It flies about making a clicking sound, and nests there—one egg to a nest. This is an adventure you'll not soon forget, nor the agility it requires.

The Tumunu or Beer School—This strenuous event takes place deep in the jungle. It's the scene of lively, illegal, homemade brew drinking. Island women are not welcome at the gathering, but visiting off-island females can go. They may or may not appreciate the unrestrained whooping variety of male laughter that ensues. If you've got the constitution, it's the quickest way to fall in (literally) with the locals. It is illegal, made that way by the first missionaries who landed on the island, but no one enforces the law now.

Air Rarotonga or Cook Island Airlines charge about $60 round trip to Atiu. When you fly there or anywhere in these islands, ask the pilot to let you sit in the co-pilot seat. Photography from there is excellent, and approaching an island from this position is an unforgettable experience.

MAUKE

Mauke, another raised reef low island, supports about 700 unspoiled and genuine Polynesians. When we arrived there the resident physician, a Scot named Archibald Guinea—portly, bearded, and 60-ish—was on hand at the airport to meet a pair of visiting doctors. With them we were loaded into his pickup and taken to his home next door to the tiny hospital. There, in disorder among his books, pictures, and memorabilia we drank beer, ate ship biscuits with cheese, and stood in a circle listening to his pungent and informative remarks. There was considerable laughter, and on departure one of the doctors dubbed him "Guinea of the Cooks."

According to Archibald Guinea, the only place to stay is either with him, he'd be delighted and his guests should be too, or with a local family.

There's a pair of villages on Mauke, small and orderly, and a large church that serves both villages. There are however two entrances, one for each village. Woe to the person who uses the wrong entrance.

MITIARO AND MANGAIA

Mitiaro is a similar raised reef low island with a population of 3,000. There's a simple guest house that goes for about $12 a double, and an unusual lake that produces a fine tasting eel. But by now the visitor may begin to have a surfeit of raised reef low islands.

Mangaia, with 1,500 people is similar again, and there are simple accommodations there. But it is a hard-working agricultural island devoted mainly to pineapples and production of the "Spirit of Pineapple," a powerful distillation that is generally called Ara. This is one of the good things to take home from the Cook Islands.

TAKUTEA AND MANUAE

Similar again, but uninhabited other than by sea birds.

THE NORTHERN COOKS

This group, some of which are 750 miles north of Rarotonga, are reached only by sea—using either the *Manuvai* or *Mataora* of the Silk and Boyd Line.

One day I sat and talked with Don Silk in his office near Rarotonga's harbor in Avarua. He spread out a large map on his desk and said, "If you want to go to sea, choose the Northern Group. It's a long voyage though, up to 18 days, may be rough too, and our ships are not known for creature comforts.

Atolls in the Cooks

But you'd see Rakahanga, Manihiki, Penrhyn, Puka Puka, maybe Suwarrow and Palmerston. They're all atolls."

"The voyage," he continued, "costs with cabin and meals about $250, or $15 a day. Deck passage is less than half of that, but I wouldn't even sell you a ticket. That sort of travel is for Polynesians who've been moving about that way since childhood. Anyway there's a voyage next week, a trading trip to pick up copra, discharge cargo, and carry deck passengers. But go aboard, have a look at the *Mataora;* she's due in Wednesday."

We did look at the vessel. We're not in the least timid about going to sea and have done so often. We've sailed on copra boats, island traders, interisland ferries, and once crewed a 40-footer across the South China Sea. But, after observation of the *Mataora* and comments from a pair of New Zealanders who'd sailed on her, we suggest that, unless you're doing some sort of penance, you give careful thought before sailing on either of these ships.

The cabins are tiny hot boxes and the plumbing facilities, which don't always work, are at a distance. The galley we were told was the source of unidentifiable food swimming in grease, and the 60 deck passengers huddled under the tarp on the foredeck were all sick. Our friends said, "You couldn't have asked for a more lively display of collective throwing up."

With apologies to Mr. Silk, who never promised us a rose garden, we declined passage. But a word about the Northern Islands is appropriate, along with the addendum that they're not entirely different from other more easily reached Pacific atolls.

PENRHYN

Penrhyn, population 530, is a lonely place, an island visited mainly by in-transit yachts, the ones sailing from Hawaii.

Copra and pearl shells keep the island going. It has one of the only natural harbors in the group. The wide lagoon is shark-infested though, by and large, not with a dangerous variety. US forces occupied the island during WW II and bits of metal from wrecked wartime equipment are still used by the islanders to fashion a range of utilitarian objects.

MANIHIKI

A stunningly beautiful island of 260 people. They dive to great depths in the lagoon to gather pearl shells, from which mother of pearl is made. The main village is Tauhunu. No safe place to anchor exists here.

PUKA PUKA

Home for 780 souls, most of whom live in three separate villages. The villages compete in everything from dancing contests to cricket matches. Copra, banana, and papaya growing are the main economic activities. The reef is extremely dangerous and the only anchorage is on the west side of Wale, the main island.

PALMERSTON

A curious atoll with a population of 50, all of whom bear

the name Marsters, and speak a sort of Victorian English. William Marsters, an Englishman, settled the island in 1862 along with his three Polynesian wives. Ships anchor off the reef every three or four months to pick up copra and deliver supplies.

SUWARROW

Suwarrow's population for some years was a total of one. The colorful New Zealander Tom Neale was the sole inhabitant. He died recently, but his book, not unnaturally titled "An Island to Oneself," is important for anyone who loves Pacific islands, particularly lonesome atolls. Ships can enter the lagoon and innumerable seabirds nest here.

Other than the dollar coin, the Tangaroa, perhaps a "Cook Islands Cook Book" and some of the above mentioned pineapple liquor, there are not a lot of exotic things you'll want to buy in the Cooks. Other islands, Samoa, Tonga, Fiji, the Solomons, and New Guinea, are more productive of native artifacts.

The main things you'll bring home from the Cook Island are warm memories.

Remember too, that when you leave Rarotonga, a New Zealand $20-per-person airport tax is collected.

3

THE KINGDOM
OF TONGA

To locate Tonga, follow the International Dateline south. Keep going past the Samoas about 600 miles, and there slightly to the west of that often inconvenient Line lies the principal island of Tonga, Tongatapu.

Following this route from Pago Pago in American Samoa, Hawaiian Airlines delivered us to Tongatapu in just under two hours, and I remember momentary surprise at the size of its flat green mass. It's a raised atoll, an island 21 miles long, and 11 miles wide at the widest.

"Welcome to the Kingdom of Tonga," a sign at the small airport proclaimed and, judging from the large crowd, we indeed felt welcomed. We asked if someone important was expected, and were told that every plane landing is important. Many Tongans consider it exciting to be at the airport just to watch planes and people appear.

Once through immigration formalities, which were simply done, and with baggage accounted for, we considered the matter of hotel accommodations. Fortunately, as in other Pacific islands, a large notice in the terminal lists all housing on Tongatapu, a substantial list. But on the subject of getting into the town of Nuku'alofa, do not as we have often done accept the first transportation that comes along. This applies to most areas in the Pacific. In the case of Tonga, it's not necessary to spend $12 for a taxi into town, because hotel minibuses meet every flight and charge $3 per person for the same service.

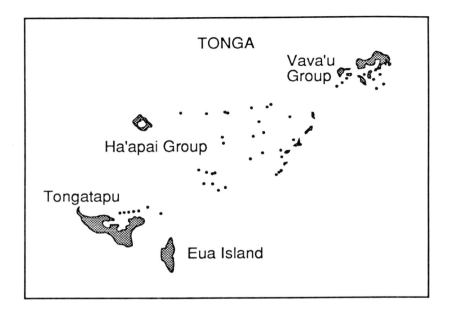

Nuku'alofa, the capital, is 15 miles from the airport. It's a tropically green flat run through country that all seems to be under cultivation with bananas, copra, taro, vanilla, beans, tomatoes, yams. The villages along the way, with their tin roofs shaded by immense breadfruit trees, are not as prosperous looking as villages in Samoa, the Cooks, or Tahiti. Tonga is poor. They don't have a paternal Uncle Sam, a benevolent New Zealand, or a thoughtful France to provide imported goodies of all sorts. They depend on income from agricultural exports, on remittances from relatives who have moved to Hawaii, California, New Zealand, and Australia. Some aid from Australia, New Zealand, Germany, Japan, and the United States also is important.

Tourism, while still small, will surely be a big thing in this kingdom by the sea. It has many attractions—the portly king himself, his palace, the beaches, lagoons, flying foxes, blowholes, ruins, exquisite outer islands, and convenient transport. There's good food, perhaps the best in the Pacific, and the weather is cooler than many other Pacific islands. Tonga has good things to bring home: tapa cloth, wood carvings, beautiful baskets, mats and, best of all, prices for everything are low. Tongans are friendly people, a quality Captain Cook recognized 200 years ago when he dubbed this group "The Friendly Islands."

The Land and its People

The Kingdom of Tonga, Polynesia's oldest monarchy, consists of three main island groups—Tongatapu-Eua, Ha'apai, Vava'u and, at a considerable distance to the north, tiny Niuafo'ou (or Tin Can Island) and Niuatoputapu Island. Within these groups there are 170 islands, 36 of which are inhabited, with a total population of 100,000.

Most of the Tongans, 65,000, live on Tongatapu, the main island. The King does too, and so do numbers of enterprising Indians, Chinese, a few Americans, New Zealanders, and Australians. Nuku'alofa, a town with a population of 25,000, is where it all happens.

Tonga's ruling monarch, King Taufa'ahau Tupou IV who can trace his ancestry back a thousand years, lives in the prominent, often photographed Victorian palace that's surrounded by Norfolk pines, near town. You can't miss it. You also can't get into it, because it's off limits to the public. The best one can do is stand outside the fence and snap photos.

The 300-pound King, his Prime Minister brother, and his nobles are totally in charge. All land is owned by the crown, the newspaper which rarely prints anything controversial is government owned, there are no labor unions, and no foreigners can own land.

The church, strict too, insists that women and girls wear ankle-length dresses, and on Sunday nobody plays games, dances, or works, and no ships, planes, buses or taxis run. Sunday is a day when you go to church, as does the King. And if you're inclined, this is a good time to see him.

Tonga is an autocratic country, a feudal system where things work, but not without some abuse of power. Some critics say that the custom of giving every Tongan boy at age 16 eight and a half acres of land has been misused by some of the nobles. They say, too, that while schools prepare young people quite well, the government hasn't attracted enough outside activity

King's Palace, Nuku'alofa, Tonga

to put all the recent graduates to work. Many young Tongans are reluctant to continue lives of farming and fishing. Unfortunately, or fortunately, farming and fishing for export is what makes Tonga go and, because of this bounty no one goes hungry.

As for outspoken critics, the government cordially invites them to go elsewhere. Many do and, ironically, the money they send back gives the economy a welcome lift.

History in Brief

Archeologists say that, while Tonga has been inhabited since the fifth century BC, details of those days belong mostly to mythology. Recorded history begins with the arrival of European explorers. Tasman arrived at Tongatapu in 1643, Wallace followed a century later, and in 1773 that most active of sailors, Captain Cook, appeared. He is the one who gave Tonga the name "Friendly Islands," an appropriate name for today, but for Cook it was a tongue-in-cheek label.

According to historians, when Cook arrived he was enthusiastically welcomed with food, dancing girls, and gifts. What he didn't know was that the Tongans were using the festivities to mask a plot to murder his crew and rob his ship. Luckily, and for obscure reasons, this didn't happen. However when the British vessel, *Port-au-Prince*, called at Tonga in 1806 she was attacked by natives and most of the crew was murdered.

Captain Bligh of the *Bounty* was in these waters too, not happily though. In 1789 near the Ha'apai group north of Tongatapu, the mutiny occurred, and Bligh with 18 of his men were set adrift in an open boat. The "Friendly Islands" weren't too friendly then either, and Bligh and his men knew better than to land. Instead they sailed their 23-foot boat an extra 3,600 miles to Timor Island. You can read the account in "Men Against the Sea," by Nordhoff and Hall.

In 1822 Wesleyan missionaries from England arrived, and their message was so successful that during the 48-year reign of King Tupou I (1845–93) he led his country from savagery to Christian peace. He was the author of the Constitution that is still used today.

His daughter, the ample and much-loved Queen Salote, led the country wisely until her death in 1965. She made headlines in 1953 when she went to London for Queen Elizabeth's coronation and rode to the function in an open carriage through driving rain, waving all the way. She earned the title "Queen without an Umbrella."

Tonga, a constitutional monarchy, the oldest one in the Pacific, and the most densely populated, has been led by King Tupou IV since 1965.

How to Get There By Air

Except for Sunday when nothing moves in or out, Tongatapu is a busy hub of air traffic. Planes arrive from nearly all directions and, while few individual airlines have daily service, something comes in or goes out nearly every day.

Several options are available coming from the States via Honolulu.

Take the Hawaiian Airlines five-hour flight from Honolulu to Pago Pago, American Samoa. Then either pause and do the Samoas, or continue on two more hours to Tongatapu.

Take South Pacific Islands Airways to Pago Pago or Apia, Western Samoa. Then fly into Tonga with Hawaiian Airlines, or consider a more exotic but slower route—fly Polynesian Airlines from Pago Pago to Tonga via Niue, Vava'u and Ha'apai. Be sure to check the schedules for flight frequency.

If you're coming from Fiji, either Suva or Nadi, Air Pacific has many flights. They'll also bring you in from Auckland.

Air New Zealand has three-hour flights from Auckland. Also fights from Rarotonga, three hours away.

Air Nauru flies to Tonga from Noumea, New Caledonia, a three-hour flight.

By Sea

There no longer are any regular passenger ships to Tonga from Fiji, the Samoas, or New Zealand. But if you're in any of these places check with the Port Authority. Occasional freighters make the run to Nuku'alofa—they're rare, austere, and spartan though. The only other sea-going opportunities are aboard cruise ships such as Sitmar, P & O, Royal Viking, or Cunard.

Immigration Formalities

Bona fide tourists and business people may enter tonga for up to 30 days, but they must have a valid passport, an onward air ticket, and proof of adequate funds. If visitors wish to extend their stay, permission is easily obtained.

Currency and Commerce

The Tongan unit of currency is the Pa'anga, and the Pa'anga is made up of 100 units, called Seniti. Currently the exchange is good for Americans—the US dollar is worth Pa'anga 1.50. But Tonga is an inexpensive place to visit anyway. Banking hours in Nuku'alofa are 9:30 AM to 3:30 PM, Monday to Friday.

Economy

The Tongan economy is based mainly on agricultural exports, and the agricultural sector employs nearly three quarters of the work force. Also there is a large cottage industry of excellent handicrafts which are either exported or sold to locals and tourists.

Time Zone

Tonga is practically on the International Dateline. Local time is 12 hours ahead of Greenwich Mean Time, 18 hours ahead of Eastern Standard Time, 21 hours ahead of Pacific Standard Time.

Radio, Newspaper and Telephone

The Tonga Broadcasting Station broadcasts in English as well as Tongan. The government-owned newspaper the *Tonga Chronicle,* published on Friday, has an edition in English and one in Tongan. Nearly all overseas newspapers are available in Nuku'alofa book stores. The Cable and Wireless office is open round the clock for long-distance calls.

Power

220 volts AC.

Health

No unusual medical problems here, and good medical and dental service available. Tap water is safe.

Language

Hawaii, Tahiti, the Cooks, the Samoas, and Tonga are all Polynesia. Many of their customs are the same, so is some of their language. And a Tongan speaking Tongan could, though with some difficulty, converse with his distant cousins. For example, the Hawaiians say "Mahalo" for thanks, the Tongans say "Malo." That's pretty close. Somewhere, sometime there was a link.

Now most Tongans speak enough English for visitors to get around easily.

What to Wear

Except for going to church on Sunday, or having an unlikely audience with the King, coats and ties are rarely worn and casual dress is in order. Brief shorts, bathing suits, bikinis are fine for the beach, but are frowned on if worn in public off the beach, and Tongan law prohibits any person from appearing in a public place without a shirt. This is strictly enforced.

In the cooler months, June to September, a sweater or jacket is recommended. And in December through March a light raincoat or umbrella would be useful.

Tipping

As in most other South Pacific areas, tipping is not encouraged.

Holidays

New Year's Day is a public holiday, as are Easter, Good Friday, and Easter Monday. This is one of the best times to hear magnificent hymn singing—sometimes with a thousand voices. April 25, as in Australia, New Zealand, Western Samoa, and the Cooks, is Anzac Day—a public military holiday with parades and wreath laying. Other holidays are July 4, which is King Tupou's birthday, November 4 (Constitution Day), and Christmas followed by December 26 (Boxing Day).

Useful Address: Tonga Visitors Bureau, PO Box 37, Nuku'alofa, Kingdom of Tonga, Tel 21733, Cable: TOUR-BUREAU.

TONGATAPU

How to Get Around

From the Airport-When you arrive by air you will land at Fua'amotu International Airport which is at the southern end of the island, 15 miles from Nuku'alofa. Once through customs, step outside the terminal and, as suggested earlier, board the appropriate minibus to your hotel. They're all plainly marked and will cost $3 per person. Unfortunately, they delay departure until everyone including crew and employees are ready to leave for town. If you're in a hurry— though you shouldn't be—take a $12 taxi.

In and Around Nuku'alofa—Nuku'alofa is considerably more spread out than Apia, Pago Pago, or Avarua in the Cooks. Walking to a restaurant on the far side of town or to a distant dock for a ferry may be a little much, and a taxi may be in order. Either hail one on the street or pick one up at your hotel. Then for the short run expect to pay $2. If you can find one of the nearly extinct three-wheelers called ve'etolus, it'll be great sport, and the fare will be $1.

There aren't any places we know of that rent motor bikes but, because the land is so flat, bicycles are ideal for middle distances or even further. Without too much complaining we once rode to and from Kolovai Beach, a total of 22 miles. Bicycles are available from a shop right next to the Dateline Hotel and cost $5 a day.

For rental cars, check with your hotel and expect to pay a flat rate, insurance included, of $45 a day. You'll need a Tongan driver's license, but with little formality this can be obtained at the Traffic Department in town. The fee is $2.

You should know too that, while most of the 150 miles of road on Tongatapu are paved, they are not well marked and, because of the numbers of horses, pigs, and chickens who stroll the roads, you'll have to be alert. Consider also that for about the same $45 you can get a car with driver, or a taxi, who'll know where he's going and who can explain the sights to you.

Public Buses—The bus terminal is in the middle of town, across the street from the public market. This is the cheapest

Street scene, Nuku'alofa, Tonga

transport. Thirty cents will take you to or from the airport, and 30¢ will take you the equivalent but opposite distance to Kolovai. Bear in mind that these buses, as in Samoa or Tahiti, play taped ear-splitting rock music en route.

Locals in rural areas use horses quite a bit. They can be rented for about $5 an hour, but often no saddles are available and the horses aren't well trained. Some riding experience comes in handy. If you're still interested, check in with the Visitors' Bureau, one block from the Dateline Hotel.

To get to the tiny within-the-reef islands in Nuku'alofa Harbor, taxi or walk to Queen Salote Wharf. Catch one of the launches; they run often to Pangaimotu or FaFa island. Round trip to either island is $6. If you're staying at one of the hotels on these islands, the trip is free.

Where to Stay

In general we approve heartily of the way Tonga houses their visitors. Accommodations cover the full spectrum of amenities and, while we have a few subjective remarks to make about hotels, we'll first provide an alphabetized list of what is available.

Beach House—PO Box 18, Nuku'alofa. One third of a mile from the center of town overlooking harbor. Ten double rooms sharing two bathrooms. $16 a double, bed and breakfast.

Captain Cook's Vacation Apartments—PO Box 838, Nuku'alofa. Six self-contained bedroom units on Nuku's waterfront, a mile from town. $20 a double.

FaFa Island Resort—PO Box 42, Nuku. Thirty minutes launch trip from town, unspoiled beaches for swimming, snorkeling. Eight Tongan thatched fales. Bar and restaurant with French and local food. Complimentary launch transport to and from Nuku. $13 a double, some with baths.

Falemaama Motel—PO Box 367, Nuku, 3 mi. from town. Three individual cottages with two bedrooms, and full kitchen facilities. $13 a double.

Fasi-Moe-Afi Guest House & Cafe Garden—PO Box 316, Nuku. Right in town. Share bath facilities. $8 a double.

Friendly Islander Motel—PO Box 142, Nuku. Two miles from town. Twelve modern suites with bathrooms, fully equipped kitchens and balconies. Swimming pool too. $20 a double.

Good Samaritan Inn—PO Box 142, Nuku. Two miles from town. Twenty-four share bath fales, dining room, lounge, picnic, swimming and barbecue facilities. $12 a double.

Ha'atafu Beach Motel—PO Box 90, Nuku. Thirteen miles west of Nuku offers seven comfortable two-bed fales overlooking magnificent Ha'atafu Beach. Share bathroom facilities, dining room. $9 a double.

International Dateline Hotel—PO Box 39, Nuku. This is the biggest hotel on the island. A third of a mile from the town center on the waterfront. Seventy-six air conditioned rooms, dining room, bar, swimming pool, tennis court, entertainment. $39 a double.

Joe's Tropicana Hotel—PO Box 1169, Nuku. A third of a mile from town. Fourteen rooms with private baths. Two bars viewing the ocean on the top floor. $19 a double with breakfast.

Keleti Beach Resort—PO Box 192, Nuku. Eight fale units with private facilities and hot water. Restaurant, lounge bar with full ocean view. Sandy beach for swimming. Weekly Tongan entertainment and feast. $19 a double.

K's Guest House—PO Box 1062, Nuku. Just over a mile from town. Five double, 4 single rooms. $19 a double with meals.

Kimiko's Guest House—PO Box 693, a mile from Nuku. Eight rooms along the waterfront. Prices start at $3 a single.

Moana Hotel—PO Box 169, one and a half miles from town overlooking Faua Harbor. Four double fales with private facilities, bar and garden available. $8 a double.

Nukama'anu Hotel—PO Box 390, Nuku. A mile from town on waterfront. Two bedroom cottage with bath, $17 a double.

Pangaimotu Island Resort—PO Box 740. Located 15 minutes by boat from Nuku. Offers 32 acres of island escape in Tongan fales. Restaurant and bar. $20 a double.

Ramanlal Hotel—PO Box 74. Center of commercial Nuku. Twenty-nine air conditioned rooms with bath. Bar, night club, and restaurant. $28 a double.

Sela's Guest House—PO Box 24, Nuku. A mile from town. Twelve double rooms and two single rooms, all with private baths. $20 double with all meals.

Sunrise Guest House—PO Box 132, Nuku. A mile from town, on the waterfront. Three single rooms, 3 doubles. $26 double with meals.

We've stayed at several of the hotels listed, have looked at others, and can report that there are good bargains to be had.

On our first trip several years ago we stayed at Joe's Hotel. It was old, scruffy, and ugly then, but the price was right and, once past the bar-dancehall on the ground floor, matters improved. The rooms were adequate, the dining room was nearly excellent, and the South Sea characters we met were straight out of a Joseph Conrad novel. The only reason I mention Joe's is that it so typifies the sort of hotel associated with the old days of beachcombing, defrocked sailors, and remittance men.

On this last trip we briefly went back to Joe's. If possible, it looked even more dissolute. The bar-dancehall throbbed with music and was filled with intertwined couples. The bar girl shrugged when we asked about accommodations and indicated that, if we insisted, she'd show us a room. We declined. Still, it's worth taking a look at this place.

We stayed instead at the Dateline, Nuku'alofa's most prestigious address. At $39 a double this hotel is a bargain. The staff is friendly and most amenities good, but on weekend nights live bands play in the open area between the bar and swimming pool. The mostly country western and island music is amplified to the point of alienating the guests in nearby rooms. Locals are in attendance on these nights, single men and women, and it's a place of some action. But compared to Joe's it's like a Sunday school.

The Ramanlal Hotel right in the center of town keeps a low profile. It's set behind the facade of buildings on the main street up a short alley, but it opens up into a pleasant leafy retreat with a pool. It has a bar and restaurant and, though it's cheaper than the Dateline, the rooms are just as nice. The food, however, is not outstanding and, although it's an Indian restaurant, don't order Indian food there. Breakfast is fine, however.

If economics are a consideration, consider the following quote from a Tourist Bureau brochure called "Tonga on $20 a Day."

"*Sample Holiday A*—Two people decide to book into a superior motel, something in the $15 to $20 a day class for a twin room. You have eight days in Tonga and decide to make the motel your base. As the motel is going to cost about $140 for the eight days, you'll have $85 left. This allows you to use taxis for local sights, to buy local handicraft and eat well.

Sample Holiday B—You're on an eight day holiday. Both of you are keen to see out of the way places, so you take a launch to one of the nearby islands. For food, transport, and hotel this is going to cost about $20 each. Then you want to see something of Tongatapu the fun way, so you hire bicycles for touring around nearby villages and beaches. This way you decide to take advantage of Tonga's good value guest houses at an average of $4 a night, and you find you still have money to buy souvenirs."

Remember that this is strictly a quote and, while we feel the above is possible, considerable discipline would be required. Nevertheless, for these purposes we can recommend a number of clean, comfortable and friendly inns:

Flame tree in Tonga

In Town—Sela's Guest House, Beach House, Kimiko's Guest House, Sunrise Guest House, and Captain Cook Apartments.

All of these inns have special rates for longer stays. They're often full, though, so it's best to write for reservations.

Out of Town—For South Sea beach exotica and for inexpensive tranquility, try the inns on FaFa or Pangaimotu. You can see both of these islands from Nuku'alofa. They stand out as tiny clumps of palms in the distance. You can walk around FaFa in 20 minutes. It has white sand swimming beaches and the FaFa Island Resort is right on the beach.

Pangaimotu is closer in to Tongatapu and offers similar accommodations, but the beach is nicer at FaFa.

To get to either island, take the launch from Queen Salote Wharf. It's free for hotel guests.

At a distance, 10 miles from town at Kolovai Beach, the Good Samaritan is a jewel. The thatched fales are comfortable, and the coastline is wildly beautiful. Best of all is the food served there.

Food

Food on Tonga runs from adequate to excellent and, like housing, is generally inexpensive. Breakfast in your hotel or inn can be either the big English style (bangers, broiled tomatoes, eggs, toast and coffee), or Continental (fruit, toast and coffee). Don't miss the fruit—papayas, melons, finger bananas, and chilled drinking coconuts.

At noon have a cold beer and a sandwich by the pool at the Dateline Hotel, or wander into town for a quick lunch at a variety of small restaurants. For example:

The USA—This spotless restaurant run by a jovial American provides good hamburgers, chili, milkshakes, and ice cream cones. This small place looks like it could be anywhere in middle America, but is slightly less expensive. It's two blocks uptown from the Dateline Hotel.

The Cafe Fakalato and Snack Bar—On Wellington Street, two blocks in from the waterfront, it has sandwiches, soup, and salads. It's good and will probably run about $3 for a respectable lunch.

The Tong Hua Restaurant—This restaurant directly behind the Dateline serves spicy Szechuan food. It's open for lunch and dinner, and reasonably inexpensive.

Fasi-Moe-Ofi Cafe Garden—Half a block from the Dateline, this is the place to go for coffee, snacks, and to watch the world go by.

Beach House—A block from the Dateline. Provides lots of good home cooking. However, it serves too much food for a light lunch, and is usually filled with hotel residents at night.

Akiko's—A Japanese restaurant five blocks up Taufa'aha Road (the main street) from the waterfront is in the basement of the Catholic Basilica. It's popular and inexpensive.

The Arcade—An upstairs restaurant next door to the Ramanlal Hotel has good sandwiches, soups, salads, some seafood. Inexpensive.

Sela's Guest House—Across town a block from the main street. Serves home-style Tongan food, featuring pork, chicken, yams, breadfruit, fish, vegetables steamed in banana leaves. Also something called Tongan pudding which nobody clearly defined for me. It's obviously starchy, probably one reason Tongans become so portly.

Dinner

A number of unusual restaurants come to mind that are especially appropriate for dinner. The Dateline isn't quite one of them and, while it's good, it can't compare with the following:

Chez Alise and André—For dinner in this small French restaurant near the King's Palace, our selection was sautéed clams on the half shell, broiled lobster with pan fried potatoes, and a salad. With it came baguettes of bread, a carafe of house wine, and for dessert a platter of local fruit and cheeses. In every sense it was excellent, and the bill came to about $20 for two.

Seaview—In the same neighborhood, the Seaview serves fine German food and is on a par with Chez Alise.

Good Samaritan—This restaurant, associated with the hotel of the same name at Kolovai Beach, serves French food too. The chef himself took our order. You can be served inside or outside by the sea. We had lobster, clams with all the trimmings and, for my first time, all the lobster I could eat. With wine, the check was about $16 for two.

Ha'atafu Motel—Excellent food—Australian style. It's also less expensive, and is not far beyond the Good Samaritan.

FaFa—The small hotel on FaFa island has a family style barbecue on Saturday afternoons and Sundays. The food is good, in quantity, and the guests generally in a festive frame of mind. Cost is about $16 for two.

Island Feasting and Kava Drinking

There's usually a feast somewhere. They're for special holidays, anniversaries, church and school functions. Check with the Visitors Bureau and your hotel for what is currently happening, then attend one, maybe at Oscar's on Oholei Beach near the airport.

The feast will probably be held outside where you'll sit crosslegged on mats and, when food appears in immense proportions, you'll eat with your fingers. Some food freshly removed from the underground oven or "umu", such as taro, breadfruit, fish, will still be wrapped in banana leaves. There'll be suckling pig, fried chicken, fresh fruit and, to end the occasion, kava, the mild intoxicant, will be passed around in coconut shells. Then usually there's singing and the traditional Tongan dance, the lakalaka. Cost for a feast will range from free to about $10 a person.

Shopping

For the usual necessities, toothpaste, postcards, clothes, and picnic supplies, visit the larger stores downtown, such as Burns Philp, Morris Hedstrom, Sanfts, E. M. Jones. They're easy to find and anyone can direct you. For liquor, cigarettes, perfume, or film, shop in the Duty Free Shop at the Dateline Hotel, the A-Z Radio Shop, or at the airport shop. Prices are low.

For gifts, handicraft of all kinds, there are at least four shops in town, all close together, where you can buy local products. They're genuine and well done, for there is no mass production of handicrafts on Tonga. It's still a cottage industry. Visit the Talamahu Market, Nuku'alofa's main fruit and vegetable market, a block from the Dateline Hotel. They have a good selection of gifts too. Try the Langa Fonua Center, the Manu-hua Women's Handicraft Center or the Fa'onelua Gardens. Be sure to examine the Tongan tapa. Tapa formed from the bark of the mulberry tree is beaten out into a fibrous fabric, then printed with brown and black designs, and sold as wall hangings or table mats. For a very large piece of tapa expect to pay about $30. Look too at the woven baskets, mats and carvings. Tonga has some fine bargains.

Entertainment

For spirited fun, for dancing, drinking, and Tongan dancing, the Dateline is active on weekends. So is the disco at the Ramanlal Hotel. The Friendly Islander, a shiny new hotel, is the weekend scene of informal island dancing as well as disco. Evenings at the off-shore inns of FaFa and Pangaimotu islands have less structured, but pleasant evenings of music and dancing. And at a distance, out past the airport at Oscar's on Oho-lei Beach they have Tongan feasts and traditional dancing on Wednesdays and Fridays. The tour desk at the Dateline Hotel can organize the evening, which will cost about $15 a person.

Making tapa

The Good Samaritan Inn has Tongan dancing, but usually not the feast.

Several notches down in couth, try Joe's Hotel. But for evenings of unrestrained sensual abandon, Tonga is not the destination of choice. Try instead Tahiti, or perhaps New Caledonia.

A Word About Tongan Dancing—Unlike the vigorous tamure of Tahiti where everything is shaken with enthusiasm, the Tongan dancing is more dignified, less sensuous, and is accompanied by drum and voice.

The 'tau'olunga is the solo dance and is done with the body glistening with oil, hair flowing, and in elaborate costume. With knees together the girl sways gently and uses her hands for emphasis. Sometimes a man or woman will spontaneously jump up and join the dance. Sometimes too a spectator overcome with enthusiasm will come forward and present the dancer with a gift. He'll paste paper money on the oiled legs, arms or chest of the dancer.

Then there are the group dances called ma'ulu'ulu. They are usually done sitting down by up to hundreds of people who use only their hands and upper bodies. This dance is often done on state occasions.

The lakalaka is an even more important group dance, generally done by men. Row upon row of dancers, all singing and dressed in costumes, act out descriptions of events from the past. It too is done on special occasions.

Boxing—Tongan boxing rules allow for a bit of mayhem here and there, like kicking one's opponent when he's down. Tongan men turn out in force and respond with gusto. The fights are usually held in a tent in a vacant lot somewhere downtown. $5 will buy a ringside seat.

Movies—There's a movie theater two blocks behind the Dateline Hotel called Loni's. It can be crowded and noisy. You may be happier watching VCR movies in the bar of the Dateline or Ramanlal Hotel. Just walk in and sit down. There is no TV yet in Tonga.

What to do on Tongatapu

By South Sea standards Tongatapu ranks only fair in beauty. There are good beaches on the island, but no hills, no rivers, and the land crowded with people looks like one big plantation. Even the lagoons are harnessed with their fence-like encirclement of fish traps.

Driving through the villages, which incline to ramshackle, visitors will see pigs, chickens, goats, children, a horse-drawn cart or two, and often a cemetery where the graves are outlined by upturned beer bottles sunk into the ground. The people you'll see wearing clumsy ankle-length flax mats over their clothes aren't exactly the glass of fashion either. They wear this attire, called ta'ovala, out of respect for the King, for elders, and sometimes as a sign of mourning.

The town of Nuku'alofa, designed for function rather than civic beauty, begins at the lagoon where wooden buildings surrounded by palms and gardens straggle along the waterfront. This is where the Dateline, the Beach, and the Friendly Islander Hotels are. Dominating the area a little further west, the Victorian King's Palace sits in a grove of Norfolk pines.

The hub of town, Talamahu market and the bus terminal, is several blocks inland. From there, spread out in squares, wooden one- and two-story shops, banks, shipping offices, restaurants, and churches line the dusty streets. In spite of this functional utility there's a sense of the orderly, the friendly, and predictable, qualities which explain the numbers of expatriates who live here and love Tonga.

Nuku'alofa

Pick up the "Walking Tour of Central Nuku'alofa" brochure at the Visitor's Bureau on Vuna Street, the coast road. Then, starting from the market area, set off by foot and, depending on time and energy, see what you want. But don't miss the following.

The Royal Palace and Chapel—The Victorian white frame building on the waterfront was pre-fabricated in New Zealand and erected in 1867. A second story was added in 1882. Unfortunately the Palace and its grounds are off-limits to visitors, but it can easily be seen from the outside fence.

The Wesley Methodist Church—The best way to see the King is to attend services at this imposing old church. The King is a big man, obese in the traditional Tongan way. He usually appears at 10 AM. With members of the royal family, he sits in an area well removed from the congregation.

The morning we were there he took his seat, trained an electric fan on himself, put on dark glasses, and I think dozed off. Music for the service was provided by a large choir which sang lustily, accompanied by a full brass band. Except for a few welcoming remarks directed to visitors, the service was conducted in Tongan.

Talamahu Market—Open every day except Sunday, this busy market sells everything locally grown or made. You can buy oranges, papayas, melons, even giant avocados, or shop for baskets, wood carvings, or tapa. Perhaps in the environs of the market you'll see women sitting crosslegged in front of a large trunk of wood beating strips of mulberry bark into tapa.

Mala'ekula, the Royal Tombs—This large park-like area surrounded by casuarina trees is sacred to Tongans as the burial

HARBOR AND LAGOON
NUKU'ALOFA TOWN

1/2 MILE

1. Royal Palace
2. Seaveiw Restaurant
3. Ramanlal Hotel
4. Bank of Tonga
5. Post Office
6. Langa Fonua Handicraft Center
7. Royal Tombs
8. Joe's Hotel
9. Date Line Hotel
10. Tong Hua Chinese Restaurant
11. Beach House

12. Kimiko's Guest House
13. Fasi-Moe Afi Guest House
14. Moana Hotel
15. Methodist Church
16. Tonga Visitors Bureau
17. Sunrise Guest House
18. Chez Alise and Andre's Restaurant
19. USA Restaurant
20. Selas Guest House
21. Fish and Meat Market
22. Bus Station and Public Market

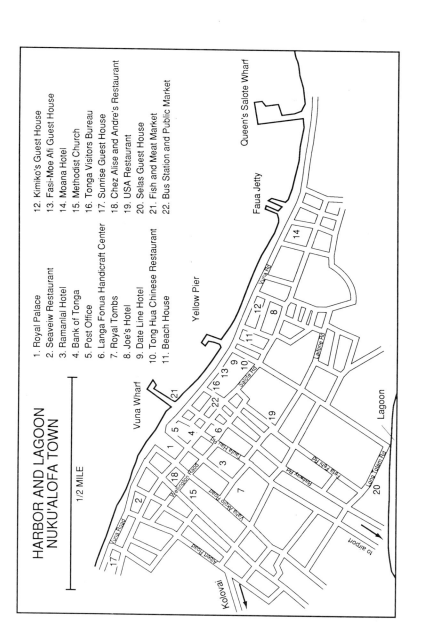

Queen's Salote Wharf

Faua Jetty

Yellow Pier

Vuna Wharf

Lagoon

Kolovai

to airport

ground for royalty since 1893. Among others, King Tupou I and Queen Salote are buried there.

Fa'onelua Tropical Gardens—Here there's a model Tongan village surrounded by beautiful vegetation typical of Tongatapu.

Vuna Market—Located on the waterfront, this market originally was the Customs House. In 1955 it was turned into a government fish and meat market. A sign outside the market indicates what is available.

Cart Factory—The horse and cart is still a popular means of transport in rural Tonga and, here with old fashioned blacksmithing and carpentry methods, you can watch skilled craftsmen construct an entire cart from raw materials.

Basilica of St. Anthony of Padua—The first basilica in the South Pacific, this magnificent building was opened in 1980 by King Tupou IV, the present king. It's probably the most impressive building on the island. Beneath the basilica there's a well-equipped community center and a Japanese restaurant.

Coconut Oil Mill—If you're interested in the most basic of South Sea industries, visit the coconut oil mill one and a half miles east of town near Queen Salote Wharf.

Pangai—This park-like waterfront area next to the Palace is where royal feasts, parades, and kava ceremonies are held. On Saturdays you can watch soccer, and sometimes cricket matches here.

You'll have done considerable walking by now. But if more civic sights are required, continue on and examine such attractions as the Audit Office, the Bank of Tonga, Tonga High School, and Queen Salote College. Without even trying, you'll no doubt stroll by Fatai, the nicely landscaped seafront residence of the King's brother, the Prime Minister.

The Eastern End of the Island

We think the obligatory sights of Tongatapu can be done fairly quickly. The best way is to see the ones to the west in one day, the ones to the east, in another.

Mua—Going east from town, the road follows the inner lagoon and comes first to Mua, 12 miles away. Captain Cook landed at Mua in 1777. It was here he rested under a banyan

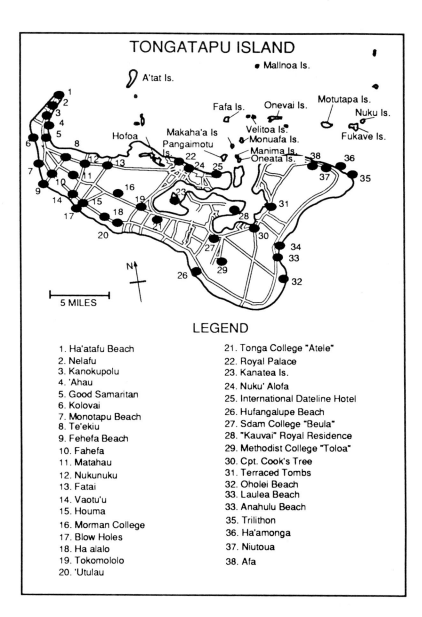

TONGATAPU ISLAND

A'tat Is.

Mallnoa Is.

Fafa Is. Onevai Is. Motutapa Is.
                              Nuku Is.
Hofoa Makaha'a Is Velitoa Is.
       Pangaimotu Monuafa Is. Fukave Is.
       Is. 22   Manima Is.
            24 25   Oneata Is. 38 36
                                37   35

31

28

30

34
33

27   29   32
26

N

5 MILES

LEGEND

1. Ha'atafu Beach
2. Nelafu
3. Kanokupolu
4. 'Ahau
5. Good Samaritan
6. Kolovai
7. Monotapu Beach
8. Te'ekiu
9. Fehefa Beach
10. Fahefa
11. Matahau
12. Nukunuku
13. Fatai
14. Vaotu'u
15. Houma
16. Morman College
17. Blow Holes
18. Ha alalo
19. Tokomololo
20. 'Utulau

21. Tonga College "Atele"
22. Royal Palace
23. Kanatea Is.
24. Nuku' Alofa
25. International Dateline Hotel
26. Hufangalupe Beach
27. Sdam College "Beula"
28. "Kauvai" Royal Residence
29. Methodist College "Toloa"
30. Cpt. Cook's Tree
31. Terraced Tombs
32. Oholei Beach
33. Laulea Beach
33. Anahulu Beach
35. Trilithon
36. Ha'amonga
37. Niutoua
38. Afa

tree, gone now, but today it takes little imagination to see the *Endeavour* swinging at anchor in the calm waters of the enclosed lagoon. There's a monument there commemorating the landing.

Langi—A little further along and just off the road, this is the burial site of ancient royalty. This is an eerie place and, because of vegetation, it's hard to see all 28 burial sites. Like the royal tombs in Nuku'alofa they are rectangular and built in terraces.

But you can get an idea of the size of these massive 30-ton blocks of stone that rise some 20 feet in height. Experts in stonemasonry express amazement that primitive Tongans with only shells and stones could have hewn these huge blocks.

Be sure not to climb on the tombs, as only Tongans of royal blood can stand on the topmost stone.

Ha'amonga—Six miles on after passing through several villages and sometimes skirting the sea, the road comes to the huge coral arch called the Trilithon. Here the ancient God Maui of Polynesian legend comes to mind. According to myth these three great slabs of coral, the uprights being 17 feet high and the horizontal slab 19 feet long, were hand carried by Maui from distant Wallis island. However, his connection with the structure is purely mythical, for its construction in about 1200 is attributed to a king named Tu'i-ta-tui. It is thought to have served as a gateway to his royal compound.

Construction of the 109-ton structure may have been accomplished in the same way the pyramids of Egypt were, by hauling the coral slabs into position on mounds of sand. As in the construction of the Egyptian pyramids, human sacrifice may have been involved in the building of the Trilithon.

The other matter of curiosity here is that, as with England's Stonehenge, there are grooves in the horizontal slab which align with the sun on the longest and shortest days of the year.

Near the Trilithon down a cleared path through the bush there are more tombs and a special stone against which Tu'i-Ta-Tui used to sit and swing his staff around him in order to clear a space. Then, according to myth, he felt safe from assassination.

The Trilithon, Tonga

Anahulu Beach—Eight miles to the south beyond Ha'amonga you'll come to Anahulu Beach. There's a cave near here; inquire locally, and ask a local or your taxi driver to accompany you into this mysterious fresh water cave. Then, if you've plenty of fortitude, you can swim into its deepest recesses. Don't forget a flashlight for this expedition.

Laulea Beach—This is one of the good beaches on Tongatapu, a mile past Anahulu Beach. A fine picnic spot.

Oholei Beach—This also is a good beach, but the importance of this area is the Wednesday and Friday beach nights which feature Tongan feasting and dancing.

Hufangalupe Beach—If you keep on going south and around the bottom of the island, continuing west another five miles, you'll come to Hufangalupe Beach. Here there are three things to see: a huge natural coral bridge under which the sea churns, a steep cliff overlooking the sea, and a pretty beach at the bottom of a downhill trail.

The Western End of the Island

For dramatic attractions, this part of the island is important. Here's where the flying foxes (fruit bats) and blowholes are found. Kolovai Beach and the best food on the island are here too and, a little further on at the very end of Tongatapu, the snorkeling at Ha'atafu Beach is excellent. Bus or taxi will deliver you to this area easily. We made the run out and back to Kolovai Beach by bicycle one day, visited Kolovai Beach and the flying foxes, and found it only mildly arduous.

The Flying Foxes of Kolovai—You'll see these fruit bats hanging by the hundreds on casuarina trees like black fruit. They're found on a short stretch of the road near Kolovai. You won't have to ask directions to find them, you'll see them plainly, perhaps smell them.

These bats, seldom seen anywhere else on the island, fly off every night to raid mango trees. Then at dawn they return, fold their wings, and hang upside down on the trees which are considered a sanctuary. No matter how much damage the bats do at night, no one molests them. It's taboo to bother them. Only members of royalty are allowed to hunt and eat them; they're considered a great delicacy. It's said that if a white bat appears, a chief will die. In 1965 this did happen: a white bat appeared a week before Queen Salote died.

Kolovai Beach—At the village of Kolovai a narrow bush road runs about a half mile to the beach. This is the location of the Good Samaritan Hotel and restaurant. The beach, while pretty, is rocky and has a sizable surf. The hotel, a pleasant place to stay, is particularly busy on weekends. Make a reservation first.

Ha'atafu Beach—This beach, with its small hotel, is about one and a half miles beyond Kolovai. Here, at the extreme end of the island, swimming and snorkeling is excellent but, like Kolovai, will require reservations.

The Blowholes—About five miles to the east, on the south coast, the road comes to the village of Houma. Here there is a path leading to the coast about 500 yards away. On the walk in, across a windy stretch of open land, you'll hear the blowholes before you see them. Then, looking down on the reef, there's a long series of circular tide pools, hundreds of them,

The Blowholes, Tonga

each with a deep hole. When the sea crashes against them there is a loud hissing sound followed by geysers of sea water. Dozens of them are active at any given time.

Using the Good Samaritan or Ha'atufu Hotel as headquarters, and with hired bicycle, you can comfortably wander these attractions and neighboring villages as well. It's a good way to briefly play at being a Tongan.

Diving—Unfortunately you seldom see or hear of organizations advertising diving gear on Tongatapu but, if gear is available, the best diving is on the reef areas north of Nuku'alofa. For snorkeling and diving, the reef that surrounds FaFa Island (six miles offshore) is good but, further out, the reef around Malinoa Island has fine drop-offs and plenty of the rare black coral. Divers are not allowed to disturb what they find there.

Deep Sea Fishing—There's a fine variety of game fish offshore, but few organized fishing vessels. The best thing is to go to Vuna Wharf where the commercial boats come in. You could hire a boat there for a reasonable amount, or ask to join one of the commercial boats.

EUA ISLAND

Eua Island, across a stretch of sea called Tonga Deep, is 14 miles southeast of Tongatapu. Born of volcanic activity, Eua is a curious island and at its highest point, 1000 feet, coral is evident. Scientists say that this 5- by 15-mile island is the oldest in the Pacific.

Coming from flat Tongatapu, Eua is a surprising contrast. There are rolling hills, towering cliffs, mountain streams, and natural forests filled with a variety of tropical birds. The locals, about 4,000 of them, are different too—more elemental and more inclined to provide uncomplicated hospitality.

All five villages, all the plantations, and most of the people are on the west side of the island. The eastern side is mountainous, heavily wooded, and some of the cliffs drop 400 sheer feet into the sea. Eua is an offbeat, away-from-it-all island.

How to Get There By Ferry

The ferry leaves Nuku'alofa from Faua Wharf (half a mile east of the Dateline Hotel) early in the morning daily except Sunday. As with all transport in Tonga, check departure times carefully as they change often. The crossing is about 25 miles and, after a three- to four-hour (sometimes rough) trip, she ties up at the town of Ohonua. The fare is $4.

By Air

Friendly Islands Airways flies to Eua from Tongatapu every Wednesday and Friday. They land at Kaufana airstrip, about two and a half miles from Ohonua. Round-trip fare $35.

Where to Stay and Eat

Eua gets few Tongan visitors. Housing and food are marginal, but there are three choices.

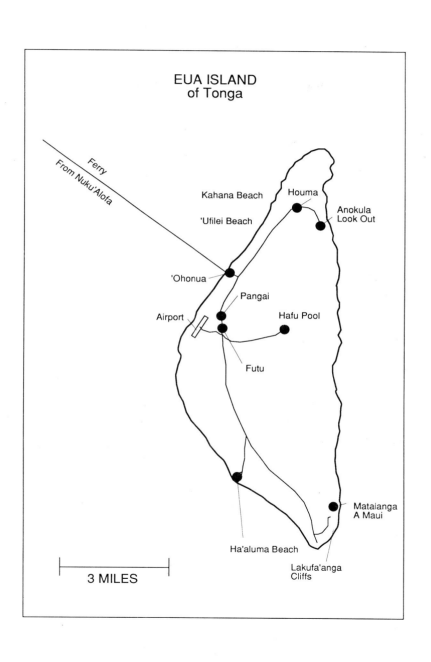

EUA ISLAND
of Tonga

Ferry
From Nuku'Alofa

Kahana Beach

'Ufilei Beach

Houma

Anokula
Look Out

'Ohonua

Pangai

Airport

Hafu Pool

Futu

Ha'aluma Beach

Matalanga
A Maui

Lakufa'anga
Cliffs

3 MILES

Fungafonua Motel—Located at Ohonua not far from the ferry dock has 10 units, all with bath, and rates are $10 a double.
  The Haukinima Guest House—This accommodation for the hardy is inland at Futu, practically on the airstrip, and about two miles from Ohuna. Meals are available on request, but they're not culinary delights. You're better off buying rations at the shops in Futu or Ohonua. Rates $7 a double.
  The Leipua Lodge—It's located at Pangai, a mile north of the airstrip, and is a shade better. Rates $15 a double. If you ask, they'll provide meals.

What to Do on Eua

Visitors don't come to Eua for swimming or lying about on beaches. There are few safe places to swim. They don't come for night life either. Other than some uninspired dancing at a local disco, there's little glitter, and they certainly don't come for gourmet dining.
  Eua is for hill climbing, forest trekking, mountain stream following, and for meeting outback Tongans. Walking will easily get you to most areas and a horse, for about $8 a day, would extend coverage. To reach the extremities at either end of the island, you can rent a Land Rover for $40 a day.
  Lakufa'anga Cliffs and Matalanga-'a Maui—For a long day on horseback, or a short one by Land Rover, set out south from Futu. Keep to the left where the road forks to Ha'aluma Beach, and continue on to the end of the island, about three miles. From here work your way northward. This is now the east coast, an area of high cliffs called the Liku. One of the first cliffs you come to will be a 300-foot drop called the Lakufa'anga. It's said that if you throw stones down into the sea from this cliff, turtles will appear. Perhaps years ago they did.
  Less than a mile onward through a fine forest, you'll come to what is known as the Matalanga'a Maui. Here there probably was a cave, but part of its roof has fallen in, leaving a bridge of earth over the entrance. Looking down through this great hole you'll see the sea crashing. According to myth, the God Maui is responsible and, for some unknown reason he became angry and picked up the missing part of the cave and flung it out to

sea. The tiny distant island to the south is said to be the result.

Hafu Pool and the Forest Reserve—This is a good area for hiking. The rain forest in the hills to the east of Futu is beautiful, as is the exotic collection of birds there. Hafu Pool is formed by the clear waters of Heike stream which comes from the eastern hills. This trek to and from Futu is easily made, a distance of about five miles round trip.

The Northern End—For perhaps the most dramatic views on Eua, go north to Houma village, then east less than a mile to Anakula.

THE HA'APAI GROUP

This archipelago scattered over a large stretch of the sea is about 100 miles north of Tongatapu. Other than cone-shaped Kao and flat-topped volcanic Tofua, most of these dozens of islands are low-lying uninhabited atolls. The 10,000 inhabitants live primarily on the seven main islands near Lifuka.

How to Get There by Air

Friendly Island Airways using the 22-seat Spanish-built Casa flies to Lifuka nearly every day except Sunday. It's the same flight that continues on to Vava'u, 100 miles to the north. One way fare to Lifuka is about $35. If you plan to stay there a day or two before going on to Vava'u, be sure to have reservations. The plane sometimes is fully booked, and you may not want additional time in the Ha'apai Group.

When we flew in I was fortunate to occupy the jump seat between Captain Bill Johns and copilot Tanoa. I had full view of the many-hued sea which was stitched with lines of surf breaking on coral reefs. To left and right lay numbers of palm-tufted reef-enclosed atolls, a magnificent sight, but perhaps not so magnificent to a sailor down there on a dark night.

Captain Johns pointed to the left, to the prominent volcanic islands, Tofua and Kao. Like a perfect cone, Kao is over 3000

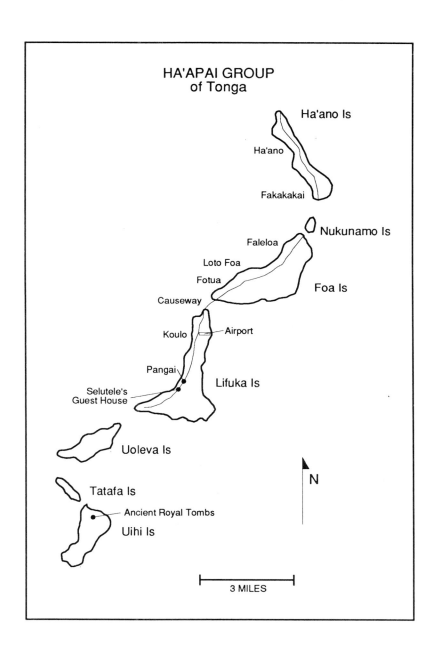

HA'APAI GROUP
of Tonga

Ha'ano Is

Ha'ano

Fakakakai

Nukunamo Is

Faleloa

Loto Foa

Fotua

Foa Is

Causeway

Koulo — Airport

Pangai

Lifuka Is

Selutele's
Guest House

Uoleva Is

Tatafa Is

Ancient Royal Tombs

Uihi Is

N

3 MILES

feet high and Tofua, with its crater lake, is about 1500 feet. I could see that Tofua was still active, with steam coming from a crater on the north side. Kao had no inhabitants other than wild pigs, and occasionally people who come from nearby islands to cultivate gardens. It was here in 1789 that the mutiny on the *Bounty* occurred and Bligh and his men were set adrift. Bligh made a brief landing on Tofua for water, but was not well received. Then off to our right in a group of seven islands was Lifuka, our destination. At the airstrip a truck was waiting which delivered us to the village of Pangai and our guest house.

By Sea

The ship, *Olovaha* sails from Nuku'alofa to Pangai, Lifuka, every Tuesday. She's a large fairly new vessel that carries a hundred or more passengers. Four of that number can occupy the two double-bunk cabins aboard. Other than a simple snack bar, passengers must bring their own food. It's 12 hours to Lifuka, then she goes on to Vava'u. Fare with cabin to Lifuka is $20.

Where to Stay

We know of three places, all simple and inexpensive and all provide meals.

Evaloni Guest House—Located in the town of Pangai, a room with shared bath and all meals is $14 a double.

Fonongava'inga Guest House—This similar establishment on the edge of Pangai is $12 a double with meals.

Selutete Guest House—This inn just across the street from the beach is probably the best address in town. We stayed there, and rather happily. The island food, reef fish, taro, breadfruit, baked bananas, prepared in a shed in the backyard, was good, the beer was cold, and the family and other guests warm and friendly. The room however was tiny, privacy scanty, and the plumbing facilities meager. Rates were $20 a double with all meals.

What to Do

In the heat of the first afternoon, we walked into Pangai town and strolled along the sleepy main street between ranks of unpainted wooden buildings. There's little to be seen. The town has a small bank, a few tiny shops, a small public market, but no restaurant, no movie house, no pub. The people on the street, mostly Tongan women under umbrellas, and a pair of men on horseback, all smiled and said hello. At the edge of town by a school, a group of children asked us our names, where we were going, and then giggled.

Just south of town are two churches, another school, a small neat hospital, and a municipal wharf, where interisland craft and the *Olovaha* tie up. On the beach in front of town where outrigger canoes are drawn up, there's an unfortunate collection of tin cans and other debris.

At the north end of town, the out-of-proportion statue of Reverend Shirley Baker will startle you. Rev. Baker, an English missionary, was an advisor to King Tupou I and in 1862 assisted in drafting the first constitution. Baker ended his days on Lifuka.

The peace and quiet of these islands may either appeal to you or drive you crazy. There are no distractions. The only animation is church-inspired and at nearly any time of the day you'll hear enthusiastic a capella singing. It's as if their voices make up a single and well-tuned instrument.

To find unspoiled beaches you have to get away from Pangai and most of Lifuka. To do this, go north or south.

North First—Hire a bicycle from Mrs. Selutete or ask the Friendly Islands Airways agent to provide his truck. Then follow the road north past the airstrip and across the causeway to Foa Island. Two miles further you'll arrive at the village of Faleloa. If you wait awhile, you'll find locals going by outboard to Ha'ano Island. It's a good trip across a transparent lagoon but, like Foa and Lifuka, Ha'ano is flat. The only difference is the lack of clutter.

Going South—Consider a combination fishing/camping trip, perhaps with a barbecue thrown in. On the wharf at Pangai ask around for a fishing boat and crew for the 15-mile sea trip, usually a calm one, to Uiha Island. You're sure to catch fish and on Uiha there's a simple guest house plus lots of places to build a fire and cook your fish. A boat for two days will cost about $70. While there, ask to see the ruins of Makahokovalu. The high islands, Tofua and Kao, are due west of Lifuka about 50 miles. To get there, an interisland boat weaves its way among coral reefs and puts you ashore on both islands. This service is sporadic. Ask the Friendly Islands agent or Mrs. Selutete for the latest information.

THE VAVA'U GROUP

This is probably the best destination in Tonga and, looking like an unfinished jigsaw puzzle, the approach to it by land or sea is magnificent. Vava'u, 100 miles north of Ha'apai, 200 from Tongatapu, is no atoll. And the hilly main island of Vava'u is surrounded by smaller islands which form intricate narrow channels, one of which leads to the principal town, Neiafu. Vava'u's population is 17,000.

The yachtsmen—fleets of them—have found Vava'u. Sometimes 100 boats are anchored in and around the Port of Refuge, which is in an arm of the harbor near Neiafu. These boats, flying the flags of New Zealand, Australia, and the United States, come in all sizes, 28-foot homemade sloops, 33-foot double ender yawls, 45-foot ketches, and 60-foot mahogany-teak schooners that cost more than Beverly Hills real estate. These "yachties" know a good thing when they see it. So will the tourist world and soon. You can't long hide a spot like Vava'u from the big beach resort interests.

How to Get There By Air

Friendly Islands Airways flies in every day except Sunday from Tongatapu, the same flight that pauses on Ha'apai. One-way fare is $70.

At least twice weekly Friendly Islands Airways flies in from Pago Pago, American Samoa. The fare is about $130.

Bus transport from the airport to Neiafu, about eight miles,

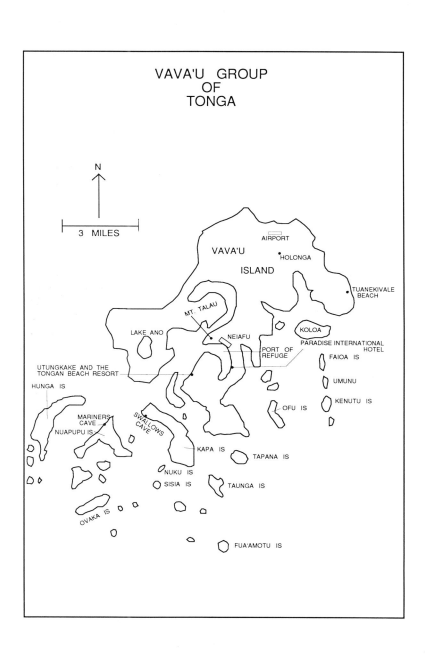

VAVA'U GROUP
OF
TONGA

N

3 MILES

AIRPORT

VAVA'U

•HOLONGA

ISLAND

TUANEKIVALE
BEACH

MT. TALAU

KOLOA

LAKE ANO

NEIAFU

PARADISE INTERNATIONAL
HOTEL

PORT OF
REFUGE

FAIOA IS

UTUNGKAKE AND THE
TONGAN BEACH RESORT

UMUNU

HUNGA IS

KENUTU IS

MARINERS
CAVE

SWALLOWS
CAVE

OFU IS

NUAPUPU IS

KAPA IS

TAPANA IS

NUKU IS

SISIA IS

TAUNGA IS

OVAKA IS

FUA'AMOTU IS

is $2. If you're staying at the Paradise International Hotel, it's free.

By Sea

Freighters are difficult to find, but from time to time one comes in from Pago Pago or Nuku'alofa. Check with the Warner Pacific Line agent in Pago Pago or Nuku'alofa. The *Olovaha* however, is a sure thing. Sailing on Tuesdays from Nuku'alofa, including a brief stop at Pangai in the Ha'apai Group, she arrives at Vava'u 22 hours later. One-way fare from Nuku'alofa is $70.

Where to Stay and Eat

As of now, the most glamorous place to stay is the *Paradise International Hotel* which is less than a mile from the town of Neiafu. The hotel has 32 units, each with its own patio. The beautiful setting overlooks the harbor and, by American standards, what you get for the little you pay is excellent. There's a pool, a pair of dining rooms, and the most popular bar on the island. The food is good. The lobby gift shop is outstanding. Rates are $39 a double.

The Vava'u Guest House—Just across the street from the Paradise, this guest house has dormitory accommodations at $8 a double. Or for $12 you can get a complete fale with its own bath. The food is Tongan, family-style, and quite good.

The Tongan Beach Resort—Run by a German named Gunther Haak, this hotel, several convoluted miles beyond town, is on the beach at the village of Utungake. It's a $3 taxi ride from Neiafu. Here there's a series of comfortable fales with full plumbing that face the beach. This spot has good snorkeling, wind surfing, beach walking, and is ideal for children. For food, it's outstanding, the best on the island, with curried seafood, sauerbraten, baked reef fish, good vegetable soup, oysters, and an extensive wine list. A meal for two with wine will be about $22. Room rates are $25 for a double.

Stowaway Village—This is right in town, has private facilities, and is $15 a double.

The Tufumolou Guest House—Near Neiafu at Neiafutahi Beach, you can stay at this spartan inn for $5 a double.

What to Do

The small handsome town of Neiafu overlooks the harbor, the Port of Refuge. It has all conveniences, airline offices, churches, banks, shops, a hospital and two cinemas. There's a good public market where carvings, mats, and tapa, some of the best, are available. And below town, at the municipal wharf, boats can be rented.

The walk from the Paradise International Hotel to Neiafu, population 6,000, takes seven minutes. From there through stands of coconut palms, patches of jungle, unpaved roads fan out to beaches, lagoons, and villages. You can walk to some of them but, for distant activities, two-seater mopeds are available in town for $14 a day.

As a preview of what you'll be doing and seeing on Vava'u, we suggest Mt. Talau as one of the first activities. In the morning when it's cool, take a taxi (a dollar ride) to the trail head just behind Neiafu. Fifteen scrambling minutes will see you to the jungly 670-foot top. From there you can examine what you'll soon be seeing on Vava'u, the best of which needs to be done by boat.

Boats—For short distances it's fine to use one of the inexpensive outboard craft available at the wharf. But some destinations are too far for this. In such cases you can hire one of the speedboats with drivers that are readily available.

For the best run, a full day of adventure, go south down the twisting channel through the changing shades of water. In about 10 miles you'll come to Kapa Island and Swallows Cave. This is a large hole in the cliff filled with electric blue water. Here the boat can go right inside where you'll see graffiti dating back to whalers of 1862.

Just across the channel on the northern end of Nuapupu Island is Mariner's Cave. Named after a British sailor who was kept captive in Vava'u in the early 1800's, this cave will separate the men from the boys. It's a diving adventure, a safe one, but with overtones of terror.

When you arrive at the cave, put on goggles, follow the leader, then dive down six feet, swim horizontally 15 feet

more, and surface in a mist-filled waterbound cave. Then you've got to get out again. If you follow instructions, and time your return with the outward surge of water, you'll be flushed out into safety and sunshine. For this effort a certificate will be issued.

With noon approaching and, assuming you've got picnic supplies, the next stop ought to be Nuku Island. This tiny white-beach island with arching palms is delightful. After lunch continue east to the larger island of Ofu and Umunu. They're pretty to look at but, if you want to go ashore, you'll probably have to swim from the boat.

This will have been a full day, but you haven't begun to see all of Vava'u's wonderful waters. Consider this solution.

The Mooring in Neiafu is one of the best yacht chartering centers in the Pacific. For example, for $1,500 a week, 37-foot fully provisioned sailboats sleeping up to six people are available. Cruising the ins and outs of the Vava'u Group is not a bad way to spend seven days, and not that expensive when the $1,500 is split several ways. For more information write: The Mooring, Neiafu, Vava'u, Kingdom of Tonga.

The best source of information on seagoing adventure is found among the "yachties" who gather at a round table in the Paradise Hotel bar for happy hour. A simple, "may we join you?" is all that's necessary. You'll be welcome, since yachts-people are generally eager to talk about their boats, their passages, and respond favorably to folks interested in such things. Someone will almost surely invite you aboard for at least a look.

We fell in with such a group. One of them, a young American "single hander" with a 30-foot boat invited us for a sail. The day we spent tacking and reaching among these vibrant islands was near perfection.

For someone seriously interested in long distance sailing, perhaps share-expense crewing, possibilities are extremely good in Vava'u.

By Road—Most of southern Vava'u can be covered by boat, but the northern end, the wild lonesome part beyond Holonga village, is best explored by foot. Take a bus to Holonga ($1) or taxi ($4), then walk in.

For feasting and island dancing, the "yachties" who ought to know say to avoid Holonga village, and go instead to nearby Tuanikavale. These more friendly villagers maintain a stretch of beach just for feasting and dancing. Ask at your hotel if something is going on there. If so, a taxi will take you there for $4. The island feast, a typical Umu operation will cost an additional $10. Be sure to arrange for return taxi transport.

THE NIUAS

NIUAFO'OU OR TIN CAN ISLAND

Niuafo'ou or Tin Can Island, surrounded by surf, has no harbor and at one time mail sealed in kerosene tins was pushed by strong swimmers from shore to and from waiting ships. As a result, the island with its postmark, "Tin Can Mail," made its mark on the philatelic world.

Closer to Fiji and Samoa than to Tonga, this flat, volcanic island is remote. The only way in is by chartered aircraft or the monthly supply ship from Nuku'alofa. But the flight between Samoa and Fiji passes right over the island. If the weather is good, its flat circular shape with a lake in the middle stands out clearly. About 700 people live there.

NIUATOPUTAPU

This small island is attractive, reasonably accessible, and very traditionally Tongan. It has good beaches and a small hotel, the Fita, that has fales at $12 double. Copra is grown, some gardening done, and the sheltered lagoon provides a good anchorage for transient yachts.

Coming or going to Vava'u from Pago Pago, this is a good pause. Schedules change often, so question Friendly Islands Airways carefully.

4

AMERICAN SAMOA

The first time we saw American Samoa was in 1968. We'd flown in from Hawaii, 2,300 miles to the northeast, and I remember how unprepared we were for the beauty that surrounded us. I remember too on the eight-mile ride into Pago Pago how the abrupt mountains and the pounding surf created an overwhelming beauty, not in the least tranquil. The greens were too green, the blues too blue, and the line of surf too creamy.

Then that night at the Rainmaker Hotel, new in those days, nature brought us out of bed with the most violent electric storm I've experienced before or since. Its fury lit up and crashed among the peaks around Pago Pago Harbor. Then, as suddenly as it began, it ended. By noon the next day we began to adjust. The colors no longer seemed so intense. The violence of nature had become tempered and the beauty, still profound, was now compatible.

That first day at the Rainmaker, with its pool, beach and spectacular location, we checked out the tourist scene. We expected that such a place would draw them in, but not so. There were a few businessmen, some off-island Samoans clad in lava lavas, some men from a tuna boat, a pair of missionaries, and a few folks like us, in transit.

We were smitten by American Samoa, and at the first opportunity I paid a visit to the Lyndon B. Johnson Tropical Memorial Hospital and asked about employment possibilities. Transient doctors and dentists suddenly enamored of Samoa had appeared there before. Like them, I was shown around,

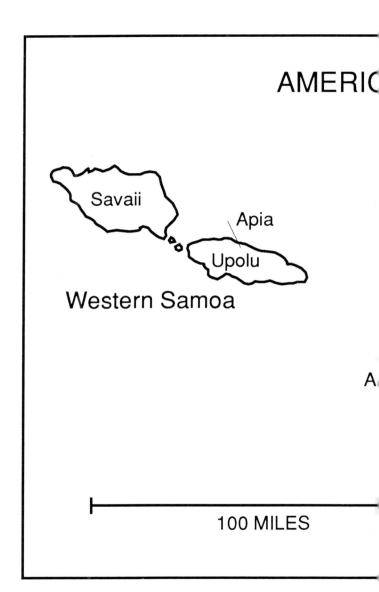

AMERIC

Savaii

Apia

Upolu

Western Samoa

A

100 MILES

SAMOA

outh Pacific Ocean

a Island

Pago
Pago

rican Samoa

Olesega

Ofu

Ta'u

Manua
Group

given a cup of coffee, and told that job openings were rare. Most of the staff tended to sign new contracts as soon as the old ones expired.

Since that brief visit we've been back several times, but in the intervening years I see few changes. There are a couple of new restaurants in Pago Pago, a new hotel near the airport, some improvements in town. There are some negative changes too. The Rainmaker Hotel now has a few wrinkles, and not the best of kitchens, the boat that used to carry passengers on a round-island supply trip no longer runs, and the cable car that ascended the mountains above Pago Pago Harbor doesn't operate anymore. But the beauty, grand as ever, is still there. There still are few tourists. Apparently the Samoans prefer it this way, but they'll put much of Hawaii to shame if they ever get around to a tourist industry.

It's a return to the familiar when you come to American Samoa from other parts of the Pacific. You're back under the American flag. There are American magazines and newspapers, American beer, coffee, and hamburgers too, and you pay for them with American currency. There are flush toilets that work, American TV and postal service, but you're also back to tipping, higher prices, and some crime as well.

What you're not back to though is an abundance of American free enterprise. Only a little copra (dried coconuts) is grown for export. And, because the land is too mountainous for serious agriculture, the few bananas, taro, and breadfruit grown are for local consumption, not export. Most of their food is imported, and nearly half of the work force depends on government jobs.

There is however one industry that pumps capital into the economy. Two tuna canneries, redolent institutions on the north shore of Pago Pago Harbor, Starkist and Samoan Packing-Ralston, hire workers who agree to can the fish, but not catch them. They leave that up to the boats manned by Chinese, Koreans, Americans, and Japanese.

This industry in 1984 exported $209 million worth of tuna. The Department of Labor says the canneries employ 32% of the work force (the Government employs 38%) and of that number one-third are Western Samoans. Here Western Samoans earn $2.82 an hour, considerably more than the 40¢ hourly wage they could expect at home. There are some, mostly US Congressmen, who say that increases in the hourly rate are needed. Lately they've suggested increases up to $3.35 an hour. The canneries objected, as did the Territorial Government. Both said such an increase would create major unemployment and perhaps drive the canneries to foreign countries with lower labor costs. This, of course, would only worsen the Territory's already weak financial condition.

American Samoa is essentially a handout society where Uncle Sam, called Uncle Sugar by many, pours millions of ill-conceived dollars into the economy. The waste is said to be impressive. But even that hasn't kept all Samoans at home as many in search of higher paychecks move to Hawaii, California, or join the military.

The future of American Samoa may involve more tourism, and even a unification with Western Samoa (which, at 1,100 square miles, is much larger). Pago Pago Harbor is a large deepwater harbor; Tafuna Airport is big enough for B52s. Since it is a US Territory, and Samoans are deeply patriotic, no one is apt to object to a nuclear presence. As an alternative US base to the Philippines, American Samoa could suddenly become very important.

The Land and Her People

The only US Territory south of the Equator, American Samoa lies 2,300 miles south of Hawaii, 4,200 miles south of San Francisco. It is a mere 77 square miles and Tutuila, the largest island, has 53 of them. Not much land is left for the other six. Total population of the seven islands, one of which (Swain's Island) is uninhabited, is 36,000. And about 6,000 live in and around the capital, Pago Pago (pronounced Pahngo Pahngo) which, with Fagatogo, is called the Bay Area.

The Samoans, about as Polynesian as they come, claim their islands as the cradle of Polynesia. Cultural evidence does indeed point to their presence there as far back as 600 B.C. Shared with Western Samoa they've got a system called Fa'a

Tutuila Island

Samoa (the Samoan Way) which is a term you'll hear often. Fa'a Samoa implies flexibility and caution as to changes that could affect traditional ways. Within these usually unwritten rules lies the essence of old Samoan life, village life, the extended family, communal ownership, all under the authority of matais (chiefs). Some of these rules apply to foreigners too, and their application is important. For example:

1. In a Samoan home do not talk to people when standing. Sit down with your legs tucked under you.

2. If you see a group of elderly men gathered in a fale (an oval high thatched roof house with no walls) the occupants are probably chiefs. Walk slowly and respectfully as you go by and,

if you're carrying an umbrella, lower it.
  3. If you arrive at a fale during family prayers, wait outside until they're over. Don't wear flowers in church. Treat Sundays with respect.
  4. Always ask permission to enter a village, to use a beach, or approach a fale.
  One final note. Samoans are polite to a fault. When you ask them a question, the answer is apt to be designed to please rather than inform.

History in Brief

In 1722, the Dutchman Jacob Roggeveen arrived in Samoa and introduced these islands to the world. In 1831, the missionaries under the influence of the London Missionary Society appeared, and the islanders took to Christianity with enthusiasm. Then in 1900, and in spite of the Germans who controlled Western Samoa, the United States took possession and the US Navy ran American Samoa until 1951. Since then it has been administered by the Department of the Interior. Officially American Samoa is a United States Incorporated Territory.

It was here too that Somerset Maugham's short story "Rain" was set, the story of the missionary and the prostitute that ended badly. At one time there was even a hotel named for the heroine, the Sadie Thompson Hotel. It's not there any more, but anyone in downtown Fagatogo can point out the site.

How to Get There

Between South Pacific Island Airways and Hawaiian Airlines, there are flights from Honolulu almost daily. Flight time is roughly five hours, about the same as to Honolulu from San Francisco.

Polynesian Airlines flies between Western and American Samoa several times daily, about a 20-minute flight.

Air Nauru, the airline with the unusual number of Pacific destinations, comes in from Auckland, Rarotonga, Tarawa, and Nauru. In the realm of flight fantasy, if you've got plenty of time and want a devious but exotic flight from Hawaii, ask Air Nauru to book you from Honolulu to Pago Pago. The flight will take you first to Majuro in the Marshall Islands, then Nauru, home of the airline—an island with an economy based on bird guano—then to Tarawa in the Gilberts, and finally Pago Pago. If you want to make the trip by sea, occasionally cruise ships, such as P & O, Sitmar, and Royal Viking call at American Samoa.

Immigration Formalities

All visitors entering American Samoa must show proof of citizenship. A passport is best.

Health

No exotic tropical diseases, but in case of medical problems, the Lyndon B. Johnson Tropical Memorial Hospital is one of the best facilities in the Pacific.

Currency

United States currency is used.

Time Zone

The local time is 11 hours behind Greenwich Mean Time, six hours behind Eastern Standard Time, and three hours behind Pacific Standard Time.

Newspapers, Radio, TV, Telephone

There is American TV and radio broadcasts are in English. The local newspaper, *The Samoan News,* is in English and all American papers are available—a day late. Make long-distance calls at the Office of Communications across from the Fono Building in Pago Pago.

Power

American Samoa uses 110 volts AC.

Climate

It can be hot and humid throughout the year. It rains a lot too, about 200 inches a year in the area around Pago Pago, but the sun shines some of every day. If there's a best time of the year, it would be April through September.

Language

English is the second language. But one would have thought, with its American school administration and American bureaucracy, English would be more prevalent. Often conversational English is poorly understood. English seems to be better understood in Western Samoa.

Holidays

All of the usual American holidays exist here, plus Samoan Flag Day on April 17, and White Sunday on the second Sunday in October. But one of the most important holidays happens in October or November when the palolo worm leaves its shell and swarms to the surface of the sea. Samoans, like other South Pacific islanders, consider the worm a delicacy and even if it weren't a holiday they'd still turn out at night en masse to gather it.

Tipping

Reasonable tipping is expected here.

TUTUILA

How to Get Around

On Tutuila, the main island, there are 50 miles of paved road. Tafuna International Airport is eight miles from Pago Pago, and by taxi the fare will be $8.

Cars can be rented at the airport, from Budget at the Rainmaker Hotel, or from Royal Samoan or Avis in downtown Fagatogo. Rates are about the same as stateside, but the price of fuel is higher in these islands. You can't go far, and it shouldn't take much.

But for local color, economy and frequency of service, try the public buses. They're not long on comfort and, with tape decks blaring rock music, they're noisy too. They'll get you anywhere on Tutuila though, and no single bus ride to and from its most distant point can possibly cost more than $1.50.

To board a bus, walk to the public market in Fagatogo. If you're staying at the Rainmaker Hotel it's a 10-minute walk. Everything in Pago Pago and Fagatogo is within walking distance of the Rainmaker. Then choose the direction you want to go, east or west. West will take you through a number of fairly uninteresting villages to the end of the line near Cape Taputapu. It's a pretty ride but our favorite, because of the beaches and views of sea and land, is to the east. It's a run that goes round the Harbor past the ripe smelling canneries, then through five or six villages, and up a lovely coast to the end of the line at Tula.

At Avasi (the bus driver will tell you when you're there) not far from Tula, ask for motorboats out to Aunu'u island. It's a short ride, a pretty one, and will cost $2 one way. For picnicking, walking, snorkeling, perhaps even spending the night at a pre-arranged local's home, Aunu'u island is good. There is a lake there too but *beware*—it is surrounded by treacherous quicksand.

Trail walking in American Samoa used to be very good. Not anymore. There are roads now to nearly all the villages, so the trails are overgrown and no longer used.

The only real hike left is the trail along the ridge behind Pago Pago to Mt. Alava where the cable car used to go. Take a taxi, about $4 from Pago Pago on the road to Fagasa. Ask the driver to let you off where the trail begins. Follow it east along the ridge to Mt. Alava. It's a fairly strenuous four-mile walk but the views will keep your mind off fatigue.

Another shorter and easier trek begins in Utulei and goes up the hill to what is known as the Naval Guns (two of them, dating from World War II). Access to the guns is a short distance from the Rainmaker Hotel, about one and a half miles toward the airport. This is a good World War II nostalgia trek.

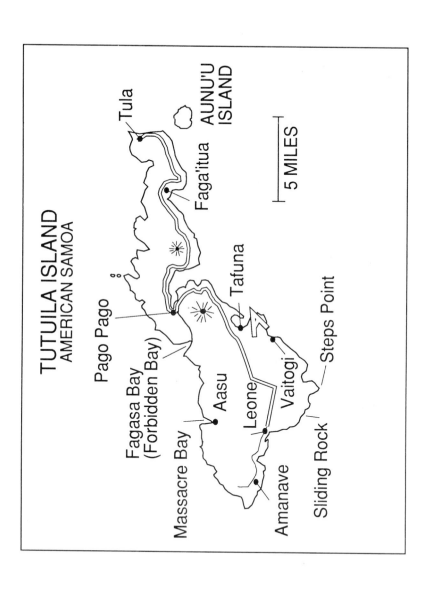

TUTUILA ISLAND
AMERICAN SAMOA

Tula

Faga'itua

AUNU'U
ISLAND

5 MILES

Pago Pago

Tafuna

Fagasa Bay
(Forbidden Bay)

Massacre Bay

Aasu

Leone

Vaitogi

Steps Point

Amanave

Sliding Rock

Where to Stay

A youth hostel or two exist on the island, as well as some inexpensive rooming houses with negotiable rates. But essentially there are only three hotels on Tutuila.

The Rainmaker—right on Pago Pago Bay, a dramatic location, it has 200 rooms, a pool, private beach, a bar and restaurant. The best on the island, it could be better. Some orders from the restaurant are not noteworthy. Rates are $52 a double.

Herb and Sias—Up an alley in Fagatogo, it is more guesthouse than hotel. Along with Joe's Hotel in Tonga, this rates near the bottom on our list. The service provided by a transvestite or two was not good, the air conditioner was faulty, and the view from the rear windows featured a junked car, tin cans and assorted trash. Rates are $25 double.

The Apiolefaga Inn—Five minutes from the airport and 30 minutes from town, this place is small, new, and staffed by

Rainmaker Hotel, the best hotel in Pago Pago

talented folks. Rates are $38 double with air conditioning. The Samoan equivalent of bed and breakfast is known as "fale, fala, ma ti," which means "mat and breakfast." They're not as elegant as mainland B & B's, but they're cheap, and the experience of living with a Samoan family in a village is worth considering.

The homes vary in style, some are modern, and others are thatched fales, most have all conveniences, though not necessarily in your room. Prices range from $10 to $25 a night, including breakfast.

Write to the Office of Tourism well ahead of arrival: Office of Tourism, PO Box 1147, Pago Pago, American Samoa 96799.

Food

Food, plentiful on Tutuila, falls well short of cordon bleu dining, but probably will improve with the new Sadie Thompson shopping center and restaurant now being built.

The Rainmaker—The setting is magnificent and evening entertainment with Samoan dancing, good. The food is fair. Expect to pay about $25 for two. Breakfast in the coffee shop is about the best meal served there.

Mark & Soli's for evening dining is the best in town. It's attractive and right on the harbor, the sort of restaurant that welcomes high school graduation parties, company functions, and where locals and expatriates gather happily. Prices are moderately expensive, but either western or Chinese food is predictably good and in quantity.

Ramona Li's, at the far end of the Bay, is an ornate Chinese restaurant. The menu is extensive and the food, when it appears, is fair. Moderately expensive. It has a band and can be noisy on weekend nights.

Shimonosaki's downtown is recommended for budget eating. This modest but satisfying restaurant-grocery store is in a clapboard building just off the main square. Good breakfasts there run about $2, either Western or Samoan. For lunch try the Samoanized version of Sukiyaki ($1.50) or the $1.95 club sandwich with cheese, ham, and a fried egg.

Ala Moana's right next door to Shimonosaki's is on the same order. It's a fast food place for take out or stand up eating. For

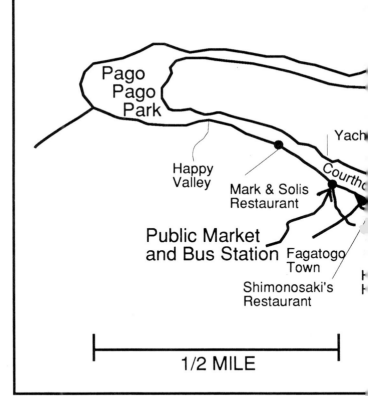

BAY AREA
PAGO PAGO

Pago Pago Park

Happy Valley

Yach

Courtho

Mark & Solis Restaurant

Public Market and Bus Station

Fagatogo Town

Shimonosaki's Restaurant

1/2 MILE

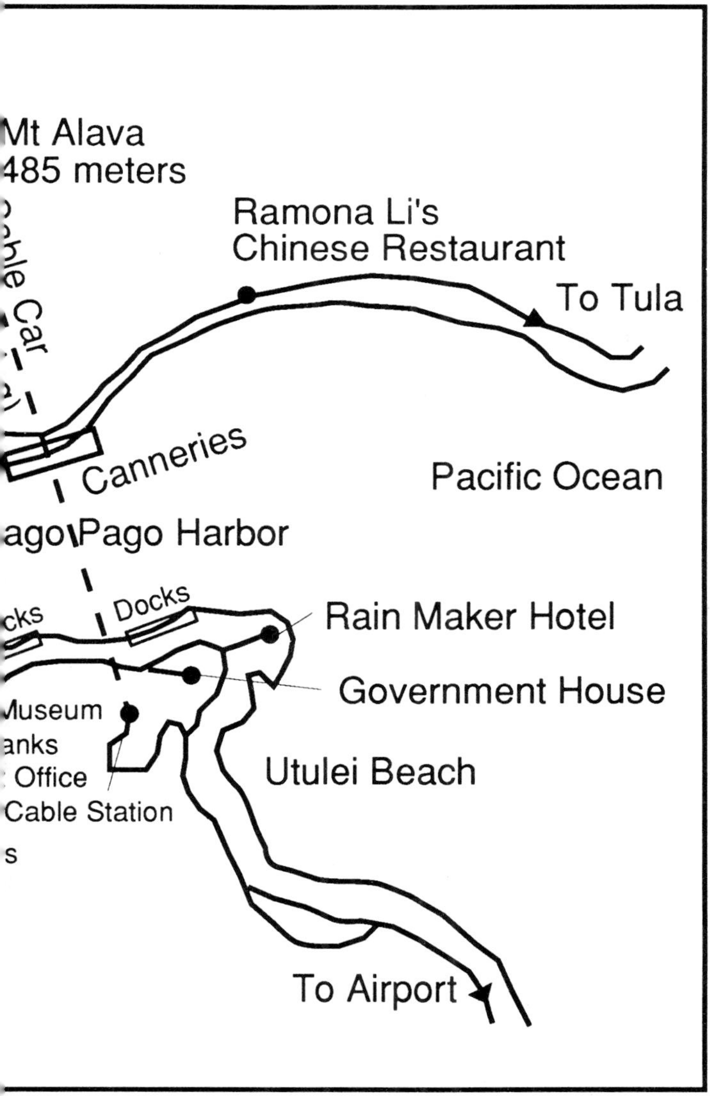

Mt Alava
485 meters

Ramona Li's
Chinese Restaurant

To Tula

Cable Car

Canneries

Pacific Ocean

ago Pago Harbor

Docks

cks

Rain Maker Hotel

Government House

Museum
anks
Office
Cable Station
s

Utulei Beach

To Airport

pizza, hot dogs, hamburgers, fish and chips, try *Matai's Pizza Parlor, Nora's Hot Dog City,* or *Milovale's.*

Evening Activities

For mixing with the locals, there are some animated and friendly spots. Food by law is supposed to be served, but you'll probably just see beer and snacks. Try the *Pago Pago* in town. This is where Sadie Thompson was supposed to have gone with her Samoan boyfriend. Now, as then, it's filled with noise and music.

A notch or two down in style, visit the *Bamboo Club.* Here you'll find happy and noisy fellowship. Then try *Caeser's Club, the Purple Onion, Christina's, the Seaside* and, 15 miles east of town, try *Tummia's Place.*

Consider too some notes taken from the column "Police Beat" in *The Samoan News.*

"Dancing is a lot of fun for some, it could mean death for others. It's good exercise to flatten your stomach, as long as you keep the distance, and don't flirt with another woman's man, you're safe. One Tafuna girl crossed into No Mans Land the other night, and was lucky to escape the jaws of death. She went dancing in a downtown night club, met a guy who told her he was single, and she waltzed into his loving arms. They were seen by relatives of the man's wife who was summoned to witness the event. The other woman barely escaped, and with nothing to cover her body, as the wife pounded, stomped, kicked and bit her."

Shopping

Shopping is not particularly exotic in American Samoa. There is a duty free store, and you can find locally made wood carvings, necklaces, and art work. Most everyday necessities are available.

What to Do on Tutuila

There aren't many ports in the South Pacific more beautiful than Pago Pago Harbor. And the combined town of Pago Pago-

Fagatogo, with its substantial public and private buildings on either side of a pretty square, compliment the setting.

There are a number of good things to do here and, because the island is compressed, it won't take long to do them. You won't need a guide either. First visit the Jean P. Haydon Museum in town. Examine the local artifacts and items of cultural history. It's five minutes by foot from the Rainmaker Hotel. Then try snorkeling at Alega, just five miles up the east coast. Do some hiking, and for island culture ask about fia fias (island dancing and feasts). Attend one, and try the taro, breadfruit, or palusami (made of coconut cream wrapped in taro leaves).

For golfers, there is the Lava Lava Golf Course, a par 70, 18-hole course. Phone 633-1191 for more information.

Other activities are listed under "How to Get Around."

With going to sea in mind, be sure to check the Transient Yacht Basin in Pago Pago Harbor. Usually several boats are anchored there and, as in the rest of the South Pacific, yachtsmen are approachable. Sometimes unpaid, or share-expense crew status is possible for passage in nearly any direction. More importantly, don't forget the outer islands. The best is yet to come.

THE OUTLYING ISLANDS

"Fa'a Samoa," the set of unwritten rules that keep Samoans cautious about changes that could affect traditional ways, has become diluted near the centers of commerce—Pago Pago, and Apia in Western Samoa. But in the Manua Group, 65 miles east of Pago Pago, "Fa'a Samoa" is alive and well, as it no doubt was in 1925 when Margaret Mead concluded in her *Coming of Age in Samoa* that adolescent sexuality flowered naturally because it was stress free.

Today not everyone agrees with her conclusions, some Samoans even dispute them, but among the 1,500 people in the Manuas where she worked, her memory is treated with warmth and respect. The Manuas are jewels, remote jewels, but happily they can be reached with two flights a day, and a

On Ofu Island

visit can be combined with pauses on both Ofu-Olesega and Ta'u. Round-trip fare from Tutuila with either South Pacific Island Airways or Manua Air is $65.

Joined by a causeway bridge, Ofu and Olesega are high islands, verdant and palm-clad with fine beaches, a quiet pair of villages, a Congregational church, and a five-unit motel only steps from the airstrip. Other than the motel, there are few amenities, no restaurants, only 500 people and, except for choir practice, no night life.

For the visitor, Talking Chief Suasili Malae is important. He owns the motel, a pickup truck for transport, and a fishing canoe. He and his wife provide food, good Polynesian fare such as fried reef fish, breadfruit, palusami, maybe peasupo (a corruption of the words pea soup), cold beer, and chilled drinking coconuts. The rooms, austere but clean and fully plumbed, are $30 a double.

We flew to Ofu on SPIA, and put down at the airstrip, practically on the beach. Chief Malae was there, and directed us, only steps away to our room. Be sure to have a reservation; it might be full of divers. Then, moments later, with the Chief's son at the wheel of the pickup, we set out through spectacular beauty along unpaved roads the length of Ofu. We rattled across the causeway bridge onto Olesega and continued to a distant village that looked orderly, but was mostly uninhabited. "Where were all the people?" we asked. He shrugged and said they were either asleep, in the hills working their yamtaro plantations, fishing, or perhaps in church.

The rest of the afternoon we wandered the beach near the motel and did some snorkeling, which was near perfect. Then, in preparation for dinner, we settled down on a low wall in front of our room and had a Scotch. But this sort of drinking is not appreciated in these islands. Visitors are advised that it's best to have a cloistered cocktail hour in your room with shades drawn.

At dinner that evening we asked about activities on Ofu-Olesega and, according to Chief Malae, this is the place to come for fine snorkeling and diving, for reef fishing from his canoe, jungle walking too, and for hunting in the hills, where wild pigs are plentiful. He said that, because the pigs damage taro-yam plantations (any small plot of ground constitutes a plantation), there's open season on them. He added that a combination of all these activities would be excellent, particularly good if it coincided with a fia fia, an island gathering complete with music, dancing, and a feast of fish, pig, lobster, and oysters.

We asked about Margaret Mead and were told that, before leaving for Ta'u—the mountainous island we could see in the distance—we should talk to High Talking Chief Toiena who lives next door to the motel. We did.

Chief Toeina, now 76 and not the least reluctant about sharing a measure of Scotch, told us about island life as it is now, told us too how abundantly grateful he was to have been born

Samoan and to live in these particular islands. Then he described the islands as they were when Margaret Mead knew them, and talked about how as a young boy he set up the mosquito net under which she typed. He suggested that Margaret—he used her first name with affection—may have been incompletely informed, since some things about Samoan culture are never revealed to palagis (foreigners).

The next day we took the 10-minute flight to Ta'u and made a heart-in-mouth landing on its mountaintop airstrip. A pickup truck was waiting and, with some returned locals, we were driven downhill to Ta'u's main town—appropriately called Ta'u.

Here, under the palms on a fine arc of beach, there was a church, a few shops, and rows of trim houses with galvanized iron roofs. Like other Samoan villages we'd seen, it was a quiet place and, other than a clutch of children who waved, some dogs who wagged tails, and a woman washing a baby under an outside tap, there were few signs of life.

Then, at the edge of town right on the beach, we were delivered to the guesthouse and given a key to the padlocked door. Once inside and with considerable difficulty, we found the right switches to produce power. And, with food in mind, we walked to a nearby shop, a South Seas mama-papa store specializing in canned food, ship's biscuits, flour, salt, kerosene, etc., and bought rations for the next few meals. The lady in charge suggested that we'd never find the guesthouse can opener, loaned us hers and, as a welcoming gift, gave us a fine fat papaya.

Our arrival had not gone unnoticed and, well before lighting the stove or opening cans, a messenger arrived with a summons for us to appear at Chief Niumata Mailo's home at 6 PM. He owns the guesthouse. We did not refuse. Most visitors to Ta'u—there are few of them—will probably receive a similar invitation. Don't count on it though; the Chief could be away or indisposed. To be on the safe side, visit the store.

Chief Mailo, a large man clad in a lava lava, greeted us in an open-air fale behind his house. We were three—the other being a fellow guesthouse resident, a Samoan school administrator.

High Talking Chief Toeina, in Ofu

There, with a view of the sea and in honor of sunset, we were given a brace of cold beers. Then, in his home surrounded by family photos, walls festooned with leis and snow scenes of the Alps, we had a prayer session. Dinner in immense proportions followed—fried reef fish, fried chicken, breadfruit, palusami and, for dessert, a puree of bananas and spices.

Then guided by our fellow guest, we paid for our lodging ($25 a double) and made a $2 gift to his daughter who had prepared and served, but not shared in, the meal.

Next came the matter of Margaret Mead. The Chief was ready for questions. He no doubt expects all palagis to be interested in the subject, and his responses bore evidence that everyone on the island loved Margaret Mead. When she reappeared on Ta'u in the '60's, a gala celebration was held.

Chief Mailo repeated some of the observations we'd heard on Ofu—that there are some matters Samoans would never tell an outsider, even Margaret Mead, and that some of her translators may have been trying to please, rather than inform her.

That night, well fed, well received, we walked quietly back to the guesthouse. It had been a good day.

Ta'u is an island of mountainous green jungle. The highest point in American Samoa, Lata Mountain (3,264 feet) is here and the interior makes for rugged hiking. Ofu-Olesega offers easier hiking and more to do. Accommodations are better, too.

After 24 hours among the gentle people on either island, you'll come to appreciate their essential wisdom and beauty. Margaret Mead found both. Still you can't help wondering how in such a fundamentally religious and structured environment, adolescent sexuality could have been stress-free, let alone flower.

The next morning the plane reappeared and made its dramatic landing which looked as hair-raising from the ground as it had seemed from the air. Moments later we were off toward Tutuila and the waiting plane for Western Samoa.

On Ta'u Island, Margaret Mead's island

5

WESTERN SAMOA

Flying between the Samoas, 80 miles from Pago Pago in American Samoa to Apia in Western Samoa takes 20 minutes. Done in daylight, the entire 47-mile length of Western Samoa's Upolu Island is exposed to view. It is a fine mountainous, jungle-covered, bay-scalloped sight. Then, with Western Samoa's largest island, Savai'i, in sight, the plane sweeps in from the sea and lands at Faleolo Airport.

Faleolo at the western end of Upolu now has a new modern terminal. About time too, for Western Samoa is beginning to burgeon.

But, on the 20-mile run into Apia, few signs of this burgeoning are apparent. Far from it, and in fact the tropics and Polynesia are at their most intense here. It's a land of luxuriant greenness and, in the dozens of villages along this coastal way, visitors see Samoan life at its traditional best.

Unlike American Samoa, thatched roof fales are everywhere here. Each neatly landscaped village has its church, village green, and shop or two. Nearly all the inhabitants are dressed Polynesian style—men in lavalavas, women in the long mumu-style dresses.

Then suddenly the road enters Apia and, lying as it does under palms and huge umbrella trees, this town of 35,000 looks as I've always imagined a South Sea town should look. Substantial buildings line the main road along the seafront, with banks, shops, shipping offices, post office, and the usual Pacific island public market where everything is sold. On the corner there's a lavalava-clad policeman directing traffic and,

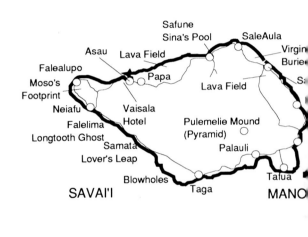

WEST

Safune
Sina's Pool   SaleAula
Asau   Lava Field   Virgin
Falealupo   Burie
Moso's   Papa   S
Footprint   Lava Field
Neiafu   Vaisala
Falelima   Hotel   Pulemelie Mound
Longtooth Ghost   (Pyramid)
            Samata   Palauli
Lover's Leap
            Blowholes   Tafua
SAVAI'I   Taga   MANO

ᴬMOA

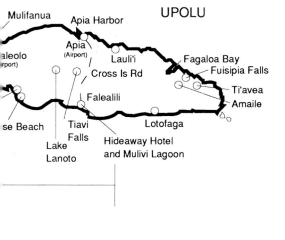

Mulifanua · Apia Harbor · **UPOLU**

aleolo Apia
rport) (Airport) · Lauli'i · Fagaloa Bay
Cross Is Rd · Fuisipia Falls

se Beach · Falealili · Ti'avea
· Amaile

Tiavi · Lotofaga
Lake Falls · Hideaway Hotel
Lanoto · and Mulivi Lagoon

sitting on the sidewalks, island women are selling such things as cocoa beans, fruit, vegetables. Compared with American Samoa, life here looks more animated, more elemental too. There are more people around, more color. Here also you'll see a good cross-section of the Samoan people and no doubt be surprised at the size of some of them. They tend to get fat. The huge intake of starchy food is said to be the reason—too much taro, breadfruit, bananas, too little exercise. One Samoan woman who died some years ago weighed 518 pounds.

The Land and Its People

Western Samoa claims the largest proportion of full-blooded Polynesians in the world—162,000 of them live on two large islands and a pair of small ones. Upolu (430 square miles), with Apia as its main town, claims 130,000 people. Savai'i, the largest island at 600 square miles, is less developed. It has a population of 30,000. The two tiny islands of Manono and Apolima have only a handful of people.

For quite a few Western Samoans the basis of happiness continues to be a healthy wife, plenty of children, a fale for living, one for cooking, some coconut trees, bananas, taro, a canoe, and a few pigs. But now Western Samoa has entered the world community, and there's more to international life than subsistence living.

In relation to other developing nations, Western Samoa is, for the time being, near the bottom of the list. Salaries are low, exports are few and, other than agriculture and some timber, there's little economic activity. As a result, quite a few Western Samoans go to American Samoa where they're willing to work in gas stations, stores, the canneries for lower wages than American Samoans.

Even so, these people show fewer signs of poverty or discontent than are seen in many successfully developing nations. They're healthier too. Most of their old medical problems, such as filariasis, TB, and yaws, have been eliminated. And the beauty of their islands surpasses that of virtually all other countries, developed or otherwise.

Tourism is probably in the future of these islands. New hotels are going up in and around Apia, the airport is being enlarged, new restaurants are appearing. It won't be long before Western Samoa becomes a thriving and important holiday destination. Luckily the country is large enough to absorb sizable numbers of tourists and, for those of the free and independent travel persuasion, there'll be plenty of unadorned Polynesia left, particularly on Savai'i.

The culture of these islands, the essence of Samoa, lies in the extended family (the aiga) and with the matai (chief) who directs the social and political affairs of the aiga. In a sense, power filters up from the aiga to the village—there are 362 villages in Western Samoa—then through the matais—12,600 of them—to the Parliament, and finally to the head of state.

Classified politically, these islands which became independent from the United Nations Trusteeship in 1962 are now a Constitutional Monarchy. The head of state is His Highness Mali etoa Tanumafili.

Downtown Apia, Western Samoa

History in Brief

Scholars believe that Western Samoa is the cradle of Polynesia and the larger, but less developed, island of Savai'i may have been the legendary Hawaiiki, the original home of the Polynesians. The first European to see these islands was the Dutch seaman, Jacob Roggeveen, in 1722. The French explorer, Bougainville appeared in 1786 and, about 1830, the missionaries—among them John Williams of the London Missionary Society—came bringing with them civilized virtues of hard work, abstention, and the fear of God.

Between about 1847 and 1899 considerable international business rivalry existed. German businesses developed about that time, and so did imported labor from China and Melanesia. Confusion existed and there was an unsuccessful attempt at constitutional government by some of the Samoan chiefs. It was not the happiest of times for Samoans, but in 1899 the Samoas were split. The Americans took the smaller islands to the east, and Germany got the bigger share, what is known as Western Samoa today.

When World War I began, New Zealand stepped in and these islands became a mandate of Britain under New Zealand supervision. During World War II the US Marines occupied the islands. Happily, the Japanese never appeared.

After the war, Western Samoa was administered by the United Nations and in 1962 they became independent. Fortunately for them, they continue to receive aid for development from New Zealand, Australia, the United Kingdom, Japan, the U.S., West Germany and the People's Republic of China.

How to Get There by Air

Coming from Honolulu, both South Pacific Island Airways and Hawaiian Airlines provide near-daily service to Apia via Pago Pago, American Samoa. From Honolulu to Pago Pago takes five hours, then a 20-minute flight will put you in Apia. Using either SPIA or Polynesian Airlines, there are four flights daily between American and Western Samoa.

Polynesian Airlines, Western Samoa's flag carrier, has four flights weekly to and from Nadi, Fiji.

Don't forget Air Nauru, the airline with more destinations than any other airline. If you're in the Solomons, Fiji, New Caledonia, even Manila, Hong Kong or Guam, Air Nauru can get you to Apia. Usually, though, it's a convoluted flight and probably will involve a stopover in Nauru. Consider Air Nauru for leaving rather than entering Western Samoa. Write them for flight information (Air Nauru, Republic of Nauru).

Air Pacific comes in from both Nadi and Suva on Fiji. Air New Zealand provides four flights a week from and to Auckland.

On departure, there is a Western Samoan airport tax of $20 per person.

By Sea

The *Queen Salamasina*, a large car and passenger ferry, comes in from Pago Pago on Mondays, Wednesdays, and Fridays. The 80-mile trip takes six hours and the fare is $15. Another newer vessel is now making the trip. Check with your hotel in either Pago Pago or Apia.

Getting to Western Samoa by freighter from other Pacific ports is difficult. But the best possibility is from Suva, Fiji, to Apia. In Suva watch the shipping news for such vessels as the *MV Sami* and the *MV Wairua*. Accommodation on these ships is possible and, with cabin and meals, this two-day voyage will run about $110.

Some cruise ships call at Apia. Have your travel agent check out P & O, Sitmar, Pacific Far East Lines, and C.T.C. Lines.

Immigration Formalities

A valid passport and a ticket to leave are required. For stays over 30 days, an entry permit must be obtained.

Health

There are no unusual medical problems here, but in case of emergency there are 31 hospitals in Western Samoa, and a big one in Apia. As to drinking water, it's potable in Apia, but in rural areas water from the tap may be questionable. Do not drink tap water on Savai'i.

Currency

The Western Samoan currency is known as the "tala" (dollar) and the "sene" (cent). 100 sene = WS $1. As of now the exchange is good for Americans. You get WS $2 for each US $1. A reminder—talas are not good currency away from Western Samoa and it's illegal to take them out of the country. American Express, Diners Club, Mastercard, and Visa are accepted at the main hotels such as Aggie's and the Tusitala. Local banks exchange foreign currency, but US dollars are accepted in many shops and hotels.

Unless otherwise stated, all costs in Western Samoa will be quoted in US dollars.

Time Zone

Local time is 11 hours behind Greenwich Mean Time, 6 hours behind Eastern Standard Time, and three hours behind Pacific Standard Time.

Newspapers, Radio, TV, and Telephone

Radio Western Samoa broadcasts in English as well as Samoan and is heard all over the Pacific. Apia receives TV broadcasts from American Samoa. Nearly all overseas newspapers are available in Apia and local newspapers publish English editions. Place long-distance calls at the International Telephone Bureau behind the main Post Office in Apia.

Power

220 volts AC.

Language

Samoan is the universal language, but English is used in commerce and government business. Illiteracy is unknown and most Samoans are competent in English.

Economy

Western Samoa's reputation as a developing country may

not head the list, but her rich soil, good climate, political stability, and healthy people, offer a promising future.

Her exports are limited to a few commercial estates—WSTC is the largest—that grow copra, coffee, cocoa, timber, and raise cattle. But most production, as in the past, still comes from the village sector—subsistence agriculture for local consumption, which involves two-thirds of the labor force.

Tourism is the coming thing.

What to Wear

Informality prevails everywhere, even in Apia. Men seldom wear ties—shorts with shirt are acceptable. Away from hotels, dresses for women are advised. Samoan women never wear shorts in public places, nor do they wear bikinis on beaches.

Tipping

It's neither encouraged nor welcomed.

Holidays

Holidays include: June 1–4, Independence Celebrations; October 14, Arbor Day; mid-November, White Sunday; Christmas, December 25; Boxing Day, December 26; New Year's Day; Commemoration Day, April 4; Good Friday; ANZAC Day, April 25. And, declared or not, it's a holiday when the palolo worm rises to the surface of the sea in October. Everyone turns out to gather this delicacy.

How to Get Around

The 30-minute run from Faleolo Airport to any of the hotels in Apia can be made by taxi or bus. A taxi will cost $6.50 per person, but comfortable buses and vans meet all flights, and the fare is $2 per person to any hotel in Apia.

Once in Apia you can walk nearly everywhere in town, but if a taxi is required, expect to pay 50¢ for short trips.

For the rest of Upolu, rental cars, taxis, public buses, tour agency buses are available.

Rental Cars—In Apia there's Avis, Gold Star, Budget, Hibiscus, and Pavatis. For an air conditioned Toyota Corolla sedan

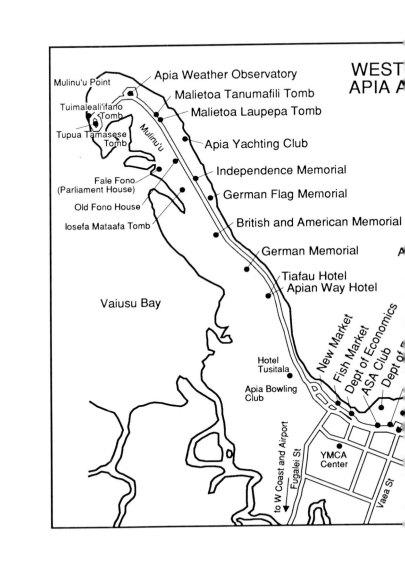

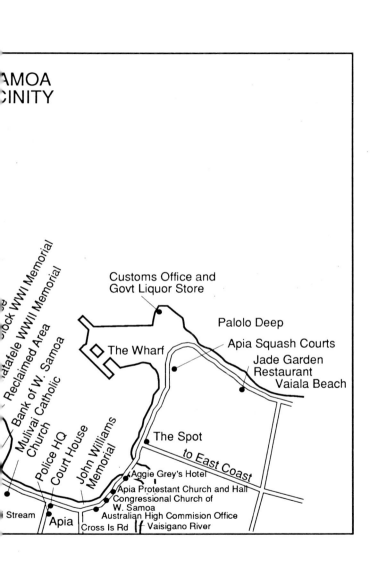

ock WWI Memorial

atafale WWII Memorial

Reclaimed Area

Bank of W. Samoa

Mulivai Catholic
Church

Police HQ

Court House

John Williams
Memorial

Customs Office and
Govt Liquor Store

Palolo Deep

Apia Squash Courts

The Wharf

Jade Garden
Restaurant
Vaiala Beach

The Spot

to East Coast

Aggie Grey's Hotel

Apia Protestant Church and Hall
Congressional Church of
W. Samoa
Australian High Commision Office
Vaisigano River

Stream

Apia

Cross Is Rd

expect to pay a flat rate, insurance included, of $40 a day. You'll need a $5 local driver's license. Remember too that not all roads are paved, far from it. Get a good map and have plenty of patience. Traffic moves on the right side of the road and all signs are in English.

Taxis—For long distances fares are negotiable and just across the street from Aggie's Hotel there's a taxi stand. Walk over and discuss the matter of a four- or five-hour cross- or round-island trip. $35 for two should be about right.

Tour Bus or Van—Four people can expect to pay about $10 per person for a four-hour tour. Check at the desk of your hotel. There are tours, including lunch, every day in all directions.

Public Buses—This is the most colorful, the most uncomfortable, least expensive way to travel, and schedules for these services are relaxed. You should go to the bus park near the public market in Apia and choose a destination. If you're interested in the far ends of the island, east or west, go early in the morning. Round trip to the most distant village on Upolu will be no more than $1.50. Our advice is to stay with the bus for the round trip. If you get off, you could get badly stranded.

To Savai'i by Air—Britten-Norman islanders of Polynesian Airlines fly from either Faleolo Airport or from Fagalii Airport, a small grass strip practically in Apia.

To Savai'i by Boat—Boats leave from the Mulifanua Wharf near Faleolo Airport. It's an hour run by the new boat, *Lady Samoa,* and an hour and a half by the vehicular ferry. Fare is $4 round trip on the vehicular ferry, and $10 round trip on the *Lady Samoa.*

Where to Stay

Rates listed below are for double rooms.

Aggie Grey's—120 air conditioned rooms with all amenities, including an iron. Pool, bar, restaurant, entertainment. $50.

Hotel Tusitala—96 AC rooms with bath and patio. Pool, bar restaurant, tennis courts, entertainment. $65.

Tiafau Hotel—30 AC rooms with bath. Pool, bar, restaurant. $25.

Apian Way Hotel—Seven AC rooms with bath. Pool, bar, restaurant. $23.

Harbour Light Hotel—30 AC rooms with bath. Bar, restaurant, nightly entertainment. $18 to $40.

Seaside Inn—Bed and breakfast, small private hotel by sea front; kitchen facilities. Near Palolo Deep Beach. $28, with bath.

Olivia Yundall's Casual & Tourist Accommodation—One unit sleeps up to four—with bath. One fully contained unit, sleeps up to 12. $10 per person. Small fale $25.

Betty Moor's Tourist Accommodations—Near Vaiala Beach. Six doubles, five singles, cooking facilities, community showers. $12.

Vaiala Beach Cottages—One mile from Apia. Near beach and Palolo Deep. $40.

Hideaway Beach Resort—30 units, 14 miles from Apia, on white coral sand beach at Mulivai Lagoon. Airport transport. A la carte dining, snorkeling, boating, fishing, billiards. $30.

The top three hotels are: The Tusitala, Aggie Grey's and the Tiafau. We've stayed at all three, found the Tusitala excellent,

Inexpensive hotel in Apia

and the Tiafau good. The Tusitala is the newest, the grounds more expansively landscaped, the rooms luxurious, and the food—especially the buffets—elegant, bountiful and delicious. They put on some good island night shows, good dancing, lots of local color and it's close to the center of town.

But, at the other end of town, there's nothing quite like Aggie's. The rooms aren't quite as nice as at the Tusitala but, when guests step through the modest entry, they pass into three acres of tropical opulence. There's a giant fale constructed in the old way without a single nail, a garlanded pool surrounded by flaming ginger and hibiscus, a bar and dining room, and a complex of comfortable rooms. Aggie's is a world in itself and guests there mingle easily within this family-style non-patronizing warmth. When they hold a fia fia in the giant fale, Aggie herself (now 89 and in a wheelchair) responds to the siva—the Samoan version of the hula—and sways her body and floats her hands.

A little of Aggie's history is important here. During World War II the US military appeared in Western Samoa. They built Faleolo Airport, constructed roads, and set up gun emplacements all over the island. American dollars flowed freely then and Aggie, seizing the moment, began selling hamburgers and coffee to the troops. Her establishment, a friendly home-away-from-home, grew and she began selling drinks too, heady home brew drinks and beer when she could get it.

It was in those days that James Michener appeared on the scene. He was beginning work about then on his "Tales of the South Pacific" and he went to Aggie's often. He went for the decent food she served, to drink good Australian beer, and to talk to Aggie. He said she was a good story teller, a good business woman, a kind person, and he credits her as playing an important role in his book.

When the Americans left in '45, what remained was only a small hotel. But little-by-little it grew, and now the only remnant of those days is the friendly environment. Guests today are well cared for, nearly pampered by a staff of 120 who look after 214 guests. As in the old days, Aggie firmly maintains the policy that girls of the village and ones of doubtful reputation in town must not enter the hotel compound at night.

Aggie Grey's, more institution than hotel, may be the happiest place to stay in the entire Pacific. One day at the bar we heard an Aussie say that he could be happy in Western Samoa without ever leaving Aggie's grounds. This may be going a little too far. We've looked at most of the hotels. Some are more elemental than others, but they're all clean, the management friendly, and no one seems to be ripping anyone off. This is true of the shops and taxis too. As the Samoans put it, this happy condition is the result of Fa'a Samoa—the Samoan way—and they expect the same from their visitors.

Food

The Tusitala—All meals excellent, dining room elegant; dinner for two about $20.

Aggie Grey's—Very good food, mostly family style; à la carte available. $18 for two.

Le Godinet—In the center of Apia, with distinctive continental dining. Famous for lobster, steaks, prawns, and a good wine list. About $24 for two with wine.

Jade Garden Restaurant—On the outskirts of Apia: 50¢ by cab from anywhere in town. The Chinese food served in this beautiful 100-year-old house is good, authentic and reasonable. Ice cold Vailima beer goes down well with what they provide.

Apia Inn—International standard of French, German, Italian and local food at reasonable prices. $25 for two with wine.

Amigos Restaurant—Samoa's original steak and seafood restaurant. Tequila cocktails. Good, and inexpensive.

There are more basic places to eat in Apia. The stalls at the public market are for the strong of stomach. The price is right though. Several notches up, there are the little cafes, coffee shops, and bars where the locals go for hamburgers, ice cream, pizza, beer, or Chinese food. Most of them are fairly good, and you can eat a pretty decent meal for under $3. Try *Otto's Reef, Tivoli Milk Bar, Fale Burger, Wong Kee's, The Burns Philp Coffee Shop,* and *Betty's.* They're all easy to find. Ask directions, if necessary.

Entertainment

For Samoan dancing, the fire dance, the siva, and for fia fia activities, the Tusitala, Aggie's, and Tiafau are hard to beat and they come with food. You should know that on weekends you can see the same things for free at the Public Market, and hear hymns as well.

For a noisy night out with the locals try Otto's Reef, Le Bistro, Mt. Vaea Club, Emilio's GoGo, or Lafayette's. All have music for dancing and a good deal of singles activity.

There are several movies in town, but in the evening you can always wander into one of the big hotels, enter the lounge, and watch a video movie for free.

The Umu and the Palolo Worm

Finally, the matter of the umu and traditional food should be mentioned. Because no work is allowed on Sunday, the umu prepared on Saturday becomes important.

The Samoan umu containing firewood and rocks is built on the ground between sections of logs. When the firewood burns down to ashes and the stones are intensely hot, food wrapped in leaves is placed around the outside.

Building the fire itself is no simple chore, but many hands are required to catch the fish, kill the chickens, slaughter a pig, and gather the yams, coconuts, bananas, breadfruit, and taro. Then all the ingredients have to be prepared and wrapped in leaves. Palusami, a mixture of coconut cream and spices wrapped in a taro leaf, is usually part of the feast as well. All of this is covered and left to cook.

On Sunday, little violation of the Sabbath is required, since uncovering the mound and eating the food takes no real work.

Another festive meal celebrated all over the Pacific involves the palolo worm. The palolo is a sea worm that lives in shells on the bottom of coral reefs. Once a year at dawn, usually following a full moon in October, the palolo swarms to the surface—an automatic holiday for all—and anyone armed with a net, even a hat, will scoop up all they can. They're then cooked and eaten like caviar, and with equal relish.

Western Samoans in their "fale", Savai'i

UPOLO ISLAND

What to do in Apia and Vicinity

Mt. Vaea—There are travelers who come to Western Samoa out of nostalgia, a second-hand sort of nostalgia based on the man who wrote *Dr. Jekyll and Mr. Hyde, Treasure Island, Ebb Tide* and, one of the best books on the Pacific, *In the South Seas*. The author, of course, is Robert Louis Stevenson and, although little mention of Western Samoa appears in *In the South Seas*, it was here that he spent his last four years. Here too that he built his home, Vailima (there's a beer made in Apia called Vailima—I don't think he'd object), and it's here on top of Mt. Vaea that he and his wife Fanny lie buried.

In those days, the 1890's, there were troubles. Samoans were caught in the middle of contesting foreign interests, they were abused and some of the chiefs were imprisoned. Stevenson, recently arrived, objected to this treatment and did what he could to improve matters. He was in this way different from most of the white men who came to these islands and earned the love of these people. They called him "Tusitala," the teller of tales.

In 1894 he died suddenly of a stroke, and was reverently carried to the top of Mt. Vaea by devoted Samoans. His wife, Fanny, died in California years later, but her ashes were taken to Apia and buried alongside her husband.

Their house, Vailima, now the residence of the Prime Minister, is mostly off-limits, but the grounds of this beautiful rambling wooden structure are open every weekday. It's Mt. Vaea though that's important, and if RLS is part of your past, set aside a morning for the trek to the summit.

We set out one morning while it was still cool, took a taxi to Vailima where the land behind Apia slants upward. There through the trees we could see the house Stevenson had built but, with 3,000-foot Mt. Vaea in mind, we followed posted signs through the landscaped grounds, past the modest waterfall and followed the footsteps of the Samoans who 93 years ago bore Stevenson's coffin to the summit.

Classified as to difficulty, this climb is mildly arduous and, along its winding path shaded by immense buttressed trees, pauses are required, some perspiration too. It's a beautiful walk though, the jungle is luxuriant, and the hour needed for the trek ends suddenly at a clearing on the summit. Apia lies at your feet, Upolu stretches out in either direction and, beyond, is the white line of breaking surf. There where we stood in the center of the clearing were the simple tombs. One could see why Stevenson had chosen this place, and on the side of his tomb we read the inscription.

> Under the wide and starry sky
> Dig the grave and let me lie,
> Glad did I live and gladly die,
> And I laid me down with a will.
>
> This be the verse you grave for me;
> Here he lies where he longed to be;
> Home is the sailor, home from the sea,
> And the hunter home from the hill.

I remember thinking as we stood by his tomb that Stevenson might be appalled at some of the sounds and sights of modern Samoa. Still he'd be happy to see that much of the essence of Samoan life, the villages, the fales, is now as it was then. The Mt. Vaea climb is a half day well spent. You'll have earned a swim and lunch. Then for the balance of the day consider seeing a bit of Apia—the public market near the clock tower and bus terminal at the western end of town is a good place to start. Everything grown on Samoa's fertile ground is displayed there, everything taken from the sea too, as well as good locally made handicrafts. Examine the kava and food bowls carved from native hardwoods, look at the shell jewelry carefully. While it's locally made, a lot of it is pure junk.

You can find here the handprinted fabrics you'll see many Samoans wearing. If you see something you like, chances are it's for sale at the public market. Check on the siapa (tapa) cloth, which is made from mulberry bark and printed with native dyes. These make exotic gifts and are easy to pack.

Mulinu'u Peninsula—From the market, it's a mile out to the end of this peninsula, the slim finger of land pointing seaward from Apia. Walk it, if you're still fresh, pause and look at the government-owned Tusitala Hotel near the market, and continue on past the Tiafau Hotel, which is named for the nearby burial grounds of Samoan royalty. The soul of Samoa, its history and culture, is concentrated on Mulinu'u—a not surprising location for the Samoan Parliament building you'll see. There is a good museum out there (open weekdays 10 AM–noon, 1 PM–4 PM). Finally at the far end, beyond the Yacht Club, you'll see the Apia Observatory. There are many impressive royal tombs out here, as you will see.

Downtown Apia—You can stroll Beach Street in 30 minutes, the length of Apia, from beyond the clock tower to Aggie's. Nearly everything you need can be found here. The shops, banks, and airline offices are open 9 AM–noon and 1 PM to 5 PM weekdays, and 9 AM to noon on Saturdays.

For newspapers, books, or cards, step into the Wesley Book Shop. Aggie Grey has a good variety shop next to her hotel. For Samoan handicraft gifts, try Western Samoa Handicrafts Corporation. For picnic food go to the Burns Philp or S. V. Mac-Kenzie supermarkets. And, for a pause, have a cup of Samoan coffee at Josie's Delicatessen. Apia is a good town for aimless wandering.

Golf—Visitors are welcome to use the course by arrangement with the Secretary of the Club. The course is just east of town near Fagali'l airstrip. Check at your hotel.

Beaches and Swimming—The beaches near Apia aren't very good. Compared with the magnificent beaches at the far side and either end of Upolu Island, they're disappointing. Still Palolo Deep, named after the reef worm that swarms to the surface in October, is good for diving. This area, called a "hole," is an unusually deep spot on the reef. There are other "holes" on the island but this one, only a mile east of Aggie's, is an organized place where you pay a fee and can rent snorkeling gear.

Papasea Sliding Rocks—You can see this anti-climactic place easily by taxi, about a dollar trip from town. You walk a short distance, pay an admission fee, and choose the appropriate rock to waterchute down.

Vaiala Beach—Just beyond Palolo Deep, this is an uninteresting beach. The undertow here can be dangerous.

OUTSIDE OF APIA

On the plane coming down from Honolulu we met the Von Reiches, a couple from Apia, who said they were associated with the government-owned Western Samoa Trust Estates Corporation, known as WSTC and pronounced Westek. These are the plantations seized from the Germans at the end of World War I.

Kurt Von Reiche, locally born of German descent, reflects those days and, as we found out later, is not only associated with WSTC but is its Chairman.

They called us one evening at Aggie's and suggested that, to examine what Samoa does best, we should see WSTC. "You could do this by tour bus," they said, "but we're available and would like to take you." We agreed with dispatch.

Kurt Von Reiche and one of his managers, Rudy Ott, picked us up next morning and we went by van to examine a large piece of the WSTC plantation which lies to the west and south of Apia. We drove past the Mormon Temple where the angel

Moroni stands on the roof blowing a horn, passed the Vailima Brewery, then turned inland into the hills and onto the plantation. We drove for miles between rows of coffee, cocoa, bananas, and among stately groves of coconut palms. By degrees, we wound into the uplands where it was cool and the grass thick and green. The only signs of life were cattle grazing on the sides of hills dotted with huge banyan and ficus trees.

Conversation between Von Reiche and Rudy Ott was carried on with an easy mixture of Samoan and English, one molding gently into the other. They talked about the condition of fences and about the fields of cocoa where new sprouts were protected by carefully placed palm fronds. Rudy, who calls Von Reiche "Mr. Chairman," was obviously well informed. His remarks, and what he pointed out seemed to please the Chairman—such things as the maturity of bananas that had been planted between rows of coffee.

Rudy turned and told us that bananas are versatile, that they shade developing plants, provide nitrogen to the soil, and they feed workers. We asked about the workers who were not in evidence. It was Saturday, and we were told that they're paid about 5 tala a day, $2.50 US, for a 40-hour week. Housing, they said, is provided.

At noon we drove onto the grounds of the coffee processing plant and the workers, the first we'd seen all morning, were playing or watching a cricket match. We were taken through the coffee plant and Rudy's description of the many processes required between the picking and drinking of coffee set me wondering how anyone thought up coffee in the first place. I remember thinking too that four hours spent examining such a plantation was a mite long. But we'd seen at first hand what a benevolent climate and intelligent humanity could produce.

AROUND UPOLU

This is an important trip, an all-day venture that should begin early in the morning. Rent a car if you must, but remember that most of the roads are unpaved, rough, and can get you hopelessly lost; and there'll be no one around to explain what you're seeing. Unless you do a tour, about which I am not enthusiastic, the easiest thing is to find another couple, negoti-

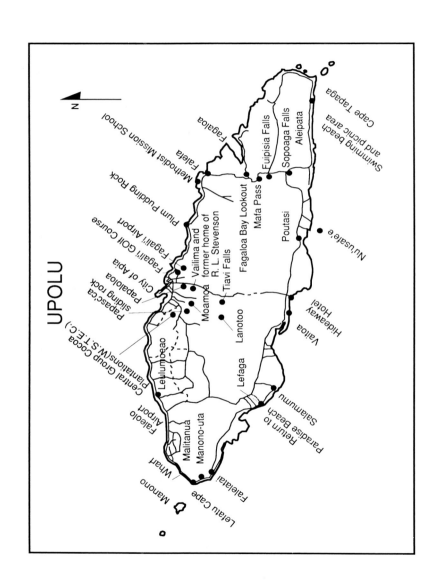

UPOLU

N

Methodist Mission School

Falefa

Fagaloa

Plum Pudding Rock

Fagali'i Airport

Fagali'i Golf Course

City of Apia

Papaseea
sliding rock

Papafoloa

Vailima and
former home of
R. L. Stevenson

Moamoa

Tiavi Falls

Fagaloa Bay Lookout

Mafa Pass

Fuipisia Falls

Sopoaga Falls

Aleipata

Swimming beach
and picnic area

Cape Tapaga

Poutasi

Nu'usafe'e

Lanotoo

Hideaway
Hotel

Vaitoa

Lefaga

Leulumoega

Central Group Cocoa
Plantations (W.S.T.E.C.)

Faleolo
Airport

Malitanua

Manono-uta

Wharf

Manono

Lelalu Cape

Falelatai

Salamumu

Return to
Paradise Beach

ate with a taxi driver for a round-island trip, and put together a lunch hamper. The taxi and a full day for four will probably come to $40 a couple. The direction you take is arbitrary, but we'll describe the trip in a counter-clockwise direction.

The first segment is to the west along the familiar road to the airport, the 20-mile village-dotted stretch that's the most heavily populated part of rural Samoa. Beyond Faleolo Airport you come to Mulifanua—the place where ferries leave for Savai'i Island. Then, just beyond Mulifanua, the road passes through the largest copra (coconut) plantation in the Southern Hemisphere—another WSTC plantation.

Next, almost at the westernmost end of Upolu, is the pretty village of Manono-Uta. If you are headed for the islands of Apolima and Manono, this is an important destination.

MANONO ISLAND

From Manono-Uta you can take the scheduled outboard (they run often), a 20-minute mostly within-the-reef run, to Manono. The water there, ideal for diving and snorkeling, has all shades of marine clarity. It's a fine mini-voyage past the islands of Apolima and Nuulopa. The fare is $2 round trip but, if you're in a hurry, boats can be chartered for $10.

Manono, the island that the legendary "Bali Hai" was modeled on, is a jewel. It's got white beaches backed with palms, clear water, idyllic villages, and no automobiles. There is little on the island except unrefined South Sea beauty. Other than swimming and snorkeling, the best thing to do is to walk the trail around the island. It'll take just over an hour.

Note that Manono is a destination in itself, not something to be done in conjunction with a one-day round-island trip.

Back on Upolu, at Manono-Uta village the road curves east and you're on the south coast now.

LEFAGA, SALAMUMU AND THE RETURN TO PARADISE BEACH

Just past the village of Lefaga a sandy track leaves the main road and runs a mile east along the coast to Salimumu. This is the "Return to Paradise" area, the scene of a 1952 Gary Cooper film. It's easy to see why Hollywood chose this place where the white sandy beach punctuated by large black rocks is overhung by arching palms and the water is as clear as gin. There are no buildings, no vendors, and the few people seen on the beach will be Samoan locals. The only evidence of commercialism is that somewhere along the road a Samoan will appear, flag you down and demand payment for entrance, usually a dollar a car.

THE MULIVAI LAGOON— THE HIDEAWAY HOTEL

The road from Lefaga leaves the sea temporarily and moves east through the jungle. There are few people, few villages, a lonesome stretch of road. But eight miles later the sea reappears in the form of the broad sparkling Mulivai Lagoon. Here, set in a grove of palms, is the *Hideaway Hotel.* With cold Vailima beer in mind, we stepped into the bar and lounge. What we saw looked inviting. You don't have to go around the

"Return to Paradise Beach", Western Samoa

island to get to the Hideaway. A cross-island road goes directly there—14 miles from Apia.

THE CROSS-ISLAND ROAD, TIAVI FALLS AND LAKE LANOTO'O

Consider the cross-island road for a separate trip. It provides access to Tiavi Falls (near the road) and to Lake Lanoto'o (some distance from the road). The Lake is an eerie body of jungle-surrounded water that contains hordes of goldfish. Getting there involves a hard walk from the mid-section of the cross-island road. A guide for this venture is probably in order.

O LE PUPU-PU'E NATIONAL PARK

Beyond the Hideaway-Mulivai area the road deteriorates. Traveling alone, I'd have considered ourselves lost. Not so though. We were on the main road, albeit narrow and rough, and it was here that the local with us said, "When I was a boy, before the war, there wasn't anything out here."

I glanced around. There certainly wasn't much now. "What I mean," he added, "this road didn't exist then—there were only trails over which my friends and I wandered on horseback. Food was never a problem, probably still isn't. But in those days you could stop at any fale and ask for food, a place to sleep, and never be refused."

After six or eight miles, we pulled up at the visitors' center which houses information for O Le Pupu-Pu'e Park. There on the walls were pictures, drawings, descriptions of local flora and fauna and of the nearby lava flow. Across the parking area was a sign indicating distance and direction to Peapea Cave, three miles uphill. This is a good hike, not arduous, but sometimes muddy. The view from the top justifies the effort.

THE LEPA COAST

The road continuing east doesn't improve, but it does at least run along the sea. The beaches here are only fair, and the sand flies aggressive. It was somewhere on the Lepa Coast that we stopped for lunch. Ahead we could see the two tiny islands of Nu'utele and Nu'ulua, pretty islands, but not nearly as inviting as Manono had been. Nevertheless we stopped, laid out our lunch and, with equal enthusiasm, ate and slapped flies.

THE EASTERN END, THE ALEIPATA COAST

Now you're at the far end of the island, about to make the final turn. Here the road becomes more precipitous, more lovely too. The beaches are whiter and the small offshore islands surrounded by many-hued reefs are more interesting. It would be a good place for a day or two of camping—for which local permission should be sought.

FUIPISIA FALLS, MAFA PASS, FALEFA FALLS, AND THE POOL AT PIULA COLLEGE

From the village of Amaile the road turns west, runs inland, and climbs through open country. The next 15 miles contain four important halts. The first, Fuipisia Falls, requires a short walk from the road, a modest admission fee is exacted by local villagers, and then you view a dramatic 180-foot plunge of water into a verdant valley.

At 700-foot Mafa Pass there is a fine view of mountain and sea. Then at Falefa Falls, right by the road, is a series of broad cataracts that end in a pool. The pool, which is said to be good for swimming, was that day roiled and too filled with jovial children to be inviting.

From Falefa the road runs down to the north coast, and at Piula there's a Methodist church-school called Piula College. This is the location of Fatumea Pool, an oval-shaped natural swimming pool filled with crystal-clear water flowing from a cave under the church. The pool has an eerie quality about it, a place some of the locals view with awe.

Beyond Piula, Apia is a half hour away. For us, daylight was waning, thirst increasing, and Aggie's never looked better.

SAVAI'I

Savai'i, Western Samoa's biggest island, lies to the west of Upolo. On a clear day you can see it from Apia. At Mulifanua, the western end of Upolu near the airport, Savai'i is only 13 miles away. Ferries run from Mulifanua to Salelologa on the Savai'i side. Several boats make this trip. One is a vehicular ferry, another is a new vessel, the *Lady Samoa*, and there are a number of smaller launches that occasionally get pressed into duty.

Schedules call for 6 AM and 1 PM departures from the Upolu side and 9 AM and 4 PM departures from the Savai'i side. Either way it's about an hour and a half, and the fare is $2 per person one way. If you're inclined to make the trip, do it in the morning when the sea is smoother. Be aware that the channel can get very rough at any time.

We made the ferry run once, on one of the smaller boats. It was packed that day with humanity. With difficulty, we found cheek-to-jowl space near the rail and in due time set off across the calm lagoon toward the reef. But once in the open sea, conditions changed and we began to pitch and roll in seas that were enormous.

As much as I love the sea and ships, I have done my share of retching in most of the major oceans. Virginia does not get sick, but I noticed that on that particular day her face was not wreathed in smiles. Someone at home had suggested the seasick remedy called Transderm by Ciba, which comes in a series of adhesive patches containing a scopalimine base and is applied to the mastoid area behind the ear. It worked for me. Our fellow passengers, however, were not free from the malady and were throwing up enthusiastically.

Unless you're an unreformed seagoing purist, avoid this run and fly instead. There's plane service several times a day from Fagali strip near Apia to Asau at the far end of Savai'i, and from Faleolo Airport to Maoto near the ferry dock.

Savai'i, roughly 48 miles long and 28 miles at its widest, is mountainous, jungle-clad, and ribbed with bleak expanses of lava flows that came from 6,000-foot Mt. Silisili. The last eruption was in 1911.

There are dozens of fine secluded beaches on Savai'i and a road of sorts circles the island and connects the villages, which are said to be the soul of Samoa and of Polynesia itself. According to experts, Savai'i is the birthplace of Polynesia, home of legendary Hawaiiki.

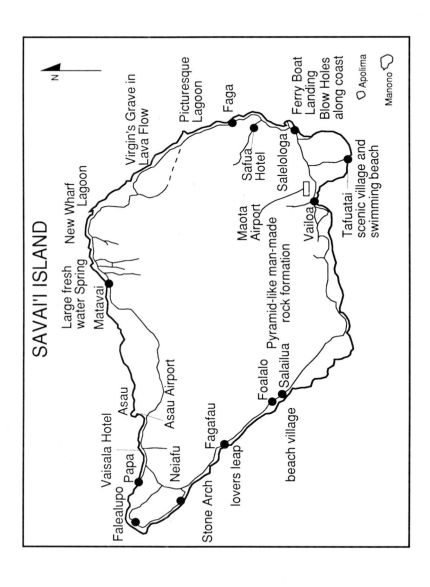

SAVAI'I ISLAND

Large fresh
water Spring

New Wharf

Lagoon

Matavai

Virgin's Grave in
Lava Flow

Picturesque
Lagoon

Faga

Safua
Hotel

Maota
Airport

Salelologa

Pyramid-like man-made
rock formation

Vailoa

Ferry Boat
Landing

Blow Holes
along coast

Tafuatai
scenic village and
swimming beach

Foalalo

Salailua

beach village

lovers leap

Fagafau

Stone Arch

Neiafu

Asau Airport

Asau

Papa

Vaisala Hotel

Falealupo

◊ Apolima

Manono

Village of Papa on Savai'i Island

On Upolu you'll see relatively few tourists, but on Savai'i their absence is total. This is because hotel accommodations are few, roads marginal, transport spotty, and there is no tourist gimmickry whatsoever.

Where to Stay

Savaiian Guest Fale—At Lalomalava near Maoto Airstrip and the ferry landing. This inn, as they say in their advertising, is for the hardy. They are right. It is cheap though.

Salafai Inn—Right in Salelologa, handy to both airstrip and ferry. Only so so. $27 a double, and not fully plumbed.

Safua Hotel—At Lalomalava, close to airstrip and ferry. Excellent. All conveniences except hot water. Double $50 with meals.

Vaisala Hotel—This hotel at the far end of the island (near Asau) is also excellent. It has a fine beach, good food, and on Friday nights locals come in for a spirited fia fia. Much laughter, music, food. Rates $53 for a double.

We've stayed at the Safua and the Vaisala and recommend both with enthusiasm. Be sure to have reservations. In a woodsy setting, the Safua has a large central thatched fale that serves as bar-dining room and library. And at a distance there are eight open-sided double bedded fales with bath. While you are dining family style, services often include a pretty Samoan girl who will fan you. She fans not to keep you cool, but to keep flies off the food.

On our first visit, our hosts at the Safua were Englishman Barry Jackson and his noble-born Samoan wife, Moelagi. Barry has since passed away, but I remember what he told us one evening about Samoan life on Savai'i. According to him the laughing, smiling Polynesian is a myth, since for a man to smile is considered unmanly, and Samoan girls are careful how and when they smile, for a smile can be an invitation to sex. Perhaps Barry was right; during his years there he dug deeply into Samoan culture, even married into it. But the Samoans we've since met show little reluctance to smile.

Moelagi Jackson still runs the Safua, still turns out fine meals and provides Samoan hospitality. In the October '85 issue of *National Geographic* she was given considerable and favorable mention.

To Get to the Safua—Fly from Faleolo Airport to Maoto Airstrip—a 10-minute flight. Fare is $30 round trip. Or take the ferry, preferably the *Lady Samoa*, and eschew the smaller craft. If you're expected, a van will meet you at either ferry landing or airstrip.

The other hotel we're familiar with is at the far end of the island near Asau. It's the Vaisala, a small hotel with 25 rooms on an excellent white beach where snorkeling is good. The hostess there is Judy Green, an Aussie from Melbourne, and the owner is Papu Vaii, a matai (chief) who's congenial and spends most of his time smiling.

There is no air conditioning, but ceiling fans and the trade-winds keep the place cool. The dining room is every bit as good as Aggie Grey's and includes Samoan dishes prepared from locally acquired sources, breadfruit, taro, raw fish in an onion-coconut marinade, local seafood, and papaya. Remember though, it's a small place and quite popular. Reservations are advised.

To Get to the Vaisala Hotel—Take the morning Polynesian Airlines flight from Fagali, the tiny airstrip near Apia, to Asau. The fare is $64 roundtrip. It's a 35-minute trip, a scenic low-level run that follows the north coast of Upolu, passes over tiny Manono and Apolima islands, then follows the entire length of Savai'i.

The anatomy of Savai'i is fully exposed on this flight. You'll see how the land slopes gradually to its high point, Mt. Silisili, and how lava found its way to the sea. There is jungle too, thick and green, white sandy, reef-protected beaches, and places where the sea crashes against lava-flow cliffs. You'll see a road, a narrow ribbon running close to the sea, that connects the villages, each with its church and village green.

Then the plane puts down on a narrow finger of land separating sea from bay. There is no terminal, just a strip and a parked van—your transport on to the hotel three miles away. This is Asau.

On Savai'i you get a feeling of space, and of variety—with volcanos, jungle, waterfalls, pristine beaches, and a prehistoric ruin or two. But when it comes to people, the variety is gone. There's an essential sameness in their neat villages, each with its imposing church. Their customs are the same, and the food they eat, usually steamed in underground ovens, is uniform and for most visitors too bland. The people, with their robust size, their elaborate tatoos, their dress, and their friendly but shy responses to strangers, are similar too. This is what Poly-nesia is all about, and on Savai'i you'll find the real unblemished article.

You can travel all the way around Savai'i by either rental car or public bus. It's a long way though, well over 100 miles, much of it by rough road.

A rental car on Savai'i can be had for a flat rate of $50 a day. The bus all the way around the island will cost no more than

$8. But bus schedules are erratic, and departures and arrivals can be in the wee hours. Don't attempt the trip in one day. Use two days for the rental car. If you travel by bus plan on four days, in which case you'll be depending on the hospitality of villagers at night—an easy thing to do. This will run $6 a night, or the equivalent in gifts. Remember too, whether by car, foot, or bus, when you appear in a village all eyes will be upon you. You simply cannot escape notice. This is the time to follow their rules of courtesy, which put simply are:

1. Always ask permission to enter a village.
2. Don't eat or talk in a fale while standing. Sit crosslegged.
3. If they offer something to drink, probably kava, tip a little of the liquid out before drinking.
4. Be particularly respectful on Sundays.

Proper conduct makes you an immediate friend; without it you could find hostility.

AROUND SAVAI'I

If you begin a round-island trip in Asau, a sawmill town with a wharf big enough for large ships to load hardwood timber, and go in a counterclockwise direction, you'll pass Vaisala where the Vaisala Hotel is. Then, five miles later at the bottom of a hill, set in tropical elegance on a fine beach, is Papa—the prettiest village in Samoa.

Continue on past the lonesome white beaches of Cape Mulinu, then follow the sea, village by village past several dramatic waterfalls, the Lover's Leap at Fagafau and past a few startling blowholes.

At Vailoa you're nearly halfway round. Here there is a pretty waterfall with an inviting pool, and you're close to the 2,000-year-old ruins of a pyramid. Chances are that someone will have to point out the pyramid since it looks like a low and not very remarkable hill. From here, some fine jungle trekking can be done. Be assured that, other than getting badly lost, there are no animals or snakes to worry about, only mosquitos (the non-virulent kind).

In Salelologa, more town than village, there's a Burns Philp department store, a Morris Hedstrom store, a Bank of New Zealand, a Polynesian Airlines office, some shops, and the

Coastal travel in Western Samoa

wharf where the ferries from Upolu tie up. Not far beyond
Salelologa you'll come to the village of Lalomala. The Safua
Hotel is near here and, by this time, you'll probably be pleased
to see it.

The rest of the way, 40 more mostly unpaved miles, you will
find intermittent fine beaches, villages, and some moonscaped
stretches of lava flow. Finally you'll close the circle at Asau
and the Vaisala Hotel.

For the dedicated traveler, the round-island trip is worthwhile, certainly a South Sea adventure. But on Savai'i my
feeling is that village life, beach wandering, and jungle trekking can be done happily near wherever you're staying. Life on

Savai'i is uniform—getting to know one area well may be sufficient. As a compromise you might do just half the island. Fly to Asau, stay at the Vaisala, then go by car or van to Maoto (stay at the Safua if time permits), then fly back from there.

THE TOKELAU ISLANDS

The Tokelaus aren't Western Samoan, but Apia is the jumping-off place for these New Zealand-administered Polynesian islands 300 miles to the north. Careful correspondence with the Office for Tokelau Affairs, Apia, Western Samoa is required. Please note their reply to my recent letter.

"Dear Mr. Booth:

Please refer to your letter of 5 September seeking passage to Tokelau on our chartered vessel. The vessel we're currently using *MV Wairua* belongs to a Suva-based shipping company. The trips for the remainder of the year are 18–23 Oct., 15–22 Nov., and 18–23 Dec. The November sailing will be a busy one for us, and suggest you make arrangement to travel, if approved by the 3 Councils in Tokelau, on the Dec. trip. The fares are NZ$200—deck, return or NZ$400 cabin, return.

The difference in fare structure relates to the type of accommodation and meals available on the ship. A deck passenger will not have any cabin-berth available to him, and the meals are of less quality than those available in the saloon.

I will not be able to confirm the availability of a cabin-berth until the week before the charter. I will tentatively book you "deck" on the December trip, and endeavor to obtain permission from the Councils in Tokelau. I am not sure how soon I will get to this, but I should be able to advise you well in advance of the actual December sailing date. If there's anything you need information on, I should be grateful if you could contact Iuta Gaualofa of this office.

Yours sincerely"

This letter held little promise but, as on each previous appearance in Apia, we approached the Office for Tokelau Affairs. It's on a back street two blocks from the Clock Tower and, each time with hat in hand, we requested sea transport to the Tokelaus. Each time they received us warmly, provided us with brochures, sold us some Tokelau postage stamps (postage stamps are important to their economy), and expressed regrets that the ship was delayed or fully booked.

Perhaps your luck will be better. If you are successful this is what to expect. The ship, a quite comfortable one, carries 12 cabin passengers, 68 deck passengers, and the voyage should take six to nine days. The ship stops at each of the three islands, Fakaofa, Nukumono, and Atafu.

These islands, all atolls, are reef-bound and have a total land area of four square miles. None have ports, so the ship must stand off while whale boats with outboard motors negotiate the surf-ridden openings in the reef, which were blasted open, to pick up their only export—copra.

Life on these islands is not idyllic but hard, since no crops other than coconuts, bananas, and taro can grow in the thin soil. For protein, fish and shellfish have to be gleaned from the reef and lagoon, a never-ending chore. Chickens and pigs contribute marginally to their diet, but these animals have to be fed, another difficulty.

There's one co-op store on each island, but the islanders can't afford much more than staples. They're poor, and many of them leave, mostly for New Zealand. We're told that if they all returned, their islands would be unable to support them.

Survival there is delicately balanced. Every man, woman, and child requires five coconuts a day, and a fixed amount of breadfruit. If a hurricane blows their trees down, they're in trouble. That is exactly what happened in 1966. Results were tragic. Why visit these islands? Anyone who loves the Pacific should at least once experience the frailty of life on an atoll. It's a sobering experience. There is a guesthouse on each island, but most visitors will want to sleep on the ship.

And on the subject of the Tokelaus, consider the maritime mystery of the *Joyita*, a puzzling event that smacks of the *Mary Celeste* incident of 1872.

One day in 1956, the *Joyita*, a small vessel designed for island trading, set out on the 300-mile voyage to the Tokelaus. She never arrived. But six weeks later, the *Joyita* was found intact and floundering near Fiji. All 27 of her people were gone. And after 32 years, the *Joyita* like the *Mary Celeste* remains a mystery.

Useful address: Visitors Information Service, PO Box 862, Apia, Western Samoa.

6

FIJI

Each time I see a new place I privately play the game of, "Would I be happy living here permanently?" My reactions for Fiji, mostly happy ones, aren't based entirely on Fiji's miles of white beaches, her rattling palms, the variety of her villages, or the dramatic hill country. I can find these things in dozens of Pacific destinations and, as much as I love most of them, none are choices for my declining years.

Fiji has the required qualities—among them, space and lots of it. Viti Levu, the big island where Suva and Nadi are, has 4,000 square miles. Vanua Levu, the next island in size, has 2,000 square miles. And then there are the smaller ones— Ovalau, Taveuni, Koro, Kandavu, Mbau, the Lau group—and hundreds of other tiny dots of land.

The people, 700,000 of them, are varied too. There are native Fijians, Polynesians, Indians, Chinese and a fair sprinkling of expatriate Australians, New Zealanders, English, and Americans. Some of them like me require a city, perhaps not to live in but at least available. Suva is such a place. It's small, in places it's tatty and hodge-podge, but it fits my specifications. When you're hungry, the best Indian and Chinese food in the Pacific is available. Mexican, Indonesian, and Italian food can be found too, or you can dine in splendor at a wide range of stylish restaurants. When you're thirsty you can drink in an English or Australian pub, and when you feel poorly, good medical and dental care is available.

For housing, something like $75,000 will provide you with a nice home in Suva, or you can live in the country-club environment of Pacific Harbor, 35 miles away. The University of the Pacific provides cultural resources if you want them and, because Fiji is such a Pacific crossroads, flights leave daily for Australia, New Zealand, Hawaii, Europe, and the Far East. But the May '87 coup which suspended the constitution and sent Fiji to the level of banana-republic military government, mars my enthusiasm. We were there at the time. More on this later.

The Land and Her People

Fiji, 5,600 miles from West Coast America, is 15 degrees south of the equator, and just the other side of the International Dateline. When it's Saturday in California, it's Sunday in Fiji.

The total land mass of Fiji's 332 islands comes to about 8,000 square miles. Viti Levu, the largest islands, is roughly 100 miles across, and a 315-mile road circles the island. Vanua Levu, the next island in size, is long rather than round, and stretches 100 miles. Then, in order of diminishing size, come the islands of Taveuni, Kadavu, Mbau, Koro, Ovalau, Rotuma, Beqa, the Lau Group, and about 100 mostly uninhabited tiny dots of land. By Pacific island standards, Fiji is large. It's bigger than Hawaii, far bigger than the Samoas, Vanuatu, New Caledonia, all of French Polynesia, and all of Micronesia. Only New Guinea, at 180,000 square miles, and the Solomons, with 12,000 square miles, are larger.

Suva, a city of 80,000, is on the wetter and more humid southeast side of Viti Levu. Lautoka, the second city at 26,000, and neighboring Nadi at 9,000, are on the drier western side. The interior of the island, with its mountains running a northeast/southwest direction, is dramatically beautiful. There's jungle in the wet (southeast) windward side, and on the leeward (northwest) side there are grassy green hills that look like California in spring. There are at least 25 peaks on Viti Levu that rise to 3,000 feet, and many rivers drain the land. For hikers and canoers Viti Levu has a lot to offer— dramatic scenery, genuine and friendly isolated villages, and no snakes or malicious animals to worry about, except for an

Fijian children

occasional mosquito. Much the same is true of Fiji's other islands.

As third-world nations go, Fiji has done remarkably well since independence in 1970. Her primarily agrarian economy—sugar cane, copra, timber, fish and food production—has performed so well that Fiji requires less foreign aid than any other Pacific nation, except Nauru. In the long run it will probably outstrip even Nauru, since the basis of that country's economy, bird guano, is exhaustible. Fiji was just starting to hit its stride when the unfortunate coup occurred. But that problem, while leaving an ugly scar, will be solved.

Then too there's tourism, and among Fiji's 4,400 resorts, hotels, and motels, something can be found for every sort of visitor. Budget-minded folks can expect to pay as little as $8 for a modest room on a good beach and they can camp for considerably less. At the other end of the spectrum, $300 a day is not considered unusual in a luxury hotel.

Tourism in Fiji is big business, not in the league of Hawaii, but bigger than Tahiti or anywhere else in the South Pacific. Most visitors, 240,000 of them in 1986, are from Australia or New Zealand (Australia is closer to Fiji than Hawaii is to California), where TV ads promote Fiji as a destination. Americans are not yet getting the "come to Fiji" message. The reason is that spot TV ads in the US cost as much as $200,000 a minute. Boosters of Fiji's tourist industry say, "Relax, we know the Americans will eventually come, and since they incline to be fussy, they'll come as package tourists and occupy the expensive resorts of Viti Levu's southwest coast around Nadi."

The big hotels and resorts are mostly foreign owned and, though some of the profit leaves the country, a lot trickles down. The tourism industry employs about 25,000 people. The waiters, guides, and reception people are Fijian. But behind the scenes in the offices, kitchens, and accounting firms, are the Indians. Even further out of sight are the non-Fijian foreigners who own and run many of the hotels and cruise ship operations.

But most of Fiji is still rural and most Fijians—real Fijians who are a handsome mixture of Melanesian and Polynesian—still live and work on communal land. Any extra money they get comes from selling part of what they produce. The soil and what it grows makes Fiji go.

Sugar cane is the most important crop and, as an export, brings in millions of dollars. Copra, cocoa, cattle, lumber, are big business too. Even so, Fiji isn't a rich country. Most Fijians live in inexpensive houses (only a few live in the old traditional mbures). They eat simply, take buses instead of owning a car, and the taxes they pay are low. Life for most Fijians has been happy.

City and town life is a little different. Here there's a multiracial, layered, and not always harmonious situation. In the years between 1879 and 1916 Indians came as indentured laborers to work the cane fields, and many stayed on. Now the Indians, who outnumber the Fijians, stand out sharply. They look and act as if they still lived in Bombay or Madras. Their women go about clad in saris, the men in the uniform of commerce, and they speak the same variety of Hindustani or Urdu as their ancestors, as well as English. Most of them live in cane growing areas—Nadi, Lautoka, Labasa—where a walk down the main road will nearly convince you you're in India. They live in Suva too, as well as anywhere business is done. The Indians aren't in big business, which is dominated by foreigners, but they do own most of the shops, restaurants, some of the banks, and many of the hotels.

The Indians acquired this commercial clout as the result of a Fijian law which states that no one can buy native Fijian communal land. So Indians, unable to obtain land, went into business and were successful. Differences of opinion between native Fijians developed in response. Should the rule of chiefs prevail on a national level or should it remain at the village level? Should the ownership of property be important in Fijian life? Why should the tribal and communal system be continued when the Indian labors under no such restriction?

In early 1987 when an election gave control to an Indian majority the Army, which is 98% Fijian, stepped in and forcibly overthrew the government.

Whether out of fear or protest, the Indian response was to close most of their shops and stop running their buses. This stirred up more resentment. We heard Fijians say, "If the Indians don't open their shops, we'll open them ourselves." Some violence did occur, Fijians attacking Indians and the Army putting the muscle on foreign newsmen. The country was badly hurt. Services came to a halt, and the life-giving flow of tourists came to a full stop.

In spite of new elections, recovery will be slow. But no matter what happens the Fijians will have to become more assertive in business matters. It's too bad to see the simplicity of their tribal life disappear but, if they want parity with the Indians, they have little choice.

History in Brief

Judging by the way native Fijians look today, the original inhabitants thousands of years ago must have come from both Polynesia and Melanesia. It was a good mixture, one that produced a highly developed society well before the first Europeans arrived.

Tasman, bound for Java in 1643, first saw the island of Taveuni. Then Captain Bligh, sailing the Bounty's launch after the mutiny, passed through and charted a few islands. But because he'd heard that the "Feegees" were cannibals, he didn't go ashore.

In the early 1800's sandalwood was discovered in Vanua Levu and, since merchants in China paid so well for it, foreign ships poured in. Sea traffic was heavy, but the sailors, whalers, and traders were not long on ethics. Guns were brought in and sold to rival chiefs. It was a bad time but gradually, with the arrival of planters intending to work and live in Fiji, and missionaries who wanted to help, matters improved slightly. Full improvement was slow though. People continued to eat missionaries and each other. But when Ratu Seru Cakobau, the cannibal king of Mbau, rose to power in 1854 tribal warfare decreased.

In 1874 England prevailed, peacefully, and Fiji was signed over to the Queen. Levuka on Ovalau became Fiji's first capital, a rough, ribald, hard drinking town. And it was from Levuka that the first ship sailed for India to bring Indian laborers back to work the cane fields. At this point one wonders why the Fijians didn't work the cane themselves. They didn't because the British Governor Sir Arthur Gordon felt that Fijians had been abused quite enough. The "blackbirding" era was still remembered—a time when Fijians were kidnapped and hauled away to work foreign cane fields. Sir Arthur's decision, humane at the time, has left its mark on modern Fiji.

In later years it was Australia rather than England that brought enterprise to Fiji, a condition that continues today. Then, during World War II, Fijian troops made a valiant name for themselves, and even improved on that image later when they acted as a peace-keeping force in Lebanon.

In 1970 Fiji, while still maintaining close ties to Britain, became independent and Queen Elizabeth II was proclaimed Queen of Fiji.

How to Get There by Air

Fiji is the hub of the entire South Pacific. Flights from every direction converge on Fiji, usually at Nadi International Airport. But some inter-island flights come in and go out of Nausori Airport on the other side of the island, near Suva. It's a 20-minute flight between the airports.

Coming from the U.S.—Qantas has three flights a week from Los Angeles, which pause in Honolulu, then go on to Nadi. Count on five hours to Honolulu, six more to Nadi. Air Pacific also has three flights a week from Honolulu.

Coming from Canada—Air New Zealand comes in from Vancouver, three times a week, with a stop in Honolulu. Canadian Pacific's DC 10's have two weekly flights with stopovers in Honolulu.

Coming from Australia or New Zealand—There is a daily flight on Air Pacific, Air New Zealand, or Canadian Pacific.

From Apia, Western Samoa—Air Pacific has two flights a

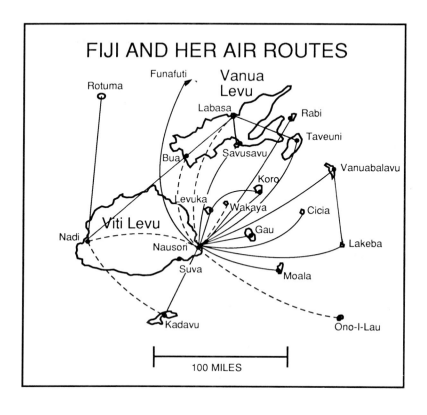

FIJI AND HER AIR ROUTES

100 MILES

week. They're two-hour flights into either Nausori (near Suva) or Nadi. If you take this flight be sure to watch for the Tongan island Niuafo'ou (Tin Can Island). In good weather it will appear at the halfway point.

From Noumea, New Caledonia—Air Caledonie flies in several times a week, a one-hour flight.

From the Solomons—Air Pacific has one three-hour flight a week.

From Vanuatu—Air Pacific has one flight a week (two hours).

Flight schedules often indicate destinations in Fiji as both Nadi and Suva. This means that after immigration clearance the plane usually goes on to the other airport. If not, there's a plane every hour for the 20-minute flight between Nadi and Nausori.

By Sea

Freighters are rare, but sometimes you can find something

Sunflower Airlines, Savusavu, Vanua Levu, Fiji

sailing from Apia, Western Samoa. There are always cruise ships, so check out Cunard, Sitmar, Five Star, P & O, or Royal Viking.

Immigration Formalities

Visitors must have a passport, onward travel tickets, and sufficient funds. A 30-day visitor's permit is issued on arrival. Extensions are easily obtained.

Health

There are no unusual problems here. There are some mosquitos, but malaria has been eliminated. Water is potable in all urban areas, but deep in the country it's best to ask.

Good medical and dental care is available, probably the best in the Pacific. The University of the South Pacific in Suva is well known for turning out capable medical people.

Currency

The local monetary unit is the Fijian dollar. It comes in denominations of 1, 2, 10 and 20. As of this writing, the F$ = US $1.25.

Time Zone

Time in Fiji is 12 hours ahead of Greenwich Mean Time, 17 hours ahead of Eastern Standard Time, 20 hours ahead of Pacific Standard Time.

Newspapers, Radio, Telephone

There is no TV, but three radio stations broadcast in English as well as in Fijian and Hindi. Newspapers are published in English and overseas newspapers are readily available. Make telephone calls round the clock at The Overseas Telephone Office in Suva.

Power

220 volts AC.

Climate

Fiji is by and large pleasantly warm, but it can be hot (upper 80's F) and humid between November and April. The cool dry season, May to October, is the choice time. But even within the country there's a difference in climate. On Viti Levu, the main island, it's drier on the western side where Nadi is, and wetter and more humid on the eastern side where Suva is.

Language

Anywhere in Fiji English will serve you well. But no matter where you go, expect to be greeted with the Fijian word, mbula. You shouldn't hesitate to reply in kind and, if you want to add a little flourish, say "bula vinaka"—hello and thank you.

As to Fijian, a few simple rules are in order. For example, the letter "d" is pronounced "nd," which makes Nadi, "Nandi." The letter "g" has an "ng" sound, so the town Sigatoka becomes "Singatoka." The letter "b" is pronounced "mb" as in mbula, for hello, or mbure for the thatched Fijian house. Don't worry too much about the silent "m", just "bula" will do nicely.

The letter "q" comes out "ngg" so the island of Beqa become "Mbengga" and the drink yacona is "yanggona."

Holidays

Most services are inconveniently closed on many holidays. They observe New Year's Day, January 1; Prophet Mohammed's Birthday, January 19; Good Friday; Easter Saturday; Easter and Easter Monday; the Queen's birthday, June 15; Bank Holiday, the first Monday in August; Fiji Day, October 12; Deepawali, October 27; Prince Charles's birthday, November 16; Christmas; and Boxing Day on December 26.

Tipping

As in the rest of the South Pacific, it's unnecessary, but the habit is catching on. Some taxi drivers will suggest that a tip would be accepted, as will the hotel staff in the larger hotels.

You'll have to be the judge, but I hope you'll regard tipping as a reward for unusually good service.

VITI LEVU, THE BIG ISLAND AND GATEWAY TO FIJI

Coming by air from Hawaii, Sydney, Auckland or Europe, you'll enter Fiji at Nadi International Airport. Nadi is truly a crossroads, an airport where many travelers en route to or from the United States, Australia, or Europe spend a zombie-like hour between the transit lounge and "duty free" shop, then reboard their plane, hardly aware they've been in Fiji.

Then there are the travelers who never get beyond this western corner of Viti Levu. Most of them are either booked for a cruise to the nearby Yasawas or Mamanucas or for a stay at one of the luxury hotels on this coast. Few of them get to the capital, Suva, fewer make the trip around Viti Levu, and fewer still get to the more distant outer islands. That's a great shame, since moving about Fiji is not difficult.

Among these 300-plus islands there are 4,400 resorts, hotels, guest houses, and restaurants of every persuasion. Because of the numerous choices, some counsel is needed. We'll assume you've just arrived at Nadi, and plan to move in a counter-clockwise direction entirely around Viti Levu.

THE NADI AREA

If you're an unstructured traveler, a pause in Nadi for rest and planning is appropriate. When you leave the customs area, the first thing to do is change money at the convenient airport bank. Next choose a hotel. This is no problem, as there are many to choose from, all between two and five miles from the airport. You'll be pleased to know that many of them provide courtesy service to local hotels. Their phone numbers and rates appear on a wall in the airport. This is a partial list with rates for doubles.

Castaway Gateway, $65.
Dominion International Hotel, $55.
Fiji Mocambo, $75.

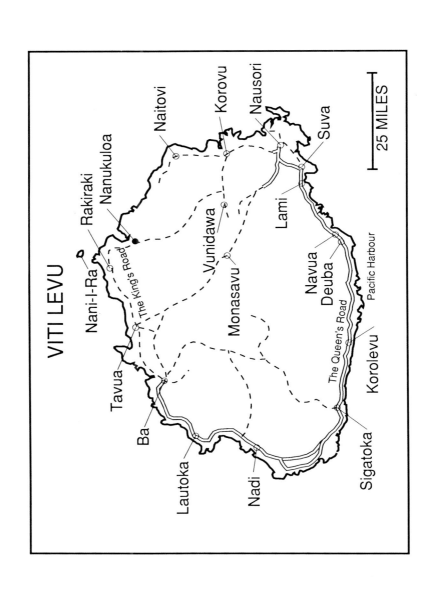

VITI LEVU

Nani-I-Ra
Rakiraki
Nanukuloa
Naitovi
Korovu
Nausori
Suva
Lami
The King's Road
Vunidawa
Tavua
Ba
Monasavu
Lautoka
Nadi
Navua
Deuba
The Queen's Road
Korolevu
Sigatoka
Pacific Harbour

25 MILES

Fijian "bure", Viti Levu

Nadi Airport Travelodge, $80. The scene of excellent curry dinners at $12.75 per person.

Sea Shell Cove Resort, $32.

Sky Lodge Hotel, $45.

Sunny Holiday Motel, $12.50. Also dormitory accommodations.

Tanoa Hotel, $75.

Fong Hing, $20.

Sandalwood Inn, $32. This is our usual hotel. It's near the airport, has free bus service to the hotel, it's close to town, has a pool, bar, good dining room, and friendly staff.

Regent of Fiji at Denaru (a suburb of Nadi). The most expensive in the area at $130.

All hotels charging over $30 have a pool, air conditioning and a restaurant.

Then comes the town of Nadi, population 10,000. It won't take long to see it. There is a main street lined with shops like a town of the same size in the American Midwest. The shops, however, are a little different. They bear such names as Mohand Lal's Jewelry, Das Gupta's Furniture, Harilala's Indian Restaurant, Khan's Hairdressers for Gents. Still there is good shopping and some good places to eat. Try *Fong Hing's* for Chinese food, inexpensive and very good. For hot spicy curries and tandoori chicken, visit the *Nadi Hotel* in town, where a meal is about $12 for two.

For dancing and entertainment, the *Bamboo Palace* will keep you mildly occupied from 8 PM to 1 AM. But most of the spirited fun takes place among the tourists at the bigger hotels.

The importance of the Nadi-Lautoka area (Lautoka, 12 miles north of Nadi, population 26,000) is that it's the jumping-off place for the Yasawa and Mamanuca Islands. They're the ones that attract most of Fiji's visitors.

THE YASAWAS AND MAMANUCAS

These islands, dozens of them, lie in a 90-mile arc off the Nadi-Lautoka coast. Tourist literature describes them as "sun-kissed islands in a placid sea." They're right, for these fun-in-the-sun places offer windsurfing, snorkeling, snowy beaches and gin-clear water. There are big hotels and scads of enthusiastic Aussies and Kiwis with peeling noses, but only an occasional American.

The easy glamorous way to these islands is to book out on one of the cruise boats that sail from Lautoka. *Blue Lagoon Cruises* ($580 per person) provides a 7-day/6-night cruise through the Yasawa group. All meals are included, staterooms are fully plumbed, with air conditioning, and shoreside excursions are provided. For $290 per person you can take a similar cruise of three days.

Contact: Blue Lagoon Cruises, Box 54, Lautoka, Fiji.

Tui Tai Explorer Cruises—Two-day/two-night cruises departing Lautoka Wharf Wednesday mornings sail among the Mamanucas and Yasawas. Fare is $220. Accommodations aboard are dormitory style, with all meals provided.

Contact: Islands in the Sun, PO Box 364, Lautoka, Fiji.

For good-value one day cruises consider the following:

Take a *Beachcomber* vessel which leaves from Lautoka at 10

AM to Beachcomber Island in the Mamanucas 12 miles out. Lots of food and swimming—a full day for $34 a person. Same address as above.

Mana Island Day Cruise—Departs daily from the Regent of Fiji Hotel in Nadi. It's a 75-foot catamaran cruise to Mana Island in the Mamanucas, 20 miles out. Food, swimming, shelling, snorkeling, $37 per person.

Contact: South Sea Cruises, Box 718, Nadi,. Fiji.

Bookings can be made for these cruises at your hotel.

The Inexpensive, More Difficult Way to the Yasawas—Go to the Lautoka Wharf in the morning and talk to some of the small boat skippers who bring in produce from the Yasawas. Dealing with them on the scene could snag you a ride to such islands as Davewa for up to $8. There is an inexpensive guesthouse out there, a good place to loaf in the sun. But save your energy for other more distant islands.

Hotels in the Mamanucas and Yasawas

This is where the big island resorts are, as shown below. Prices listed are for doubles.

Beachcomber Island Resort, $106.

Castaway, $90.

Club Naitasi, $90.

Matamanoa, $125.

Navini Island Resort, $92.

Plantation Island Resort, $95.

Treasure Island Resort, $92.

And the daddy of them all, *Turtle Island Lagoon Lodge* in the Yasawas, with rates of $398 a couple. This includes all drinks and meals.

Abatha

Located in a mountain valley eight miles from Lautoka there is a small village called Abatha. Surrounded by waterfalls and mountain peaks, this village is a good place to start hiking. You're welcome to hike there every day except Sunday but, if you swim in one of the nearby waterfalls, don't do it in the nude.

Traditionally when visiting any Fijian village, a gift or "sevusevu" of yagona root is presented. This is a must for obtaining permission to hike on the village lands. For this purpose, you buy a small bundle of root in any market. When you arrive in Abatha, ask to see the village mayor. You will be shown to his house and, at this point, take off your shoes before entering, then sit crosslegged on the floor. When the mayor arrives give him the present plus one dollar for a hiking fee. If you want to spend a night or eat there, this is the time to ask.

To get to Abatha, take the Queen's Road to Lautoka, 20 miles north of Nadi Airport. At the first roundabout before town, bear right. Proceed about a mile, then turn right on Tavakubu Road. The road isn't good, and it fords two streams, but in about seven miles it ends at the village of Abatha.

Coming from Lautoka, ask at the bus station, and board the appropriate van. Fare should be about $8 each way, and most drivers will gladly wait while you hike.

NADI TO SUVA ON THE QUEEN'S ROAD

It's 120 miles from Nadi to Suva on the Queen's Road. This is the main well-paved route, one you can do easily by rental car or public bus.

Rental Car—The best place for rentals is at Nadi Airport. Try Hertz, Avis, Jans, or Dominion. $110 will provide a Toyota Starlet Wagon for three days, unlimited mileage. For a week it'll cost $175.

For driving the Queen's Road, remember that most of the bridges are one way. Treat them with caution and, if there's any question about right-of-way, yield. Watch for trucks and buses; they often hog the road. Watch out for animals too. A reminder for Americans—be sure to drive on the left.

Buses—Between Nadi and Suva there are 11 daily trips by air conditioned luxury buses. The roughly five-hour trip will cost $25. For less than half of that you can take a local bus. They're open air, have harder seats, and may take eight hours to make the run.

When we did it, the luxury bus picked us up at our hotel at

7:30 AM then, after stopping at several hotels for other passengers, proceeded down the road towards Suva. It's rather dull at first, the way is flat, mostly cane fields, barren country and occasional tiny villages, each with an Indian shop and sometimes a mosque or Hindu temple.

Sigatoka is the first town of any size along this coast, an attractive (2,000 population) community on the banks of the Sigatoka River which has a one-way bridge across it. You could spend a night there at the Sigatoka Hotel which is inexpensive, quietly pleasant, and has good food. There are good boat rides you can take upriver to quaint villages where Fijian pottery is sold.

The Coral Coast begins at Korotogo, a small community seven miles beyond Sigatoka. Reef exploring and snorkeling are excellent, and the scent of suntan oil is strong. The coral beaches are white, the water transparent, reasons enough for the existence of several beach resorts.

Casablanca Beach Hotel, $65.

Hyatt Regency, $94.

Hide-a-Way Resort, $65. Also dormitory-type accommodations, $7.

Naviti Beach Resort, $70.

Reef Resort, $80.

Tambua Sands Beach Resort, $58. Also dormitory accommodations, $8.

The Crow's Nest, $66.

Fijian Resort Hotel, $120.

Tubakula Beach Resort, $35. Also dormitory, $6.

Horseback riding is available at the Casablanca Beach Hotel, the Naviti Beach Resort has tennis and golf, as does the Fijian Resort Hotel. Other hotels can make arrangements for such activities.

About here the vegetation changes from dry to jungle-like rain forest. When we first traveled this road some years ago, the road was unpaved and the most prestigious hotel was the Korolevu Beach Hotel. It's gone now, but the town of Korolevu offers a pair of good things to do.

First, you can hike to an excellent waterfall. Ask in Korolevu for directions to Biausevu village, less than a mile. There you pay a dollar for a guide to lead you on another two miles to the waterfall. It's an easy trek, but it does involve wading numerous streams.

The other activity is to visit Vatulele island 25 miles due south of Korolevu. Vatulele is the home of Fiji's Red Prawns which come from a grotto on the coast. The lagoon here is good for snorkeling, and the island has an away-from-it-all character. You can get here cheaply by small boats from Korolevu, or more stylishly aboard the 140-foot 3-masted schooner *Tui Tai* that leaves on Saturday mornings from the nearby Naviti Beach Resort. A full day aboard, including food and shoreside activities, will be $34 per person.

Pacific Harbor is next, and it's well worth a pause. There's golf, game fishing, and a recreated Fijian village with attendant shops—a good place for a trip into Fiji's past. The Fijian village is open daily, except Sunday, from 9:30 AM to 2:00 PM. Pacific Harbor, a half hour from Suva, is Suva's playground.

The Navua River—Six miles beyond Pacific Harbor the road crosses the muddy Navua River. It's not a scene of overpowering beauty, but upstream the river runs fast and clear offering rafters or canoers all levels of challenge. A day spent there, 20 minutes from Suva, provides beauty and adventure.

For $45 per person you can be picked up at your hotel in Suva and taken to the upper reaches of the Navua River. Then with guide, you paddle downriver through gorges, past waterfalls and villages, for 15 to 20 miles. At mid-point the guide will cook lunch and by 4 PM you're at the end of the run.

The folks who operate this wet run say that participants should be in the 15–45 age group, but I think they're flexible about this. Contact: Wilderness Adventures, PO Box 1389, Suva, Fiji.

This trip probably can be arranged for you at your hotel.

Beqa Island—It is from Navua's wharf that boats leave for Beqa Island (pronounced Mbengga), the legendary home of Fiji's firewalkers. The boats that make this run for about $5 tend to be small. I'm constantly startled at the distances some small boats in these islands travel and, if the sea is up, I recommend caution. You'll be in for a wet and rough 10-mile passage.

As to firewalking out there, a little background might help.

Legend has it that, in return for a favor, a spirit god gave a Beqa native called Tui the power over fire. To prove his gift a pit was dug, lined with stones, and a great fire was lit. When the stones were white with heat, the spirit leapt on them and invited Tui to join him. Tui did, and was surprised that he felt no pain and suffered no burns. To this day members of his tribe, the Sawaus, are able to walk on white hot stones.

Chances are that you won't see any firewalking on Beqa. They're rather sensitive about doing it for strangers, but not about exporting it to the big hotels in Nadi or Suva.

There is good walking of the more conventional sort on Beqa, some hill climbing too, but it's best to mind your manners and avoid wandering into villages unless invited by one of the village elders.

Some experts classify this island as one of the five best dive spots in the world. A boat and two dives will cost you $50. The dive boats leave from Pacific Harbor, not Navua.

From Navua to Suva is about 18 miles, a pretty run for much of the way, but soon you're in lively traffic and then in the big city—Suva.

SUVA

Lying as it does between hills and the harbor, Suva is attractive. The way its streets wind down from green hills to the city center is pleasant to the eye. So is the way downtown Suva has developed, with its hodgepodge of high-rise office buildings, residual colonial buildings with second story verandas, and the planned dignity of her parks and houses of government.

If you include the suburbs in the hills east and north of town, the population of greater Suva is 156,000. It's a bustling place, but it has no beaches and no resort-type hotels. It's a seaport, a commercial center, a university town, the seat of government, and not a bad place to spend a weekend.

If you were to walk the length of town, paying due attention to the lively traffic, and keeping the harbor to the right, the stroll would take about 25 minutes. You'd see the essence of Suva, the sprawling public market, the wharves where freighters, cruise ships, and inter-island vessels tie up. You'd see the business area with its Indian shops, banks, and airline offices,

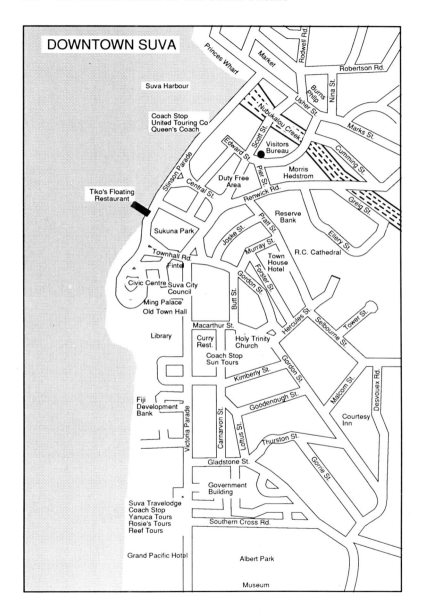

DOWNTOWN SUVA

Suva Harbour

Princes Wharf

Market

Rodwell Rd.

Robertson Rd.

Coach Stop
United Touring Co
Queen's Coach

Nubukalou Creek

Burns
Philp

Usher St.

Nina St.

Marks St.

Scott St.

Edward St.

Visitors
Bureau

Cumming St.

Stinson Parade

Central St.

Duty Free
Area

Pier St.

Morris
Hedstrom

Tiko's Floating
Restaurant

Renwick Rd.

Greig St.

Sukuna Park

Joske St.

Pratt St.

Reserve
Bank

Ellery St.

Townhall Rd.

Murray St.

Town
House
Hotel

R.C. Cathedral

Finte

Foster St.

Gordon St.

Civic Centre Suva City
Council

Ming Palace
Old Town Hall

Butt St.

Hercules St.

Selbourne St.

Tower St.

Macarthur St.

Library

Curry
Rest.

Holy Trinity
Church

Coach Stop
Sun Tours

Gordon St.

Kimberly St.

Malcom St.

Desvouex Rd.

Fiji
Development
Bank

Victoria Parade

Carnarvon St.

Goodenough St.

Lottus St.

Courtesy
Inn

Thurston St.

Gorrie St.

Gladstone St.

Suva Travelodge
Coach Stop
Yanuca Tours
Rosie's Tours
Reef Tours

Government
Building

Southern Cross Rd.

Grand Pacific Hotel

Albert Park

Museum

the shiny new Travelodge, the venerable old Grand Pacific Hotel, the government buildings, and finally Albert Park where Kingsford Smith landed the *Southern Cross* on his epic flight in 1928.

There's more to Suva than that though, for in the suburbs reaching into the hills, there are shopping centers, churches, parks, schools, Hindu temples, Moslem mosques, and neighborhoods ranging from shabby to affluent.

Where to Stay

Hotels are no problem in Suva. There are at least 12 choices, and most are within walking distance from the center of town, or at most a $1 taxi fare away. Going from the least to most expensive, this list covers most housing in Suva.

South Seas Private Hotel—$5 single, $11 double. Dormitory-type accommodations and cooking facilities.

Suva Apartments—$20 double, private bath and cooking facilities.

Grand Pacific Hotel, Suva

Pacific Grand Apts.—$21 double, private bath and cooking facilities.

Tropic Towers—$25 double, private bath and cooking facilities.

Grand Pacific Hotel—On Victoria Parade right next to the Travelodge. Built in 1914, this white, crenellated hotel of Edwardian elegance belongs in the dignified company of old colonial hotels such as the Peninsula in Hong Kong, the now demolished Repulse Bay Hotel in Hong Kong, Raffles in Singapore, and the Eastern and Oriental in Penang. The GPH is a bit frayed, but I admire its gracious simplicity with no flamboyance, no flaming sauces and no electronic band. As on a pilgrimage, we always go there for at least a drink, and sometimes we stay. Rooms are about $55 double, but they also have "thrift rooms" at $35 double. No cooking facilities, but they do have bar, pool, restaurant, with video movies at night.

Suva Peninsula Hotel—$38 double. Cooking facilities, bar, pool and restaurant.

Sunset Apartment Motel—$40 double with bath, cooking facilities.

Outrigger Apt. Hotel—$40 double with bath and cooking facilities.

Capricorn Apt. Hotel—$45 double; all conveniences including cooking and pool.

Southern Cross Hotel—$45 double with bath, cooking facilities, pool, bar, restaurant.

Town House Apt. Hotel—$48 double with cooking facilities. We've stayed here a number of times and like it. It's five minutes from the center of town, the bar is congenial, and the restaurant serves good food, particularly curries. No pool.

Suva Courtesy Inn—$65 double. No cooking facilities. Pool, restaurant, bar.

Travelodge—This most elegant of Suva's hotels is $90 double. Has all services, pool, several dining rooms, active bar, convention facilities, guest laundry.

Food

The restaurants in hotels such as the Travelodge, Grand Pacific, Townhouse, Courtesy Inn, or Southern Cross serve food primarily based on European tastes.

Gordon's Restaurant (Courtesy Inn)—Dinner for two about $22.

The Townhouse Restaurant—Dinner for two about $22.

The Grand Pacific Hotel Restaurant we found to be only fair and recommend it mostly for light snacks or lunch poolside.

The Travelodge's Lali Restaurant is formal. Try it when they do Island Night or Indian buffets—about $35 for two.

Penney's Restaurant—This is the coffee shop at the Travelodge, and it provides one of the best bargains in town. For an excellent club sandwich and an extensive salad bar expect to pay $11 for two.

Local restaurants serve Chinese, Indian, Mexican, fish and continental food.

The Zichuan Palace on the second floor of one of the old colonial buildings downtown is excellent. Accompanied by Fiji Bitters beer, two can eat extremely well for $15.

The Ming Palace—An ornate establishment on Victoria Parade in the center of town serves fine Cantonese food—about $15 for two.

The Curry Place—There are two downtown. They serve curried goat, lamb, chicken, and prawns. Their dahl soup is hot and spicy and the vegetarian samosas are excellent. It's a bring-your-own-bottle place. Dinner or lunch for two about $8.

The Red Lion—On Victoria Parade it is moderately expensive, and has good seafood and steaks.

Trap's Mexican-American Restaurant is fair but, combined with music and night life, it becomes better. On Victoria Parade downtown.

Tiko's Floating Restaurant is actually a small ship tied up to the seawall in the center of town. Mostly it's an after-hours night spot, but you can dine well and fashionably on steaks and seafood. Fairly expensive.

Scott's Restaurant specializes in continental cuisine and is away from the center of town, about a $1 taxi ride. Stylish and somewhat expensive.

Le Normandie in Cumming Street—the only French restaurant in town. Moderately expensive.

For Fast Foods
Downtown there's *Kentucky Fried Chicken, Jude's, Palm Court,* and the *Pizza King.*

If you're staying in a hotel with cooking facilities, all groceries you will need are available in Suva. Try the Burns Philp Supermarket or Hedstrom's, both downtown.

The cheapest place in town to eat would be in the stalls near the public market. The food is nourishing and abundant.

What to See in Suva

Suva is a good town for strolling and, if you start at the south end of town near the Grand Pacific Hotel, walk into the Botanical Gardens. Examine the labeled flora and fauna in this lovely area. Then step into the museum on the same grounds. They've got the best collection of Melanesian artifacts in the South Pacific. Open weekdays and Saturday mornings.

Public Market, Suva

Government House is a block South and, if you're there at noon, you'll see the Changing of the Guard, nearly as good as at Buckingham Palace.

Go north on Victoria Parade, past the government buildings (they could use a scrub down), then wander through the commercial part of town. Check out the duty free shopping around Thomson Street. Jewelry, cameras, perfume, etc. are sold at Boomerang Duty Free, Caines Jannif, or Tapoo Duty Free. There are some good values, but examine prices critically.

In the same area, pay a visit to the Fiji Visitors' Bureau. It's the friendliest and most helpful in the Pacific. Their address is GPO Box 92, Suva, Fiji.

A word of caution—be wary of young men on the street who strike up a conversation with "G'day mate, what part of Australia you from? What's your name?" and attempt conversation. They may claim to be local guides, they may offer you a free gift. Do not encourage them. Smile broadly and walk away. They're professional touts.

For genuine Fijian artifacts visit Fiji Arts and Crafts Center behind the Post Office near the seawall. Lots of wood carvings, baskets, and the like.

One of Suva's biggest attractions is City Market. It's at the north end of town and is well worth seeing. The display of fruit and vegetables is dramatic, as are the flowers. You can also buy some good and authentic souvenirs there—tapa cloth, woven mats, and baskets. Best time to go is in the morning.

Prince's Wharf is just across the street. This is where you'll find inter-island ships of all kinds. You can walk aboard most of them, ask where they're going, ask to see accommodations, and even consider sailing on an appropriate ship. Some are quite good, some quite bad.

The Yacht Club and prison are at the north end of town. A cold beer, perhaps with lunch, at the Yacht Club after a long walk is refreshing and you'll probably meet some of the members. They like to talk about their boats and such conversations often lead to share-expense sailing possibilities.

The prison is noteworthy only because it looks so much like a prison, with harsh stone walls, iron bars, and barbed wire.

For a short side trip out of Suva, eight miles, take a taxi for $9 or the Tacirua bus or 50¢, from the public market out to the

Patterson Brothers Ferry in Savusavu

Colo-i-suva Nature Reserve. You'll find woodsy walking among the streams and waterfalls there—a peaceful spot. For picnicking and barbecuing there are covered bures (typical thatched native-style houses) complete with grill and cut wood. Entry to the reserve is free.

Overseas Phone Calls

To make overseas phone calls, visit the Overseas Telephone Office on Victoria Parade in the center of town. They provide quick, comfortable and private service. A three-minute call to West Coast America runs $8.

Post Office

The Post Office is at the north end of town. Stamps are usually available at the larger hotels.

Travel Agents

There are any number of travel agents in the downtown area. We've had good service with Thomas Cook Travel near the Post Office on Victoria Parade. They'll change money for you too.

Suva After Dark

Suva swings at night. From raunchy to respectable, there are a number of places to go. Most of the hotels with restaurants have bars where locals and expats congregate. You could go to the movies but, for more spirited activity, consider the following.

Chequers—This downtown club classifies itself as having a "slightly raw atmosphere." They have a band, are open seven nights a week til 1 AM, and gentlemen requiring female companionship will find a friendly environment there.

Lucky Eddie's—Downtown too, this place provides lively fun. They have a live band and a $2 cover charge.

Screwz—In town and has country-western music. An active place with a $2 cover charge.

Rockefellers—I'm not sure what they mean, but this place is described as "for the more sophisticated person." They add that they've got both waiters and waitresses. For the same $2.50 cover charge you can also get into Lucky Eddie's.

Golden Dragon—This is a more formal night club—good music, ample dance floor, close to the Travelodge.

If you're still out and about after 1 AM, go aboard *Tiko's Floating Restaurant* and visit the "Engine Room." It's Suva's best after-hours spot. Good for dinner too.

SUVA TO NADI ON THE KING'S ROAD

From Suva to Nadi via the north coast or the King's Road is 180 miles. Most of it is unpaved, often narrow, windy, and precipitous. It can be a horror and, along its rock strewn, extremely beautiful length, there are a few confusing spots marked with ambiguous directions. I don't mind driving the south coast, but in the north I leave the driving to even the most ancient of overland buses rather than risk it myself.

Sunbeam Bus Lines, which does the Suva-Lautoka run, departs from the Bus Terminal at the public market and makes six trips daily. Three of them are express, three are local.

The express runs are more comfortable, faster, and have softer seats. Fare is $18. Local runs use open-air buses with plastic side curtains that can be lowered in case of rain. Seats are harder and, because of more stops, are slower. You might try it once, however. It's more fun and you see more of Fiji this way. Fare is $7.

We set out one morning on the local and rattled out of town on the road to Nausori. In Suva we made all the stops, but beyond town they became further apart, and 12 miles out we crossed the Rewa River and pulled into Nausori, a rice shipping town better known as the place to turn right to go to Nausori Airport. There's little to do in town, and no good hotels, but you can get outboard-driven boats for trips down the muddy Rewa to a number of interesting villages in the delta area.

Mbau Island off the coast near Nausori is where the cannibal king Cacobau lived. He ruled over much of western Fiji from here in the mid-19th century. Coming in to Nausori by air you can often see this small circular island with a curious line of posts between it and the mainland. By following the posts at low tide you can wade across to Mbau. Take a bus to the wading point. Mbau is, however, not high on the list of things to do in Fiji.

Toberua Island is a four-acre island resort on the eastern side of Viti Levu, and has been called one of the 12 best resorts in the world. Beaches and all amenities are excellent. Rates are $150 for a double room. To get there take a bus or taxi from Nausori to nearby Nakelo (taxi from Suva to Nausori is $11). From Nakelo it's a 30-minute boat ride to Toberua. This isn't something to do on the spur of the moment. Reservations are required. Make them through your hotel or travel agent. Or contact: Toberua Island Resort, PO Box 567, Suva, Fiji.

Beyond Nausori by Bus—After Nausori the paved road doesn't last long, and soon the bus is moving through wooded country on a single-lane dirt road. Korovou, a dairy town and district center, is the next stop—a 15-minute halt. Then the bus pushes on through increasingly beautiful and verdant hills and soon follows the course of the Wainimbuka River where you'll see locals transporting produce, mostly bananas, down river on bamboo rafts.

The villages along the way are small, numerous, and orderly, all with a school, church, and shop. On the local bus we stopped often and briefly. Then, approaching Viti Levu Bay, there's evidence of serious farming—sugar cane, rice, cattle grazing—and not far beyond, we come to Navunibitu Catholic Mission School. Here there is a mural portraying the Madonna and Christ as black. It's known as the church of the Black Christ.

The road at this point is at its worst, but we were close to Raki Raki, which has a good hotel and was our destination. There, five and a half hours after departure, dusty, tired, thirsty, but happy, we debarked.

Raki Raki Hotel and Environs—At Raki Raki you're halfway to Nadi, 90 more miles to go. Like an oasis, this is a welcome pause, and the hotel provides all comforts. The rooms are attractive, the pool refreshing, and the dining room, excellent. Rates are $50 for a double.

From Raki Raki consider several days of do-it-yourself island life. Nearby Nanana-i-ra Island offers solitude, good beaches, and a group of housekeeping bungalows referred to as *Kon Tiki Lodge*. Rates are $15 for a double. Be sure to have reservations, and go armed with everything you need to eat and drink. There are no shops on the island. To get there, take a taxi from Raki Raki to the wharf ($7), where boats to the island are available at $9 per person for the short run. Contact: Kon Tiki Lodge, Raki Raki, Fiji.

On to Nadi by Bus—From Raki Raki on, the sea is never far out of sight, and the country begins to change from wet to dry. At Narewa village, four miles past Raki Raki, it looks like cowboy country. There are flat-topped mesas, lots of cattle and plenty of dust. Then suddenly the road is paved again and remains so all the way to Nadi.

Now it's sugar cane country and the bus moves at full tilt through little towns that are more Indian than Fijian—Tongowere, Rambulu, Korovou, Tavua. Then in sizeable Mba, the bus stops and we get off to stretch.

Mba is comfortably functional, and its hotel, the *Ba*, with

Raki Raki Hotel, North Coast, Viti Levu

pool and good dining room ($28 for a double), is headquarters for folks who are into river running. From here a road goes inland 25 hard miles to the village of Navala, where the Mba River provides rafting with plenty of excitement and foam. Contact Wilderness Adventures (see below).

From Mba to Lautoka it's rolling hills and sugar cane all the way. Then you're in Lautoka. "Welcome to the Sugar City," the sign says, and here it's necessary to change buses for the short run into Nadi. You've closed the circle.

Viti Levu's Interior—You can cross the island south to north from Sigatoka to Mba, a distance of about 85 miles. It's a rough, spectacular trip, and the villages in the further reaches of this route are as they were 200 years ago. But don't attempt this venture in a rental car; do it with guide and four-wheel drive vehicle. There are few roadside conveniences, and a breakdown could be disastrous.

An even longer, rougher route through more extensive jungle would be the long haul from east to northwest across the center of Viti Levu, Nausori via Monosavu to Tavua, a good 100 bone-shaking miles. A guide is necessary here too.

But as an alternative to uncomfortable and menacing car trips, try a more enlightening variation: a four-day walking trip.

Nadi to Sigatoka—Richard Slatter, a young part-Fijian who lives in Nadi, takes up to 15 people by four-wheel drive deep into the highlands behind Nadi to the village of Naidarivatu. There the track becomes trail and, with packhorses, cooks, and Slatter himself as guide, the group sets off by foot.

At night the hikers sleep on the ground in sleeping bags. By day, with breaks for three big meals, they walk about six miles (total trip 25 miles). They walk through shoulder-high grass, bush country, highland forest filled with mango trees, and thickets of bamboo. There are orchids to be seen, tree frogs, and the occasional iguana. Hikers wade streams, cross the Sigatoka River 17 times and, best of all, they stop in remote villages and go through the kava ceremony with village chiefs.

Kava Ceremony—Kava or yaqona is made from the crushed roots of the piper methysticum root. The crushed roots are tied into a cloth and further wrung out. The results look like muddy water. This liquid is then placed in a large wooden bowl which is put on the floor of the house, ready for the proper occasion.

The proper occasion occurs when a group of visitors such as the above hikers appear. They enter the chief's house and sit crosslegged in a semicircle with the chief seated in the center. The chief claps his hands once, then drinks all of his yaqona from a cup made of a coconut shell. Everyone claps and calls out "maca"—"it is drained." Cups of yaqona then make the rounds, and the ritual is repeated.

Most visitors consider the non-alcoholic drink mild and tasteless. But it does have a slight narcotic effect. Those who drink a lot of it develop a stunned expression and tend to fall down a lot.

The hike ends at the village of Nabutautau where the last missionary was eaten in 1871. Then, by four-wheel drive, the group is driven out onto the Coral Coast road at Sigatoka. The cost of the trip is $260 per person, and Slatter suggests an upper age limit of 50, but if you're fit he's flexible about that requirement. All gear is furnished, and is carried by pack horses. Hikers carry only their personal effects. Contact: Richard Slatter, c/o Sandalwood Hotel, Nadi, Fiji.

For this trip, rafting the Mba River, or canoeing the Navua River, also contact: Wilderness Adventures, PO Box 1389, Suva, Fiji.

THE OUTER ISLANDS

How to Get There by Air

With economics in mind, there are few deals in the Pacific better than Fiji Air's Fiji Island Pass. For $100 they offer a one-month pass to Fiji's outer islands from Suva, excluding Ono-i-Lau, Rotuma, and Funafuti. Funafuti is in Tuvalu, outside the country, and Rotuma and Ono-i-Lau are too distant to qualify for such a ticket. Some of the flights, especially to the Lau Group, get fully booked early, so make your reservations as soon as possible.

Sunflower Airlines flies to the islands from Nadi.

By Sea

There are a variety of ships that sail, most from Suva, to the outer islands. Some sail on schedule, such as Patterson Lines and Northwest Shipping which serve Vanua Leva, Taveuni, and Ovalau. Others, like the *Kaunitoni* which serves the Lau Group, or the *Belama* which goes to Kadavu, sail according to weather and cargo commitments. None of these ships wins awards for comfort. They're all working vessels and in no way compare to the tourist oriented and opulent Blue Lagoon boats. They have a cabin or two, but most passengers sleep on deck.

VANUA LEVU

Vanua Levu to the northeast of Viti Levu is Fiji's second island in size, 2,000 square miles. It's less developed by far than Viti Levu, and comparatively few visitors go there. This is unfortunate, as Vanua Levu has much to offer.

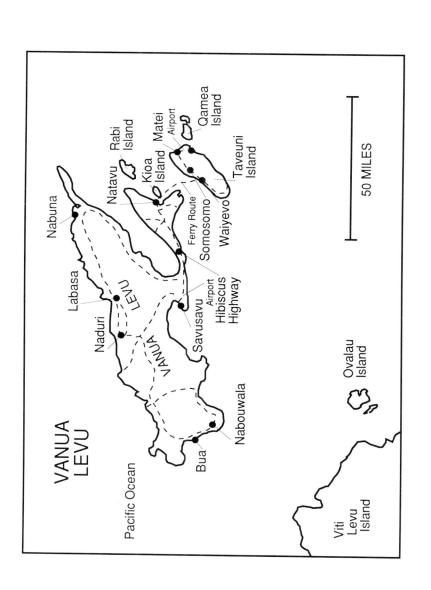

VANUA LEVU

Pacific Ocean

Nabuna

Labasa

Naduri

VANUA LEVU

Bua

Nabouwala

Savusavu Airport
Hibiscus Highway

Natavu

Kioa Island

Ferry Route
Somosomo
Waiyevo

Rabi Island

Matei Airport

Qamea Island

Taveuni Island

Ovalau Island

Viti Levu Island

50 MILES

Labasa, a sugar cane town in the north is on the drier side of the island, and is the largest settlement with 5,000 population. It's a business town, and is dominated by the Indian community, a pleasant place but not noted for tourist attractions.

How to Get There by Air

Sunflower Airlines flying out of Nadi goes to Labasa, an hour and 15 minute flight. Fare: $65 one way.

Where to Stay

There is a pair of hotels, each with restaurant, that will put you up comfortably.

The Grand Eastern: 16 rooms with bath, $25 double.

The Hotel Takia: 34 rooms with bath, $46 double.

From Labasa, roads connect most parts of the island. Scheduled buses and rental cars are available. But Savusavu in the south is the choice destination on Vanua Leva.

SAVUSAVU

How to Get There by Air

Air Fiji flies from Suva's Nausori Airport to Savusavu daily, a 50-minute flight that lands at an airstrip surrounded by palms, one and a half miles out of town. The fare is $55 one way, if you don't have the Fiji Air Pass.

By Sea

Northwest Shipping has a big ferry that sails from Suva via Ovalau Island three times a week, an overnight trip. There are no private cabins aboard, but they do have dormitory style bunks, and a snack bar. Fare is $20 one way.

Where to Stay

A $2 taxi fare from the airport will deliver you to any of the three hotels in town.

The Harbor Inn—A small clean hotel where pictures of religious personalities look down on the guests who pay $12 double. No alcoholic beverages are sold or allowed there. *The Savusavu Holiday House*—Has five rooms. This is a notch higher at $30 a day.
The Hot Springs Hotel—The rooms all have balconies, are comfortable, and overlook the harbor. It has a good dining room, a pool, and a friendly bar frequented by the local yachting people, occasional commercial travelers, and people like us traveling for pleasure. Rates are $50 double.

Resorts and Hotels at a Distance from Savusavu

Namale Plantation—Run by Curly Carswell, this is four miles from Savusavu. This resort on an excellent beach has accommodations for 20 people in eight thatched bures, with all possible conveniences. It even has a special honeymoon bure. There's a swimming pool, fishing, boating, horses, all water sports, bar, restaurant, and library. Including all meals, rates are $165 a double.
Kon Tiki—About seven miles from town, this hotel is in a grove of palms on a good beach. It has thatched bures for accommodations, but they are fully equipped for cooking at $25 double. If you're going to stay here, buy your food supplies in Savusavu, as there are no shops near the hotel.
Na Koro Hotel Resort—Has individual bures, beautiful beach, pool, in a working copra plantation and is a pretty away-from-it-all place. $145 double including all meals.
Lesiaceva Point Beach Apartments, on a point of land at the far end of Savusavu peninsula, have two units with cooking facilities for $25 double. Be sure to buy groceries in Savusavu. A good value.

Dining in Savusavu

Other than the Hot Springs Hotel, try either the *Wine and Dine* or *Ping Ho's* for Chinese food. Both are good and inexpensive.

Grounds of the Na Koro Hotel, Savusavu, Vanua Levu

For an Evening Out

Visit the *Planter's Club* near the Hot Springs Hotel. It's private, but the bartender will make you a member quickly. This is a happy spot for after-dinner drinking, mostly Fiji Bitters Beer.

Savusavu, lying on perhaps the most beautiful harbor in Fiji, is a compact little town. It has the usual collection of small Indian and Chinese shops along the waterfront. There's a good bakery in town, a general store, public market, and a wharf much used by local fishermen.

Sailing—These waters, with associated reefs, tiny islands and remote bays, offer some of the most compact sailing in the South Pacific. For this purpose *Emerald Yacht Charters* (Box 15, Savusavu, Fiji) has 35–44-foot sailboats that are fully provisioned. With skippers, they charter for about $1,500 per week.

Don Hounsell, associated with this organization and a New Zealand yachtsman of experience, tells us that every year more and more privately owned cruising boats appear in the South Pacific. He says that visitors seriously interested in sailing and with time to spare, can eventually find a share-expense berth. Savusavu is one of the good places to look, according to Don.

Diving—From Savusavu, *Pacific Island Divers* use an excellent nearby reef. Boat, equipment, and two dives are $50. They also have a PADI certification course available.

Hot Springs—Next to the Hot Springs Hotel, these are untidy bubbling pools where locals steam their food, wrapped in burlap.

Outside of Savusavu

Going east from Savusavu there is an unpaved road called the Hibiscus Highway. It's one of the most tropically lush roads in the Pacific and, along its 50-mile length to Natavu, there are magnificent stretches of coastline, punctuated by unchanged Fijian villages—about as far off the beaten path as you'll get in Fiji.

The importance of the road is that at Natavu there's a ferry across to Taveuni Island. You can easily fly from Savusavu to Taveuni, but consider the following day-long venture.

Go to the bus terminal in Savusavu at 10:30 AM and board the bus to Natavu, a three-hour trip for $3. Don't worry about missing the ferry at the end of the run—it waits for the bus.

At Natavu don't expect to find a vessel that looks like a ferry, since what you'll find is a 30-foot covered launch with seats. Fare is $3. Please note, *don't* leave Savusavu by bus if the weather looks threatening, as the boat trip across Somosomo Straits to Taveuni can be hair-raising in bad weather. But it's a delight in fine weather.

Leaving Natavu the roughly 20-mile voyage ($20 round trip) winds its way through multi-hued water past Kioa Island where several hundred Polynesians from Tuvalu live. This is an island worth visiting. People are hospitable and, although there are no hotels, locals will probably put you up.

Beyond Kioa Island there are about 12 miles of open water and, when the boat comes into Waiyevo on Taveuni, passengers are transferred to a rowboat which puts into the beach. The last few steps to shore are by wading.

TAVEUNI ISLAND

Taveuni ranks third in size and is known as Fiji's "Garden Island"—every characteristic of Fijian scenery and vegetation is found here. The main activity on this 26-mile-long and 7-mile-wide island is copra growing.

Getting There by Air

Sunflower Airlines flies from Savusavu to Mareau Airstrip on the north end of Taveuni, a daily 30-minute flight at $30 one way.

Passengers from the Vanua Levu Ferry coming ashore in Taveuni

From Suva—It's about an hour and 15 minutes on Fiji Air, $60 one way, if you don't have a Fiji Air Pass.

From Nadi—Sunflower Airlines flies in almost daily.

By Sea

Patterson Bros. Ferry services Taveuni three times a week.

Where to Stay

Valentine's Place, where for $4 you can pitch a tent. It's close to one of the best beaches on Taveuni—Prince Charles Beach, on the northwest side of the island.

The Kaba Hotel—A simple, clean hotel in Somosomo for the hardy. $15 double.

The Matei Lagoon—Directly across the road from the airstrip at the northern tip of the island. It has nice cottages overlooking the ocean for $54 double.

Castaway Hotel—This pleasant hotel with pool, restaurant, bar, and a poor beach is a half hour south of the airstrip. They provide free airport transfers. The ferry from Vanua Levu comes in near here. $54 double.

Dive Taveuni—Run by New Zealanders Ric and Do Cammick, this nicely landscaped hotel has four bures and is near the airport. Rates are $75 per person including meals and diving. They take only certified divers, and operate off 19-mile coral Rainbow Reef on the south coast.

Maravu Plantation Resort—A shiny place on a well-mowed hillside (near the airport) under palm trees where guests stay in well appointed bures. Complementary airport transfer, pool, all sport activities. $150 double with all meals.

Dining on Taveuni

Other than an inexpensive but good Indian "take out" place at Waiyevo, there are no restaurants on the island. The hotels are where you'll eat, and well—but not inexpensively. Dinner for two at the Castaway will run $35 with wine. It'll be more expensive, but we hear excellent, at the Maravu Plantation.

Grounds of Maravu Plantation Resort, Taveuni

What to Do

Taveuni Island, of volcanic formation, may be the most beautiful island in Fiji. Up till now it has been one of the least developed for tourists.

Along the northwest coast there are some good but not outstanding beaches, Prince Charles Beach near the north end being the best. For ocean activities it's the reef that is the attraction.

The opposite coast on the southeast side, where sheer volcanic cliffs drop to the sea, is almost completely undeveloped. To get to most of this area, you have to hike in or approach it by boat, which brings up the subject of kayak camping.

Kayak camping is a way of getting to otherwise inaccessible places such as this coast, by sea and putting ashore for exotic camping. The people at the Maravu Plantation Resort say they can arrange such details. John Grey (PO Box 61609, Honolulu, HI 96882) runs an organization called Pacific Outdoors Adventures. It's a sea kayaking outfit. John says that using three guides and several boats he can take up to 10 people along an area such as Taveuni's southeast coast. As to costs, he just says that his clientele are people who can afford and appreciate some of the most beautiful and remote places on earth.

I am sure that some of the local Fijians on or near this coast could provide similar services for a more modest fee.

One village you're sure to drive through is *Somosomo*. This pretty village, divided by a fast-flowing river filled with romping children and matrons bathing, is called a "chiefly village." It's the home of Fiji's Governor General, Ratu Sir Penaia Ganilau.

Wander through Somosomo and, if you're fit and ambitious, get a guide (about $10) and set off inland behind Somosomo to *Lake Tangimauthia* in the mountains to the east. It's an all-day venture but, if you're successful, you'll see the flowering plant tagimaucia that grows nowhere else in the world.

Bouma Waterfall—A bus or taxi will take you around the north end of the island to Bouma. This cascade is impressive, a fine place for a picnic and a swim in its pool.

Wairiki—Just south of Waiyevo on the west coast, visit the 300-year-old Catholic Mission. The old limestone church here is magnificent. Here too notice the memorial to a very old battle, the last battle between Fijians and Tongans. The Fijians won, and are said to have eaten the Tongans.

A little further south on this coast is an unusually pretty golf course and some handsome condominiums. Both looked abandoned. You'd think the time-share people would be enthusiastic about them, but Taveuni doesn't have the required boutiques, restaurants, and trendy shops to attract such people. Taveuni is unadorned Fiji.

Near here is a marker indicating the location of the International Dateline.

Nggamea Island—This nearby small island off the northeast coast of Taveuni is owned by the American Malcolm Forbes. You can go there inexpensively by outboard boat from Navakathoa village on Taveuni's east coast. Or, for $140 per person per day, the Qamea Beach Club launch will deliver you to the Club where you'll be given all meals, provided with dive boat, and all gear necessary for diving. As they say, this is a special place for special people.

OVALAU ISLAND IN THE LOMAIVITI GROUP

How to Get There by Air

Air Fiji has two flights daily except Sunday from Suva's Nausori Airport, 20 minutes and $25 one way, if you don't have the Fiji Air monthly pass. It lands on the opposite side of the island from Levuka, and a waiting minibus transfers passengers into Levuka.

By Sea

The *Princess Ashika* has regular sailings from Suva, and Patterson Brothers operates the *Ovalau* daily from Natovi Wharf (60 miles north of Suva).

By Combination Bus and Ferry from Suva

This is the adventurous way to Levuka on Ovalau. Take the early morning bus from Suva's bus terminal to Natovi, 60 miles up the north coast of Viti Levu. The first part of this run follows the route of the bus to Lautoka, but at Korovou it turns off and continues to Natovi. Fare is $5. At Natovi the Ferry *Ovalau* sets off for the 3-hour voyage to Levuka. Fare is $7 one way. When we went, the blue sea was calm, flying fish performed, and we lolled on deck soaking up the sun.

Where to Stay

The classic place to stay is the old *Royal Hotel.* This two-story building with colonial flavor has been around since Levuka was the hard-drinking, renegade-filled former capital of Fiji. We stayed there, and happily. They've got 15 rooms, most with baths. It has a bar and restaurant, with rates $16 double.

Ovalau Holiday Resort—Five units, $42 double.

Ruku Ruku Resort—Six apartments with cooking facilities. This hotel is on the northwest coast about 15 miles northwest

of Levuka. The beach is fair. But, if you can negotiate the shallows to the reef, the snorkeling is good. $55 double.
Mavida Guest House—$15 double includes breakfast.
Old Capital Inn—In the center of town, this place is the most economical at $3 to $5. You can eat here too. When we were here it was filled with young Americans, British, and Australians, traveling on severe budgets.

Where to Eat

The Royal Hotel (make a reservation), *The Old Capital Inn,* and the *Ruku Ruku* provide restaurant services. There are shops in town where groceries are sold.

For Evening Entertainment

Visit the *Ovalau Club,* a congenial place that reflects the past. Examine the photos on the walls, and read the letter from Count Luckner, the World War I German sea raider who was captured nearby.

What to Do

Levuka, the old capital of Fiji, now a by-passed town, but there was a time when its many saloons were filled with roistering whalers and sailors. Today the town is a sleepy, old fashioned seaport like Lahaina was before it was reborn. Levuka may yet be. The main industrial activity is fish processing and you'll probably smell the plant before you see it at the south end of town.
Going south from town past the fish cannery, there is a monument marking the spot where in 1874 the "deed of cession" was signed by Ratu Seru Cakobau, the Cannibal King, that made Fiji part of Queen Victoria's British Empire.
Continue on to the Draiba Cemetery where the headstones of past pioneers are worth examining. Just beyond is a Catholic Mission where a printing press produced the first Gospel in the Fijian language.
Three or four miles south on the coast road will bring you opposite the island of Moturiki. On the east side of Moturiki facing Ovalau there are some good beaches. Go there by a

Main street, Levuka, Ovalau

launch available in the area. It's a good day trip for picnicking and swimming. Bring all supplies as there are no services on Moturiki.

Near the old Methodist church in town there is the longest flight of steps in Fiji—199 of them that climb through verdant forest to Mission Hill. From there the view of the harbor and distant reef is excellent, and in the far distance you can see the islands of Makogai and Wakaya. Makogai at one time was a leper colony and housed hundreds of patients, but now is mostly uninhabited. It was on the other island, Wakaya, that the feared German naval captain, Count Luckner, who roamed the Pacific in World War I, was captured. This island is being developed for possible tourist use.

Beyond Mission Hill there is a confusing path that goes on into the mountains. With a guide and perseverance, you could hike on through the forest to Lovoni village in the center of the island. From there a road descends through a lovely valley to the coast near Levuka. Buses are available in Lovoni.

OTHER ISLANDS IN THE LOMAIVITI GROUP

The only other island in this group that has been developed for tourism is the small island of *Naigani.* It has beautiful beaches and can be reached by ferry from Natovi on Viti Levu, a 12-mile run at $15 round trip.

Naigani Island Resort provides all activities, restaurant, bar, dance band, baby sitters, swimming pool, snorkeling, glass bottom boats—something for everyone. Rates are $60 double, and dormitory accommodations are available at $6.50 per person.

Koro Island is about 30 miles northeast of Ovalau. Flying between Suva and Taveuni you fly right over this mountainous 10-by-5-mile jungle island. There are no resorts or hotels. If you want to go there (Air Fiji flies in three times weekly) ask Air Fiji to organize housing with a villager. Beaches are so-so, but there's good hiking to waterfalls and isolated villages.

Ngau Island, nine miles long and three miles wide, is 25 miles south of Koro. No hotels on Ngau, but at Waikama village six miles up the coast from the airstrip there's an inn that'll put you up and provide meals for $24 double. Other than hiking, there's not much to do on Ngau.

Air Fiji goes in three times a week, a 20-minute flight from Suva. Boats go in on an irregular schedule from Suva and Ovalau.

Mbatiki and *Nairai*—To get entirely away, and to follow the traditional route of the copra gathering boats, ask around Levuka for the next sailing to Mbatiki and Nairai. If successful, you'll find a small vessel, perhaps powered by sail, that goes to these two islands for the express purpose of gathering copra. The essence of the South Pacific is out there. There are no roads or cars on either island and no air transport to them. Stay with the ship; the next one could be many days later.

KADAVU ISLAND

Kadavu, pronounced Kandavu, is a large mountainous island 60 miles south of Viti Levu. Timber for export is grown on the thickly wooded hills in the south, and along the windward side there are a number of copra and banana plantations.

It's a handsome away-from-the-tourists island with friendly people, good beaches, and some of the best diving in Fiji.

How to Get There by Air

Air Fiji flies in from Suva every day except Sunday. Fare is $30 one way (included in Pass). Sunflower Airlines goes in twice a week from Nadi at $40 one way.

Where to Stay and Eat

There are two places, but the hospitality and quality of the food at *Reece's Place* is more popular. Reece's has four units at $18 double and is on the tiny island of Ngaloa, a short boat ride from the airport. Be sure to make reservations. Ask Air Fiji to help.

The other hotel is the *Plantation Hideaway*. For $20 double they provide bungalows with cooking facilities. There are two general stores in Vunisea for groceries, near the airport. Make reservations here too.

What to Do

There is good hiking from easy to difficult, and close to Reece's Place there is a fine beach with unusually good snorkeling.

For turtle calling visit nearby *Namuana*. Turtle calling, whether it works or not, is a form of ancestor worship. Here, as in other parts of the Pacific, young women call this ancestral animal by singing or making magical sounds and turtles often appear. In the old days this was never done in front of strangers or for money. Now it is.

Astrolabe Reef—For divers or anyone interested in barrier reefs Astrolabe, to the north of Kadavu, is important. On the blue open-ocean side of this reef, the sea plunges to thousands of feet. On the landward side you can stand in emerald water to your waist. Sharks are thick on the ocean side, absent on the landward side.

To get to the reef ask at Reece's Place. Boats are available on a catch-as-catch-can basis.

THE LAU GROUP

The 50 small islands in this group are scattered in an arc to the east of Fiji, and are closer to Tonga than to Suva. They reflect more a Polynesian-Tongan influence than Fijian.

To Get There by Air

Fiji Air flies to five of the 50 islands:
Moala—In the south (twice a week).
Ono-i-lau—By charter only.
Lakeba—Central islands (three times a week).
Cecia—Central islands (twice weekly).
Vanuabalavu—In the north (three times a week).
These flights are all a little over an hour from Suva. Fares are about $65 one way. They're often booked up well ahead of time.

By Sea

If you can mesh with the sailing of the *Kaunitoni*, you've got a winner. She's one of the better cargo passenger ships and has several reasonably comfortable cabins without baths. Food at one time was provided but now all passengers, cabin and deck, have to furnish their own meals—an inconvenience when you consider it's a 10-day voyage. Still it can be done, and the ship does provide hot water and a few cooking aids.

The *Kaunitoni* makes two voyages, one to the northern Laus, another to the southern group, about 12 stops on each trip. Unfortunately schedules are relaxed and space is often fully booked, but it's worth a try. The purpose of each trip is to pick up copra, deliver cargo, and carry passengers (mostly deck). Fare for the 10-day round trip is $150 cabin, $50 deck.

Most of the Lau Group are of mixed volcanic and limestone formation, but there are coral atolls too, which are often uninhabited. *Vanuabalavu* is the largest in the group, a raised coral island. The beaches are good, the lagoon extensive, and the people in Lomolomo, the biggest village, live in Tongan homes rather than Fijian bures. Air Fiji can arrange housing there for you.

Like too much of a good thing, the rest of the Lau Group offers an unending array of perfect beaches, sparkling lagoons, and stands of swaying palms. Get on the *Kaunitoni*, if possible. Otherwise settle for an island or two served by air. Try *Moala* in the south or *Lakeba* in the central group, both high islands. To long remember the Lau Group bring home a locally made tanoa bowl, the one with legs, carved out of a single block of wood.

ROTUMA

Rotuma is a small volcanic island about 240 miles north of Viti Levu. The island is a Fijian dependency, but the Rotumans are of Polynesian stock and many for some reason tend to become administrators within the Fijian government.

How to Get There by Air

Air Fiji flies there from Nadi twice a week, a two-hour flight.

By Sea

Service is irregular, but the *Wairua*, a fairly good passenger-carrying ship, does the trip occasionally. There's no hotel and little tourist activity. The Rotumans want to keep it that way.

Recently, however, there has been a confrontation between a large cruise ship company and the elders of Rotuma. The company wanted to send the cruise ship *Fairstar* with 1,000 Aussies for an eight-hour visit to Rotuma. Some Rotumans said they wanted the visit, and reasoned the Aussies would buy handcrafts, cold beer, and food, leaving the islanders $15,000 richer. Other Rotumans argued that their culture and tradition was at stake. This has so far not been resolved, but it is a sign of the times.

For further detailed background on these islands, see *The Fiji Explorer's Handbook* by Kim Gravelle, available in Fiji bookstores.

Final Note: when you leave Fiji by air there is a $10 per person airport tax.

7

NEW CALEDONIA

New Caledonia consists of a large island, Grande Terre, and a group of small islands called dependencies—the Loyalty Group, Ouen, the Isle of Pines, Huon Islands, and the Chesterfields. Grande Terre is as big in land mass as the whole state of Hawaii. Its capital Nouméa, with 70,000 people, looks big too. There are imposing buildings, freeways, traffic lights, escalators and, in the center of town there is a large bowered park called the Place des Cocotiers.

Nouméa has sidewalk cafes, little corner bistros, boulangeries, patisseries and, if it weren't for the black faces and the climate, you could be in a French provincial town. The white inhabitants have a Gallic look, the slight difference around nose and mouth that perhaps comes from a nasal approach to words. Some look as if they had just left the farm, some are conservatively well dressed, and many of the young people are clad in the latest mod-chic.

Then there are others. You see them and hear them in the bars and bistros. They are usually bearded and have a military appearance. They are clearly soldiers, perhaps of the Foreign Legion. New Caledonia needs them now and perhaps will in the future.

Arrival in New Caledonia is attended by the feeling that you've arrived somewhere very colonial, very French, where everything works, except during the awkward hours from 11:30 AM to 1:30 PM when everything is closed. You'll soon become aware that the standard of living is much higher in New Caledonia than on other Pacific islands, except Guam and Hawaii. They've got television, lots of cars, good housing, big hospitals, and a form of government that's run as an overseas territory of France. What the French say about égalité they apparently mean, for all New Caledonians are full citizens of France, though this doesn't mean that everyone has a say in what's happening in New Caledonia now. The problem is that, out of a population of 145,000, the 60,000 native Melanesians known as Kanaks constitute a 40% minority. They want independence, and a few are extremely militant about the matter. Because they know they would lose in a referendum, they say they'll boycott the polls and threaten violence at the outcome.

The other 60%—French, Asian, Vietnamese, Algerian—prefer French rule and are of the opinion that the Kanak life style is not oriented toward self-government. Kanak workers, they say, tend to be more interested in a rural life than in acquiring technical skills or material possessions.

According to the French, the Kanaks don't want to work. According to the Kanaks, they don't get the chance. They say they just get the dirty low-paying jobs, and they add that France is exploiting them by reaping millions of dollars from their mines which produce high-grade nickel ore. The Kanaks have a point. France's economy would be hurt if the mines were lost to an independent New Caledonia.

On the other hand, when you look around this colony at the roads, the public buildings, schools, and hospitals, it's evident that a lot of money has been spent on public works, money that undoubtedly came from the mines. Even so there are rural Kanaks who claim they've never seen any of the benefits. Both sides have legitimate arguments. Perhaps these problems can be resolved without violence, the sort of violence that occurred years ago in Algeria. Nevertheless in an autonomy-conscious world, it's hard to imagine a long and sustained colonial future for New Caledonia.

For the present, New Caledonia is a great place for a vacation. For Aussies and New Zealanders it's a sort of Hawaii, but closer. Nouméa is less than 1,000 miles from Australia. In Nouméa you'll find the big hotels, the boutiques, the casinos, the beaches, and the restaurants. Half of the population lives

Bus to the outlying areas

there. That leaves a lot of empty space on the rest of the big island and the tiny islands around it.

The Land and Her People

New Caledonia and its dependencies are an island group in the southwest Pacific that forms part of Melanesia. The big island called Grande Terre has a land area of 12,000 square miles, and is the third largest island in the South Pacific after New Guinea and New Zealand.

Along the entire length of New Caledonia runs a chain of mountains. Mt. Passie in the north and Mt. Humbolt in the south are nearly 5,000 feet high and this chain divides the island into climatic areas. In the west on the leeward side, looking like the Australian outback, there are wide stretches of dry savannah land dotted with eucalyptus trees. This is

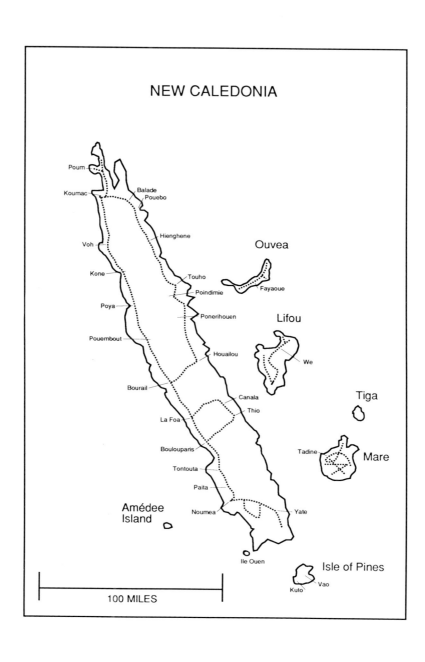

NEW CALEDONIA

Poum
Koumac
Balade
Pouebo
Hienghene
Voh
Ouvea
Kone
Touho
Poindimie
Fayaoue
Poya
Ponerihouen
Lifou
Pouembout
Houailou
We
Bourail
Canala
Tiga
Thio
La Foa
Boulouparis
Tadine
Mare
Tontouta
Paita
Amédee
Island
Noumea
Yate
Ile Ouen
Isle of Pines
Kuto
Vao

100 MILES

good cattle country but, because of invasive mangrove swamps along this coast, there are few good beaches.

On the east coast where it rains over 100 inches a year, there are coconut plantations, rivers with waterfalls, and 150-foot-tall Norfolk Pines. This is where most of the rural Melanesians live.

Around both sides of the island, there is a protective barrier reef, the second largest barrier reef in the world.

The Economy—Mining, mainly nickel ore, represents the most important export by far. The island provides 30% of the world's nickel. Secondary resources are cattle, copra, fish farming, and tourism. But since locally grown products are insufficient for local needs, meat, groceries, and manufactured products are imported from France, the European Economic Community, Australia, and New Zealand.

The People—Half of the 145,000 people live in and around Nouméa. About 60,000 are Melanesian, 50,000 European, 17,500 are Wallis Islanders and Tahitians, and 12,000 are Indonesians and Vietnamese.

Government—New Caledonia is part of the Republic of France, and the head of the Territory is an appointed High Commissioner. He has considerable power and runs such things as defense, education, public works, agriculture, and mines. Then there's an executive council, and finally an elected Territorial Congress consisting of 46 members. There is some criticism, perhaps justified, for it's said that the High Commissioner can alter anything the Territorial Congress does. The French for the moment are in full charge.

The real Melanesians, most of whom live on the east coast or in the south, grow manioc, yams, taro, sweet potatoes, bananas, and coconuts. They raise chickens and pigs, and their national dish bounia, which is similar to that in the other island groups, is a steamed leaf-wrapped mixture of taro, yams, manioc, chicken, fish or pork laced with coconut milk.

Their traditional culture is also similar to that found in the other islands. They call it "la coutume." In independent Vanuatu it's called "custom," and now with independence, it's given room to breathe. In New Caledonia a return to the old ways is sought after, but any success they have with this seems to be in spite of the government.

Then there are the small islands, the ones they call dependencies. To the south there is the volcanic Isle of Pines and Ouen Island. To the north there are the Loyalty Islands, Ouvea, Maré, Lifou and Tiga, all upraised coral atolls which are covered mostly with coconut palms, hibiscus and sandalwood.

Finally there's Nouméa, the capital, where it all happens. From a point downtown opposite the old town hall all road distances on the island are measured. By road to the furthest point is a distance of 240 miles. Most visitors never get that far from town.

History in Brief

In most Pacific island groups the chain of historic events has followed a similar sequence:
1. Pre-recorded history
2. The explorers
3. The traders
4. The missionaries
5. Reaction to stages 2, 3, and 4.
6. Colonization
7. Independence
8. Dependence

New Caledonia has come as far as stage 6.

Before the white man arrived, some 60,000 agrarian people called Canaques lived there. Canaque (now called Kanak) is the indigenous word for man, and they made up small, often unfriendly, tribes who spoke a variety of languages.

In 1774 the explorer Captain Cook landed at the Balade area on the northeast coast and, because the land reminded him of the Scottish Highlands, he named his discovery New Caledonia. Cook is also reported to have been surprised that the people there had neither pigs, nor goats, nor dogs, nor cats, and it's said that he presented them with a pair of both pigs and dogs. We hear about him making gifts of animals to other islanders as well from the livestock he carried on board. One wonders if these acts of generosity have any bearing on the present day importance of pigs in the rural Pacific lifestyle.

Eighteen years after Cook, the Frenchman D'Entrecasteaux,

who was searching for a missing navigator named Laperouse, stopped at the same area. Other explorers came too, and the charts and observations they made were extremely accurate. These in turn drew traders who, with profit in mind, came looking for sandalwood and bèche de mer (sea cucumber).

Next, right on schedule, the missionaries arrived. First the Protestants landed in the Loyalty Islands in 1841. Then in 1843 the Catholics appeared and went ashore at Balade.

Native reaction was distinctly unenthusiastic. Some of the missionaries and settlers were eaten and the others, feeling unwelcome, soon left. In the name of order, and in competition with British activity elsewhere in the Pacific, Napoleon III sent Admiral Despointes to Balade, where in 1853 he declared the islands a French Territory.

One slight variation from the normal sequence of events then occurred. A penal colony was established. As a result of the Paris Commune uprising of 1872–78, as many as 40,000 prisoners were transported to New Caledonia where they did manual labor on the Isle of Pines and on an island in Nouméa Harbor. For these prisoners life was hard, but perhaps a shade better than in Australian penal colonies and considerably better than at Devil's Island in French Guiana. At any event, in 1897 the transportation of prisoners from France ended.

According to French historians, after 1900 New Caledonia developed slowly, not without difficulties, until the outbreak of World War II. The main difficulties were matters of land use. The discovery of nickel created land tenure problems, and land-hungry, cattle-farming immigrants from France alienated the Kanaks by taking some of the best land. This led to violence, and many Kanaks were forced into reservations—the beginning of today's problems.

Eventually there was land reform, high time too, but results were too little and too late for the militant Kanaks.

In 1940 New Caledonia was one of the first French colonies to join De Gaulle's Free France. Then from 1942 to 1945 the territory became an important American military base and this pushed New Caledonia into modern day development.

Next in the sequence of events should come independence, but this won't happen soon. The French on New Caledonia maintain a strong military presence. Even so there have been clashes between Kanaks and the military, as well as clashes between Kanaks and right wing groups. Kanak leaders have been assassinated and now that there are rumors of a militant socialist Kanak connection with Libyan terrorist groups, the plot thickens and the world watches.

How to Get There by Air

From Nadi, Fiji—Air Calédonie flies in once a week. That's how we arrived recently, and on the two-hour flight which originated in the French Wallis and Futuna Islands numbers of handsome French-speaking Polynesians were aboard. It was a festive flight, and courtesy of generously-poured Air Calédonie champagne, a merry group left the plane at Tontouta International Airport. Unfortunately, from there Nouméa is still 32 miles away.

From Los Angeles via Papeete, Tahiti—UTA makes the long trip twice a week. It's a good way to see both French island groups, then continue on to Australia.

From Singapore—UTA comes in twice a week.

From Australia—Qantas flies in five times a week from Sydney, once a week from Brisbane, once a week from Melbourne.

From Auckland, New Zealand—Air New Zealand has two flights a week.

From Vila, Vanuatu—Air Calédonie has five flights a week.

Before booking, be sure to ask your travel agent about triangle or APEX fare flights that include New Caledonia.

By Sea

Cruise ships come in reasonably often. Check with Cunard, Sitmar, Five Star, P & O, Royal Viking. It's practically impossible to find a freighter unless you sail from Europe, specifically France. We met some French people in Nouméa who had come by freighter the slow way from Marseille through the Caribbean, Panama, the Marquésas, and Tahiti. Look up a freighter travel specialist in New York, Los Angeles, San Francisco or Seattle.

Immigration

A valid passport and an onward or return ticket is required for stays up to 30 days.

Health

There is no malaria in New Caledonia, nor are there any unusual health problems. For those who need care, excellent pharmacy, medical and dental facilities are available. Tap water is safe to drink.

Currency

New Caledonia's monetary unit is the French Pacific Franc (the CFP) the same currency that's used in French Polynesia (Tahiti).

The denomination of notes are 10,000, 5,000, 1,000 and 500 CFP. The coins are 100, 50, 20, 10, 5, and 2 francs.

As of this writing, $1 US = 100 CFPs. Exchange of money is usually done through banks and there always is a charge. You're better off changing large amounts since a CFP 370 or $3.70 charge is levied for each transaction. Most shops and hotels will accept US dollars.

Time Zone

Local time is 11 hours ahead of Greenwich Mean Time, 16 hours ahead of Eastern Standard Time, 19 hours ahead of Pacific Standard Time.

Climate

New Caledonia is far enough south of the equator to get some changes of season. It's like Hawaii in that regard, pleasant all the time, but the best months when it is dry and cool are April to November.

For this climate light informal clothes are adequate all year round, but in the cooler months a sweater in the evening will be welcome.

Languages

French is the official language, but in most hotels and associated restaurants English will be understood. Elsewhere, some knowledge of French comes in very handy. Melanesian is spoken by the indigenous people and there are 30 different dialects.

Holidays

New Year's Day; Easter Monday; Labor Day (May 1); Ascension Day (May 28); Whit Day (June 8); Bastille Day (July 14); Assumption Day (August 15); New Caledonia Day (September 24); All Saints Day (November 1); Armistice Day (November 11); Christmas Day (December 25).

On these holidays all offices and shops are closed.

Newspapers, Radio, TV, and Telephone

There is a daily newspaper, *Les Nouvelles Caledoniennes* and a weekly paper called *Tele 7 Jours*. Both are in French.

A local station broadcasts radio from 6 AM to 10 PM. TV in color is seen from 4 to 10 PM.

New Caledonia has a sophisticated satellite telephone communication system. Calls go through quickly from your hotel room or from the Post Office downtown.

Power

220 volts AC; 50 cycles. Two-prong plugs.

Tipping

There is no tipping in New Caledonia.

NOUMÉA AND ENVIRONS

Nouméa is by no means off-the-beaten-path. It's a popular holiday destination for Australians, New Zealanders, and hordes of Japanese tour group honeymooners. Therefore don't

Nouméa

arrive without hotel reservations. But if you do, go directly to the travel assistance booth in the airport terminal. They have a list of all hotels, with rates, and will make necessary calls to obtain a room.

Then comes the matter of getting into Nouméa which is 32 miles from Tontouta International Airport. You could get there on a local bus for $3.50 but this is the slow way and they don't often run at night. It's a colorful run, but one best done going *from* town to the airport when you leave.

The sure solution is to pay $10 per person and go quickly and comfortably to your hotel on the hotel transfer minibus.

Is your destination the beach or town? They're worlds apart. Staying in town means surrounding yourself with shopping, restaurants, parks, pleasant wandering. In the city you're well removed from carnival-type beach activities, from the "glass bottom boat people," tour groups, and the same folks you see in Waikiki, Coney Island, Surfer's Paradise or Moorea. On the other hand, that may be exactly what you want.

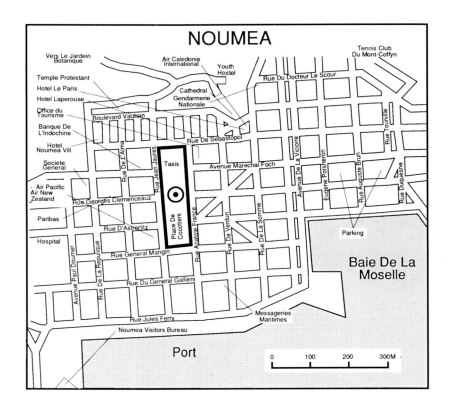

NOUMEA

Tennis Club
Du Mont-Coffyn

Vers Le Jardein
Botanique

Air Caledonie
International

Youth
Hostel

Rue Du Docteur Le Scour

Temple Protestant

Cathedral

Hotel Le Paris

Gendarmerie
Nationale

Hotel Laperouse

Office du
Tourisme

Boulevard Vauban

Banque De
L'Indochine

Rue De Sebastopol

Rue Tourville

Hotel
Noumea Vill.

Rue De L'Alma

Societe
General

Rue Jean Jaures

Taxis

Avenue Marechal Foch

Avenue De La Victoire

Eugene Porsteron

Rue Auguste Brun

Rue Duquesne

Air Pacific
Air New
Zealand

Rue Georges Clemenceauz

Paribas

Rue D'Astrerlitz

Place De
Cocohiers

Rue Anatole France

Rue De Verdun

Rue De La Somme

Parking

Hospital

Rue De La Repuique

Avenue Paul Doumer

Rue General Mangin

Baie De La
Moselle

Rue Du General Gallieni

Rue Jules Ferry

Noumea Visitors Bureau

Messageries
Maritimes

Port

| 0 | 100 | 200 | 300M |

Where to Stay

At the Beach

Anse Vata, three miles from the city center is an attractive, beautifully landscaped beach area. It's where Admiral Halsey made his headquarters during World War II, and now it's where most of the beach hotels are.

The Nouvata Beach Hotel—The beach is directly across the street, a good Chinese restaurant is on one side, and on the other a little cafe that sells fruit juice, omelets, breakfast croissants, and pungent French coffee. It has 50 rooms and 36 bungalows, all with fridges. There is a pool, bar, and dining room. Rates are $52 double for bungalows, $80 for rooms. Rooms have color TV. This is where we stayed and it was a good choice.

Club Med—A mile beyond the Nouvata Hotel at the tip of Anse Vata on an extremely good beach, stands the Club Mediterrannée. According to their brochure, guests are provided with sailing, windsurfing, tennis, disco, squash, archery, aerobics, shows and more. We strolled over and asked to be shown around. After a two-minute tour through the mostly Japanese-filled establishment, we were out the back door. Club Meds are like cloistered monasteries devoted to pleasure rather than sanctity. The brotherhood-sisterhood is protected from tiresome worldly intrusions including curious visitors like us. Club Med is its own world, a world apart where you pay for a drink at the bar with beads.

Le Surf Novotel—On the expensive side, this three-star hotel has a piano bar, conference facilities, boutiques, good beach, pool and casino. Rates are $105 to $200 double.

Isle de France TraveLodge—This three-star hotel has a pool, bar-restaurant, boutiques. It's not quite on the beach. Rates are $90 to $109 double.

Nouméa Beach Hotel—On adjoining Baie des Citrons (Lemon Beach) this hotel has all conveniences including a Japanese restaurant. $88 double.

Hotel Mocambo—On Lemon Beach, it has all conveniences, but no pool. There are 38 rooms and it's a short walk to the beach. Rates are $70 to $100 double.

Hotel Le Lagon—Situated near Anse Vata, 300 feet from the beach; no pool, but all other amenities. $76 a double.

Lantana Beach Hotel—Across the street from Anse Vata Beach, a good location. No pool, but everything else. $70 double.

Hotels in Town

Paradise Park Motel—This nicely landscaped hotel is a mile out of town in the suburb, Valée des Colons. Including a pool, it has all amenities, some with kitchens. There is a supermarket nearby. $64 a double.

Nouméa Village Hotel—In the center of town handy to stores, restaurants, duty free shops. There's a swimming pool, bar and restaurant. Rates, including a continental breakfast, are $60 double.

Hotel Le Paris—In the city center this hotel has a pool, bar, restaurant, and three discos. Rates are $60 double.

Caledonia Hotel—Located in the "Latin Quarter," this budget hotel has 19 rooms, 10 with private facilities. It's near the Post Office. Rates are $20 a double.

Hotel La Perouse—In the city center, with a bar, snack cafe, and TV lounge. $50 double.

Trianon—In the suburbs on Route de Trianon. $30 double.

Youth Hostel—Near the city center, dormitory-style accommodations for $8 per person.

Dining in and Around Nouméa

There are so many restaurants that the best approach is to visit the New Caledonia Tourist Bureau on Avenue Foch, half a block from the Place de Cocotiers (the central square) and ask for the brochure "Bon Appetit," which is the guide to eating out in Nouméa.

In this brochure the restaurants are classified as "snack" (55 of them) or "full restaurants" (64 more). Location, prices, styles of food and telephone numbers are listed. There is even a section on "How to say it in French."

Snack restaurants are usually open from 11:30 AM to 2 PM and 7 PM to 11 PM. You might want to go downtown and try

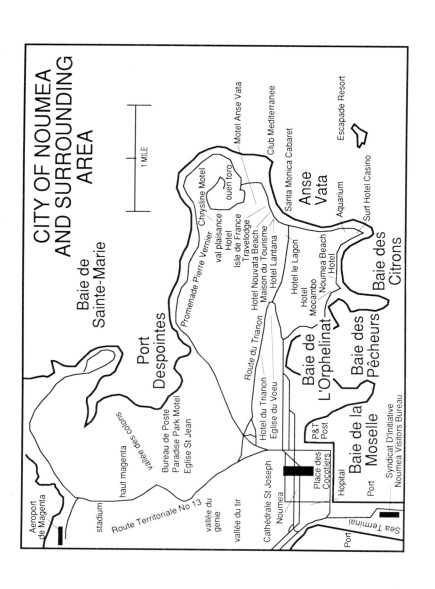

CITY OF NOUMEA AND SURROUNDING AREA

1 MILE

Baie de Sainte-Marie

Port Despointes

Aeroport de Magenta

haut magenta

vallée des colons

stadium

Route Territoriale No 13

Bureau de Poste
Paradise Park Motel
Eglise St Jean

vallée du genie

vallée du tir

Promenade Pierre Vernier

Chrysline Motel

val plaisance
Hotel

ouen toro

Isle de France
Travelodge
Hotel Nouvata Beach
Maison du Tourisme
Hotel Lantana

Motel Anse Vata

Club Mediterranee

Santa Monica Cabaret

Anse Vata

Hotel le Lagon

Hotel Mocambo
Noumea Beach Hotel

Aquarium

Surf Hotel Casino

Escapade Resort

Route du Trianon

Hotel du Trianon
Eglise du Voeu

Baie de L'Orphelinat

Baie des Pêcheurs

Baie des Citrons

Cathédrale St Joseph

Noumea

Place des Cocotiers

P&T Post

Hopital

Baie de la Moselle

Port

Syndicat D'Initiative
Noumea Visitors Bureau

Port

Sea Terminal

Le Bearno. Order a "croque monsieur" (a toasted ham and cheese sandwich) for $2.20. On the beach at *Le Bambino* in the Nouvata Beach Hotel a cold beer and French style hamburger will cost $4.00.

You could splurge a bit by going downtown to the *Café Moustache* and ordering a pepper steak with fries and a glass of wine for about $16.00. Hot dogs are available at *Julius's* in the Lantana Beach Hotel for $1.50. At *Le Gibus* in town the lunch is $7.50; all fish and meat main courses are served with vegetable.

If you want budget food, try the *Indian Curry House* near the interurban bus station in town. And, as elsewhere in the Pacific, extremely cheap food is available at the Public Market downtown. You'll have no trouble finding good restaurants and bistros.

For evening dining, Chinese, French, Indonesian, Vietnamese, Japanese, Indian, Italian, Greek, and Moroccan cuisine are all available. Needless to say, French food should head the list. Some visitors come to Nouméa mainly for the restaurants, such as the *Dodin Bouffant* in the Latin Quarter, where you'll find foie gras, soup, Duck Magret, dessert, cheeses and wine at $72.00 for two.

At *L'Eau Vive,* a restaurant run by nuns, you should be prepared to sing "Ave Maria" while dining on grilled fish, roast veal or seafood pancakes. $10.00 per person is an average cost.

We particularly enjoyed *Le Bilboquet* a French restaurant on Avenue Foch. An appetizer, mixed salad, grilled steak, dessert and wine was $40.00 for two.

For Vietnamese food, which is like Chinese only spicier, go into town and try *Tan Viet.* $30.00 for two will yield Prawns Saigon, skewered beef, spring rolls, Vietnamese salad, rice and enough cold beer to put out the fires.

For North African food, especially for couscous lovers, visit *La Couscoussière* in Anse Vata. A selection of prawns, Couscous Royal, brochette of beef, and some hearty table wine, will come to $50.00 for two.

New Caledonia isn't as expensive as Tahiti, but as you can see it's a lot steeper than Fiji, Vanuatu, the Solomons or nearly anywhere else in the South Pacific.

Evening Entertainment

Nouméa offers lively night life. Some of the night clubs, usually small ones, stage the sort of shows you'll see anywhere in Europe. Others feature Polynesian spectaculars, the sort with vigorous sensual Tamure dancing. These clubs dotted throughout the city and beach areas are expensive and few Melanesians attend them.

Nearly all the hotels, particularly in the Anse Vata Beach area, have bar-discos that offer merriment. We bear witness to the one at the Nouvata Beach Hotel. Our bungalow was within ear shot of the bar which on Saturday nights sounded like they were doing the chariot race scene from *Ben Hur.*

There are four movie theatres in town, The City 1 and 2, the Liberté, and the Rex. They open at 8 PM and all have dubbed-in French.

Unusually for the South Pacific, there are gambling casinos in Nouméa. Try your luck at blackjack, baccarat, roulette, chemin de fer, and slot machines. To get in, take your passport and wear a jacket and tie.

For something milder, cheaper too, bingo is available. Visit #7 Rue Jules Ferry on the waterfront. They're open Sunday through Thursday from 2 PM till midnight. Cards cost $1.00 each (100 CFPs).

What to do in the Nouméa Area

Nouméa's location was selected in 1852 by an English sandalwood merchant, James Paddon, who settled on the harbor island of Nou which later became a prison colony. Two years later French Captain Tardy de Montravel arrived, and more accurately defined what is today Nouméa. But the city developed into a mosquito-filled backwater not noted for civic beauty. When Robert Louis Stevenson was there in 1890, he sarcastically referred to it as "a town built from Vermouth cases."

Since then, because of the discovery of nickel and the activities of World War II, Nouméa has progressed. It's now a city of beauty, particularly from November through January when the flame trees (poincianas) turn red.

Getting around in Nouméa is easily accomplished. A taxi to or from the beach area and town will cost about $3.50. By other island standards, this is expensive. The bus system works well; the fare is 80¢.

To get the feel of town, go directly to the Place des Cocotiers. From this lovely central square at kilometer zero all distances on the island are measured. Since downtown is laid out in squares, getting around is easy. Begin by standing at the top of the Place facing the harbor. Look up to the left and view the two square towers of St. Joseph's Cathedral, built in 1893. Then look down the square through the flamboyant trees and notice the Fontaine Monumentale, the focal point of the square. Below and to the left where Rue d'Austerlitz joins Rue Anatole France (the main taxi terminal is there) is the older section of town, where vine-covered colonial buildings mix with modern structures. In the same block stands the *Public Market* where from 5 AM on matrons and cooks bargain for fish, meat, poultry, vegetables, and fruit.

The *Museum of Nouméa* is to the left. Walk down the square to Avenue Foch, turn left and continue four blocks. On the ground floor of this admission-free museum there is an unusually good presentation of New Caledonia Melanesian culture. The thematic presentation covers all aspects of life from the making of tools, to agriculture, the arts, and rituals. In the adjoining courtyard there are examples of plants used for food, ornamentation and medicine. Open hours are 9 to 11:30 AM and 2 to 5:30 PM daily except Sunday and Monday.

For art work done by contemporary local artists, go to the Old Town Hall on the right side of the Place at the corner of Avenue Foch. Then settle down at a handy bistro for coffee or a cold drink and some people-watching before going off to more distant attractions.

The *Aquarium* is located just beyond the point separating Lemon Bay from Anse Vata. It's 80¢ by public bus or 45 brisk minutes by foot from town. Particularly important to see is the display of fluorescent coral formations. The Aquarium is open afternoons except Monday and Tuesday.

The Botanical Garden and Zoo—To get there, walk or bus along La Route Territoriale three miles northeast of town, with many good views along the way. Other than a few deer there won't be any large animals in the zoo since there aren't any in New Caledonia. But you will see plenty of colorful parrots, some flying foxes, and the curious national bird called the cagou. If you've been staying out of the center of town, you'll undoubtedly have heard the cry of this flightless bird, which sounds like the barking of a dog.

Ile Nou (Nou Island)—In the early days this was a separate island, but now you can go there by bus. There's a hospital on the site of the old penal colony, but evidence of the prison remains. Most visitors to Ile Nou go for the uncrowded beach at Kuendu at the far western end of what is now the peninsula.

Amedée Lighthouse—This tiny island 18 miles south of Nouméa consists of about a square mile of uninspired land. Dominating the scene is an old lighthouse that dates back to the 1860's. Amedée has a good beach, and for snorkeling the water is excellent. In tourist season the beach barbecues never go out, the Polynesian music never stops, and the tour boats

Outrigger sailing canoe, Isle of Pines

come and go. Count on 8 hours and $35.00 for the trip, including lunch.

Duty Free Shopping—There are plenty of modern department stores and chic boutiques in Nouméa, but for serious shopping visit the duty free shops where prices are 20–30% off for purchases over $20. Be sure to bring your passport when you shop in these stores.

According to the Visitor's Bureau, there are at least 45 duty free stores. You can tell them by the red, white, and blue signs they display. Begin by strolling the Rue de l'Alma, a block west of the Place des Cocotiers.

For jewelry, gifts, watches, try *Bijouterie Gaspard,* 23 Rue de l'Alma. For clothes, perfume, lingerie, shoes, watches, step into *Adam Des Isles,* 35 Rue de l'Alma. To buy liquor, go to *Gaspards* in Le Village, 35 Avenue Foch. For cameras, try *La Caméra* in the Latin Quarter.

On the nearby Rue de Sebastopol and Rue Anatole France there are more duty free shops, and in the Anse Vata Beach area try the *Drug Shop* in the Novotel Hotel, a good place for leather goods and liquor.

To take something home representative of New Caledonia, wood carvings, shell necklaces, model canoes, or clubs, visit the department stores in the downtown area. Be aware that these items are not duty free.

Sports Activities

Horse Racing—Your visit may coincide with one of several annual race meets. If they're being held, you'll know about it.

Cricket and Soccer—For noisy spectator sports, these games are hard to beat. Cricket is probably the most fun to watch, and one of the best scenes to photograph. These games, held Saturday afternoons at the Terrain de Cricket, are colorfully informal and bear little resemblance to the proper and stiff performances of British cricket.

Tennis—There are six courts available next to the Chateau Royale on the beach at Anse Vata. Phone 26–45–32 for reservations.

Golf—There's a nine-hole course at the Dumbea Golf Club, 15 minutes west of town. Phone 36–83–03.

Car Rentals

Hertz—Telephone 26–18–22. Flat rate, insurance included for a two-door Fiat Uno will be $75 a day. A Peugeot 505, four-door, will be $97 a day. Offices at the airport and downtown. Open daily, including Saturdays and Sundays, but on holidays only until 11:30 AM.

Avis—Telephone 27–54–84. A two-door Innocenti will be $23 per day, plus 26¢ per kilometer and $10 a day for insurance. There is a downtown and an airport office. Open daily except 11 AM to 1:30 PM, but closed Sundays. Saturdays 7:30 AM to 11 AM only.

Europcar—Telephone 26–24–14. Their largest car will cost $50 per day, 50¢ a km, plus $14 for insurance. The smallest will cost $25 a day, 28¢ a km, and $10 for insurance. Offices downtown and at the airport. Open weekdays except for lunch, Saturday until 11:30 AM. Closed on Sundays.

AB Location—21 Rue Jules Ferry by the Quai. Telephone 28–12–12. A two-door Fiat Uno is $25 per day, plus 28¢ a km and $8.50 a day for insurance.

Credit cards are accepted; gas costs are not included. The minimum age to rent a car is 25. They drive on the right and your home driver's license is accepted.

THE ISLAND KNOWN AS GRANDE TERRE

If you speak some French, and have plenty of time, give thought to driving around Grande Terre by rental car. Remember though that driving on the narrow mostly unpaved roads requires attention and, because there are several stretches that are one-way areas, delays are possible.

As an alternative to driving there are buses, the long-distance variety, that leave from the bus terminal on Rue Clemenceau, three blocks east of the Square. Consider, for example, the bus that departs about noon and goes up the west coast to Koumac, 230 miles away. By traveling only parts of this distance, then using other buses, you could leapfrog your way up one coast and down the other. This isn't comfortable traveling, but it does reduce the responsibilities of driving. And the price is right, for $32 should pay the fare to and from the most distant point on the island. A reminder about bus travel—to get a good seat, always be at the terminal well in advance of departure time.

By Rental Car the Long Way Around

Going west from Nouméa, the underside of the island, with its hilly savannah land dotted with fire-resistant Niauly gum trees, looks just like the Australian outback. But 45 paved miles later at the *Hotel Les Paillotes* in Boulapari you could easily be in France. In such rural inns as this one, with pool, bar and restaurant, the meals incline toward local seafood and good country-style French cooking. Rates are $45 a double.

From Boulapari you have options. Either continue along the main road toward Bourail or turn north and drive over the central mountain chain to Thio, 47 unpaved miles away.

The Thio Option—On this road there is a scheduled one-way stretch. Inquire about one-way schedules before leaving Boulapari, then drive with care. Thio is where nickel-bearing ore was discovered in 1876, and is still the most prominent mining area in New Caledonia. You'll be able to see the workings as you enter the area, but they don't mar the beauty of this picturesque valley with its pretty river and nearby beach. This is the lush green side of the island.

For accommodations, stay at the *Ouroue Hotel* right on the beach, 10 minutes from town. Rooms with bath and cooking facilities are $30 a double.

From Thio you don't have to retrace your route. You can continue on to Canala, and then go south to the pastureland on the other side. Unfortunately, there is an eight-mile gap on this northeast coastal road that prevents you from continuing on to Houailou. Nevertheless on the slow 22-mile run to Canala, (there's a one-way patch here too) the country is verdant, and just one and a half miles shy of Canala you can stretch your legs on a three-mile walk to Ciu Falls.

The town of Bourail, 63 miles from Canala, is back on the main road and a good stopping point. The town itself isn't noteworthy, but on the coast five miles away there are two guidebook attractions. One is Pierced Rock where the sea forced its way through a high cliff; the other is Turtle Bay which has a good beach and, occasionally, turtles. Both are fine for picnics. Note too that in the open country around Bourail you can see villages with the traditional beehive Melanesian huts—round, high-roofed thatched huts built from bamboo and grass. In Bourail there are three inns.

Le Niauly with restaurant and bar; $32 double.

Hotel Douyere with restaurant and bar; $30 double.

El Kantara with restaurant, bar, pool, tennis; $41 double.

Continuing west from Bourail to Koumac it's 113 miles of tedious dry cattle country. In Koumac, where the paved road ends, you're 230 miles from Nouméa. From Koumac, as an option, you could continue west 35 miles to Poum which is the end of the line for Grande Terre Island. Or you could stay at one of Koumac's inns, all with bar-restaurants.

The Coppelia, $30 double.

The Madonna, $30 double.

The Passiflore, $20 double.

Le Grand Cerf, $35 double.

From Koumac, the now unpaved road turns north toward the eastern top of the island, 35 miles to the Balade area where Captain Cook first saw New Caledonia. This is the green verdant side of the island again, and along this coast there are towering mountains, one of which is the highest on the island, Mt. Pasie. I was told it can be climbed without a guide. There are inviting beaches, rivers, and waterfalls along this coast. And in the jungle there are isolated Melanesian villages where traditional ways are still practiced. Then 43 miles beyond Balade you enter a village of startling beauty, Hienghene. The coast here is wildly dramatic, and the town's setting at the mouth of a river has a quality of great serenity. For housing there is a pair of inns, both moderately priced. *The Relais Koulnoue* and *Chez Maitre Pierre.*

By foot from Hienghene several ambitious treks are possible. One is across the mountains all the way to Voh on the other coast. On the map this looks like 25 miles; by foot it's probably double that. For this sort of trekking, find a guide locally, or contact an agency that specializes in camping expeditions. In

Nouméa try *Aline-Raid,* 13 Rue Tabou.

Driving east of Hienghene the road passes through tiny jungle villages, the heart of New Caledonia's Kanak area. You'll see people working copra, tending fields of coffee and, along the way, parrots and exotic birds will take to the air in front of the car.

Then, after two ferry boat river crossings, and after passing the towns of Touho, Poindime, and Ponerihouen, you'll arrive in Houailou. In this town, surrounded by Norfolk Pines and sustained by coffee growing, there is a modest inn with bar and restaurant, the *Bel Aire.* Rates are $28 double.

From Houailou back to Nouméa, 114 miles away, you cross the island to Bourail and take the same road into Nouméa you used coming out. Once you get back, you'll have done a total of 500 hard, mostly unpaved miles. For any but the most dedicated explorers this may be a little much. An alternative would be to fly to one outstanding area. Hienghene on the east coast is such a place and, once there, you could see the area on foot and by bus—in depth. A three-day trip from Nouméa to Hienghene would cost $250 per person, including accommodations.

Another worthwhile trip is the 45-mile drive from Nouméa to Yate. It's a pretty drive, lots of sweeping views of the landscape and of 18-mile-long Lake Yate, a lake with an important hydroelectric plant at one end. You return to Nouméa by the same road.

Yate is just beyond the lake and near a good beach. This area, with its reputed 2,000 varieties of plants, is a paradise for botanists. For accommodations, the *Gite St. Gabriel* on the beach is $25 a double.

Check at your hotel for tours to these areas, also local tours around Nouméa.

NEW CALEDONIA'S
OUTER ISLANDS

Travelers will be happy to know that flying to the outer islands does not require you to make the 32-mile trip to Tontouta Airport. Domestic flights leave from Magenta Airport, only six miles from Nouméa.

A taxi to Magenta from the Anse Vata beach area will cost about $7, or $6 from town. The Number 7 bus makes these same runs every 30 minutes for $1.

THE ISLE OF PINES

The most popular outer island destination is the Isle of Pines, known as Kounie. This irregularly shaped 10-mile-long and 7-mile-wide island is just 65 miles from Nouméa. It is a

Beach at Isle of Pines

30-minute twice-daily Air Calédonie flight from Magenta Airport. The fare is $71 round trip.

An elemental "deck passage" ship, the *Boulari* makes the trip from Nouméa, an eight-hour voyage, every other Monday night, and goes to Kuto Bay. The one-way fare is $16.

The Isle of Pines, named by Captain Cook because of the stands of indigenous pines, is far enough south of the equator to have pronounced changes of season (the opposite of our seasons.) It's a healthy beautiful island with vegetation that includes wild orchids, tree ferns, coconut palms, banyans, sandalwood, and the curious pine tree, *araucaria cooki,* which is often close to 200 feet tall. There are beaches too, lots of them with fine white sand washed by a sea of many colors.

But it hasn't always been a happy island. The first missionaries to arrive in 1841 were murdered a year later by the Melanesian natives, and from 1871–79 France sent at least 3,000 prisoners to the island. The prison ruins and the prison cemetery, which you can visit, speak eloquently of those days. You'll also undoubtedly notice the ruins of a hotel in the Kuta-Kanumera area—the product of recent Kanak unrest.

The people who live on the Isle of Pines, only about 1,400 now, are Melanesians and the land they live on is held for them in perpetuity.

An only passable way to see this island is to pay $150 per person, including air fare, and do a one-day tour. This is a 10-hour junket, probably with a group of Japanese honeymooners. On such a tour you'll be met at the airport, and then briefly shown Queen Hortense's Cave—an interesting grotto deep in a tropical vale—several Melanesian villages in the center of the island, and the village at St. Joseph's Beach where you'll be given a short outrigger sailboat ride. Next there'll be an elegant meal at one of the inns, with lobster, grilled fish, vegetables, salad, dessert and wine served family style. Afterwards you'll be taken to one of the fine beaches in the Kuto-Kanumera area, then eventually to the airport for the return to Nouméa.

Consider instead of the day tour a more personal venture, a two- or three-day trip using one of the following inns (called gites ruraux or rural lodgings) as your base.

Kodjeue—Native style bungalows with bath at $36 double.

This comfortable inn is on a pretty beach five miles north of Kuto. The bungalows have cooking facilities, and there is a general store nearby. Bikes for hire.

Manamaky—In the south of the island at St. Joseph's Bay, $36 double. Cooking facilities and a small restaurant.

Nataiwatch—At Kanumera Bay, four bungalows with bath and kitchenettes, plus a restaurant. Near a good beach and with cars to hire. $36 double.

Oure—At Kanumera Bay two bungalows with bath, $25 a double; four bungalows without bath $15 double; four rooms with toilet/shower nearby, $12. Restaurant and camp ground.

Reine Hortense—On the beach at Kuto Bay, three plumbed bungalows with kitchen facilities. $36 double. 220 v. electricity, camp grounds and tent rentals.

Be sure to make reservations in advance for all the outer islands. You'll be met at the airport.

Instead of the $150 per person one-day honeymoon tour, you and a companion could spend two nights and three days in one

Kodjeue Inn, Isle of Pines

of the gites ruraux on the Isle of Pines for about $275, including airfare. This would allow time to wander the island, preferably by bicycle, do the pair of good caves in the center of the island, and spend the right amount of time on the exquisite beaches of the Kuto-Kanumera area. From Kuto you could spend an hour climbing 850-foot peak Nga—good views from there. To step into the past, the 40-minute walk toward the airport from Kuto would bring you to the convict cemetery. At Upi Bay, six miles from Kuto, outrigger canoes are available to examine the enormous coral outcroppings. At Oro Bay just north of Kuto there's good rain forest walking, with plenty of places for picnics and ad lib wandering.

For Divers—The Nauticlub (B.P. 18, Isle of Pines, New Caledonia) offers package holidays, two dives per day, meals, and accommodations. Rates for diving only are $70 for two dives.

One of the best dive areas is at False Pass in the Gadji area in the north. Underwater visibility there is 200 feet with plenty of parrot fish, turtles, Moorish idols, and huge heads of yellow brain coral. For a different sort of dive experience try one of the caves. You're supposed to be unusually qualified to make these dives which involve entering a pool within a cave and, aided by a flashlight, maneuvering among eerie underwater stalactites.

Island Shopping—Remember that, while basic foods are sold on the islands (including excellent French bread), no liquor is sold at the shops. So bring your own.

OUEN ISLAND

This island is just 23 miles off the southeast coast of Grande Terre and is 15 minutes by air. It's a good place for peace and quiet, certainly not on the tourist route. They have one small resort on Ouen, the *Turtle Club,* with facilities for boating, diving, and fishing. Rates are $30 double.

THE LOYALTY ISLANDS

This group (Ouvea, Mare, Lifou and Tiga) are upraised coral atolls 65 miles off the northeast coast of Grande Terre. Kanak

Melanesians and some Polynesians live on these low islands where nature kindly provides all necessities: yams, manioc, bananas, coconuts, and fish from the sea. Visitors come here for sunshine, fine beaches, and to see a measure of what is, for the moment, genuine island life.

Ouvea is a slender 30-mile-long island with nearly 3,000 people who live off the land and export copra. A paved road runs down the west side of this narrow island and connects the villages. The beaches, mostly on the western lagoon side, are excellent. The entire wooded island is beautiful, but the best scenery is to the north of the administration center, Fayahoue, toward St. Joseph where there are several tiny jewel-like islands.

In the far south of the island there is a causeway called Lekine Bridge that connects with Mouli Island where the beaches and snorkeling are nearly perfect.

Air Calédonie flies to Ouvea two or three times daily, a 45-minute flight. Fare is $80 round trip.

Where to Stay

Loka in the north of the island at St. Joseph's village has beach bungalows with bath at a distance. There is a restaurant, and they provide free airport transfers. $23 double.

Guei at Fayahoue Beach has bungalows, with bath at a distance, restaurant, bike rentals. $31 double.

Watau at Fayahoue Beach has bungalows without bath, restaurant. $29 double.

Fleury at Fayahoue Beach has two bungalows with bath, restaurant, bike rentals. $29 double.

Beaupré at Fayahoue Beach has three bungalows with bath, restaurant, bar, bikes for rent. $35 double.

MARÉ ISLAND

This 20-mile-long by 10-mile-wide island has a population of 4,400. The town of Tedine on the west coast is the port and commercial center. The airport is on the other side of the island at La Roche. Here, behind an impressive Catholic Mission, there is a hill that provides a view of all Maré. The island is laced with roads between villages. There are beaches, but not nearly as good as Ouvea's.

Air Calédonie flies to Maré every day. The flight takes 45 minutes and the fare is $80 round trip.

Where to Stay

Si Med—Three bungalows with bath on the beach at Ceingeite Beach on the west side of the island. Restaurant, airport transfers, island tours. $35 double.

Yedjele—Two bungalows with baths, kitchen facilities. No restaurant, but host will prepare meals. $36 double.

LIFOU ISLAND

Lifou is the largest and most popular of the Loyalty Group. 8,600 people live on this 25-mile-long, 11-mile-wide island. Situated in the Bay of Chateaubriand on the east side is the administrative center, called We.

There are interesting caves on the island (nearly all upraised coral islands have a cave or two) and there are lots of traditional Melanesian beehive huts too. Be sure to see the Lourdes Chapel on the western side at Sandalwood Bay. Excellent beaches in this area.

Air Calédonie comes in twice a day. Fare is $80 round trip.

Where to Stay

Les Cocotiers at We has 10 bungalows with bath, restaurant-bar, free airport transfer. $25 double.

Gite de Luecilla—On the beach at Luecilla, four bungalows with bath, kitchen facilities. Restaurant, bar camping ground, 220 v. electricity, hot water. $30 double.

TIGA ISLAND

This tiny three-by-one-mile island just north of Maré is covered with tropical vegetation. About 150 people live here and their main source of revenue is copra. There is one good beach on the island. Planes come in twice a week but, since there are no accommodations here, you may be satisfied just seeing Tiga from the air.

8

THE SOLOMON ISLANDS

Nature is excessive, lovely, and ominous in the Solomons and the Melanesians who live there, often blond or redheaded, are the blackest of all people.

Before World War II such names as Guadalcanal, Savo, Munda were rarely heard. So rarely that, as the story goes, one Englishman, or perhaps he was an Australian, became concerned about the developing war. He wanted no part of such an activity, and cast about for a remote place to hide. To him the Solomons seemed the ideal choice. And they were until suddenly in 1942 the Japanese Army and Navy appeared in strength.

According to the story, our escapee from unpleasantness then strapped a transmitting radio to his back and, with a handful of others, mostly Australians, took to the hills. He became an intelligence agent, a "coastwatcher" for the allies. It was a job not known for comfort or longevity.

Now 36 years later the Solomons have regained "back of beyond" status, and a modern day escapist might again look at these islands with interest.

Honiara, the capital of Guadalcanal, didn't exist when I was there during World War II. They were the British Solomon Islands then, and the hardware of war that littered the land still bore the scent of death. That debris is still there, but now it's rusty, coral-encrusted, and softened with time. When asked about these remnants, most islanders, not even born at the

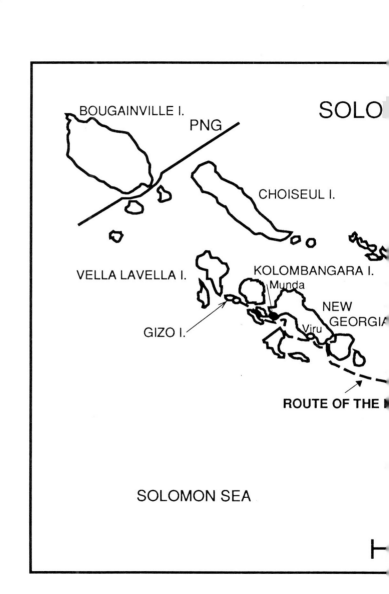

BOUGAINVILLE I.

PNG

SOLO

CHOISEUL I.

VELLA LAVELLA I.

KOLOMBANGARA I.

Munda

NEW
GEORGIA

GIZO I.

Viru

ROUTE OF THE

SOLOMON SEA

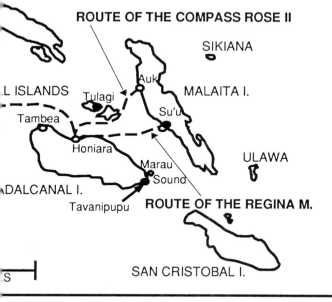

ONTONG JAVA

A YSABEL I.

ROUTE OF THE COMPASS ROSE II

SIKIANA

L ISLANDS

Tulagi

Auk

Tambea

Su'u

MALAITA I.

Honiara

Marau

ULAWA

DALCANAL I.

Sound

Tavanipupu **ROUTE OF THE REGINA M.**

S

SAN CRISTOBAL I.

time of that war, will shrug as if to say, "Don't all beaches have rusting landing craft? Aren't there rotting field pieces, aircraft and tanks in all jungles?" Today even the most remote islands have usable airstrips that date back to those ancient days.

In 1944, courtesy of the *USS Acontius,* the Solomons were my first South Sea islands. I'd never seen a coconut palm, or a reef with translucent water, a man with a bone in his nose, a thatched village on stilts under palms on a white beach, and I'd never felt the violence of a South Pacific rain squall.

In spite of the war I was impressed, hooked and, after several subsequent trips, remain hooked. Still these islands aren't for everyone. There are few activity-filled resorts, it can be hot and humid, the inter-island seas can be rough, there aren't many roads, and there is some malaria. But it's real Melanesia, and for "do it yourself travel" there are plenty of inter-island boats, adequate housing, gentle people, and beauty. And, thanks to World War II, you can get nearly everywhere by air.

The Land and Her People

Two hundred fifty thousand Solomon Islanders live on the six main islands and associated clusters that slant across the Coral Sea for 900 miles. Ninety-four per cent of them are black Melanesians, but a small fraction are Micronesian, Chinese, a few are European, and curiously some are Polynesian. Of the Polynesians, more later.

Guadalcanal, over 100 miles long by 30 miles wide, is the largest island. Then in descending order there's Malaita, San Cristobal, Choiseul, New Georgia, and Santa Ysabel. All of them are mountainous, covered with rain forest, and laced with rivers. The remaining hundreds of islands range from substantial, to mere dots of coral.

Most of the people who live in this fragmented country speak English as well as one of 90 other languages. But, when it becomes necessary to cross language barriers, they use the colorful lingua franca called "Pijin" that was developed in collaboration by blacks and whites.

Solomon Island children, Auki, Malaita

Honiara on Guadalcanal, the capital of this now independent nation as of 1978, lies between grassy hills and the sea, eight miles from the airport. Along its main street, shaded by poincianas, and palms, there's a Chinatown, a bowered park, a river, the harbor, a collection of shops, and the public market. At the far end of town is a dignified pair of government buildings and the Mendana, the best hotel in the Solomons.

By South Sea standards, this 17,000-population town is unspoiled. There are no touts, no tourist gimmickry on the streets, tipping is discouraged and, other than on rare cruise ship days, few tourists are seen.

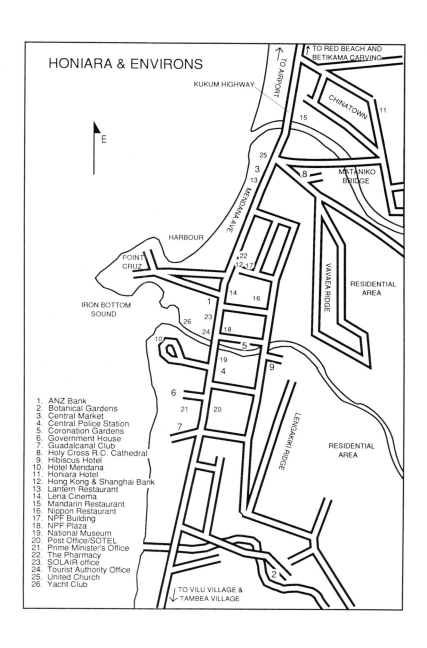

HONIARA & ENVIRONS

KUKUM HIGHWAY

TO AIRPORT

TO RED BEACH AND
BETIKAMA CARVING

CHINATOWN

E

15

11

25

3
13

8

MATANIKO
BRIDGE

MENDANA AVE.

HARBOUR

POINT
CRUZ

22
12 17

VAVAEA RIDGE

RESIDENTIAL
AREA

14   16

IRON BOTTOM
SOUND

1

23

26

24   18

5

10

19

4

9

6

21   20

7

LENGAKIKI RIDGE

RESIDENTIAL
AREA

1. ANZ Bank
2. Botanical Gardens
3. Central Market
4. Central Police Station
5. Coronation Gardens
6. Government House
7. Guadalcanal Club
8. Holy Cross R.C. Cathedral
9. Hibiscus Hotel
10. Hotel Mendana
11. Honiara Hotel
12. Hong Kong & Shanghai Bank
13. Lantern Restaurant
14. Lena Cinema
15. Mandarin Restaurant
16. Nippon Restaurant
17. NPF Building
18. NPF Plaza
19. National Museum
20. Post Office/SOTEL
21. Prime Minister's Office
22. The Pharmacy
23. SOLAIR office
24. Tourist Authority Office
25. United Church
26. Yacht Club

2

TO VILU VILLAGE &
TAMBEA VILLAGE

At a distance from Honiara life goes on the same as it always has. Most areas are still without electricity, there are few roads, social services are scanty, and the new nation with an economy based on copra, palm oil, fish, timber, and some cattle, emerges slowly. But at the village level the land and sea fully provide the basics—bananas, coconuts, papayas, yams, and fish. Pigs and chickens are kept, there's hunting too, and any money gained from the sale of surplus crops (usually copra, is used to buy rice, canned meat, kerosene, and beer. Beer, you'll undoubtedly notice, is consumed with enthusiasm.

Visitors traveling away from Honiara will find creature comforts rather bleak, but the hospitality of the islanders, the special smiles you get when they find you're American, and the beauty of the land and sea, make up for the deficiencies in comfort.

History in Brief

The first European to see the islands was the Spaniard Alvaro Mendana who came in 1567. While on Guadalcanal he apparently found gold in the rivers, and named the islands after King Solomon's mines, rather than after his king. In later years the Dutch, French, and British spasmodically appeared.

In the nineteenth century European recruiters arrived, and sometimes abducted Solomon Islanders to work in Australian cane fields. This was called "blackbirding," an activity the white man cannot look back on with pride. The British stopped this practice in 1893, and at the same time made the islands a British Protectorate. But in those days the Protectorate had only enough funds for police and administrative purposes, nothing for education or social welfare. This responsibility was left entirely to the church, which no doubt accounts for the islanders' close attachment to Christianity. Notice that at some point in conversation with a Solomon Islander you'll nearly always be asked your religious persuasion.

The administration of these islands in the early days of this century was neither easy nor smooth. The missionaries brought education and improved health, but they also condemned the old ways, and unfortunately the new converts tended to be ashamed of their culture, and rejected it. Then too, there were foreign-introduced epidemics in those years that killed thousands. There was tribal warfare, blood feuds, head hunting, and missionaries and administrators murdered.

The planters came in about that time too, mostly to grow copra. This created employment, but with the Depression came reduced prices for copra, and laborers were laid off or poorly paid, producing more resentment.

War came to the Solomons in 1942, and some of history's fiercest sea, land, and air battles were fought here. The Americans, the Australians, New Zealanders, and the Fijians, finally prevailed. It's an accepted fact that Guadalcanal was the turning point of the war against Japan.

No mention of that campaign would be complete without mentioning Sergeant Major Jacob Vouza, a member of the Solomon Islands Armed Constabulary. When the Japanese invaded the Solomons, Vouza volunteered to act as scout, and in so doing he had considerable information about the disposition of American troops. Unfortunately he was captured by the Japanese, but refused to betray the whereabouts of the Americans. He was tortured, tied to a tree, bayoneted and left for dead. Escaping, he made his way back to American lines where he made a full report before allowing himself to be taken to the hospital. For this exploit he was awarded the British George Medal, made a Member of the Order of the British Empire, and given the American Silver Star. He died in 1984.

Peace came in 1945, but not the end of the islanders' problems. Most of them wanted the Americans to stay, and there was considerable disappointment when they didn't. Some islanders were convinced that the Americans would return one day and bring with them all the goods they'd been so generous with during the war—food, clothing, equipment, radios, housing. This belief was transformed into a "Cargo Cult" movement that somehow came to be called the "Marching Rule."

The origins of the term "Marching Rule" have never been clear, but newspaper people in England at the time claimed that it was a corruption of the words "Marxian Rule." Whatever the meaning, the cult grew, became organized, leaders were chosen, and its adherents refused to accept the authority of the British Government. "Marching Rule" took over whole villages and built towns surrounded by palisades. They even built warehouses to store gifts that would surely arrive from America.

The authorities finally decided that the movement was getting out of hand, and by making judicious arrests, they put a stop to the problem, or almost did—some islanders say that elements of the "Marching Rule" still smoulder quietly in the Solomons.

But positive things happened in those post-war days and, with the world becoming more autonomy-conscious, the Solomons sought freedom. In 1978 they became independent. Their government, as with many Commonwealth countries, retains the Queen of England as head of state, but has as the working head of government their own elected prime minister.

How to Get There by Air

Coming into the Solomons you'll probably land at Henderson Airport of World War II fame, eight miles from Honiara.

Coming from the US—Fly to Nadi, Fiji, then take Air Pacific's once-a-week flight to Honiara (three hours).

Coming from Australia—Using Qantas or Ansett Air Lines, you can get into Honiara from either Sydney or Brisbane daily.

Coming from Port Villa, Vanuatu—Air Nauru flies in once a week, but Solair, the Solomon's own airline plans additional flights from Vila soon (two hours).

Coming from Guam or Majuro in the Marshalls—One of the best bargains in the Pacific is Air Nauru's flight from Majuro or Guam via Nauru into Honiara. Flights on Wednesday and Saturday. Majuro—Nauru—Honiara fare is about $200. Guam—Nauru—Honiara is about $300.

Coming from Port Moresby, Papua New Guinea—You can fly in with Air Niugini twice weekly. The most dramatic air route to the Solomons is via Kieta on Bougainville (Papua New Guinea) to Munda (Solomons), then to Honiara. It's more expensive than the direct flight, but worth it.

Leaving Kieta, the flight follows Bougainville's lovely south coast, then flies low over the Shortlands, above tiny green

Solomon islanders in war paint

atolls and down "the slot" between Choiseul and Vella Lavella. Kolombangara comes next, and the plane flashes over the town and island of Gizo, then drops down into Munda for entrance formalities into the Solomons.

By this time you'll have been visually reminded that airstrips courtesy of World War II link these islands and exist in the most unlikely places. After Munda the flight continues over Rendova (in the Russells) and terminates at Henderson Airport, Honiara.

By Sea

If you're in Port Moresby, Kieta, Port Vila, or Suva, there

could be a chance of finding a cargo vessel bound for Honiara. Most of them say they don't carry passengers, but if a ship is ready to sail, go aboard, and in your most winning way talk to the captain. There are also cruise ships and, as suggested in other chapters, you can contact the appropriate cruise lines.

Immigration

Visitors must have a valid passport, onward tickets, and adequate funds for support.

Health

The main problem in the Solomons is malaria; there's even some in Honiara. The best thing to do is visit a clinic in your home town that specializes in providing inoculations and counsel for overseas traveling. For the Solomons you'll probably be given chloroquine tablets and instructions to take the proper dosage two weeks before arrival, during your stay, and two weeks after it. The problem is that some Solomon Island malaria is chloroquine-resistant, and another prophylaxis must be taken, such as fansidar. But fansidar has side effects, and should be taken only if malaria occurs. Talk this over with medical people before leaving home. We've never had a problem.

Good medical care is available in Honiara, but it's a little spotty away from town. Water in Honiara is potable, but not always elsewhere. Inquire locally or drink beer and soft drinks. Be careful of cuts and abrasions, as infections occur easily in this climate.

Currency

As of this writing the exchange is very good for Americans. One US dollar equals two Solomon Island dollars. Solomon Island paper money comes as $2, $5, and $10 notes. Coins are $1, 20¢, 10¢, 5¢, 2¢ and 1¢.

American Express and Visa credit cards are accepted at most hotels in Honiara, but not always in the outer islands.

There are four commercial banks in Honiara—The National Bank of Solomons, Australian New Zealand Banking Corp.,

Hong Kong and Shanghai Banking Corp. and the Westpac Banking Corp.

Time Zone

Local time is 11 hours ahead of Greenwich Mean Time, 16 hours ahead of Eastern Standard Time, 19 hours ahead of Pacific Standard Time.

Newspapers, Radio, TV, and Telephones

The *Solomon Star* and the *Solomon Tok Tok* are weekly newspapers with English editions. The country has its own broadcasting service, a large portion of which is in English. Overseas newspapers are available in Honiara. No TV. The telephone system, using a satellite service, puts world-wide calls through 24 hours a day.

Power

230/415 volts at 50 Hz.

Holidays

There are 10 public holidays in the Solomons each year: New Years Day; Good Friday; Easter Saturday; Easter Sunday; Easter Monday; Whit Monday in May; Queen's Birthday in June; Solomon Islands Independence Day (July 7); Christmas Day; Boxing Day (December 26).

Climate

Weather here is warm and humid, but there are breezes that temper the heat. Daytime temperatures are consistently about 82 F, and 72 F at night. When it rains, it rains hard and long. The wettest months are January through March and the driest July through September.

Language

As discussed earlier, English is spoken widely, and Pijin, an easy to acquire language, is used too.

Deck passengers on the M.V. Iuminao

Tipping

A bit of island philosophy about giving and receiving may be important here. Nearly all Pacific islanders are very generous, and those that receive, feel obliged to reciprocate, but not necessarily at that same time. This may partially explain the attitude that tipping is not necessary or expected.

HONIARA, GUADALCANAL AND ENVIRONS

After you've stepped off the plane at Henderson Airport, gone through customs, and changed some money, go out the front entrance of the terminal and board one of the waiting airport minibuses. For $3 Solomon Island or $1.50 US they'll take you the eight miles to your hotel in Honiara.

Hotels in Honiara

There are three major hotels in Honiara, all good and, listed in order of cost, they are:

The Mendana—This hotel of international standard lies under the palms by the sea. It has 101 air conditioned rooms, restaurant, bar, terrace lounge, and swimming pool. Rates are $35 US (or $70 SI).

Honiara Hotel—At the opposite end of town from the Mendana, this comfortable hotel has 48 air conditioned rooms with private facilities at $25 US double. They've got a pool, bar, and restaurant where good western and Chinese food is served.

Hibiscus Hotel—This peaceful budget hotel is across the street from the Mendana. It has a bar, an unusually good restaurant and is close to town. Some but not all rooms are air conditioned. Some have cooking facilities. $18 US double.

Hostels and Inexpensive Housing

Check with the United Church in Honiara or ask at the Solomon Island Visitors Bureau. Better yet, write them: Solomon Island Tourist Authority, BOX 321, Honiara, Solomon Islands.

Inns and Hotels at a Distance from Honiara, but Still on Guadalcanal

Tambea Village Resort—Thirty miles west of Honiara, this simple resort thatched in the native style, lit by kerosene lamps, cooled by the tradewinds, has 24 plumbed bungalows. It has a cocktail lounge, dining room, a barbecue area famed for whole roasted pigs, and a library filled with dog-eared paperbacks. Tambea is on a good swimming-snorkeling beach. Rates $30 US double.

Tavanipupu Island Resort—At the far end of Guadalcanal to the east, 70 miles from Honiara. This small inn on a 40-acre island in Marau Sound has two fully equipped cottages. Each accommodates four adults. There is no hot water or electricity, and kerosene provides for cooking and light. Guests must bring their own food supply, except for fresh fruit and vegetables, as there are no sources of food on the island. Good planning suggests that supplies be sent on ahead of time by boat from Honiara, a free service. There isn't a road, but you could go by boat, definitely a no-frills trip, or do it by the once-a-week Solair flight. Fare is $60 US round trip. A full week on Tavanipupu for up to four people comes to about $200 US.

Dining in Honiara

The three main hotels all have restaurants of good standard. The *Mendana* has good buffets, the *Hibiscus* does excellent coconut crab and seafood, rather expensive, and the *Honiara* is well known for good Chinese food.

The *Mandarin, Lantern* and *Jade Garden* all in Honiara are typical Chinese restaurants and are quite inexpensive.

The *Nippon* serves authentic Japanese food and caters to the Japanese that appear in the Solomons out of war nostalgia.

For fast food, fish and chips, hamburgers, or Australian meat pies, try *Kingsley's* and *Maggie's Kitchen*, both inexpensive and downtown. By American standards, most eating in Honiara is moderately inexpensive.

Evening Entertainment

Honiara is not a swinging town. It compares in no way with Papeete, Suva, Nouméa, or even Port Villa and Apia. There are a couple of movie houses, the Kukum and the Lena, both open in the evening. But there aren't any local discos or lively bars. Nearly all evening activities take place in the hotels and a couple of clubs.

The *Honiara Hotel* has a congenial bar, and once or twice a week they put on some Gilbertese dancing. They're Micronesians but their music, with its Polynesian lilt and style, is very good and something you can dance to.

The *Mendana* features the same sort of activities, perhaps on a larger scale. They also have video movies some evenings.

The Yacht Club (next door to the Mendana) is a good spot to meet some of the local expats. The bartender will quickly organize membership. Much the same thing is true of the Guadalcanal Club. They have a pool too, and some evenings show video movies.

How to Get Around in Honiara and on Guadalcanal

There are plenty of taxis in town, you can usually hail one on the street, and they're nearly always parked outside the Mendana Hotel, or can quickly be summoned. Taxis here have no meters, so it's best to negotiate fares before setting out but, for a short run in town, expect to pay 50¢. For longer hauls, about $6 an hour.

Car Rentals—Both Budget and Avis have operations in Honiara. Find them at either the airport or the Mendana Hotel. Rates for a compact car, insurance included, will be about $30 a day. And Americans should be reminded to stay on the left while driving.

What to Do

After settling in at your hotel, the first thing to do is to visit the Solomon Islands Visitors Bureau. It's a block toward town from the Mendana. Ask for the General Manager, Wilson Maelaua. He'll make suggestions, reinforce them with brochures and, if necessary, provide letters of introduction to appropriate people. He's an important first contact.

As for shopping, some good handicrafts can be purchased—baskets, shell money (the kind used as bride-price money), ebony or other wood carvings of fish, turtles, and birds, all inlaid with shell. But the most unusual item you can buy in the Solomons is the grotesque spirit figure called the Nguzunguzu. When these elaborately carved figures of a human head or bird are attached to the prow of a canoe they give protection against enemies or bad weather. A small Nguzunguzu placed on your coffee table will insure the same protection.

These artifacts are available in downtown Honiara. Try the Handicraft Shop and Museum across the street from the Mendana. A little further into town visit the BJS Arts and Craft Shop, The Honiara Coin Center, or the Village Craft Center. They're all open weekdays and until noon on Saturday.

The very best place to examine the full spectrum of island craft is at Betikama village, which is slightly out of town on the way to the airport. Betikama is an Adventist high school, but it houses the biggest range of carvings in the islands. And on the same property there's one of the best collections of World War II weaponry—field guns, crashed planes, mortars, uniforms, and so forth. A taxi there will be about $1 US.

For duty free shopping try the Technique Radio Centre, QQQ Wholesale, or The Pharmacy. All are in town and sell liquor, cigarettes, perfume, cameras, and watches. Purchases should be made 24 hours before departure, and can be collected on departure at the airport.

You can't miss the post office in town—it's open daily and half a day on Saturdays. For pharmaceutical supplies there are any number of shops along the main street.

Visitors are welcome at the Anglican, Catholic, Methodist, and Seventh Day Adventist churches. As a rule services are in Pijin on Sunday morning, in English in the evening. Ask at your hotel.

For people preoccupied with ships and the sea, the harbor in the center of town has a great deal to offer. All sorts of vessels provide transport. Canoes and launches move up and down the coast or out to Savo Island. Larger boats sail to nearby islands, and reasonably substantial ships sail to the distant islands.

Chinatown at the far end of town, with its collection of wooden verandahed shops, lies alongside the Mataniko River. There's a strong South Sea flavor about this part of town. It's quite near the Honiara Hotel.

The Botanical Gardens are at the west end of town just past the post office. Turn inland and follow the signs to the Gardens about a quarter mile from the turn off. There, in a fine rainforest with a meandering stream, most of the Solomon Island flora can be examined. There's even a reasonably typical island village on the grounds.

You'll like Honiara. It's a pleasant, safe, utilitarian town. It's not exotic though, and it is most certainly not affluent. Most of the people who live there have simple tastes, little money, and are not apt to be seen in the bar-dining rooms of the three hotels. The expensive material things in life are still limited to a few upper-income islanders, resident expatriates, and tourists.

The Compass Rose *in Honiara*

GUADALCANAL

Guadalcanal is 100 miles long. Along part of its northern coast, where Honiara is, a road runs about 75 miles. To put it another way, from Honiara you can drive west and then south about 35 miles, or east 40. Beyond these limits, access is by foot, air, or sea.

For Americans and Japanese veterans of World War II, the battlegrounds are a sort of pilgrimage, and the best way to visit these scenes is with a well-informed guide. You'll be apt to see a clutch of Japanese there—any number of agencies in Honiara do this well.

Such a trip runs about four hours and will take you east across the Lunga River toward the airport where there'll be a brief halt to see the original "Foxhole," a bunker used by the Marine Commanding Officer of Henderson Airport, Colonel

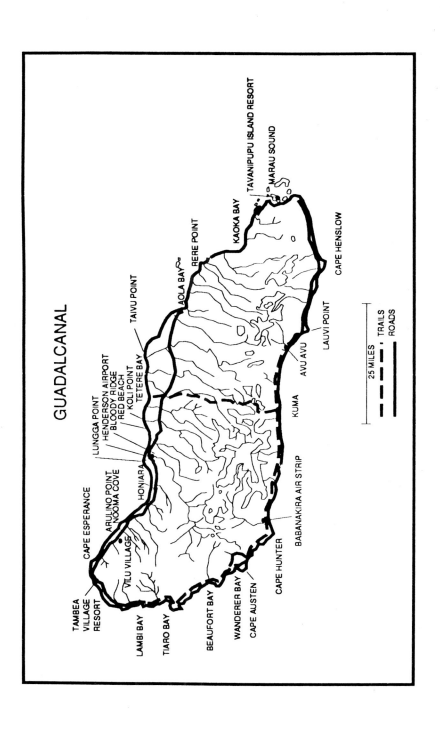

GUADALCANAL

TAMBEA
VILLAGE
RESORT

CAPE ESPERANCE

LAMBI BAY

TIARO BAY

BEAUFORT BAY

WANDERER BAY

CAPE AUSTEN

CAPE HUNTER

BABANAKIRA AIR STRIP

ARULINO POINT
NOOMA COVE

VILU VILLAGE

HONIARA

LUNGGA POINT
HENDERSON AIRPORT
BLOODY RIDGE
RED BEACH
KOLI POINT
TETERE BAY

TAIVU POINT

AOLA BAY

RERE POINT

KUMA

AVU AVU

LAUVI POINT

KAOKA BAY

CAPE HENSLOW

TAVANIPUPU ISLAND RESORT
MARAU SOUND

25 MILES

TRAILS
ROADS

Fox. Using flashlights, the nearby underground hospital will be examined. Then, without need of explanation, visitors will see the skeletal remains of Henderson's old control tower.

"Bloody Ridge," where the Americans defended Henderson is next and, at "Red Beach" four miles beyond, a solitary Japanese cannon pointing out to sea marks the landing place of US Marines on August 7, 1942.

Finally there'll be a stop at Betikama village for a look at its impressive collection of war relics, and for shopping if you have an interest.

If this hasn't been enough of World War II nostalgia, plan a walking trip on your own to see the last Japanese stronghold, the Gifu. To do this cross the Mataniko River east of town, turn south and follow the road about a quarter mile to the Vara Housing Estate. Cross the bridge there and follow a footpath up and over the grassy hills. Stop often enough to rest and enjoy good views of sea and land, then continue on past several patches of World War II barbed wire entanglements, to the village of Barana. Keep going up the hill—this is the Gifu, the anticlimactic scene of the Japanese last gasp in 1943. Allow three hours for this trip.

Mt. Austin is just beyond. You could continue walking and gain the summit from which five views of coastal Guadalcanal and most of the battlefields can be seen. Or, since there is a road all the way to the summit, a taxi from Honiara will take you there for a couple of dollars.

For a further taste of bushwalking, the sort there's lots of on Guadalcanal, set aside a full day and, with guide, do the *Mataniko Valley Gorge and Cave Trek*. First taxi to Tuvuruku which is inland from Chinatown. Get a guide there. You follow him over some grassy hills and descend into heavy jungle near the river. You'll follow the river, ford it up to your waist six or eight times, and finally arrive at a spectacular gorge with a double-sided waterfall. By this time a rewarding swim has been earned. There's a cave nearby too, a curious cave through which a branch of the river flows. A word of caution: do not attempt this excursion if there have been recent heavy rains, or if it looks like a storm is developing. Fording the river on dry days is exciting enough.

WEST OF HONIARA

By driving or taxiing west of town, the road goes about 35 miles to Lambi. It's a peacefully scenic run that passes through Kakambono where the Japanese had their headquarters during the war. Beyond, the road fords several rivers (don't go if it's raining heavily), passes through a number of pretty villages, some stately coconut plantations and, at Vilu 16 miles from Honiara, visitors should stop off at Fred Kona's War Museum. Pay a small admission, and wander about his grounds where there are downed aircraft, weapons of all sorts, uniforms, helmets with bullet holes in them, and other relics.

At the town of Visale, 25 miles from town, there is an old and photogenic Catholic church. Then almost immediately you're at Tambea Village, a community famed for its hotel resort complex and the good diving offshore. This area has some good wreck diving, excellent reefs, and drop offs. They charge about $40 for two tanks, and offer a certification course. Contact: Rick Belmare, Island Dive Service, PO Box 414, Honiara, Solomon Islands (Also at Mendana Hotel and Anuha Island Resort).

Tambea Village Resort on an exceptionally fine beach is an ideal place for complete withdrawal. It's unspoiled, unpretentious, inexpensive, a good base from which to study village life, for bushwalking, swimming, reading, and eating well. The only flaw with Tambea is that there are some troublesome sand flies. Take along some Cutters insect repellant.

Beyond Tambea the road curves around the western end of Guadalcanal at Cape Esperance and ends at Lambi Bay. To keep going from here, walking becomes necessary and, to do the south coast village-by-village, you should have a guide and should be a trail-wise camper with good equipment.

Four days along this route would bring you to Babanakira airstrip where the walker is less than halfway to the eastern end of Guadalcanal. Here there is a once-a-week plane back to Honiara. A trip such as this requires pre-planning and, as the guidebook says, "Keep a good lookout for crocodiles when you cross the Variana River near Tiaro Bay."

From Babanakira Airstrip hikers could continue on another

three or four days to Avu Avu on the southeast coast. From there a sort of road goes on to Marau Sound at the eastern tip. You can then return to Honiara by boat or plane.

Trekking on Guadalcanal

J. L. O. Tedder in his very excellent "Walks on Guadalcanal" discusses the essentials of trekking, and suggests the following:

Guides—Recruit guides in the village of departure. To do so, inquire at the local village council. You should be prepared to feed guides en route, and pay them a modest sum too, but often they'll go along without charge just for the trip.

Food—Plan to carry as little as possible. When you are staying in villages simple foods are usually available—yams, taro, green vegetables. This will nicely augment the canned or dried food you're carrying.

Sleeping—Fortunately there are quite a few villages, and good planning suggests that you aim for one each evening. There you'll be invited to sleep in a thatched hut. On leaving, guests are expected to give a gift, generally a can of food or a stick of "trade tobacco."

Gear—Staying dry and keeping gear dry is very important. Whenever possible wrap equipment in plastic, or pack it in a metal box which can be strapped to a pack frame.

Speed—Distances from village to village are usually calculated in hours rather than miles or kilometers. But a speed of one and a half miles an hour is considered comfortable.

Drinking Water—Guides will know about safe sources of water, but generally most springs are safe. Avoid river water near villages—rivers are often used as latrines.

A drinking coconut cut from a tree, opened with a machete, and put to lips is also an unforgettably refreshing way to quench your thirst.

Hazards—There are two poisonous snakes on the island, but they're rare and usually will move away. Centipedes can also be a problem. They cause a very painful bite. Some are as much as a foot long and dark green in color. When possible, sleep under mosquito netting; centipedes come out at night.

Rivers—Most are swift and can flood without warning.

Where possible cross in the shallows, and move diagonally downstream.

Village Etiquette—Always ask permission to enter a village. Tell them where you've been and where you're bound. Always ask for the village leader, and remain seated while he consults with other villagers about where you'll be sleeping. Do not pick anything from village gardens without asking permission.

GOING EAST FROM HONIARA

The road east goes along flats where there's rice growing, crosses the Nalimbu River and, at a point about twelve miles beyond Honiara, there is access to a wearisome but magnificent hike across the center of the island to Kuma.

To get to the trail head, turn south beyond the Little Tenaru River. Continue on for two and a half miles until you come to the Kongga Resthouse. With a guide and bearers, start walking and plan on three hard days to Kuma on the south coast of Guadalcanal. From there, go west to Babanakira Airstrip or east to Marau Sound.

Continuing east by road from Honiara, the road terminates at Aola Bay. There is an onward trail to Marau Sound at the eastern tip of Guadalcanal, but this four-day walk is less interesting, and requires that you swim several rivers. *Marau Sound*—Tavanipupu Island in Marau Sound is called the Jewel of Guadalcanal. Accommodations there were discussed earlier. Plane service in or out is just once a week, but in such an unusual retreat, a week should be about right. You could return earlier by boat.

THE OUTER ISLANDS

While in Honiara, go to the Coral Sea Shipping Company office on the main street in the center of town. Ask about the sailing of the *MV Iuminao*. For air services visit the Solair office in town. Solair is the domestic airline that serves 22 Solomon Island destinations. Ask to see John Baura, the manager, who'll give good air transport advice. Using these two sources, plus the Visitor's Bureau, your future in the Solomons will be well taken care of.

SAVO ISLAND AND IRON BOTTOM SOUND

The waters north and west of Honiara are known as Iron Bottom Sound. This was the scene of violent naval battles with an incredible loss of life. Here the hulks of fighting ships form artificial reefs, and have attracted hordes of fish and a variety of coral life. Some of the wrecks are quite shallow and these scenes of death and destruction draw divers from all over the world. The water here is clear and warm.

Beyond Iron Bottom Sound, otherwise known as the "Slot," the small volcanic island of Savo stands out sharply. The special attraction of this island, other than the nearby naval battles, are the megapode birds who bury their eggs in the sand. You can negotiate the often choppy 22 miles by small boat from Honiara in three or four hours. But, unless you're into bleak islands, strange birds, and wet sea trips, you may be happier elsewhere.

THE WESTERN PROVINCES

The Western Provinces encompass the islands of Rendova, New Georgia, Kolombangara, Gizo, Ranogga, Vella Lavella, Choiseul, Treasury and Shortlands. Some of the loveliest lagoons and coral islands are in this area. Marovo Lagoon is one of the largest in the world and is dotted with scores of tiny atolls.

To get there, consider one of the best short sea trips in the Pacific, the voyage of the *Iuminao*. Having done it, we recommend it highly. But before describing the voyage a few remarks about going to sea in the Solomons are necessary. First, the vessels that serve the outer islands are working ships of about 150 feet and smaller that carry cargo and 50 or so deck passengers. Some of them like the *Iuminao* have two first class cabins, but meals are not provided. This sounds awkward, but isn't. Think of it as going camping. On the *Iuminao* it's camping in an air conditioned cabin with white sheets on the bunks, a small refrigerator, and a fully plumbed bath.

Coming into Viru, New Georgia on the M.V. Iuminao

For the trip we purchased all provisions at Honiara shops, found fresh fruit available at stops along the way, and forgotten essentials were available from a small snack bar aboard.

This ship sails at 2:30 PM on Sundays, and arrives in Gizo late afternoon on Monday. En route it makes 11 stops, then returns on Wednesday. Round-trip fare is about $80 per person.

A brief narrative of that voyage may help. In the straits between Guadalcanal and the Russell Islands we did some pitching and rolling, then pulled into Yandina in the Russells. I remember this small group from the war but now as then, other than the big Lever Coconut plantation, there's little to do or see. The trip improves after Yandina.

From the Russells the voyage continued across 80 or so miles of the Solomon Sea, a rough patch occasionally, into Blanche Channel southwest of Vanguna Island. Viru, in a placidly pretty harbor, was next. From this picture-postcard village, you can go by canoe or small boat to Seghe, a nearby village, and from there to the *Uepi Island Resort*. Plenty of white beaches at Uepi, and extremely good diving, but you must bring your own gear. Rates are $60 a double including meals. From Honiara you can fly there on one of Solair's nine-seater Islander Aircraft. Contact: Roco Ltd., Seghe, Marovo Lagoon, Solomon Islands.

From Viru the ship continued up sparkling Blanche Channel between Rendova and New Georgia. We paused at Egelo on Rendova where passengers came and went and cargo was shuttled. Then came Sasavele, followed by Munda which is close to vibrant Roviana Lagoon. Here there's another good inn, the *Munda Rest House*. They have 10 self-contained rooms, at $18 a double. Power canoes are available for excursions into the lagoon, including the half-day trip to Plum Pudding Island where John F. Kennedy swam ashore the night his PT boat was hit by the Japanese destroyer. The coral and marine life makes this area exceptionally good for snorkeling. Meals will be provided on these excursions. You could leave the ship at Munda and fly back to Honiara, or wait until the ship reappears a week later.

After Munda the ship calls at Nora on New Georgia, Ringi on Rendova, and at sunset pulls into the small island and town of Gizo.

Gizo

This second largest town in the Solomons is the administrative center for the Western Provinces. The pretty little island of Gizo itself measures about three miles by seven miles. It's also the last stop for the *Iuminao* which ties up at the wharf for the night. Here the best thing to do is sleep aboard (if you're returning with the ship) but, for happy hour and dinner, go ashore. Only steps from the wharf there is a comfortable and friendly hotel, the *Gizo*, which is the gathering place for most of the local expats. Clustered round the bar you'll find them eager, as the Aussies say, to "shout" or "be shouted a drink." With little encouragement, they'll point out the area's possibilities, the best being easy access by powered canoe to dozens of tiny islands with fine beaches. There's good fishing and snorkeling, as well as villages where you can buy fine ebony carvings.

Food at the Gizo is good, not outstanding, but far better than the cold food you've been eating on the *Iuminao.* Passengers who leave the ship in order to fly back to Honiara will find the rooms fully plumbed, comfortable, and cooled by fans. Rates are $35 a double.

Our evening at the Gizo was filled with good cheer, and the next morning, feeling a little the worse for wear, we sailed for Honiara, a day and a half away.

Visitors who stay in Gizo can continue west to Vella Lavella Island by unscheduled copra boat or canoe. The point of arrival will probably be Liapari village, 10 miles away at the south end of the island. Fare will be no more than $10 round trip. Accommodations there range from meager to non-existent, which makes it good for examining outback island life. Best thing to do is ask around Gizo for a round-trip sailing, pack a lunch, and do the trip in one day.

For visitors returning to Honiara by air, there is daily service from Gizo's Nusatupe Airstrip on a nearby island. En route to Honiara, Solair usually stops at Ringi, Munda, Seghe, and perhaps Yandina in the Russells.

Choiseul

The big island north of Vella Lavella is best reached by air from Gizo. The problem is that when you land at Choiseul Bay at the far western end of the island, you're really nowhere. There are few roads, no services, a hard place to deal with. Unless you're a dedicated trailwise trekker, you'll be happier elsewhere.

Santa Ysabel

The long island southeast of Choiseul is well off beaten paths too, but at the Buala-Fera area where the plane from Honiara lands there are simple and inexpensive rest houses. This is where most of the Ysabel people live. Headhunters years ago from the Roviana area to the south are said to have killed off most of the inhabitants in the northwest. Solomon Island culture here is pure and undiluted, the very place for serious study, but perhaps not aimless wandering.

The Florida Islands

Tulagi, which until 1942 was the capital of the Solomon Islands, was my first South Pacific landfall in 1944. Then it was the scene of considerable military activity. Now it's a sleepy backwater where, other than the Japanese fish processing plant and a marine repair slipway, there's little to see. Ships from Honiara go to Tulagi twice a week, about 35 sea miles across historic Iron Bottom Sound.

The other two large Florida Islands, Nggela and Small Nggela, are beautifully scenic and have interesting villages, but there are few amenities and very few roads. You commute to these islands by boat from Tulagi, then walk or travel the coast by canoe.

For accommodations in this area, the *Anuha Island Resort* has recently been built on a 150-acre island off the north coast of Nggela. It's 15 minutes from Honiara by Solair, and this world-class holiday facility, with windsurfing, scuba diving, water skiing, pool lounging, and evening entertainment, may now be the most prestigious hotel in the Solomons. Contact: Anuha Island Resort, PO Box 133, Honiara, Solomon Islands.

Malaita Island

This second largest of the Solomon Islands is jungle-covered, mountainous, and inhabited by nearly 80,000—making it more populous than even Guadalcanal. But because there's not enough arable land, many people leave for employment elsewhere. A lot of them are in Honiara.

In the past Malaitans have been feared and disliked by other islanders. Their quick response to a slight, their pride and overstrong adherence to tradition, has given them poor press away from Malaita. Even among Malaitans there is rivalry. Coastal people don't get along with the mountain dwellers, a sort of mutual intolerance exists, and there are still Malaitans in the back country whom it's best to avoid.

To Malaita by Air—There is a daily flight from Honiara to Auki on the southwest coast, a 30-minute flight that goes over the Florida Islands. $85 round trip.

Getting off the small inter-island plane at Auki, one is sharply reminded of its remoteness. Directly behind the termi-

Village in Langa Langa Lagoon, Malaita Island

nal shed is a timeless Solomon Island village, thatched and on stilts. Here the essence of the tropics is strong—a blending of the scent of cooking fires, the moist odor of vegetation, the busy sounds of chickens, and the distant laughter of children. By minibus, the ride to Auki seven miles away is $1.50.

Coming from or Going to Auki by Sea—Take time to make the seven-hour sea trip one way. We recommend the trip from Auki to Honiara since it's done in daylight, departs Auki at 9:30 AM and arrives at 4:30 PM.

A night at sea aboard the *Compass Rose II* is not what dreams are made of. There are no private cabins, only deck and first class. Deck is just that, and first class entitles you to occupy a tattered, usually crowded lounge. There is no food available, no water, and the fetid toilets are awash.

During the day, if it's not rough, the blue sea and magnificent views of the Florida Islands make the trip well worthwhile. Go prepared with lunch, some beverages, then find a place on the boat deck and settle in. Fare first class is $12 per person.

Where to Stay in Auki—Run by kind and thoughtful Malaitans, the *Auki Lodge* has six twin rooms with fans and cold water baths. Rates are $17.50 double. Food is adequate, but the best thing to order is chicken curry, then ask for the curry powder and lace it up again. Their beef is tough or, as another guest described it, "resilient." For breakfast if you order fruit you'll get wonderful papaya, lots of pineapple and, if you ask, even a chilled drinking coconut. There's a comfortable veranda at the Lodge, a good place to sit in the cool of the evening and watch the sun sink over the palms by the harbor.

Set in considerable beauty on Langa Langa Lagoon, Auki has no frills whatsoever. Several years ago there were a couple of simple restaurants, but they're gone now and, other than a pair of shops selling canned food, bread, kerosene, and beer or the market—selling fish, taro, yams, and betel nuts—the only place to eat and sleep is the Auki Lodge.

Langa Langa Lagoon, the Artificial Islands, Shell Money, Shark Worship—The artificial islands of Langa Langa Lagoon

Auki Lodge, the only accommodation in Auki

and the Lau Lagoon in northeast Malaita are among the most unusual destinations in these islands. Langa Langa at Auki is the most accessible, and the trip down this lagoon by long skinny outboard canoe is a worthwhile (and often wet) run. The people at the Lodge can organize a canoe and guide for the three-hour round trip. Mornings are preferable. Cost is $22.50 for two.

Some of the man-made islands you'll see are fairly new, others over a hundred years old, but all were constructed by building up coral boulders on a shallow reef. Sand was then brought from shore and used to fill in the gaps. Next houses were built and sometimes palm trees grew, but for water the people had to depend on rain. Why were they built? Some say they were constructed to provide safety from marauding hill people. Current belief is they were built to get away from shoreside mosquitoes. If you choose not to take the entire canoe trip, one such man-made island is right across the harbor from Auki. To go ashore there you'll have to pay $1 to a dour looking man.

At the far end of the canoe run in Langa Langa is the Laulasi-Alite area. Here visitors are taken ashore, where they can watch women drill holes in tiny shells and string them together on lengths of jungle vine, each one about a fathom long. They're referred to as fathoms, and can be used as cash, or more importantly as bride price money. The going bride price on Malaita is now 10 sets of shell money at $150 each.

Here at Laulasi priests used to call sharks by beating gongs, and the sharks were said to appear. Shark calling, a form of ancestor worship, has been called off, at least for visiting outsiders. Our boatman frowned and said it was taboo.

A Note on Lagoon Trips—When thinking about lagoon trips, you may visualize gliding over clear smooth water to reasonably close destinations. Not always so. The water in lagoons can chop up smartly, depending on the tide. There may be swift currents and a trip, often several hours long, can be wet, uncomfortable, and sometimes perilous. Remember too that you have to go back the same way. Boatmen in Langa Langa do predictably safe work, but it's always best to ask a number of questions before setting out.

Visitors could do the Langa Langa junket in one full day from Honiara. For $85 per person, Solair will fly you to Auki, arrange for the canoe, provide lunch, and fly you back to Honiara.

Near Auki-Lilisiana Village—Lilisiana is a large thatched and stilted village inhabited by people who used to live on Langa Langa's artificial islands. To get there, ask someone to paddle you over. It's very close. You can wander about, observe island life, examine their shell money, and stroll to a very good beach. You can then walk back along the coast to Auki, about a mile and a half.

The Kwaibala River—If you walk south from Auki toward nearby Ambu village, you'll pass a bit of the Kwaibala River, a restful walk along this clear stream with a rock-strewn bottom. It's quite shallow, but there are a couple of good pools to loll in.

For a good difficult trek ask at the Lodge for a guide to *Riba Cave*. It's on the road toward Dukwari village about an hour and a half away. If you're into wet sloppy caves filled with swallows, you'll be delighted with this one.

Lilisiana village, Auki, Malaita

Other Parts of Malaita

Depending on weather, roads on Malaita are either slow or impassable. Going north from Auki the road runs up and around the north end to Fouia, about 75 miles. South of Auki a track runs some 50 miles. The rest of Malaita, filled with mountains and rain forests, is accessible only by foot, air and sea. It's a wild, often inhospitable island.

Going north from Auki, it's 50 bouncy miles to Malu'u. The bus costs $4, but sometimes you can get a boat from Auki to Malu'u, or even beyond. These are boats, not canoes, small trading vessels 40 to 50 feet long that are safe, raw, and inexpensive.

At Malu'u there's a rest house, clean and adequate, for $18 double. They'll provide food, if asked.

From Malu'u you can hire canoes for the trip to Lau Lagoon, but it's a long boat ride. You could, if transport is available, continue on another 25–30 miles to Fouia, only a short boat ride to the big artificial island of Sulufou. The only problem then is that there is no place to stay at Fouia. If you can arrange the logistics, the Lau Lagoon is worthwhile. They say there are 50 artificial islands in this lagoon.

Going south from Auki, the road, mostly a track, runs south about 60 miles to Su'u, a jungly trip with good views of the sea and lots of coastal villages. But the best way to get at this area is by boat. Check out the sailing of the *Regina M.* from Honiara, a deck-passage boat even more basic than the *Compass Rose II.* Check out sailings of boats from Auki too. Either way plan to take your own food and camp out on deck.

San Cristobal Island, Santa Cruz and Reef Islands

San Cristobal to the south of Malaita shares with Malaita a violent past. Professional island murderers were still in business on San Cristobal at the turn of the century, and fighting was active between coastal and hill people.

As to cannibalism, some experts say that islanders ate their enemies to emphasize supremacy. Others say that by eating an enemy you acquired his *mana* or spiritual power, his "face" or reputation. Those days are gone now.

Solair flies to the district center, Kira Kira, on the north coast of San Cristobal where simple housing is available. But, if you are seeking the most remote destination in the Solomon Islands, continue on another 310 miles to the *Ngarando Island Resort* at Mohawk Bay in the Reef Islands. This off-the-map place has two furnished bed-sitting rooms with kitchen and bath. Rates are $30 double.

The Ngarando is located on an unusually rich coral lagoon that's filled with marine life and fat crayfish. Boats and canoes are obtainable, and the folks who operate the resort also run a trading post. You'll hear nothing but Pijin spoken, and you can watch the day-to-day dealings in copra, turtle shells, crocodile skins and other exotica. For special people, this is a special place. To get there, fly from Kira Kira, or take the twice-monthly ship from Honiara.

THE POLYNESIAN OUTLIERS

If you're lucky, very patient, or both, the epitome of going to sea in the Solomons is aboard one of the government ships that sails to the Polynesian Outliers—to Sikaiana, Rennell, Tikopea, Bellona, Ontong Java. No one quite knows why these Polynesian enclaves exist on the fringes of black Melanesia, but they're Polynesian nonetheless—albeit not as sophisticated as their Samoan, Tongan, Cook or Society Island cousins.

Rennell Island

One hundred-twenty-five miles south of Honiara, Rennell (50 by 10 miles wide) is not a rich island. Growing food is difficult, but enough coconuts, papaya, yams, and other crops are grown to sustain life. Other than the big lake on the island, the bauxite that's mined there, and the fact that these people are Polynesian, Rennell has little to offer.

Because at one time Rennell's culture was considered fragile, the islands were closed to all Europeans for about 25 years, nearly until World War II. This added a mystique to the island which it probably doesn't deserve. You can fly to Rennell on Solair from Honiara, or take the twice-monthly government ship. Once there, you'll have to find an islander to put you up.

Bellona

Nature on Bellona (six miles by two), a close neighbor of Rennell, has been a little more benevolent. Crops grow well and there's plenty of spring water. But Bellonans, like the Rennellese are inclined to be testy with each other and strangers. And like other Polynesians, they share a mutual distrust of Melanesian Solomon Islanders.

Check with Solair for flights to Bellona from Honiara.

Tikopea

Six hundred miles east of Honiara, Tikopea is well off by itself. It's reported to be a happy, prosperous place, and the folks there live well on what their volcanic island produces. They're also known for their kindness to each other and to strangers. The only way in is by sea.

Sikiaina

Small and crowded Sikiaina lies 130 miles east of Malaita Island. It's a pretty island inhabited by handsome men and women who love music and dancing in a very Polynesian way. Sikiaina has no airport or hotel, and the only access is by sea.

Ontong Java

Three hundred miles north of Honiara, this coral atoll, also known as Lord Howe Island, consists of several small coral islands set around the lagoon. The handsome, heavily tattooed locals sustain themselves by gardening, fishing, and selling copra and trochus shells, from which buttons are made.

These Polynesians are extremely isolated and, other than the government ship, some copra boats, and a few yachts sailing south from Micronesia, they have little contact with the outside world. There's no hotel or rest house, but a trip to this atoll on the bi-monthly government ship would be something to remember.

Final note—When you leave the Solomons, be prepared to pay a $10 Solomon Island airport departure tax.

9

VANUATU

Vanuatu, a cluster of 13 islands and 16 small ones in the southwest Pacific, 1,300 miles east of Australia, has had a kaleidoscopic past. Formerly known as the New Hebrides, it was administered as a British-French Condominium, referred to as "pandemonium," and the events surrounding independence in 1980 had Gilbert and Sullivan qualities. Then there are the languages they speak: French, English, 105 indigenous tongues, and the wonderful common language, Bislama.

The drama and color continue. There are still plots, counterplots, and the present Prime Minister, Father Walter Lini, a New Zealand-trained Anglican priest from Pentecost Island, tends to make everyone a little nervous. He worries Australia and New Zealand by accusing them of neo-colonialism and of failure to provide independence to the Aboriginals and Maoris. Father Lini antagonizes the French by saying their activities in Tahiti and New Caledonia are militaristic and that they should provide autonomy to the rebel Kanaks in New Caledonia.

As far as I know, he hasn't yet suggested an independent state for the American Indians, but he's got a lot of people concerned about Vanuatu's alliance and solidarity with Libya, his accepting guidance from Cuba, and offering Libyan-trained Vanuatans to help in New Caledonia's Kanak independence movement. Father Lini also suggests that, while he sees little future for white people on Vanuatu, he is not reluctant about accepting aid from them. Vanuatu exists almost entirely on aid from the developed countries and on what the tourists, mostly from New Zealand and Australia, leave behind. There are problems in Vanuatu. They sound malignant when read about in the press. But arrival in Port Vila, Vanuatu's capital and usual port of entry on the island of Efate, is accomplished quickly and easily. Port Vila, as it has for years, looks like a tropical version of a French Mediterranean resort. Its setting at the foot of green hills within a magnificent natural harbor makes it one of the most beautiful capitals in the Pacific. And when it comes to the amenities sophisticated travelers require, Port Vila has them all—fine restaurants, French, American, Chinese, Mexican, or Aussie-style food, palatial resort hotels, smart shops, trendy bars, and a harbor filled with foreign yachts.

Unfortunately they do have storms, and on our last visit we saw the results. Three months after the fact, Vila still looked war-torn. There were houses in town with roofs missing, shops with all their windows out, warehouses along the docks buckled in. Several yachts were beached, and the interisland ship *Konanda* lay wounded at her dock.

It takes time to recover from such an event, but nature is more resilient than man. On the day after the storm all the leaves were blown from the trees, banana trees were left bare, most of the fronds from coconut palms were carried away. But a week later new buds were out and nature was busily repairing herself.

Man's efforts are somewhat slower, and many buildings we'd known before were in shambles and in need of repair. Rossi's Hotel, known as the Raffles of Port Vila, was tattered but still housing guests and turning out good food. The Solaise, a moderately priced hotel, our favorite in town, was out of commission completely, and so were a number of other restaurants, hotels, and public buildings. But day by day as Father Lini made his inflammatory pronouncements, repairs were made and, when we left, Vila was busily entertaining visitors. The *Fairstar* had sailed into port with 1,500 Aussies, Japanese tourists were appearing, as were planeloads of enthusiastic Aussies and Kiwis. Yachts were filling the harbor and everyone was having a good time. We were too.

The Land and Her People

The 73 islands of Vanuatu, formerly called the New Hebrides, stretch in a north-south direction for 500 miles, and have a land mass of 6,500 square miles. Some of the small islands are coral atolls, the larger ones are volcanic in origin, and the terrain ranges from forest-covered mountains to grassy uplands to tiny reef-enclosed islets.

As to their volcanic origin, the process continues, and these islands are referred to as being within a "ring of fire." Literally they are, for five of the 500 active volcanoes of the world are here—Benbow on Ambryn, Yasur on Tanna, Lopevi and Gaua and a submarine volcano off Tongoa Island.

Port Vila on Efate has a population of 15,000 and it's here most of the foreigners live and most of the holiday activities happen. Away from Port Vila conditions change rapidly and, other than two or three resorts at a distance from town, the island reverts to elemental Melanesian life style. There are some copra, coffee, and cacao plantations, subsistence plots of land growing yams, taro, manioc, bananas, and a number of isolated villages. All of them are connected by a 90-mile road that circles the island. The interior is mountainous, jungle-covered, and mostly uninhabited.

Next in importance after Port Vila is the town of Luganville, called Santo, a town of 5,500 on the south coast of the biggest island in the group, Espiritu Santo. Here and nearby 125,000 Americans, Australians, and New Zealanders were stationed during World War II. It was a staging area for the Pacific campaign, and it was from several airfields near Luganville that bombers conducted raids on Japanese-held islands.

Evidence of those days lingers, there are Quonset huts still in use as warehouses, some overgrown air raid shelters, and all over the island you'll see lengths of the meshwork steel once used to surface the runways of hastily built airstrips. It's used now for fences, walkways and small bridges.

Copra, some fish processing, and cattle keep Luganville going, but only just, for life there looks somnolent. Except for the divers who come to explore "Million Dollar Point," and the wreck of the *President Coolidge*, there are few tourists. Except

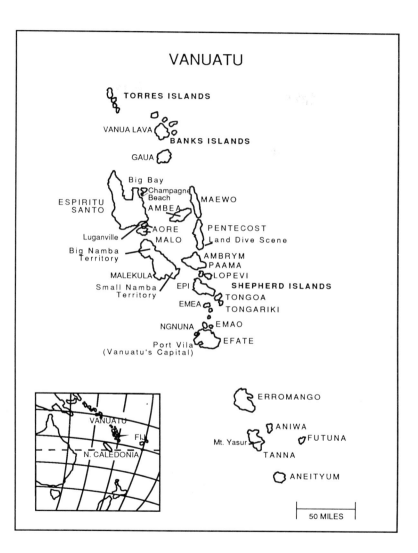

VANUATU

TORRES ISLANDS

VANUA LAVA
BANKS ISLANDS

GAUA

Big Bay
Champagne
Beach
MAEWO
ESPIRITU
SANTO
AMBEA

AORE
PENTECOST
Luganville
MALO
Land Dive Scene

Big Namba
Territory
AMBRYM
PAAMA
MALEKULA
LOPEVI
Small Namba
EPI
SHEPHERD ISLANDS
Territory
TONGOA
EMEA
TONGARIKI

NGNUNA
EMAO
Port Vila
EFATE
(Vanuatu's Capital)

VANUATU
FIJI
N. CALEDONIA

ERROMANGO

ANIWA
FUTUNA
Mt. Yasur
TANNA

ANEITYUM

50 MILES

Coastal scene, Vanuatu

for this southwest corner of 75-mile long, 45-mile wide Espiritu Santo, the island is one of mountainous jungle and life for the tribespeople in the interior is much the same as it's always been.

It was on Espiritu Santo that the pre-independence comic opera occurred, events that escalated into what is now called the Coconut War. Roughly this is what happened.

Life for the French and British under the pre-independence Condominium had been confusing enough, but they were badly alarmed when Father Lini became head of the Independence Party circa 1979 and said that after independence foreign-held land would be returned to the indigenous people.

Enter at this point Jimmy Stevens, a bearded nonconformist who was part-English and part-islander and who lived on Espiritu Santo. Jimmy had at one time felt that the black man should have the land the white man had taken from him. He'd even urged his people to go and squat on French-owned land, which they did, and for which Jimmy was thrown in jail. Released, he continued his protest and was in trouble once more. But by now he was an established martyr.

A strange thing happened though, for Jimmy changed his point of view and began to support the efforts of a group of Americans to buy land on Espiritu Santo. The Americans were planning to buy lots that could eventually be used for retirement or holiday purposes. But that ended badly because when officials in Vila heard about this, they became fearful of an American colony in their backyard, and instituted new regulations and taxes. Most Americans pulled out. The French land owners, however, saw possibilities of staying on after independence. Jimmy Stevens not only said this was possible, but he drew up a separate constitution for Espiritu Santo, called the country *Vemarana*, and declared himself head of the new state.

On May 27, 1980 Jimmy Stevens' men, armed with bows and arrows, entered Luganville and took it over. The comic-opera war was underway but, other than bloody noses, hurt feelings, and the exodus of hundreds of Luganville residents, no one was hurt or killed. Jimmy was in full power, but the act killed the economy on Espiritu Santo. No copra was going out, nothing was coming in.

On the eve of independence there were mixed feelings about the revolt. Some of the French, seeing the possibility of Espiritu Santo becoming a French colony, were elated. The British saw it as a troublesome inconvenience and Father Lini, concerned about a rift in the new country, appealed to the British and French for military force to put Jimmy down. At first they weren't enthusiastic but finally, with independence a week away, troops were sent to put down the revolt. A short time later a force from Papua New Guinea arrived, completed the job, and arrested Jimmy Stevens. The Coconut War was over. The only casualties were a death on Tanna Island, where there was a movement sympathetic to the attempt, and Jimmy's son who was killed while trying to run a roadblock.

Jimmy Stevens was sent to prison at Port Vila, where he remains to this day. And the country under Father Lini is, with the exception of possible links with Libya and Cuba, a non-aligned parliamentary nation.

In spite of plots, counterplots, even independence, most of the native people, called Ni-Vanuatans, live as they always have by subsistence farming—taro, yams, manioc, bananas, fish, and pork. But with independence, the question of just who owned which parcels of land became a problem. So far the matter has not been solved, nor has all foreign-owned property been turned over to the people. By law, the new government got the property back, but most of the big copra plantations have been leased back to the original owners.

There are areas in Vanuatu where independence makes not a whit of difference. The tradition-bound remote people on Pentecost, Malekula, Ambrym, Erromanga, and Tanna are little changed. Most of the Big Namba tribesmen in north Malekula could care less who runs the country. The Little Nambas in the south feel the same way—they just want to be left alone to follow the ways of "custom."

In distant regions women still wear fiber mats or grass skirts, some of the men like the Big Nambas wear penis sheaths, which polite Victorian explorers had great difficulty describing and contented themselves with mentioning the women's skirts.

Some Malekula men still pierce their nasal septa and insert pieces of wood or bone. They encourage the tusks of hogs to grow in a full circle, unpleasant for the pig. And they communicate with the ghosts of ancestors by drinking kava. More of kava later. The circumcision ceremony, lengthy and arduous, the "boot camp of adolescence," is still practiced, and those who don't finish can't marry. Life in some parts of Vanuatu is still brutal and short. The rules of "custom" are many but, as those who still practice "custom" say, "The custom road is very hard, very strict, it allows no chance of escape. If I make a mistake I will die. But custom is strong, and if you are loyal to its rules, you will be strong. Custom will protect you."

Then there is the Pidgin language, Bislama, which probably is a corruption of the name of the sea slug, "Beche de mer"—the delicacy New Hebrideans sold to Chinese and European traders. The language developed from these early contacts is marvelously creative and descriptive. Try your hand at it. For example:

A saw—"pull em e com, push em e go."

A brassiere—"basket blong titty"

Thank you very much—"Tangku tumas"

How much?—"Hamas long hem"

Something wrong with the car engine—"Engine blong car bagarap"

Goodbye—"Tata"

What is your name?—"Wanem nem blong yu?"

Food—"Kae kae"

And with kae kae in mind, the national dish is called lap lap. Lap lap is a melange of yams, manioc, and taro, to which coconut milk and sometimes fish and pork are added. It's then folded into a banana leaf and steamed. It tastes better than it looks.

History in Brief

The man who put the New Hebrides on the map was Pedro Ferdinand de Quiros, a navigator working for the King of Spain. The King wanted to colonize some islands in the Pacific, the Solomons in particular and, with that in mind, de Quiros was sent out in 1605.

His fleet of three ships, which carried assorted priests, sailors, and soldiers, somehow missed the Solomons. Instead they found the island now known as Espiritu Santo in 1606. De Quiros was delighted with his find, and decided to establish a colony which he named "*Tierra Austral del Espiritu Santo.*" But things began to go wrong. Spaniards stole from the natives, who responded in kind, and fighting started. Then the Spaniards became sick from eating poisonous fish, probably from malaria too, and in the end the Spaniards left in disillusionment.

It wasn't until 160 years later that the Frenchman Bougainville sailed in. He was unenthusiastic, but looked and charted, before he left. Captain Cook arrived in 1768. He went ashore on Espiritu Santo and later on Erromanga, which he found to be hostile. Then, after naming the group the New Hebrides, after Scotland, he too sailed away.

In 1825, 57 years later, Peter Dillon an explorer, discovered sandalwood on Erromanga. This was a profitable discovery, for the British found that the Chinese would trade large amounts of tea for sandalwood which they used for cabinets, coffins, perfume and incense. As a result, foreign ships and traders poured in and hungrily gathered sandalwood. They cheated, bribed, and stole, and in no time relations between the natives and traders were strained. Natives killed and ate white men. White men responded with epidemics of smallpox, measles, and venereal disease, then added insult to injury by kidnapping the natives for work in Australian cane fields. This practice was referred to as "blackbirding."

Nevertheless, between "blackbirding" and gathering sandalwood, the white man was profitably busy in these islands. Then a third dimension arrived—the missionaries. In 1839 Reverend John Williams of the London Missionary Society landed on Erromanga. His reception ashore was not a happy one, for he was set upon, clubbed and killed. For organized Christianity in England, this was a challenge, and soon more missionaries came. And as competitors, so did British and French trading companies.

French immigrants began to land about 1883. In 1887 the British government, not wanting French supremacy, joined

France and set up a joint Naval Commission, the grandparent of the Condominium. Its purpose was to protect lives and property. With two battleships (one French, one British) and the pro-British Presbyterians, they made a ludicrous attempt at creating order and in 1906 the French-British team officially became the Condominium.

The result was two governors—British and French—two judges, and down the line, with two police departments, two currencies, two departments of education, even two sets of laws. Among other problems, British law was stricter than French, a bone of contention.

It seemed however, that the French were more serious about their future, for by 1920 there were six times as many French as British. In this way the New Hebrides limped along until 1970, when the New Hebrideans began to show interest in running their own country. in response, both Britain and France sent men to assist in the eventual transition.

Andrew Stuart came from Britain and Jean Jacques Robert from France. But unfortunately they had different points of view. Socially and politically, they saw each other as little as possible. It was an association that became even more strained when English-speaking Father Lini won an election and became head of the Vanuaaku Independence Party.

The French, hoping to maintain their presence after independence, were disturbed particularly by the thought that a poor position in the New Hebrides would create problems for them in troubled New Caledonia, thereby threatening the loss of New Caledonia's rich gold and manganese mines.

At this point, as we saw earlier, Jimmy Stevens and his Coconut War entered the drama, eventually leading to independence in 1980 and the curious posture of Vanuatu today. It's a country that bears watching. For the present though, it's a cracking good place for a holiday.

How to Get There by Air

From the U.S.—Fiji is sure to be a jumping-off place. Get there as discussed in the Fiji chapter, then come to Vanuatu on the once-a-week Air Pacific flight from Nadi (two hours).

From Nouméa, New Caledonia—U.T.A. flies in daily to Port Vila (50 minutes). Air Caledonia flies in once a week.

From Honiara, the Solomons—Air Nauru has two flights a week (two hours). Solair, the Solomon Islands airline, plans a weekly flight to Port Vila via Espiritu Santo.

From Sydney or Brisbane, Australia—Ansett flies in and out every Sunday.

By Sea

Occasional freighters will carry passengers from Suva, Honiara, Port Moresby, or Apia. They're rare though. But if you're inclined to cruise ships, 30 to 40 of them, each carrying up to 1,600 usually jovial Aussies, come in each year. Ask your travel agent about Cunard, Sitmar, Five Star, P & O, Royal Viking. For shorter trips among Vanuatu's islands, many trading vessels in Vila harbor take passengers. See section on "The Outer Islands."

Inter-island ship, The Konanda—*the best for passenger travel*

Immigration

All visitors must have valid passports, onward tickets, and sufficient funds for support. No visas required for up to 30 days.

Health

Basic medical services are available in most areas. Good medical and dental care are available in Port Vila and Luganville. If visiting the outer islands anti-malarial prophylaxis should be taken. Talk this matter over with your doctor before leaving home.

Water is potable in Vila and Luganville, but check locally in remote areas. There are no dangerous animals in Vanuatu.

Currency

The Vatu, almost on a par with the U.S. dollar, is the local currency. American Express, Visa, Diner's Card, and Mastercard are accepted in most restaurants and hotels. There are plenty of banks in Port Vila and Luganville for most transactions. Australian dollars are also accepted. Westpac Bank is open 8:30 AM to 3 PM, ANZ from 8 PM to 2 PM, Hong Kong and Shanghai Bank from 8:30 AM to 11:30 AM and from 1:30 PM to 3:30 PM, and Banque Indosuez de Vanuatu from 8 AM to 11 AM and 1:30 PM to 3 PM.

Time Zone

Time is 11 hours ahead of Greenwich Mean Time, 16 hours ahead of Eastern Standard Time, 19 hours ahead of Pacific Standard Time.

Newspapers, Radio, & Telephone

The *Tam Tam Newspaper* put out by the government comes out weekly in English, Bislama, and French. It's fine for local news but, for international news, pick up an Australian or New Zealand paper at one of the big hotels. Radio Vila broadcasts in three languages twice a day. Telephone service for overseas calls goes by relay through Fiji or Australia.

Power

220 volts AC.

Climate

The best weather is May through October, averaging 74°F/ 20°C. It's hot, rainy and humid January through April and averages 85°F/23°C.

Languages

English, French and colorful Bislama are spoken.

Holidays

New Year's Day; Good Friday; Easter Monday; Labor Day (May 1); Independence Day (July 30); Assumption Day; Constitution Day (October 5); Unity Day (November 29); Christmas; and Boxing Day (December 26).

Tipping

As in most of Oceania, tipping is not necessary and not advised. Also there is no bargaining, except with taxi drivers.

PORT VILA

After going through customs at Bauerfield Airport, four miles from Port Vila, go to the Snack Bar and change enough dollars or Traveler's Checks into Vatus for the $4 taxi ride into town. Money can be changed later at your hotel or a bank— usually the bank exchange is better. Then, if you don't have a reservation, check the airport list of hotels; it's on a wall near the exit.

Where to Stay

If you want room service, a swimming pool, in-room video, a choice of dining rooms, and a beach with watersports, you need an international class hotel. These are your choices. Keep in

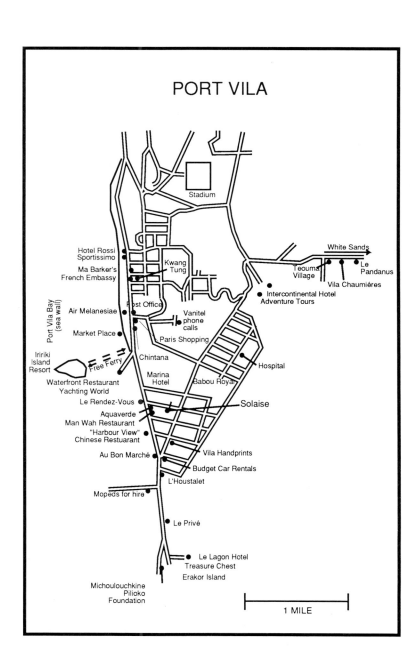

PORT VILA

Stadium

Hotel Rossi
Sportissimo

Ma Barker's
French Embassy

Kwang
Tung

White Sands

Teouma
Village

Le
Pandanus

Vila Chaumiéres

Intercontinental Hotel
Adventure Tours

Air Melanesiae

Post Office

Port Vila Bay
(sea wall)

Market Place

Vanitel
phone
calls

Paris Shopping

Iririki
Island
Resort

Chintana

Free Ferry

Hospital

Waterfront Restaurant
Yachting World

Marina
Hotel

Babou Royal

Le Rendez-Vous

Solaise

Aquaverde
Man Wah Restaurant
"Harbour View"
Chinese Restuarant

Au Bon Marché

Vila Handprints

Budget Car Rentals

L'Houstalet

Mopeds for hire

Le Privé

Le Lagon Hotel
Treasure Chest
Erakor Island

Michoulouchkine
Pilioko
Foundation

1 MILE

mind that there is a 10% government hotel tax wherever you stay.

Le Lagon—Located at the mouth of Erakor Lagoon two miles from Port Vila, this hotel has 145 rooms and bungalows. All resort amenities are here. Rates are $85 a double.

Intercontinental Island Inn—This is on a lagoon with beach two miles from town. It has four restaurants, three bars, entertainment, pool, tennis courts, and a convention center. VCR for your room is $2.75. $90 a double.

Iririki Island Resort—On an island in Port Vila harbor, this hotel is connected by a free ferry from town. Rooms are in bungalows with views of the sea and town. All amenities are colorfully provided. $125 a double.

White Sands Country Club—This accommodation is 11 miles from town and is $135 a double. It provides a dignified sort of opulence, set in a grove of coconut palms by a good beach. There is a restaurant, and the hotel provides transport to and from town.

Port Vila in the distance

For hotels that are less pricey, and perhaps with self-contained cooking facilities, consider these choices.

Solaise Hotel—This has long been our favorite and, although it was badly damaged in a recent storm, it's back in business now and better than ever. It has regular hotel rooms, and also rooms with cooking facilities. On the garden-like grounds there is a swimming pool, and the restaurant is excellent. $40 a double.

Hotel Rossi—Rossi's, with its Terrace Bar facing the sea and its entrance facing the main street, is a well loved institution that's seen the ebb and flow of Pacific history, including World War II. But partly because of age, partly because of that last storm, Rossi's has deteriorated. You can still get good lobster, coconut crab and sandwiches here. The beer is still cold, the company usually good, and prices continue to be modest. Just try to ignore the exposed wires in the bar, the shameful state of the toilets, the peeling paint, and the weeds where flowers were. The rooms at $32 a double are clean.

The Marina Motel—Run by amiable New Zealanders, Alwyn and Roger Elliot, these self-contained units are clean, comfortable, and you can do your own cooking. Then in the evening, sit on your own balcony and enjoy the best view in Port Vila. The Marina is right in town, handy to everything. $40 a double.

Teouma Village Resort—Located on a lagoon two miles from town, these bungalows or townhouses surrounded by gardens are good group or family choices. There is a pool, but no restaurant, $35 a double.

Vila Chaumiere's—Next door to the Teouma, this place has a series of hexagonal-shaped bungalows for up to four people. They have waterbeds, fully equipped kitchens, and a swimming pool. $32 a double.

Olympic Hotel—Located in the center of town, this hotel has rooms with or without cooking facilities. With its central location, its restaurant, and international dial telephones, it is particularly good for the business traveler. $45 a double.

Erakor Island Resort—This is an idyllic retreat on an island two miles from Vila. Housing is in bungalows, some classified as honeymoon bungalows. Restaurant, all watersports, and constant ferry service to and from the mainland. $50 double.

Manuro Paradise—Thirty miles from Vila, this hotel is on a remote stretch of coastline where guests sleep in Melanesian-style bungalows. Restaurant and good snorkeling. Rates are moderate.

Takara Lodge Resort—This resort is 38 miles from town on the north coast of Efate. If you aren't inclined to make the slow trip by road, Air Melanesia will fly you there for $60 round trip. Staying in very basic ocean front bungalows will cost $25 double. Food is excellent. As they say, "We do beasts roasted whole on the spit, roasts stuffed with shellfish or paté, and in season wild pigeon, and fresh-water prawns." If you are driving around the island, this is a welcome spot.

Hideaway Island Resort—Five miles by road and ferry from town, this inn has bungalows, restaurant, and a good beach. Very popular with scuba people. $52 double.

For the very low budget traveler, there are the following (we suggest you write before arrival).

Ron Graham Guest House—Box 229, Port Vila, Vanuatu. They have six simple rooms at $10 double.

Kalfabun Guest House—Box 494, Port Vila, Vanuatu. There are three simple rooms there, north of town on the way to the airport. $10 double.

Camping is not encouraged in Vanuatu, although at Takara Beach Resort they do have inexpensive tents for rent.

Dining in and Around Port Vila

Dining, eating, snacking, or in-room cooking are easily accomplished in Port Vila. The list of possibilities is lengthy and covers the entire spectrum. There's French, Vietnamese, Japanese, Chinese, Aussie, American, and plenty of local delicacies, such as coconut crab, lobsters, oyster, and flying foxes.

The following restaurants, based on a meal for two, are rated: Expensive—$25 to $50; Moderate—$15 to $25; Inexpensive—$5 to $15; and Budget—$1 to $5.

The Tassiriki and the Tuku Tuku—These restaurants are in the Intercontinental Hotel. The Tassiriki specializes in continental cuisine—seafood, steaks, fine wines, flambé desserts. The Tuku Tuku has specialty buffet dinners each night—

Italian, Asian, Melanesian, etc., and often during dinner you can watch a group of male dancers from Ambrym Island do such all-time favorites as the circumcision or pig killing dance. Food is excellent and expensive. Breakfast is moderate.

Iririki Resort—Take the free ferry, a three-minute voyage from downtown to this island and hotel where good continental food is served in lush surroundings. A fine view of the harbor and town. Expensive for dinner.

Solaise Hotel—They have a family-style restaurant with good seafood, excellent curries, fine Italian cooking. The Solaise is high on our list. Moderate.

Ma Barker's—An institution right in the heart of town, with an American decor; be sure to look at the clock above the door. They serve good fish curries and steaks. Probably best for lunch. Try their $3.25 hamburger, immense and with all the trimmings including a fried egg. Inexpensive.

Rossi's—As described earlier, they serve predictably good sandwiches, seafood, curries—all in sizable portions. Inexpensive.

Waterfront Bar and Grill—One of the best watering places in Vila. This open-air bar-restaurant on the seafront has a good salad bar, and an outside grill where you can watch your steak, fish or chicken being grilled. It's one of our favorites and a good place to meet the yachties. Across from the Marina Motel. Moderate.

Bloody Mary's—An outdoor fast-food place on the waterfront next to the public market. The sign over the entrance says "Namba wan kae kae quik taem," or "Number one fast food." they have hamburgers, fish and chips, milkshakes, ice cream. Popular with the locals. Budget.

Reflection—A French restaurant in the Olympic Hotel. Quite good. Reservations needed. Expensive.

Cottage Restaurant—In the center of town across from the post office, this place has Australian food—teas, breakfast, lunch and dinner. Not exciting, but not at all bad. Inexpensive.

Le Rendezvous—Overlooking Vila's bay, this combination French and Oriental restaurant serves good food in an atmosphere of old world sophistication. Reservations required. Moderately expensive.

Le Pandanus—On a lagoon near town, this continental-style restaurant does flambé dishes at your table. It has a romantic setting, fine wine list, and reservations are required. Expensive.

Bamboo Royal—Chinese food is served in an impressive style. Cantonese. Take-away food too. Fair. Moderate.

Harbour View—Chinese food served in a private house. There are fine views of the bay. Good. Moderate.

For ultra-budget dining try the stalls on the waterfront behind the public market. Eighty cents will buy a plate of lap lap, some rice and fish, plus fruit. It doesn't look too appetizing, but it's filling and the price is right.

Preparing Your Own Food

Because so many hotels provide cooking facilities, cooking for yourself is a simple matter. Port Vila's public market on the waterfront in the center of town is open every Wednesday, Friday, and Saturday morning. There you can buy all varieties of shellfish, fish, poultry, vegetables, and fruit. Next go to one of the nearby grocery stores such as Burns Philp, Hebrida, or Ballandes where Vanuatu's French past is evident in their fine selection of cheeses, wine, wonderful baguettes of French bread, and deli food. All the ingredients for do-it-yourself gourmet dining are available in Vila.

Business hours for shops are "flexible." They usually run from 7:30 AM to 11:30 AM. Then there is siesta till 1:30 PM, when they open again until 5-7 PM. Most shops are closed Saturday afternoons, and Sundays.

Evening Entertainment

There are several discos in Vila where the contemporary sound of music goes on from 10 PM to 3 AM every night except Sunday. You can have fun in these spots but, by Suva, Papeete, or Nouméa standards, they're fairly mild and not frequented by indigenous Vanuatuans. Foreigners and Vanuatuans are friendly, but relations between them are not as animated and informal as in Fiji, Tonga, Samoa or Tahiti. Here your play-mates will mostly be Aussies, New Zealanders, some French from New Caledonia, and the occasional American.

The three big hotels in town, the Intercontinental, Le Lagon, and the Iririki all have discos. Just appear, and follow the sounds of merriment to their source. Then try Vila's top French night club, the *Club le Privé*, on the road to Erakor. In the same area, drop in to *Le Palace* and dance to the latest trendy music. Drinks at all these places are moderately priced.

For a night spot catering mainly to Melanesians, try the *Sol Wata Klab*—in other words, the Salt Water Club. Here they won't fall all over you, but you'll be welcome. It's a good place to try a cup or two of kava—but beware of more than two.

At the *Iorana* on the outskirts of town there's an unusual sort of disco-roller skating. It's popular with the locals and is open from 4 to 11 PM.

For a traditional island evening, the people at Mele village three miles north of Vila put on a lap lap dinner every Friday at 7 PM. This affair, complete with a wide selection of island food and music played by a local band, makes you feel like a tourist but it's a very good evening.

Our choice for a lively evening in Vila is the *Waterfront Bar and Grill* on the seafront in town. From dinner time on a cross-section of Vanuatu gathers under the stars by the bay and handy to a congenial bar. It's the best place to meet the yachties, local expats, other visitors, and a few locals.

There are two theaters in town—Ciné Pacifique and Ciné Hickson. Most of the films are in French. The best place to see movies is via video in the lounges of the bigger hotels. No charge for attending; just walk in and settle down.

How to Get Around in Port Vila and Efate

From one end of Port Vila, north to south along the harbor, it's a very walkable three miles. From the Intercontinental or Le Lagon into town it's two miles—a fine but hot walk. Chances are you'll usually take a taxi, for about 50¢. All taxis have meters and can be called (ring 2979 or 2870) or hail one on the street. They happen along frequently.

The central part of Port Vila is only a block or two wide, but stretches along the harbor for a mile. This part of town is always colorful. Beginning at Rossi's Hotel at the north end you'll stroll by Handikraf Blong Vanuatu (Vanuatu Handicraft Store), a good public library, an interesting museum, Ma Barker's restaurant, and several smaller ones. You'll pass the government buildings. We were lucky and saw their opening of Parliament ceremony. Then there's the French Embassy, several airline offices, banks, general stores, the public market and the wharves with interisland ships alongside. The National Tourism Office is along the way, as is Hertz, several duty free shops and, if thirst develops, a number of bistros

Free ferry to Iririki Island from Port Vila

304 Adventure Guide to the South Pacific

await. You'll notice that folks on the street nod, smile, and often say hello.

Toward the far end of downtown Vila, you could detour and take the free ferry over to Iririki Island for a cold drink, lunch, or merely for a boat ride. Finally, just opposite the Marina Hotel, is the *Waterfront Bar and Grill,* another happy solution for warm walking. Beyond, along the curve of the harbor toward the cruise ship dock, or on to Le Lagon or the Erakor Hotel, distances become more pronounced and a taxi is useful.

*Beyond Vila—*An 82-mile, mostly rough, road runs around Efate Island. There aren't any scheduled buses that make the run, as in Fiji or Samoa. A few trucks do segments of the round-island road, but none are dependable. Choices are to rent a car or moped, hire a taxi, or take an organized sightseeing tour.

*Car Rentals—*There are three car rental sources in Vila: Budget, Avis, and Hertz. Hertz claims to have the cheapest rates, but in fact the charges are similar. A four-seat compact will cost about $42 per day, insurance included. Budget offers a special weekly rate, seven days for the cost of five, or $210 a week. Avis says they'll pick up or drop off anywhere. They all have offices at the airport, in town, and at the Intercontinental and Le Lagon hotels. Remember that traffic moves on the right hand side of the road. United States driver's licenses are accepted.

*Mopeds—*The economical way to get around is by moped or motorbike. They're available at Moped Rentals on the corner of Wharf Road next to the Ichise Japanese Restaurant. Phone 2699. Rates for mopeds with insurance are $16 a day plus $30 deposit. Motorbikes are $20 per day. Drive them with care on the rough country roads.

*Hire Car or Taxi—*Bargaining, like tipping, is usually not done in Vanuatu but, when hiring a taxi or car for long distance excursions, establish the fare ahead of time. About $10 an hour should be right.

Organized Sight Seeing

We know of four reputable tour agencies in Vila.

Island Holidays—At the Intercontinental Hotel.

Hibiscus Tours—At Le Lagon Hotel.

Tour Vanuatu—In town opposite the French Pharmacy.

Frank King Tours—In the center of town next to the post office.

All of these agencies provide similar services, are competitive and generally do a good job. We've used Tour Vanuatu and were pleased, but people we've met who are into touring and group travel have unusually kind words about Frank King's services. For $100 you can buy a seven-day pass for any tours King offers. Be sure to go the Vanuatu Visitors Bureau in the center of town, and they'll give you suggestions and advice.

If you plan to take a tour, you'd have the following choices.

*By Bus—Vila City Tour—*A short but concise examination of the French and British parts of Vila—the market, shopping center, and a side trip to nearby Mele village. $7 per person.

*Manuro Resort—*A 68-mile round trip to Manuro with a swim at a white beach and bay. Lunch, either Melanesian or French, is served there. $15 per person, lunch extra.

*By Bus Around Efate Island—*A seven-hour trip all the way around the island. En route they provide morning coffee, lunch, a swim at a good snorkeling beach, stops at panoramic points and interesting villages. Frank King does this trip five days a week leaving at 9:30 AM. Cost is $27 per person including lunch.

*By Boat—*The *Coral Sea* is a 40-foot fun boat equipped with glass bottom for reef viewing. Refreshments are served aboard, and the two-hour cruise costs $8.50 per person.

The Sea Star is a schooner that sails off to Mele Bay for a half day of lounging and snorkeling over a good reef. Refreshments are available and a barbecue lunch is provided at a total of $24 per person.

The Escapade is a 42-foot cruiser used for fishing and scuba diving. For fishing they provide five lines and, for catching the big ones, there are two chairs aboard. Lunch is served and the seven-hour trip costs $55 per person.

There are cruising sailboats, the *Coongoola* and the *Vaimiti,* that charter out for longer trips including other islands. Also there are several fully equipped dive boats.

What to Do in Vila

Port Vila may be the prettiest capital town in the South Pacific and there are many things to do, other than sitting quietly on the sea front watching the blue bay roil up from schools of mullet. Food, as we've discussed, is one of Vila's most obvious attractions. Simple strolling in this compact bougainvillia- and frangipani-garlanded town is another. But perhaps your first obligation after visiting the Visitors Bureau is to look into Vanuatu's culture, past and present.

The Museum and Cultural Center is right downtown on the main street a block south of Rossi's Hotel. Because these islands are so rich in customs, carvings, masks, clothing, spears, and artifacts still used today, the information this center provides is good conditioning for what comes later. Ask to see the curator, a knowledgable young American named Kirk Huffman.

Then, to read a little about these islands, step next door to the public library and briefly study a little local history. There perhaps you'll learn that the white man's origin was in these islands. According to Tanna Island custom, when men and women set out (it's not clear from where) to settle the earth, many of them lost their boats and spent a long time in the sea. That is how the white man came about, bleached by sea and sun.

To buy authentic artifacts such as slit gongs, bowls, carvings, model canoes, war clubs, masks, necklaces, and the prized full-circle boar tusks, go next door to the Handikraf Blong Vanuatu (Vanuatu Handicraft Store.) Since it's run on a non-profit basis to provide an outlet for outer islanders, you get the best prices in Vila.

The Michoutouchkine and Pilioka Art Gallery—For a more modern approach to Pacific art, take a 50¢ taxi ride to this flower-filled verdant gallery on the south end of town. Here, promoted by Nikolai Michoutouchkine, you can examine and buy the sketches, paintings, and tapestries of Aloi Pilioka, a possible modern-day Gauguin whose works represent a blend of Polynesian and Melanesian cultures.

Duty Free Shopping—Because Vila is a duty-free port, there are bargains to be had, and shoppers with visions of outwitting the tax people find Vila attractive. Bear in mind that you don't just walk into a store and exit with all these goodies. To make purchases you show outgoing air tickets, then pay for the articles which are put in sealed bags to be picked up two days before departure. They must then be carried unopened through exit customs. Prices for these items are fixed and there is no bargaining. Following are the names of a few duty-free shops.

Fung Kuei's Store—This is on the main street next to the ANZ Bank. check their cameras, Mikimoto jewelry, compact disc players, liquors, and cigarettes.

Ballandes Duty Free—Sportswear, shoes.

Burns Philp—Nearly everything.

Pierre's Bijoux—Watches, pens, cameras, and books.

Optique Port Vila—On the main street opposite the Indosuez Bank. Jewelry, leather goods, and sun glasses.

The Nautilus Dive Shop—Next door to Ma Barker's restaurant. A good selection of diving gear.

Vanuatu as a Tax-free Finance Center—Speaking of outwitting the tax people, Vanuatu claims to be a pure tax haven. According to brochures, the Government Finance Center provides secrecy and offers freedom from income tax, capital gains taxes, estate taxes, and other taxes. For more information write to Investors Trust Ltd., GPO Box 211, Port Vila, Vanuatu.

Golf—There are several golf courses. The *White Sands* course with its par 36 is probably the best. It's 20 minutes from Vila. The *Vila Golf Club* is popular too and invites overseas golfers to join them every Saturday at 1 PM for their weekly competition. Greens fees are moderate.

Tennis—There are two courts at the Intercontinental Hotel. Make arrangements there.

Diving—Vila is filled with diving operators and, for novices, this could be the place to learn. A dive course costs about the same as in the States, but here the water is warmer, clearer and more accessible. At Mele Bay, four miles north of Vila, water visibility is more than 80 feet, and there are coral gardens, tame fish, and some interesting wrecks of ships and planes to dive on.

Trips to these areas are done by boats geared for diving. Try

Dive Action on the waterfront near the Visitors Bureau, *Scuba Holidays, Island Divers,* or *Nautilus.* All these organizations are in or near town and for about $30 they'll take certified divers for a morning or afternoon trip to Mele Bay or perhaps south of town to examine the wreckage of the Star of Russia which sank in 1874. Snorkelers can go along on the boat for about $10.

For a full PADI certification course contact *Nautilus Scuba Diving School,* PO Box 78, Port Vila, Vanuatu. It costs about $250.

Horseback Riding—There are several possibilities, but best is probably White Sands Country Club. Some good trails are there, as well as rides on the beach. Contact Frank King Tours for this activity and for rates.

Churches—Anglican, Catholic, and Presbyterian churches are all in Vila, and welcome visitors. All have services in English, French and Bislama. More information at your hotel.

You can see that Vila is productive of nearly everything anyone could require, but the real Vanuatu lies beyond Vila's city limits and over the horizon to her outer islands.

EFATE ISLAND

Taken clockwise from Vila, the trip around Efate Island should be done in no less than two days. En route there are two good inns for stopovers, *Takara Lodge* and the *Manuro Hotel.* In between there are plenty of good beaches, a few interesting villages and several offshore islands with no accommodations whatsoever that few people visit. Most of the 82-mile road is rough, slow going, and there are few services available. Take some emergency rations along.

Leaving Vila, the first village along the way is Mele, the biggest on Efate. This is an uninteresting cluster of wooden houses with galvanized tin roofs and inhabited by hard working farmers. At Mele a short road leads off to the coast where a ferry connects with the *Hideaway Island Resort.* The snorkeling is good there, but it's not the place to go if you want to learn about Vanuatu.

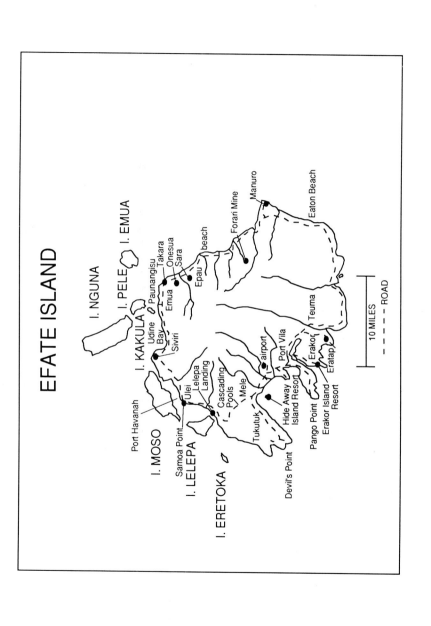

EFATE ISLAND

I. NGUNA

I. PELE

I. EMUA

Port Havanah

I. MOSO

Samoa Point

I. LELEPA

I. ERETOKA

I. KAKULA

Udine
Bay

Siviri

Ulei

Lelepa
Landing

Cascading
Pools

Mele

Tukutuk

Devil's Point

Hide Away
Island Resort

Pango Point

Erakor Island
Resort

Eratap

Erakor

Port Vila

airport

Teuma

Paunangisu

Emua

Takara
Onesua
Sara

Epau

beach

Forari Mine

Manuro

Eaton Beach

10 MILES

– – – ROAD

Just beyond Mele and visible from the road is a cascading body of water surrounded by verdant jungle. There's a path from the road that leads down to the first of several clear water pools and short falls. It's beautiful, peaceful and quiet.

From these pools the road winds upward, with plenty of good views, then it passes through bushy lonely country. Note the trees festooned in Christmas-tree style with beer cans. Exuberant passersby have consumed beer, and in honor of the occasion, bedecked a tree.

At Lelepa Landing, seven miles from Mele, walk down to the beach where there'll be a collection of outrigger canoes and small boats pulled up on the sand. This is the take-off point for Lelepa Island a mile across the channel. One of these boats will take you to the island where there's a seafront cave and where diving is excellent. Avoid the trip if it looks rough, especially in the afternoon, as the channel is tricky. Do not make the crossing in a paddle-type outrigger, and do not pay $10 for the trip, as we did. Pay $1 round trip.

Jungle pool near Mele, Efate Island

At Samoa Point, three miles from Lelepa, you can stop and swim on an exceptionally good beach. Continue on then to Port Havvanah, a sleepy town with links to the past. Here, during World War II, elements of the US 7th Fleet lay anchored, and in the jungle behind town there's an abandoned American airstrip.

Three miles beyond at Siviri village you can see offshore islands, and enter a cave where folklore tells us that children once lit the inside by pounding on the ground.

The road becomes even more marginal about here and in nine miles comes to the village of Emua. There canoes and boats are available to take you the four miles out to the islands of Nguna and Pele. The reef is pretty and rich.

At Takara you've come 37 miles from Vila. As mentioned earlier, the food at the *Takara Lodge* is excellent and the accommodations basic, but adequate. Along this coast there are fine white beaches, long stands of coconut palms, lots of immense banyan trees and, inland, thick virgin rain forest.

Beach at Lelepa Landing, Efate Island

Further on, set in the magnificence of the rain forest, there are several small villages. Remember to mind your manners, and always ask permission before wandering into these villages or using their beaches. There's an abandoned manganese mine along this road near Forari.

At Manuro, 25 miles from Vila, you'll find the *Manuro Hotel* where you can stay overnight. Food and accommodations are good, as are the snorkeling and shelling on this reef-protected beach.

The next day continue on along the south coast past Eton Beach, then some flatlands, and finally you're back in Port Vila.

THE OUTER ISLANDS

How to Get There By Air

The easy way to the outer islands is in Air Melanesiae's small aircraft, usually Twin Otters that fly up and down this 500-mile chain of islands. They go to unimaginably remote areas almost every day.

Go to Air Melanesiae's office in Vila opposite the post office (phone 2643). Plan your itinerary and ask for schedules and fares. As a rule of thumb you'll notice that fares work out to about a dollar a minute. For example, flying from Vila to Santo, 190 miles, will take 70 minutes and costs $67.

By Sea

The romantic purist way to the outer islands is by sea, but travel aboard the trading vessels and copra boats that serve Vanuatu's islands may not be for everyone. Creature comforts aboard are few, standards of hygiene are relaxed, and seas can be rough.

But for those who are interested, Vila's harbor is right in the center of town and vessels tied up there are available for informal examination. Step aboard any of them, talk to the captain, inquire about destinations, accommodations, food, and fares.

Air Melanesiae (for domestic flights)

If she's been repaired since a recent storm, the *Konanda* is the most comfortable ship to sail on. The Ininsco Co. owns this 800-ton vessel which has one first class cabin with a sink and two bunks. The toilet is down the passageway.

Unlike Solomon Island ships, the *Konanda* and a few others provide meals for cabin passengers. Quality varies, but passengers can count on boiled rice, canned mackerel, occasionally fresh fish and a little beef. Fresh fruit is not provided but is easily obtained before sailing. A large papaya will cost 20¢, two oranges 20¢, bananas and breadfruit only pennies.

The *Konanda's* usual two-week voyage, for $11 a day, visits Nguna Island just north of Efate, Nataso, Makura, Emal, Tongoa—all tiny islands. Then it goes on to Epi, Ambrym, and Malekula. The purpose of the voyage is to pick up copra, deliver supplies, and give islanders a chance to shop at the complete store *Konanda* carries on board.

Most of the stops are without benefit of wharf, so you'll be taken ashore by canoe. You'll be stared at, smiled at, have a chance to buy some fruit and maybe some carvings, then take a swim and you'll be off to the next island for some more of the same. For the right kind of traveler, there's no better way to spend 14 days.

At Burns Philp Co. in Vila ask about the somewhat smaller *Lali* and *Onma* II. Sometimes there's an available cabin. The *Lali* sails from Vila on Saturdays for Malekula, Ambrym, Pentecost, Aoba, Espiritu Santo, and returns on Fridays. The *Onma* II does the same ports, but returns a day sooner. Consider either of these ships for a one-way run, then fly back.

TANNA ISLAND

For our first outer island we boarded the 3 PM flight to Tanna and, with a chain-smoking pilot at the controls, made the 160-mile trip in one hour. The fare is $59. After Efate Island, Tanna is supposed to be the most visited island. But we didn't find it that way. Far from it. There may have been other visitors, but they weren't in evidence, and in the simple, but comfortable *White Grass Bungalows,* 15 miles north of the airport, we received the exclusive attentions of the Melanesian owners. Our fully plumbed quarters in one of several thatched bungalows were in full view of the sea, and a walk across neatly trimmed flowered grounds brought us to the bar-dining room where we sat in solitude. The food was good, and reasonably priced. Onion soup was $2.50, a plate full of ham sandwiches $3.50, fried fish $5.00, and cold Foster's beer $1.50 a can. Bungalow rates were $35 a double.

There are other places to stay on Tanna. *The Tanna Beach Resort,* the best, is only two miles from the airport at the tiny town of Lenakel. It has a pool, thatched bungalows, and is nicely set in a palm-fringed coral cove. Rates are $44 a double.

Across the island at White Sands there are some simple accommodations to be had with local people, and at bargain prices. Camping is no longer allowed there. Get information at Air Melanesiae before leaving Vila.

How to Get Around on Tanna

Roads of a sort, none paved, run up and down Tanna's west coast from Black Sands Beach in the north all the way around

White Grass Bungalows, Tanna Island

the bottom of the island to the Hot Springs—Yasur—Port Reso-
lution area. Another road just across the center of the island
from Lenakel, the administrative center, to the Mt. Yasur
area.

There aren't any taxis on Tanna, but several minibuses are
available. Either of the hotels can get you one, and there'll
always be a van at the airport when you arrive. Wherever you
go, always arrange round-trip transportation to be sure you've
got a way back. A fare of $10–$15 per person will get you to
and from the most distant place.

Walking on Tanna is excellent. The island is laced with
trails that pass through primitive "custom" villages. But
these villages should be approached with care and preferably
with a guide. Without knowing it, an outsider could break a
taboo or two and, although you wouldn't be harmed, you certainly wouldn't be embraced.

Tanna, 23 miles long by 12 miles wide, is an island filled
with myths, rich with history, and the current scene of curious

customs. Along the coast there are black volcanic beaches, heavy jungle in the interior, upland grassy hills where wild horses roam. And on the eastern side of the island opposite the airport is the Yasur volcano, said to be the home of Tannese spirits.

Tanna's Curiosities

The John Frum Society—No one knows exactly who John Frum was or where he came from. Some think he could have been a black American GI during World War II. Whoever he was, there are some people on Tanna and other Pacific islands who are sure this Messiah will return and bring all sorts of wonderful goodies.

On Tanna the John Frum phenomenon, call it a Cargo Cult if you will, had its origin early in the 20th century when islanders got the impression that wonderful things were given to the white man by God. This made the Presbyterian missionaries' task a little easier and, to get these possessions, the Tannese agreed to give up pagan practices. They stopped drinking kava, they covered their nakedness, they stopped wild and abandoned dancing, no more skinny dipping, no more worshipping spirits. And they went to work for the white planters.

For their pains, their attention to Christianity, their hard work, what they got was trade tobacco, some mirrors, beads, hatchets, and a few knives. They felt cheated and in time became anti-white, anti-missionary. Gradually they went back to their old ways—to kava, penis sheaths, dancing and spirits.

Then came the apocalypse of World War II and with it planes, ships, jeeps, radios, GI food and movies. Employment came too, and this time they weren't cheated. American GI's were generous to a fault. But the GI's left at the end of the war. So the John Frum islanders began their long wait and with it came another breakdown of customs, a deterioration of sanitation, a defiance of law and general sloth.

Since then conditions have improved, but there are still practicing John Frum villages on Tanna. One of these is Ipekel near Sulphur Bay. The new more tolerant government allows the practice. A recent visitor asked why they waited for someone who would surely never appear. The answer was that they'd been waiting a much shorter time than the Christians have been waiting for the second coming of Christ.

Custom Villages—Tanna has a population of over 20,000 and most of them still live their lives according to custom. They still practice circumcision rites, the ceremonial killing of pigs, primitive marriage ceremonies, dancing with painted faces, and the drinking of kava.

Kava Drinking—This is one very good way to communicate with the ghosts of ancestors, and also a good way to simply get stoned. On Tanna, their kava, which is unusually strong, is prepared by the chewing or pounding of piper methysticum root. It's then put in a bowl and fibers of the plant are further squeezed to extract the juices to which water has been added.

Then at night village men gather at the Nakamal, the Men's Hut, and begin the ritual drinking of kava. The kava causes them to become quieter, more withdrawn, rather than noisy and ribald. Women in Vanuatu are absolutely prohibited from drinking kava and in the old days were buried alive for doing so.

The drinking of kava on Tanna is something outsiders should never interfere with. A kava drinker should respect-fully be left alone. If you travel the dark jungle roads at night, you'll see clutches of men walking slowly bearing faggots with burning embers. They'll turn their backs to you as you pass. If you're in a car, the driver will take the high beam off them, and may quietly say, "They've been drinking kava."

Mt. Yasur—Coming from the airport side of Tanna, Mt. Yasur is a long way off—not far in miles, but over the grim roads it seems a long way. You cross the central range of mountains, drive through thick jungle, and suddenly emerge on a desert of volcanic ash hard by a gloomy lake, called Siwi. Mt. Yasur, with its pall of smoke, looms overhead and there is no trace of a road. Wind and ashes cover any recent tracks. Chances are you'll get stuck and that you'll have to get out and help push the van out.

Well shy of the summit the road stops. From there it's a matter of climbing, a stiff but manageable climb to the rim of the volcano. During the assault the mountain shudders, booms, and dark clouds billow out. At the top, the 1,400-foot mountain gave me a feeling of dread. Nature there is raw, overwhelming, and each time the volcano erupts you can see rocks flying skyward. The smell of sulfur is marked, the scent of the underworld, and it's easy to see why Yasur is considered the home of the spirits by the Tannese. All tours can be arranged at your hotel. Our minibus trip was $24 per person.

The Wild Horses—We were told that from our White Grass Bungalow Hotel we could easily walk to the plains that were visible in the distance. Here is where we would find the horses. We followed directions, walked a mile down the jungle road, stopped often to marvel at some of the largest banyans we'd ever seen and, at a point that seemed to agree with directions, we left the road, entered the jungle, and struggled through the bush to a dead end. It was hot work, we finally gave up, and irritably returned to the hotel. "Sorry tu mas," the Melanesian who'd given us instructions said. He'd told us a mile short of the correct turn off. It took two cold Fosters to cool me down. The horses are there, though. Just follow good instructions.

ERROMONGO ISLAND

Erromongo, just north of Tanna, is where Peter Dillon's discovery of sandalwood in 1825 created such turmoil. It's also the island where the Presbyterian missionaries Williams and Harris were killed by natives who had little enthusiasm for religion or the sandalwood trade. Erromongo has had a stormy past, but now it languishes quietly and mostly unvisited.

Coming or going to Tanna from Vila, a twice-weekly plane drops down at either Dillon Bay on the west side, or Ipota on the east coast. One thousand people live on this jungle island 28 miles long by 13 miles wide.

Near Dillon Bay there is an accommodation called *Meteson's Guest House*. It has comfortable though simple Melanesian-style bungalows. The main activities are bush-walking and snorkeling. Rates with meals are $32 a double.

On Erromongo it's bush-walking and canoe-camping that attract visitors. The bush-walking is for hardy trekkers who with or without guide put a pack on their back and cross the spine of the island from Dillon Bay to the east coast and beyond. It's hard punishing work.

Canoe-camping is a combination sea-land trip by canoe or small boat down the coast, village by village. The best route with the most villages and the most beautiful reach of coast is the 20-mile stretch from Dillon Bay south to Ponumbia. Since there are no roads, boats do this often. The cost is minimal and, because of the villages, little camping gear is required.

ESPIRITU SANTO

At 80 miles long and 24 miles at its widest, Espiritu Santo is Vanuatu's largest island. Delightful but sleepy, (6,500 population) Luganville—called Santo—is the main town. Other than the east coast, the island consists of impassable jungle and mountains.

We flew up from Vila to Santo on the daily *Air Melanesiae* flight (65 minutes, fare $66 one way), passed over Malekula, Norsup, Malo, and put down at the World War II bomber field near Luganville. Taxi fare into town was less than a dollar.

Long rather than wide, Luganville lies on a pretty island-dotted coastline. Right in the center of town there's a grassy restful park, and the shops along the main street, run by Chinese and Vietnamese, have the musty nostalgic odor associated with country town general stores.

In the style of the '50s, the *Santo Hotel* ($68 double) is the best in town. The rooms are attractive, all have balconies, and the staff are hospitable. But the hotel is unusually quiet and few people frolic in the pool or at the bar. Other than divers, businessmen, and backland adventurers, few outsiders come to Luganville.

In spite of numerous World War II Quonset huts in town, it's hard to imagine a time when over 100,000 allied troops were there, a time when James Michener was immortalizing his Bloody Mary.

For housing, a notch down in price from the Santo, the *New Look Motel* in the center of town has rooms with baths at $25 double. The *Jaranmoli Rest House* has very basic accommodations for $12 double.

Copra cutters, Espiritu Santo

For Food—The *Santo Hotel* offers full service and good, but lonesome, dining. Just a block away you'll find more local activity at two restaurants, both Chinese, the *Ocean House* and the *Formosa.* Both are all right, and inexpensive.

For Evening Fun—There are a couple of movies in town, with most films in English (the French aren't all that popular in Santo). There isn't much in the way of spirited fun anymore and most of the discos have closed. There is one four blocks east of the Santo Hotel that's open occasionally. They may show a video movie at the Santo Hotel, but this is a quiet town.

Banks—For changing money, there's a bank right next door to the Santo Hotel, and others down the main street.

Activities on Espiritu Santo

Our taxi driver, a man worth knowing named Peter Tari, charged $10 an hour. He called for us the next morning and we set out north from town along blue Segond Channel. Just past the airport on Palikulo Point we came to the resting place of the troop transport and former luxury liner, *President Coolidge*. In 1942, the *Coolidge* hit a mine and, with the loss of two men out of the 5,000 aboard, sank in 100 feet of water.

Today the *Coolidge* is home to grouper, shark, barracuda, trevally, and many exotically colored fish of the South Seas. Visibility in these water ranges up to 150 feet. At 80 feet the *Coolidge's* number one hold which contains jeeps, trucks, aircraft parts, and rifles is within reach of trained divers. Contact Alan Power at the *Santo Hotel* who runs the most professional dive service in the Pacific.

The next stop, less than a mile further on, is *Million Dollar Point*. There US Forces at war's end outwitted French planters who attempted to buy surplus supplies at rock bottom prices. The Americans refused their offer, and instead pushed all this equipment into the sea. It's an amazing sight—rusted machinery, aircraft, trucks, Coca Cola bottles, jeeps, litter the shallow

Million Dollar Point, Espiritu Santo

waters which are now home to coral, colorful fish, and scuba divers.

We continued on, past the abandoned Pacific Fish Packing Co. (now moved to American Samoa), past Club Nautique's yacht harbor and beach, past coconut plantations (Espiritu Santo exists mainly on copra), and finally arrived at the most beautiful beach in the South Pacific, aptly named *Champagne Beach.*

Champagne Beach, 34 miles north of Luganville, is a long arc of beach with powdery white sand at the edge of the jungle. The water is magically clear, there is no hard-to-negotiate coral in the shallows, and for swimming and picnicking it's absolutely perfect. The locals charge $1.00 entrance fee per car.

Until five years ago there was a resort-type hotel there, but politics and the Coconut War caused its demise. Now, other than an occasional cruise ship which anchors for the day, and rare individual travelers, few people see this beach. No camping is permitted. The locals are markedly opposed to it.

For a bit of Jimmy Stevens Coconut War nostalgia, take the rough road 14 miles out of Luganville to the village of Tanafo. There you can stand in a cleared square under the big banyan tree where Jimmy was captured at the end of his war in 1980. Beyond Tanafo you will encounter only jungle, mountains, footpaths and, deep in the interior, primitive people, including pygmies.

For the adventurous, attempt a visit to the villages in Big Bay north of Luganville. You can get to the nearest part of Big Bay by a four-wheel drive track, but it's better to go by boat. Ask around Luganville for the *Kismet* or the *Henry Bonneaud.* These ships go to this area to collect copra, which is then put into burlap sacks and put aboard ship.

At villages where copra is being taken aboard, there'll be brisk beach trading of other commodities such as canned mackerel, kerosene, sugarcane, bags of flour, bullets, and beer. This is the noisy, colorful, essential Vanuatu.

PENTECOST ISLAND

The most spectacular of Vanuatu's Melanesian customs

Champagne Beach, Espiritu Santo

takes place on the southern part of Pentecost Island in April or May, their autumn months. It's called the Pentecost Jump or Land Dive, a traditional custom that is supposed to assure a successful yam harvest and make men out of boys. To understand the dive, some lore is important.

Legend tells of a woman who ran away from an abusing husband several times. Each time, he caught her and took her home. Finally she took refuge in a tall tree, but her husband followed her. Just as he reached the top she jumped, and miraculously reached the ground unhurt. She dared her husband to follow. He did and was killed.

What he didn't know, was that his wife had tied vines from the tree to her ankles, which broke her fall. The Jump goes on today, but now it's a test of courage for men only.

For the event, towers of up to 90 feet are built of tree branches lashed together with lianas. Then each man builds his own platform and chooses vines of the right length and strength which bind his ankles. If they're too long, he'll smash into the ground; if too short, he'll be snapped back against the tower. Fortunately, by the time a young man makes his first dive, he's been well trained and the jump goes off without a hitch. Only rarely is anyone even slightly hurt. When the missionaries arrived in the 19th century, they were appalled by the dive, (called the N'gol) and were successful in almost stopping it. Only the village of Bunlap persisted. With independence for Vanuatu, a freedom from these restrictions occurred. Earlier forbidden practices were, while not encouraged, allowed. The John Frum Society is an example, as are the land divers in Bunlap and now in other Pentecost villages too.

How to Get There—There's a hard way to see the dives, and an easier way. The hard way requires permission from the Chief of Bunlap, and then a six-hour jungle trek with guide from Pentecost Airport to Bunlap. Or, on appropriate days, you can fly to Lononore airstrip and continue on by van to Wali where the easier-to-get-to dives are performed.

As much as we dislike guided tours, an even easier way to see the dives is to buy a package, which will take you over and back to Vila the same day. It'll probably cost about $265 per person, plus an additional charge of $65 to watch the dive ($85 if you have a camera). If the weather turns bad, you'll be forced to stay overnight, an inconvenience since there are only two or three units at the *Maru Bungalows,* and there'll no doubt be a sizeable group of tourists.

Ask around Vila about yachts sailing up for the dives, or the charter boat *Coongoola.*

MALEKULA ISLAND

Fifty-six miles long, 18 miles at its widest, Malekula lies 18 miles south of Espiritu Santo. It's not far in miles, but a long leap into a primitive world. They were busy killing and eating each other as recently as 1930.

You can fly from Santo to Norsup on the northeast coast or to Lamap at the southeast end. Either Air Melanesiae flight will cost about $25, and simple housing in both places will cost $5 or $6 per couple. Food is available from small shops.

Most people come to Malekula to see, or attempt to see, the Big Nambas who live in the jungly northern interior, or the Small Nambas who live in similar surroundings in the south. Neither trip is to be taken lightly and can be done only after talking with government officials in Vila. Chances are they'll be reluctant to let you proceed. But, if you do get permission, it'll be to the Big Nambas only.

The Big Nambas live in and near Amok, 12 rough miles by vehicle from Norsup. Prices for this run are negotiable, but realistic. If you go, you'll see men wearing penis sheaths, women with their two front teeth knocked out, pigs growing their tusks painfully in a full circle, five-foot yams, and a society that missionaries have been unable to break.

There is little chance you'll be allowed to visit the Small Nambas. There's no road in, the way is perilous, and the Small Nambas, hidden behind what is known as "The Banana Curtain," want to be left alone. Don't even consider making the attempt on your own.

AMBRYM ISLAND

Triangular-shaped Ambrym, 18 miles from apex to base, 25 miles along the base, is another primitive island. But there the missionaries, mostly Catholic, have left their mark. Even so Ambrym Island is the best place in Vanuatu to buy handicrafts such as drums, slit gongs, carving, weaving.

To get there fly Air Melanesaie from Santo to Craig Cove in the west for $41. You could fly to Ulei on the southeast coast, but there's no housing there. Alternatively, you could come in by ship to Craig Cove from Vila, or by small craft across the 15-mile channel from Lamap on Malekula, an often rough trip.

The only place we know to stay is the surprisingly good *Relais d'Ambrym,* seven miles east of the airstrip at Craig Cove. Rates are $42 double, including airport transfer.

There are some good "custom" villages on Ambrym, but they are no better than those on Tanna or Pentecost. It's the Benbow Volcano, with its associated ash plain, that's the attraction. The volcano is hard to get to and something of an

Vanuatan spirit masks

anticlimax, but the Relais d'Ambrym people will organize the trip. Yasur Volcano on Tanna is much more accessible.

AOBA

On Aoba (population 7,800) nature provides a number of attractions for active people who require no amenities. There are volcanoes, lakes bubbling with steam, and "custom" villages reached only by footpaths. You can get there by boat from Santo 30 miles away or fly into Walaha from Santo. We know of no accommodations on Aoba.

Big Namba, Malekula Island

THE BANKS AND TORRES ISLANDS

This group in the far north, named after Captain Cook's botanist Joseph Banks, has a strange brooding sort of beauty. The cloud-shrouded peaks of Vanua Lava, the biggest island, look like something designed by Hollywood. Further north Ureparara Island, the summit of an ancient volcano, has one of its sides caved in, and the walls form a large horseshoe bay. Nothing tranquil about this island, which Captain Bligh saw on his epic post-mutiny passage in 1789.

Unfortunately there's little of interest other than the scenery in these islands. The people are not very animated. Other than powerful Quat, the god of nearly everything in this group, nothing seems particularly important to the locals.

You can fly to Vanua Lava from Vila once or twice a week on Air Melanesiae. There's a very basic guest house there.

There are scores of other islands in Vanuatu that we've neglected, but eventually a sense of sameness begins to develop. Unless you've got unlimited time, perhaps your own yacht to live on while looking at these myriad dots of land, save your energies for other areas.

When you return to Port Vila after a spell in the outer islands, it's truly a return to the bright lights, and to a creature comforts that look better than ever.

Final Note—There is a $10 per person Airport Tax to be paid on departure.

10

PAPUA NEW GUINEA

Papua New Guinea, the eastern half of the second largest island in the world, includes a cluster of islands off its northeast coast—New Britain, New Ireland, Bougainville, Manus, the Trobriands, and scores of smaller islands.

The other half of the island, the western part—Indonesian Irian Jaya—is another story and, other than brief remarks about it, this chapter is confined to Papua New Guinea. However, when you put both halves of the island together, notice how in profile it resembles a huge bird taking off. The head of the bird, a place the Dutch called Vogelskopf (bird's head) is on the Indonesian side. The other end, given no anatomical name by the Australians, is in newly independent Papua New Guinea.

The Dutch left their half of the island after World War II, and things have changed. Vogelskopf is called Manokwari and the town Pacific veterans knew as Hollandia is called Jayapura.

In 1944 when I first saw Hollandia it was suffering from the excesses of war. Seen recently, the same town still suffers, but now it's from Indonesian neglect and a curious military problem on its border.

The eastern half has changed too and as of 1975 Papua New Guinea, calling itself Niugini and its airline Air Niugini, became independent. Fortunately the Australian presence lingers and in a generous way controls the purse-strings. Without Australia Papua New Guinea would probably fall apart. And

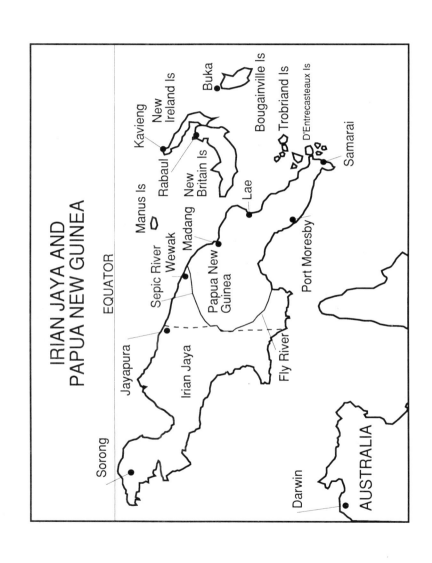

IRIAN JAYA AND
PAPUA NEW GUINEA

EQUATOR

Sorong

Jayapura

Irian Jaya

Darwin

AUSTRALIA

Manus Is

Sepic River

Wewak

Madang

Papua New
Guinea

Fly River

Port Moresby

Kavieng

New
Ireland Is

Rabaul

New
Britain Is

Lae

Buka

Bougainville Is

Trobriand Is

D'Entrecasteaux Is

Samarai

you're sure to hear commentary on all of this moments after stepping off the plane in Port Moresby, the usual port of entry—particularly if, with an icy South Pacific lager in mind, you go directly across the street and enter the public room of the Gateway Hotel.

There, standing at the bar, you'll almost certainly find a clutch of Aussies, many of them smartly turned out in Aussie gear—shorts, white shirt, and knee-length white stockings. They're sociable people, particularly when they're drinking, and being a newly arrived Yank is apt to get you a slap on the back, a "Good on ya mate," and another beer.

Then, attended by appropriate ribaldry without which Aussie drinking cannot be sustained, you'll hear a mixed bag of remarks. You may hear that, while matters aren't going flat out for the new government, there's hope, even progress. Perhaps too, you'll hear the other point of view—the Aussie who'll say what bloody cheek the United Nations had to suggest independence for this lot, some of whom a generation ago were stealing each others' pigs and wives and blipping each other on the head.

For a newly arrived American this is a time for listening. Our point of view is neither required nor recommended. In time someone will sum up all points of view by offering, "But don't get us wrong, mate, this is a good country, and we wish them the very best of luck."

We once fell in with such a group, and in time they asked why we were in Papua New Guinea. I explained that World War II nostalgia drew at me a little, but mostly we wanted to see the Sepik River, the Trobriands, the Highlands, maybe the Kokoda Trail. They approved with noisy enthusiasm, but one of them added, "You're just scratching the surface of this country, mate. There are other rivers to be seen, trails to be walked, mountains climbed, some snow-clad, and with valleys so remote that Stone-Age people live in them. There are jungles with birds of paradise in them, cassowaries, wallabies, little pigmy blokes too. And don't forget the hundreds of islands in the Bismarck Sea off the North Coast that are like little jewels. Remember too that over 700 linguistic groups and cultures share this country."

Someone else broke in, "If it's the Kokoda Trail you're interested in, you'd better come home with us. We're doing a mixed grill, we've got plenty of grog, and Bert here has done the Trail."

We went. It was a fine happy evening, and we awoke the next morning feeling delicate, but enthused about what we'd heard. And our Aussies were right. Two subsequent trips convinced us that New Guinea has everything an adventurer or escapist from the usual could want. But, on balance, Papua New Guinea has far better amenities and transportation facilities than Irian Jaya, the western half. The 1987 *World Status Map* and their Official Advisories for International Travelers does advise that, "Papua New Guinea has continuing crime problems in both urban and rural areas." They recommend travel with in-country tours instead of independent moving about. This we admit is cause for concern, but it has never stopped us from traveling independently. We've done it with caution, but happily and safely.

Near Madang, Papua New Guinea

History in Brief

Most of the early people were hunters and gatherers who used stones, bones, and wood for tools and weapons, as some still do. Each group was self contained, about 700 separate and exclusive groups who spoke 700 different dialects, and often knew as little about each other as they knew about the existence of England or Holland.

The first European probably came ashore on the western end of the island, in what is now Indonesian Irian Jaya. That honor goes to a Portuguese sailor, Jorg de Meneses, who arrived in 1526. Then a few years later the name New Guinea was bestowed on the island by a Spaniard, Ortiz Retes, who thought the natives similar to those on the Guinea coast of Africa. It's now thought that some of these early Europeans introduced the pig and sweet potato to these and other South Pacific Islands.

The cast of foreign visitors continued with Dampier, Bougainville, Schouten and, of course, Cook. They came to chart the coastline and rivers of this very large island, but it wasn't until 1939 that the interior of New Guinea was fully charted. Even now there are areas where no white man has yet stood.

In 1828 the Dutch annexed the western half, leaving the eastern part in a state of colonial confusion. Finally in 1883 England took over the part not claimed by Holland—today's Papua New Guinea. Then there were problems with Germany which, in 1885 after talks with Britain, took over the northeast part of New Guinea.

When World War I broke out in 1914, the Australians made a landing at the German administration center at Kokopo on New Britain and the Germans, who had more pressing matters in Europe, surrendered quickly.

In 1920, the League of Nations gave England the mandate to govern the former German colony. At this point the entire eastern half was under the British-Australian flag and was administered by Australia. The southern part was called Papua, the northern part, New Guinea.

It was in January of 1942 that Japanese troops and their navy landed at Rabaul on New Britain island, capturing 300 civilians and 900 soldiers. Tragically, most of them later lost their lives when their prison ship en route to Japan was torpedoed and sunk.

From Rabaul, Japanese troops moved south to the main island of New Guinea and fanned out, attempting to cross the Owen Stanley mountains and take Port Moresby. They nearly did so, but were halted by Australian-American forces in the Kokoda area. The Japanese then withdrew and were pushed all the way back to Rabaul where they had started. There they dug in and remained until the war's end.

During the 50's and 60's there was considerable commercial and agricultural development from outsiders, but native New Guineans were being encouraged to become active in the development of the territory and on September 16, 1975 Papua New Guinea became independent. The first general elections were held in 1977, and Michael Somare was elected Prime Minister.

In the opinion of this writer, considerable credit should go to Australia for its orderly, generous approach during the transition period and its continuing support of the new country. Equal credit should be given Papua New Guinea for the responsible way it achieved independence.

But problems remain, one of which is unity, or the lack of it. The New Guineans have always been communally exclusive. The people in one valley often speak a different language from the people in the next valley, and their relationship may not always be harmonious. To get ahead in such an environment requires skill, strength, and wealth. Heredity—important in other parts of Melanesia or Polynesia—does not determine who succeeds in new Guinea.

Christianity, mutual trade and the development of a common language (Pidgin or English) have helped, but differences persist among the highlanders, coastal people, and outer islanders. There is also a wide gap between town people and rural dwellers, as well as between the native population and the 35,000 Australians, Europeans, and Chinese who work there.

Before independence there were considerably more foreigners than there are now. For many of them Papua New Guinea was home. They owned property and had a vested interest in the territory. Now most off-islanders are employed on short term contracts and put down few roots.

Another problem, one common to other emerging nations, is the matter of public harmony, safety in the streets or at home. Unfortunately Papua New Guinea is having more than its fair share of violence and crime, so much so that traveler's warnings have had to be issued. Put simply, young people hoping for economic success abandon tribal life and go to the centers of commerce, to Port Moresby, Lae, or Mt. Hagen. There, when they are unable to achieve material success, frustration, anger, resentment, and crime result.

It's hoped that these problems are merely symptoms of development, like having measles in childhood. But eventually Papua New Guinea, with all of her resources of timber, fishing, agriculture, mining and hydro-electric power, will no doubt find the necessary unity to become a stable society.

How to Get There By Air

From Honolulu to Port Moresby via other Pacific islands, the best route would be by Quantas, Air New Zealand, or Air Pacific to Nadi, Fiji. Air Pacific has a once-a-week flight to Honiara in the Solomons. From Honiara take the several-times-a-week Air Niugini flight on to Port Moresby.

An alternate route from the Solomons is the three-times-weekly scenic Solair flight from Honiara to Kieta, Bougainville, Papua New Guinea. If you plan to make this trip, be sure to have a pre-issued visa for Papua New Guinea. Kieta is not permitted to provide entry permits.

To New Guinea from Australia or New Zealand—Fly from Sydney, Brisbane, or Cairns, Australia to Port Moresby on daily Qantas or Air Niugini flights.

To New Guinea from Hong Kong, Manila or Jayapura, Irian Jaya—Air Niugini and Cathay Pacific provide service.

By Sea

Check on cruise ship schedules. Some make calls at Port Moresby, Lae, Madang, or Rabaul. Sitmar, P & O, Cunard, Royal Viking and Five Star are possibilities.

From Sydney, Australia, contact the Karlander New Guinea Line in Port Moresby, Papua New Guinea. This freighter line sometimes carries six to eight passengers.

Immigration

No visa is required if visitors carry a US passport and enter the country at Port Moresby. If there's a chance that you might enter from Kieta, Bougainville, or come in through Vanimo from West Irian (the Indonesian part of the island), be sure you have a visa obtained from the Papua New Guinea embassy in Washington, DC.

You must also have an ongoing or round-trip ticket and evidence of sufficient funds for support.

Health

There is malaria in some regions, the Sepik River area included. Preventive medication is necessary. Two chloroquine (Aralen) tablets should be taken on the same day each week, starting two weeks before arrival, until two weeks after departure. Water is generally potable in Papua New Guinea, hardly ever in Irian Jaya on the Indonesian side.

Good medical and dental care is available nearly everywhere.

Currency

The monetary unit is the kina. One K is worth about 98¢ US. The word kina comes from the pearl shell used in the highlands as traditional money. The K is issued in denominations of K2, K5, K10 and K20. Coins are Toeas—1, 2, 5, 10, 20, 50, and a K1 coin.

Time Zone

Ten hours ahead of Greenwich Mean Time, 15 hours ahead of Eastern Standard Time, 18 hours ahead of Pacific Standard Time.

Carrying produce on the Sepik River

Newspapers, Radio, TV, and Telephones

Papua New Guinea has two English language newspapers: *The Papua New Guinea Post* and *The Niugini Nius.* The National Broadcasting Commission of New Guinea operates a series of English speaking broadcasts seven days a week. There is world-wide telephone service from most sizeable towns in the country.

Power

220 volts AC.

Climate

Tropically warm and humid in the lowlands, cool sometimes snappy in the highlands. April to October are the best months.

Languages

English is widely spoken, as is colorful Pidgin and 700 other languages that you're not apt to understand. English will get you by nicely.

Tipping

As in other parts of the South Pacific, tipping is neither encouraged nor expected.

Holidays

January 1, New Year's Day; Good Friday; Easter Sunday; Queen Elizabeth II's Birthday in June; Independence Day, September 16; Christmas; Boxing Day, December 26.

Other events prompting local ceremonies: Chinese New Year, the end of January or early February. National Capital Show in Port Moresby, mid-June. Highlands Singsing, every August.

PORT MORESBY AND ENVIRONS

Port Moresby, the capital on the south coast, has a population of about 150,000 which includes some 11,000 Australians,

Europeans, and Chinese expatriates. This community, sometimes called the National Capital District, may not be the serene place it was before independence but, warts and all, it's a city that provides all comforts with a solid Australian flair. It's a gateway city, a port, the center of commerce, and there's even a university. It's also the most expensive city. But usually visitors who land at Jackson International Airport seven miles from town are only there briefly, practically in transit. Still two or three days in Port Moresby is worthwhile and is good conditioning for what lies ahead.

The city which used to straggle over the promontory separating Fairfax Harbor and Walter's Bay has remnants of the past. The old Moresby and Papua Hotels, a block apart, still stand on Musgrave Street, and expats of 20 years ago will remember them. Also the RSL Club (Returned Service League) and the

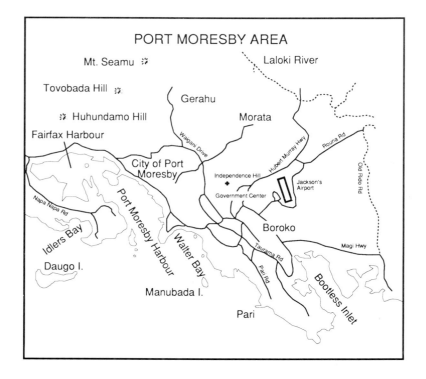

PORT MORESBY AREA

Yacht Club are long-time sources of refreshment, still producing lively conversation and behavior. I remember when $13.50 per person provided a room and three meals at the Papua Hotel; now it's $50 a double without meals. The old four-faced clock on Musgrave Street is still the business and geographic center of town. The traditional department stores, Burns Philp and Steamships, remain active. So do several banks and shops. But the profile of town has changed. The white 12-storey Australia New Guinea building, the Bank of Papua New Guinea, the Papua New Guinea Banking Corporation and the new international-standard Travelodge dominate the scene.

The suburb of Boroko has a shiny new shopping area. At Waigani, connected to town by a multi-lane highway, there's the new 12-storey Australian High Commission Building, the Port Moresby Council Theatre, the Supreme Court Building, and a National Museum under construction. At Tougaba Hill, practically in the center of town, luxurious new housing is going up.

Not all recent development is attractive, and old time expats would be appalled by the new squatter areas, squalid communities inhabited by unemployed drifters who were lured to the city where they have become, to say the least, social problems.

Where to Stay in Port Moresby

The Gateway Hotel—After leaving the plane at Jackson International Airport, the most convenient place to stay is just across the street from the terminal, at the Gateway. This pleasant hotel with bar-dining facilities provides free minibus service into Port Moresby, seven miles away. Rates with bath, about $65 double.

The Travelodge—This most prestigious hotel is right in the center of town, a high rise with sweeping views of harbor and ocean. All amenities are provided, with rates about $100 double.

The Hotel Moresby—This is an old landmark hotel in the center of town, with bar-restaurant. Rates $45 double.

The Papua Hotel—This is another remnant of old days, and

still the scene of congenial gatherings. It has music, dancing, bar and an unusually good restaurant. Rates $50 double.

The Davara Motel—This hotel is on Ela Beach Road, 10 minutes walk from the town center. Good sea views, pool. Rates $50 double.

Islander Hotel—It's in Boroko, halfway between town and the airport. Close to the new Waigani Commercial Center, it has pool, bar and restaurant. About $75 double.

The Loloata Island Resort—This resort, 14 miles from Port Moresby, is on an island in Bootless Bay. It's considered an escapist resort where you can swim, snorkel, fish and loaf. Rooms with all meals included are $75 double. Reservations are recommended. Write to PO Box 5290, Port Moresby, or phone from the airport, 258590.

The Boroko Hotel—Near the airport, it has a restaurant-bar. Rates $55 double.

Budget Accommodations

The YWCA Hostel—This is located between town and Boroko and is not licensed (no bar) but it has a restaurant. $25 double.

The Salvation Army Hostel—It's close to town and has kitchen facilities. $40 double.

The Civic Guest House—In Boroko, it's inexpensive and serves meals. Rates on request. Write PO Box 1139, Boroko, Papua New Guinea, or phone 255091.

The Konedobu Hotel—This is in the old colonial part of town among mango and rain trees. It's inexpensive.

Dining in and Around Port Moresby

Dining in Port Moresby is much the same as dining in a similar size Australian city. You'll eat well, but are generally limited to two types of cooking—Chinese or Australian. Both offer excellent local seafood.

As to typical native New Guinea dishes, few restaurants serve their "cooked in the earth" root crop dishes. When this food is eaten by off-islanders, it's out of curiosity, not hunger.

The smartest, best turned out restaurants are at the big hotels: The *Travelodge*, the *Davara*, the *Gateway*, the *Islander*, the *Boroko*, the *Moresby*, and the *Papua*. All except the Papua are fairly expensive, but the Papua in our opinion is one of the best. An evening meal in these restaurants will average about $35 for two with wine. The Chinese restaurants are less expensive, but very good. There are at least six of them. Try the *Moonlight* in town. For dining more modestly and with spirited local company, try the *Royal Yacht Club* on the harbor side of town. Or visit the *RSL Club* (Returned Service Men's Club) on Ela Beach.

Evening Entertainment

An evening out in Port Moresby is like an evening out in Cairns, Alice Springs, Wagga Wagga, Adelaide or even Sydney, Australia. You can have fun, the sort of fun inspired by bar-cabaret activities. The RSL Club is a friendly, noisy places where considerable beer is consumed. The same is true of the Yacht Club where you'll meet, drink, and have fun with congenial people, mostly Aussies.

Or you could go to the movies. There are several theaters in town.

Other than a few squalid indigenous night spots where you wouldn't be welcome, there are no hostess-filled bar-clubs in the area.

What to Do in the Port Moresby Area

The landscape around Port Moresby is attractive, but there is no jungle there. Its wooded and grassy-patched hills give it an Australian appearance, which is understandable because Australia is only 250 miles away. Along the coast there are some good beaches. In daylight this is a good area for strolling. For longer distances taxis, more expensive than in other Pacific areas, are available. But buses and PMVs (public motor vehicles) are cheap and run often. Start out by doing the town on foot.

Touaguba Hill—To get your bearings, leave the center of town and take the easy footpath to the summit of this hill. From there Port Moresby lies at your feet.

Ela Beach—Go the short distance from town to the beach,

then walk under the casuarinas. If the tide is in and there's not too much seaweed, you can go for a swim.

Koki Market—Continue down Ela Beach a mile or so, to one of the most colorful markets in the Pacific. Everything from the land and sea is sold there including native string bags (bilum bags,) grass skirts, baskets, and carvings. While there, be sure to check out the arrivals of the "lakatoi people" (sailing canoe people) who bring their produce from up and down the coast. For a taste of their life, adventurous travelers could make arrangements to sail away with these people when they return home up or down the coast, a hundred or more miles.

Hanuabada and the Konedobu Cultural Center—From town this is rather far to walk. You can take a taxi or bus from the harbor side of town to the north about three miles. At crowded, old Hanuabada Village see the series of houses built on stilts out over the harbor. This is how Port Moresby looked way back when.

In the same area, near Konedobu, visit the Cultural Center and examine the Papuan artifacts including trading canoes (lakatois)—the same sort you saw being used at Koki Market. The admission fee is 20 toea (about 20¢). There is good shopping here.

The University of New Guinea—This is 10 miles from town. Wander the campus grounds, then visit its Botanic Gardens and see the collection of native orchids and local flora.

The National Museum and Art Gallery—This is in the new part of town, Waigani, which is eight miles out. The area is worth visiting just to see the new construction. The National Museum has a collection of artifacts from all over the country and is excellent. Admission is free.

Post Office—Stamp collectors should visit the post office in town on Champion Street, and ask about new issues; they're extraordinarily colorful. Remember too that you can make overseas calls from here.

Outside of Port Moresby

Roads from Port Moresby don't go far. None of them go north all the way across the island, none go to the far eastern end, nor anywhere near the Indonesian border in the west. About

Road sign, Papua New Guinea

the best you can do by car is down the coast through lowland forest by *Rigo,* about 51 miles, or northwest up the coast nearly to *Yule Island,* about 38 miles. There's a small inn on Yule Island, an inexpensive away-from-it-all spot.

The other road, and the best trip in the area, is up the Sogeri Road northeast of town. There are worthwhile places to see on this route. The first one, 11 miles from town, is *Bomana War Cemetery.* It's a moving, well-kept memorial to the dead of the World War II New Guinea Campaign. Nine miles further is the bushland park of *Rouna Falls.* There the air is cooler, the Falls beautiful, and there are miles of bushwalking for those who want to explore.

The *Kokoda Monument* is about seven miles further on, but to get to where the Kokoda Trail begins you turn left at the monument, and follow a rough track nine miles to Owens Corner, where the walking starts. Near the Monument and the Sogeri Market there is a hospitable inn run by colorful Aussies, *The Kokoda Trail Motel.* The beer is cold, the food is good, and you'll get plenty of free (mostly true) information about walking the Kokoda Trail. Rates at this nicely landscaped riverside retreat are $50 a double with bath.

The 40-mile trip will cost about $2 per person by PMV or $22 by taxi.

To *rent cars* check with Avis in town or at the airport, Budget in town and at the Gateway Hotel, Hertz in Boroko. Rates will work out to $50-$70 a day (insurance and mileage included). Remember, they drive on the left side of the road in PNG.

The Kokoda Trail

The Kokoda Trail was the route taken by Australian soldiers in 1942 to stop the Japanese who were coming down the Trail in an attempt to take Port Moresby. When the two forces met, a bloody battle ensued, and the Japanese were halted just 45 miles from Port Moresby. Then Australian and American troops clawed their way back up and over toward the north coast. Months and many lives were required.

The Trail, perhaps not in as good condition as it was in the '40s, is now available to backpackers. The rugged trek passes through magnificent rain forests, across dozens of streams, along ridges with views forever, and through a number of villages inhabited by friendly people, few old enough to remember anything about the war.

Most hikers today fly to the far end of the Trail, at Kokoda, and then walk back downhill toward Port Moresby. Depending on fitness, between five days and two weeks are required to walk the 58 miles. Do not attempt the walk in the wet season, between December and March.

The trip isn't difficult if you know what to expect, but it isn't to be taken lightly. Take a guide if you're not trailwise. Happily though, most villagers along the Trail understand English, and since the villages en route can usually provide shelter, a tent is not needed. Even if it's necessary to spend a night between villages, there are lean-tos at regular intervals. Food and water are available along the way and, in case of emergency, there are several airstrips with radio communication. If soldiers could do it, fight too, and carry all essentials, fit travelers should not have a problem.

THE NORTH COAST OF PAPUA NEW GUINEA

The parts of Papua New Guinea accessible by sea are our choice areas. Port Moresby is an exception. It's not that we're unenthusiastic about that city, but shipping people there tend to be uncooperative when it comes to carrying passengers. If you insist on leaving Port Moresby by ship, make the rounds of the shipping offices—Burns Philp, Steamships, Coastal Shipping. Question them about passage around the eastern tip to Samarai. Then wander about the harbor, go aboard a few ships and, hat in hand, talk to the captain.

On the other hand, it's as well to postpone seagoing activities until arrival on the north coast, nearer the good things of PNG. Adventure coupled with reasonable creature comforts is plentiful there and, other than a measure of resilience, no jungle survival skills are required. One can expect a good meal, a cold drink, a fair bed every night, unless you volunteer to do some cross-country trekking.

Ships are fairly easy to come by in this area, land transport too, where there are roads. Where no roads exist, you can usually get there by air. And by way of example, consider doing the north coast, or pieces of it, by moving in an erratic east-to-west direction.

Before departure from Port Moresby, a few words about language may be helpful. English will get you by nicely in most areas, probably everywhere. However, without trying at all, you'll absorb bits and pieces of a compromise language that cuts across the 717 actual languages of PNG. It's Melanesian

Pidgin, "Pisin", and about a million Niuginians use this descriptive "trade language." With apologies to Berlitz, please note the following brief vocabulary lesson.

Go isi	Go slowly, as on road sign
Meri	Woman
Ples	Please
Bilong	Belongs
Kai kai	Food
Buggerdup	Broken, not working
Shit bilong im	Garbage
Wan tok	Conversation, meeting
Mi pela laikum turist	We like tourists

MILNE BAY PROVINCE

The tiny island of Samarai which lies at the extreme southeastern tip of Papua New Guinea, the bird's tail, is the best place to start a meandering east-to-west journey. And it's the most productive place to find vessels sailing into some of the most exotic of Papua New Guinea's islands.

To get there take the daily Air Niugini flight from Port Moresby to Alotau, 20 miles from Samarai. The fare is about $65 US. If enough light remains, take the scheduled launch on to Samarai, about two hours distant. If necessary you can spend the night at an inexpensive guesthouse in Alotau.

Samarai is palm-clad and so small you can walk around it in 20 minutes. It's a district center, a base for shipping the area's most important crop, copra (coconuts). There's a comfortable guesthouse, *The Pacific View,* with rates $40 double.

Down the hill in town there's a pleasant club which will require all of three minutes to negotiate membership. There you'll meet most of the Australian community, a congenial but island-bound lot whose activities lean toward VCR, the club and gossip. They're always glad to see a new face though, and you won't get bored.

But the main reason for coming to Samarai is to find onward transport by sea to some of the finest Papua New Guinea islands, the nearby D'Entrecasteaux and Trobriand Islands. Check in with Burns Philp and Steamships shipping offices, or

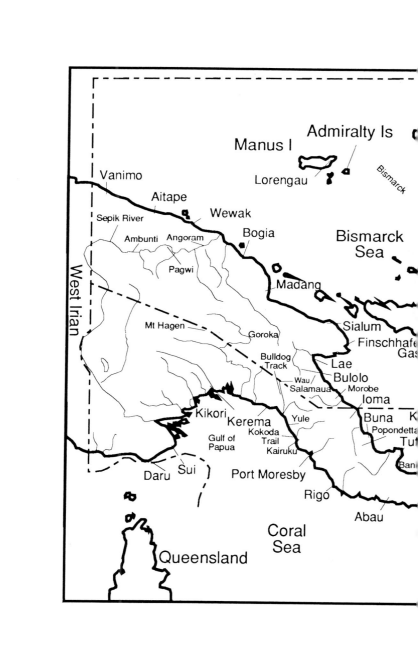

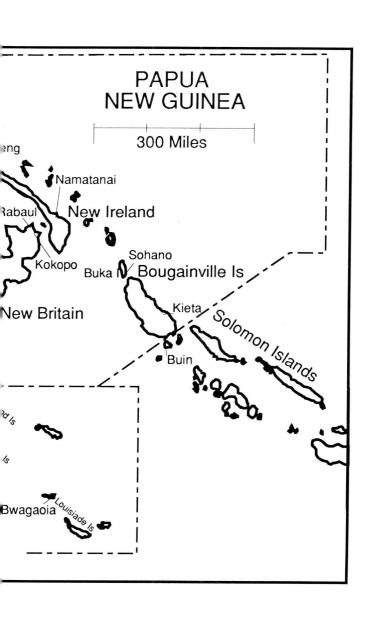

PAPUA
NEW GUINEA

|— 300 Miles —|

eng

Namatanai

New Ireland

Rabaul

Kokopo
Buka
Sohano
Bougainville Is

New Britain
Kieta
Solomon Islands

Buin

d Is

Is

Bwagaoia Louisiade Is

approach the vessels that come in. It won't take long to find something. On our second day there we saw tied up at the wharf a small Burns Philp copra boat named the *"Lakatoi."* Her deckhouse was set well aft, the cargo space forward, and there was about her solid 85-foot length a no-nonsense seagoing look.

Her captain, a Rossel islander named Abel Cain, said they were off to the Trobriands via the D'Entrecasteaux on a five-day voyage to deliver supplies, pick up copra and carry native deck passengers. He said that if we provided our own food, we were welcome to occupy the only passenger cabin. And he added that a cookboy would be assigned to prepare our food.

Without delay we bought the necessary supplies—rice, canned meats, vegetables, cheese, ships' biscuits, beer, and enough Scotch to see us through. Fresh fruit we were told would be available along the way (it was).

Thus provisioned, we enjoyed a final evening at the club, and early the next morning we were at sea.

THE D'ENTRECASTEAUX ISLANDS

The map of Papua New Guinea plainly displays to the north of Samarai the three main islands of this group—Normanby, Fergusson, and Goodenough. You may have to squint a little to see the tiny Amphletts a little further to the north but, large or small, these islands are far from beaten paths.

Getting across the straits from Samarai to Normanby, the first of these islands, can be rough going if the sea is up. When it is, life aboard small trading vessels will not fill hearts with hosannahs.

Fortunately, our six-hour passage to Esa Ala on the northern end of the Normanby was benevolent—a day of indolence with blue seas, flying fish, and two good meals prepared by the cookboy.

At Esa Ala, a modest village near modest thermal springs, cargo was unloaded, copra taken on, and because the *Lakatoi* moved only by day, we stayed for the night. And that pause provides a good moment to clarify seagoing activities in the Milne Bay area. First of all because there's copra to be gathered and supplies to be delivered, a fair number of vessels move about in all directions. most of them carry deck passengers and, for the slightly more affluent as on the *Lakatoi,* provide cabin space. But these boats are spartan, and even cabin class is rugged. It's like going camping.

Our cabin had four bunks, a hot plate, and a refrigerator that was never quite successful with ice cubes. For plumbing, there was a bucket with rope attached. For lighting we had the stars and a kerosene lamp. Captain Abel Cain, sharing sundown Scotches, kept us well informed and the cookboy, when he wasn't clinically involved with one of the topless female deck passengers, rivalled Julia Child.

From Esa Ala we sailed erratically, village-by-village, up the west coast of Fergusson, then to Goodenough, and finally due north through the jewel-like Amphletts. We stopped at places with names like Nau Nau, Bula Bula, Wakabi. We loaded copra and, with tears and wails to mark departures and arrivals, we took on and discharged deck passengers.

A passenger-carrying coastal freighter

Some of the islands had peaks with smoking volcanoes. On others there were lacy waterfalls. The tiny green Amphletts had talcum-white beaches, coconut palms, and colored parrots. Eventually, on approaching an island we'd leap into the gin-clear sea and swim to the beach ahead of the ship.

These people, the Melanesians, depend on the sea for fish and the land for yams, bananas, and breadfruit. For such luxuries as rice, kerosene, tinned fish, and beer, they depend on the sale of copra—which is one reason boats ply these waters.

Some of these folks succeed admirably, some fail terribly. There are squalid villages to be seen huddled at the edge of malignant jungle. Other villages, perhaps close by, lie in splendor under the palms—neat airy settlements where paths of crushed coral lead to a well-mowed central square and tidy thatched buildings labelled "Native Women's Club" or "Village Council Center."

There was one evening en route when an Aussie who ran a trading center rowed out to where we lay anchored and took us ashore for dinner. During that happy evening his mother, remarking about the island life expectancy, said that at 72 she was the oldest human being on Goodenough.

THE TROBRIAND ISLANDS

The Trobriand Islands, 22 of them, lie 100 miles off the north coast of Papua New Guinea in the Solomon Sea. Some anthropologists refer to the people who live on these lovely green coral islands as Polynesians. If that's true, they're the darkest Polynesians I've ever seen. Nevertheless they're handsome folks, and according to the anthropologist Malinowski who was interned there during World War I, they're affectionate too. In his book he calls the Trobriands the "Islands of Love."

Proud people live on these islands. They're justifiably proud of their traditional villages, their woodcarvings, and the soul of the villages—their yam houses—which trigger a lively festival when they are filled.

With the same sort of pride, and with surplus yams, the Trobrianders keep alive the "Kula Ring" trading ritual. This annual sea voyage by trading canoe among neighboring islands embodies a spiritual approach to barter, one that involves trading yams for ornamental shell necklaces and pottery.

Outsiders, casual visitors, will find that the islanders are a little sensitive about strangers who appear uninvited in their villages and they're not pleased with people who snap photos of their nubile bare-breasted women.

My impression of these admirable people is that they covet neither our possessions nor our culture. In a kindly way they keep the outside world at arm's length.

The main things to see here are: the people themselves, their traditional villages, yam houses, and dances, as well as the good beaches and lush tropical beauty. Good carvings can be bought in the Trobriands as well.

To Get There

Air Niugini has regular flights from Port Moresby to Kiriwina, the main Trobriand Island. This is about an hour flight and the fare is $120 round trip.

The *Melanesian Explorer* also has trips to these islands, which will be described later.

Where to Stay

The Kiriwina Lodge accommodates 30 people. Rates with all meals are $60 double and include airport transfer.

Note—The Trobriands are on the tour circuit now, and the guesthouse fills up quickly. Reservations are advised. Ask about special tours. As much as I hate to admit it, a tour is often cheaper than do-it-yourself travel.

From the Trobriands—Fly on from there in any direction, or if you wait long enough some sort of ship will appear and you can continue on to Lae or Samarai. There isn't a road between the Samarai-Alotau area and Lae. All transport is by air or sea.

We were lucky in the Trobriands and sailed away on a coastal freighter bound for Lae. En route we slept between sheets, ate Aussie meat pies, drank Victoria Bitters and, courtesy of a waggish Australian Captain, laughed all the way to Lae.

MOROBE PROVINCE

Lae, Papua New Guinea's second city at 35,000 population, has changed considerably since the day in 1937 when Amelia Earhart and her navigator, Fred Noonan, took off for Howland Island and were never seen again. Then came World War II, and subsequent bombings flattened Lae. Since then it's been entirely rebuilt and now resembles any comparable Australian town.

Travelers don't usually go to Lae for Lae's sake. They treat it as a way station. Still it has everything comfort requires: restaurants, movies, shops, golf courses, tree-lined streets, as well as good onward transport by air, sea, and road.

The Botanical Gardens are one of the best in the South Pacific. They have 140 acres of exotic plants and the largest collection of orchids in the world.

The War Cemetery next to the Botanical Gardens is a well cared for cemetery with the graves of 2,804 servicemen who died in the World War II New Guinea Campaign.

Where to Stay

The Huon Gulf Motel—Near the airport, which is practically in town. This nicely landscaped hotel with pool has all amenities. About $75 double.

The Lae Lodge—Not far from the town center and set in pretty grounds. Pool and tennis courts. $70 double.

Melanesian Hotel—Centrally located, comfortable rooms with baths. $50 double.

Klinkii Lodge—Near the golf course. Comfortable rooms with baths. $40 double.

Hotel Cecil—In town near the wharf. Comfortable rooms with baths. $35 double.

Budget Accommodations

Buabling Haus—A simple hospitable inn run by a church group. $8 per person.

Salvation Army Tourist Flats—They're on Huon Road. Rooms, some with cooking facilities, about $25 double.

Dining in Lae

There are plenty of Aussie-style fast-food restaurants for sandwiches, fish and chips, and meat pies—all inexpensive. In Chinatown there's at least one good inexpensive Chinese restaurant. For good fellowship, plus reasonably priced good meals, visit the RSL Club. Most of the hotels serve meals in extremely pleasant surroundings. They are moderate to expensive.

Shopping

The best place to buy native artifacts at a bargain price is from the street peddlers outside the Burns Philp store downtown.

OUTSIDE OF LAE

The Siassi Islands—A series of tiny islands 90 miles north of Lae, they're white-sanded, palmed and beautiful. A number of boats, usually copra boats, will carry you there for about $20 one way. Talair also flies from Lae. Accommodations range from marginal, to none and, if you've just done the Milne Bay Islands, something else may be preferable.

Finschaven—Seventy miles from Lae at the northern top of the Huon Gulf is an attractive coastal town, an old German colonial settlement where copra and coffee are grown. "Finsch" will be fondly or otherwise remembered by many World War II sailors and soldiers.

You can fly there from Lae by Talair or catch one of the Lutheran Shipping Co. vessels from Lae's wharf. Fare is about $10 one way.

Stay at the *Dregerhaven Lodge,* PO Box 126, Finschaven (phone 44-7050). This place is inexpensive and popular for fishing, snorkeling. Make reservations.

Sialum—This area is 30 miles up the coast from Finschaven, is strikingly beautiful, and has good beach activities. You can fly there, about $55 round trip from Lae, or go by car from Finschaven if the road has been completed.

Stay at the *Paradise Spring Inn.* For a weekend, meals, morning and afternoon tea included, the rate is $250 double.

For 5 days it's $580, or $60 per day double without meals. Make reservations in Lae for this popular resort (phone 019).

Salamaua—This peninsula 25 miles south of Lae is spectacular, a place probably destined to have a Club Med or a posh diving club. Now it's perfect for indolent walking, picnicking, and snorkeling on the reef.

There is no road to Salamaua from Lae; it has to be done by boat. Best thing to do is walk down to Voco Point from downtown Lae and ask around for a boat. If one is leaving, expect to pay about $4 round trip. You should probably make the round trip in one day as housing is difficult to find there.

BULOLO, WAU, AND THE BULLDOG TRACK

In the 1920s gold was discovered in the Bulolo-Wau area, and large numbers of gold-fevered men went there the hard way. They came by foot ten days over the mountains, through the jungle from Salamaua 55 miles away. The miners and the mines were successful, but after the war operating costs in-

Outrigger canoe, near Madang

creased and, with gold fixed at $35 an ounce, mining became a waning industry. There is still some mining activity, but timber and coffee production are the mainstays.

Because of a military need during the war, a road was pushed through south from Lae to Wau via Bulolo—a distance of 93 miles. You can travel there by either PMV, bus or rental car. Or, for hardy bush-skilled walkers, the Bulldog Track is a 50-mile challenge.

This trail begins at Edie Creek near Wau and continues on to Bulldog. The jungles are thick, the country uninhabited, the trail poorly marked and, to make matters more challenging, locals are reluctant to act as bearer-guides. The Kokoda Trail, in comparison, is a Sunday walk in the park.

Where to Stay

Bed and breakfast rates are $50 double at the *Pine Lodge Hotel* in Bulolo.

In Wau stay at the *Wau Lodge* which the management refers to as a "Game Safari Lodge." Rates are moderate.

RABAUL, NEW BRITAIN

The 300-mile-long island of New Britain is north and east of Lae. It's about 390 miles from Lae to Rabaul. The easiest access is by air from Lae or Port Moresby, but note that long distance air travel in PNG isn't cheap. Port Moresby to Lae one-way is about $160, from Lae to Rabaul is about $90. But any number of ships make the Lae-Rabaul run. Contact Burns Philp, the Nambuna Line, and Coastal Shipping. The two-day passage, meals included, is about $50.

Rabaul in West New Britain Province has a population of 25,000 and is one of the prettiest ports in the Pacific. It's also off the beaten track and, because of recent volcanic rumblings, travel there was discouraged. Apparently it's all right now and Rabaul, on Simpson Harbor at the foot of three volcanic peaks, stands ready to receive visitors.

The People—The dominant group are the Tolai People, about 70,000 unusually productive folks who import unskilled labor from other areas. Their highly successful activities are mainly agricultural—copra, cocoa, and garden produce. Rabaul has had a colorful past. It was German until 1914, then Australian. Between 1942 and 1945 it was in Japanese hands and was under constant attack by the Allies. The old town was completely destroyed. What you'll see now is a new and well-laid-out community.

Where to Stay

Rabaul Travelodge—It's the best in town, has all amenities, and is about $65 double.
Motel Kaivuna—In the center of town; $50 double.
Hamamas Hotel—In town by the sea; $48 double.

Budget Accommodations

Rabaul Community Hostel—Rooms and dormitory facilities. $24 double with all meals.
New Guinea Club—Bed and breakfast; $25 double.

What to Do

Rabaul's *Simpson Harbor* is excellent for sailing, boating, and game fishing. Ashore there's golf, tennis and good walking. For magnificent avocados, mangos, and immense papayas, visit the *public market*. East of town a short distance at *Kokopo,* you can see the ruins of Japanese air raid tunnels from World War II.

For snorkeling and diving, go to the old *Japanese submarine base.* The water there is clear electric blue and has some eerie dropoffs.

Rabaul is famous for volcanos. The last major eruption was in 1937. You can visit *Matupit* crater, which is still active. Someone can paddle you across from Matupit Island (near the airport). *Mt. Kombiu* (the mother) is the highest nonactive volcano in the area at 2,100 feet. Taxi or bus out to Nordup north of town, and start walking at the Nordup United Church. Go early in the morning when it's cool. The walking is hard work, but the views from Mt. Kombiu make it all worthwhile.

THE DUKE OF YORK ISLANDS

For good snorkeling and picnicking, take a launch from town to islands called "the Pigeons" which are halfway from Rabaul to Duke of York Island. Visit nearby Mioko Island where you can see remnants of the fabled *Queen Emma's house*. Queen Emma was a part-Samoan woman colorfully prominent in trading history of the late 1800's. You can stay at a small resort on Mioka.

WEST NEW BRITAIN PROVINCE

A road now under consideration may someday connect Rabaul to West New Britain's major shipping area, the three towns on Stettin Bay, Talasea, Kimbe and Hoskins. The distance is about 185 miles. Now only air and sea transport is available, but once you are there an all-weather road connects the towns.

Nearly 90,000 people live in West New Britain and, other than some primitives deep in the jungle, most are involved in the production of copra, cocoa, palm oil, and subsistence gardening. There are some underground hot springs near Hoskins and Talasea which may be of interest, there is good snorkeling on Stettin Bay's coral reefs, and some fine wood carvings are available here. This province is definitely not the most popular destination in Papua New Guinea.

Where to Stay

Hoskins Hotel—Near the airport; a double room with bath and meals included is $65.

Palm Lodge Motel—In Kimbe, this bed and breakfast is about $40 double.

NEW IRELAND

New Ireland is the skinny 200-mile-long island just north of New Britain. The population is 58,000, and some of them have retained their traditional culture as reflected in the wood carvings which you will see for sale. Most of the locals are involved in subsistence farming, and the area's economy is based on copra, fisheries, cocoa, timber and rubber.

Kavieng at the western end is the administrative center. This is a sleepy little town well away from the hue and cry.

Where to Stay

Kavieng Hotel—It has all comforts, plus unusually good buffet meals. $52 double.

Namatanai Hotel—This hotel, in the town of the same name, is about 160 miles by road southeast of Kavieng. Rates $40 double.

MANUS ISLAND, THE ADMIRALTY GROUP

Manus island, 190 miles off the north coast of Papua New Guinea, ranks high in beauty. Its surrounding satellite islands and coral reefs are delightful and the inhabitants, more Micronesian than Melanesian, are handsome and congenial.

Manus is 65 miles long—it's where Margaret Mead did some of her best anthropological work. Pacific veterans will remember Manus as the place where the ammunition ship *Mt. Hood* blew up, with the loss of all on board.

Lorengau, the main town (population 4,000) is served by air and sea from Lae.

Where to Stay

The Seaadler Lodge—On the waterfront; $50 double.

BOUGAINVILLE ISLAND

The combination of Buka and Bougainville Islands (connected by a ferry) extends about 150 miles and, although this group belongs to PNG, it is geographically part of the Solomon Islands. More than 100,000, mostly Melanesians, live there and the administrative center is at Arawa-Kieta.

You can fly in from Port Moresby ($180 one way) or from Honiara in the Solomons, one of the most spectacular flights in the Pacific. By sea, Bougainville is served by numbers of ships. Coming from Lae by sea is the easiest and is much cheaper than flying. Check with the Nambuna Shipping Co. in Lae.

If you're into mines, there is a huge open pit copper and gold mine at Panguna in the interior, not far from Arawa. Because of the mine the quality of life has changed, and now there are supermarkets, impressive housing areas, schools, new roads, and a burgeoning economy.

The interior of Bougainville is mountainous, covered by dense rain forests and laced with rivers that flow down the mountains into the sea. Because of this, there are few good beaches and much of the coast is mangrove swamp.

Traveling overland you can go by bus all the way to Buka in the north or to Buin in the south, where you will be far from the influence of the mines.

Plenty of World War II remains are on the island, including Admiral Yamamoto's plane which was shot down by the Allies. Locals will guide you to the scene of the crash where the Admiral was killed.

Where to Stay

The Davara Hotel—Comfortable, with a bar-restaurant and pool. About $70 double.

Hotel Kieta—Near the waterfront, with a bar-restaurant. $65 double.

Buka Loman Soho Guest House—This is at Buka in the north. $20 double.

GOING TO SEA FROM BOUGAINVILLE

To the north and east of Bougainville there are three of the most unspoiled atolls in the world. Kilinailau (population 1,000) is mostly Melanesian; Tauu has 500 people, mostly Polynesian; and Nukumanu has 300 almost pure Polynesians. Each of these groups has fine circular lagoons dotted with tiny islands. For survival, the islanders depend on the sea and what they can grow on their thin soil—including copra for export.

When we were in Bougainville a fair-sized copra ship was ready to sail to these islands and, other than deck passage possibilities, there was one modest cabin aboard. Passengers were required to furnish their own food. Fare for the week-or ten-day voyage was about $70 per person. It's an adventure worth considering. Since we had just completed a similar voyage, we declined this one.

THE ROAD TO NEW GUINEA'S HIGHLANDS

Some travel writers suggest flying directly from Moresby to Goroka or Mt. Hagen, and this is too bad, for there is nothing like spending a day watching the land change from lowland jungle to highland forest. From Lae this is what happens on the daily 200-mile bus run to Goroka, eight hours away. Then the next day there's another 140 mostly unpaved miles, five hours on to Mt. Hagen. Fare for the entire run will be about $50, or half that amount by PMV.

GOROKA

We recommend spending the first night in Goroka which is a completely westernized town of 19,000 at a comfortable altitude of 5,000 feet. It's in coffee growing country.

Where to Stay

Bird of Paradise Hotel—In the center of town, it has a bar-restaurant. $55 a double.

Lantern Lodge—In town, with a bar-restaurant. $50 a double.

Minogere Lodge—Close to downtown; bed and breakfast. $46 a double.

Salvation Army Flats—In the northern part of town. $12 per person.

What to See

The *J. K. McCarthy Museum* has an excellent display of the area's early civilization. Also good artifact shopping there.

MT. HAGEN

By road, from Goroka through Chimbu to Mt. Hagen the going gets rougher, more mountainous, but the scenery is majestic, and the villages unspoiled and genuine.

At 6,000-foot Mt. Hagen (population 44,000 including the urban area), you'll see the real highland life and ferocious looking bearded men with bones in their noses. And at the public market, open only in the mornings, signs proclaim "Noken Sipetim, Baim Kot, K10, Order Hagen Council," or "No spitting, if you get caught, 10 Kina fine (about $10)."

Coffee, tea, pyrethrum and market garden crops are important commodities in the market.

Market, Mt. Hagen

Where to Stay

Plumes and Arrows Inn—Near the Airport with all comforts; bar-restaurant. $55 double.

Highlander Hotel—Near the center of town; bar-restaurant. $58 double.

Hagen Park Motel—Downtown, with a bar-restaurant. $58 double.

Kimininga Hotel—Near center of town; bed and breakfast. $15 per person.

What to Do in Mt. Hagen

The most famous wildlife sanctuary in Papua New Guinea is at the *Baiyer River Wildlife and Bird of Paradise Sanctuary,* 30 miles north of Mt. Hagen. There are 90 species of native birds and animals in their natural surroundings. Take a PMV out there. The cost will be roughly $3 per person.

For a singsing or festival, *Minj* is a good possibility. It's a 55-mile run through tea and coffee country.

The big event, probably the biggest in PNG, is the *Highland Singsing* in August. Goroka has it one year, Mt. Hagen the next. This is a two-day celebration attended by nearly 100,000 tribespeople from all over PNG. They come decked out in their very best—mudmen from Goroka, the basket men of Minj, tribesmen with their faces painted, others covered with bird of paradise feathers or with shells. With the sound of drums, stamping of feet, singing, confusion, and color, there's nothing like it.

MADANG

The open-air bus that leaves Lae in the morning for Madang 220 miles away goes up the Markham Valley. It travels past the World War II airport at Nadzab, still in use today. It continues on through cattle-farming country past the turnoff to Goroka then, after following the Ramu River for a time, it enters the coastal range and winds through the sort of jungle seen in Tarzan films. At about 5 PM, after fording countless streams and pausing in village after village, it rattles into Madang. The trip fare is approximately $16 per person.

The bus, an open air variety, is generally filled with Melanesians and their "kargo" of vegetables, rice, kerosene, and fruit. On departure these fellow passengers will probably avoid eye contact with you, but at the lunch halt near the Goroka junction, there'll be a tentative smile or two. Then, at the first river ford rest stop where men disappear into the bush to the left and women to the right, there'll be outright grins. Before long they'll be sharing food with you and by Madang, you'll all be first cousins.

Madang, set as it is on Astrolabe Bay, is called "the jewel of PNG"—an apt description and for such a place of beauty we were surprised at the lack of tourist gimmickery. Including the urban area, 24,000 people live there, 1,200 of whom are foreign expatriates.

On the Lae-Madang road

When we arrived, the bus delivered us directly to our hotel, *The Coastwatcher,* which had been chosen at random. And 20 minutes later we stood freshly showered and thirsty at the Coastwatcher bar, an institution filled with locals and Aussies, not a tourist among them. In another 20 minutes we had firm friends.

We met teachers, administrators, planters, miners, businesspeople, and pilots. With some of them at our elbow, we played tennis or strolled under buttressed towering trees—mango, palm, and breadfruit. In the market we bought finger bananas, papayas, and drinking coconuts. At Kraenket Island just offshore, we lounged on white beaches and snorkeled on the reef. One day we drove north up the coast to the old German Mission of Alexishaven, a place of quiet worship where cocoa and copra are grown. Here there is a cemetery filled with priests and nuns from the past.

Then, back in Madang, tied up at the wharf, we found the *Melanesian Explorer.*

Where to Stay

Madang Resort Hotel—On the waterfront with pool, bar-restaurant; about $85 double. This is where you can contact the *Melanesian Explorer* operators, Jan and Peter Barter.

Coastwatcher Motel—Within walking distance of town, it has pool, bar-restaurant, and a pleasant atmosphere. $50 double.

Madang Lodge—In town on the beach. $28 a double.

CWA Cottage—Near town. $28 a double.

Dining

Dine at most of the hotels, a couple of fast food spots in town, or buy what you want at the public market.

THE SEPIK RIVER

The Sepik River is a monster waterway, a 600-mile river that, like the Nile, nourishes a variety of people and cultures.

When Margaret Mead was there circa 1926, no white man had been up the river more than 300 miles. Now, with some efforts you can travel all the way to the Indonesian border—a good 600 miles.

For travelers doing the Sepik on their own (we'll talk about the *Melanesian Explorer* later) Wewak, 180 miles up the coast west of Madang, is the usual starting point. Air Niugini flies from Madang to Wewak, about $40 US, or there's a two-day voyage from Madang aboard a spartan Lutheran Shipping Co. vessel that costs $35 US.

Wewak is a delightful little town with magnificent sandy beaches, unusually good coral reefs for divers and, like Samarai, it has a congenial club.

Where to Stay

Wewak Hotel—On a hill overlooking town, it has a restaurant-bar, and is $60 double.

Windjammer Beach Motel—On the beach, it has a restaurant-bar and is a bed and breakfast. $55 double.

Sepik Motel—Overlooks the sea, has a restaurant-bar, and is $50 double.

TO THE RIVER

From Wewak to the Sepik matters get a little "iffy," but visitors can hire a car (rather expensive) or take the PMV bus via Maprik to Pagwi on the river. Fare for the PMV trip will be about $10.

In Pagwi the simplest method to experience the river is to hire a motorized canoe with guide and spend two days going downriver to *Angoram*. Gasoline (petrol) is expensive, and that trip will cost about $150 US. This may be enough to provide you with a feel for the river. Along the way you'll stop often enough for a close look at village life, to buy carvings, and examine the richly carved and decorated haus tambarans (spirit houses), some as tall as an eight-storey building. There is nothing quite like them, or the primitive art stored there.

There are fair hotels at Pagwi, Angoram too, and en route there are "adequate" accommodations. A road leads from Angoram to Wewak for your return.

THE MELANESIAN EXPLORER

On the other hand, for ease in logistics and less wear and tear on the body, consider the *Melanesian Explorer,* and do an even more extensive Sepik trip in comfort. It is, however, much more expensive than the first way, and fellow passengers are more likely to be "tourists" than "travelers."

The *Melanesian Explorer* is the ship that does the Trobriands and the D'Entrecasteaux. The Sepik River part from Madang via Manum Island takes five days, and is an extension of the Trobriand trip. (The whole voyage takes 16 days.)

Passengers for the Sepik River increment board early evening in Madang and the ship proceeds westward up the coast. After a fine meal, perhaps a comradely nightcap, sleep with the roll of the ship comes easily.

Before dawn everyone's called on deck to view the 6,000-foot volcano on Manum Island. As dawn approaches, its cone glows bright red, then wanes. Hollywood could do no better. Seen in daylight Manum is as dramatic—a green-jungled remote island dominated by its smoke-plumed mountain. On the walk from the black sandy beach to a primitive village, children will approach and take you by the hand.

By noon with the diminishing volcano astern, the mouth of the Sepik appears. The sea there is muddy and in it float clumps of the hyacinth-like *salvinia molesta.* This plant is called "the curse of the river," a menace to navigation that can double its size in 48 hours.

For four days the *Melanesian Explorer* ascends the river, travelling only by day. Each day there are trips to villages, to haus tambarans, and even a crocodile hunt at night. The ship's speedboats carry passengers up jungled canals, into hyacinth-bound lakes, and there's a guide aboard who gives appropriate lectures. Happily too at the end of each trip ashore, the ship is waiting with air conditioning, hot showers, and glasses tinkling with ice.

Finally at Ambunti, 200 miles upriver, where hills appear and the river narrows, passengers debark and fly by ten-seater

---

Spirit house in the Sepik region, used for men's meetings and storage of cultural objects

Sepik artifacts offered for sale

aircraft over mountains, jungle, and twisting rivers to Mt. Hagen. Another hour by air from Mt. Hagen, and you're in Port Moresby.

As of April, 1988, a new first class luxury vessel will replace the existing *Melanesian Explorer,* the ship that's been plying the waters off the north coast of PNG for eight years. We liked the old one, but the new ship will provide even more creature comforts, though at somewhat increased costs.

The full cruise which includes the Trobriand Islands, other islands off the north coast, and the Sepik River will take 16 days and cost $3,000 per person.

The Trobriand leg of the cruise that begins in Madang and ends in Alotau (or vice versa) takes seven days. The fare is $1,890.

The five-day Sepik River cruise (Madang to Ambunti) will cost $1,350. And a short three-day cruise from Madang to such offshore islands as Manum and Karkar will be $825. For fur-

ther information contact Melanesian Tourist Services, PO Box
707, Madang, Papua New Guinea.

THE GULF DISTRICT

Few travel writers even mention the south coast of Papua
New Guinea, the Papua Gulf District. Perhaps with good reason, they ignore such rivers as the Fly which flows through
lowland swamps, then through a confusion of mangroves to a
muddy sea.

Only the most dedicated adventurers wander this area, some
successfully, some tragically like Michael Rockefeller who in
1961 disappeared on the Indonesian side of this region.

Still the future holds promise. There may be oil in the Gulf
of Papua, and the promise of hydroelectric power from dam-
ming the Purari River could bring wealth to Papua New
Guinea.

INDONESIAN IRIAN JAYA—
THE BIRD'S HEAD

If you're going from Papua New Guinea toward Indonesia,
planning to visit the Moluccas, Sulawesi, Bali, and Java, you'll
be pleased with this route. You will need a measure of resilience though. Irian Jaya is not like Papua New Guinea.

Once a week Air Niugini flies from Wewak to Jayapura, the
capital of Irian Jaya and a place with which I have a lively
love-hate relationship. The adjacent beaches, with never a
tourist in sight, are excellent, and Lake Sentani near the airport is magnificent—though completely undeveloped. During
World War II General MacArthur had his headquarters near
there. By air, usually by missionary aircraft, you can visit the
remote Baliem Valley where the Stone Age Danis live.

But Jayapura itself is a shabby neglected town. The best
hotel is the *Dafonsoro* which provides little comfort, no hot
water, cockroaches the size of Buicks, and costs $60 US for a
double.

On arrival in Jayapura, go directly to the Police Department and get their blessing on paper. I neglected that formality, and was fined $50 US for the lapse.

Be very careful taking photos, particularly near the harbor. The military are much in evidence and are sensitive to the sight of a foreigner with cameras. I was picked up for that too, and locked up. An unpleasant hour followed, but fortunately the Indonesian naval officer who questioned me turned out to be my contemporary and, like me, had been in Hollandia during the war. He ordered my release.

Jayapura, as you get to know it, does get better. The non-government locals are friendly, as are the resident American missionaries.

There's sin too. One source is directly across the street from the American Missionary headquarters, where a number of commercial ladies await. But the girls at a watering spot in

World War II military remains near Jayapura, Hollandia, Indonesian New Guinea

town called Scorpio's are a little more refined, and will dance with you too. If you want to escape from here by sea, there are a number of alternatives. An unpleasant way to go to sea from Jayapura would be aboard one of the big passenger vessels bound back to Surabaya or Jakarta. We went aboard the *MV Tolando* for a look, and were shown a small hot cabin as well as the redolent toilet down the passageway. Hordes of passengers were already aboard—congestion prevailed. The two-week voyage would be like doing penance.

One of the good ones—a 1,500-ton government vessel we went aboard—was sailing for Sulawesi with stops at Biak, Manokwari, Sorong, and Ujung Pandang. She was clean, the cabins roomy, and we would have been her only passengers. But we were bound in the other direction.

Useful Addresses

For tour information to the Highlands, to remote lodges, the Sepik River, and elsewhere contact: Air Niugini, PO Box 7186, Boroko, Papua New Guinea; or The Office of Tourism; PO Box 5644, Boroko, Papua New Guinea.

Final Note—There is a $10 per person airport tax to be paid on departure from Papua New Guinea.

11

MICRONESIA

Micronesia, or the "tiny islands," is a collection of 2,100 islands with a total land mass of 700 square miles. Those islands are scattered over an expanse of three million square miles of Pacific Ocean, lying on both sides of the equator and stretching nearly from Hawaii to the Philippines. From the furthest eastern edge to the western tip it's nearly 3,000 miles. The 148,000 people who live on the 125 inhabited islands of Micronesia come in all sizes and colors, speaking at least nine different languages.

There are, however, things the islands do have in common. The most obvious is beauty. Then in varying amounts they share elements of bureaucracy, corruption, backwardness, a lack of industry, few roads, and a dependence on Uncle Sam. But changes are taking place in Micronesia. No longer are these islands lumped together in what has been called since 1947 "The Trust Territory of the Pacific Islands." Now there are four new countries among them, albeit countries heavily dependent on the United States.

The Republic of the Marshall Islands. Its capital is Majuro Island.

The Federated States of Micronesia which includes Ponape, Truk, Kosrae, and Yap. Its capital is Ponape.

The Republic of Palau. Its capital is Koror.

These three new states have agreed to allow the United States full military access to their islands, and as a result will receive considerable financial assistance.

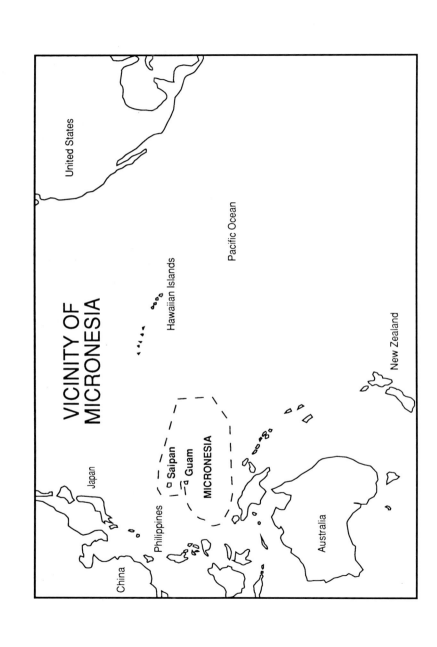

VICINITY OF
MICRONESIA

United States

Pacific Ocean

Hawaiian Islands

Japan

China

Philippines

□ Saipan
□ Guam

MICRONESIA

Australia

New Zealand

The Northern Marianas Islands. With its capital at Saipan, it has entered Commonwealth status with the United States and has agreed to the presence of US military bases.

The largest island of Micronesia is Guam, but Guam has an entirely different status. It's a Territory of the US and, while Guam calls itself "The Gateway to Micronesia," it is in no way connected to the new governments. Being on Guam is like being in the USA and, as her Chamber of Commerce says, "Guam is where America's day begins."

Some of the islands of Micronesia are not much interested in the kinds of development that will disrupt traditional culture. Yap, Ponape (now called Pohnpei) and perhaps Kosrae are good examples. Luckily there are some leaders who suggest that a few things the developed world has—such as refrigeration, public health, and schools—are sensible and will only enhance tradition.

Other islands (Saipan, Tinian, Palau, Majuro) look with enthusiasm on what developed countries can deliver. Now that they know about TV, McDonald's hamburgers, discos, designer jeans, and country-western music, they're losing interest in fishing from a canoe on the reef, living on taro and breadfruit, or sitting about stringing leis. Fortunately, even on the islands that favor progress, there are wiser heads who caution against changing too quickly.

Now is the time to see Micronesia. It's a trip best done as a free and independent traveler. You don't need a tour leader to herd you about, because there aren't that many decisions to make. There are only a few hotels and restaurants. It's no trick finding a beach to loaf on, a reef to dive on, or someone with a boat for transport. Even inter-island trips are easy: you fly from one group to another by Continental's Air Micronesia, affectionately referred to as "Air Mike." And if you're lucky enough to find a ship sailing to more remote areas, it won't be because you've used a travel agent. The ship will just suddenly appear, an event no travel agent could have predicted.

You can have good fun in Micronesia. You'll see these islands in comfort and without hardship. The hotels and food are good, people are friendly, English is spoken, there are no unusual health problems and American currency is used.

History in Brief

The original home of these people was probably near Malaysia. They appeared in the Marshalls, Carolines, Marianas, Gilbert and Ellice Islands as early as 1,500 BC. While there may have been more people on some of these islands than there are today, there probably never was a "golden age" civilization. In spite of the presence of the Nan Madol ruins on Ponape, the Latte Stones on Guam, and the artifacts on Palau, the early people did not build an impressive civilization.

Recorded history begins with the sighting of some of these islands by Magellan in the 16th century and, while successive Spaniards did little to colonize the islands, they did leave their religion behind, and today almost half the population is Roman Catholic.

Spain's rule, beginning in the 18th century, was ended by the Spanish-American War at the beginning of the 20th century. Germany, by purchase, took over some of the islands and, while imposing a stern discipline, maintained a thriving copra trade.

When World War I began, Japan moved in and under a League of Nations mandate the islands (except Guam) were entrusted to Japan. Like the Germans before them, they ran the islands with a firm hand. Those are the years (1914 to 1945) that some Micronesians look back on with nostalgia. Japan was a harsh ruler, but the system worked and so did the islanders. Today most adults over 45 still speak some Japanese.

During World War II many of these islands were in the news and still remain in the memory of thousands of Americans. Guam was lost to the Japanese early in the war, then dramatically taken back in 1944. There were battles fought in Saipan, in the Marshalls, and there was the long grinding conflict among Peleliu's limestone ridges (part of Palau.) At Truk, Japan's Gibraltar, an entire enemy fleet was sunk in the lagoon. It was from Tinian in the Marianas, 125 miles north of Guam, that on August 6, 1945, the B-29 *Enola Gay* took off, set course for Japan, and dropped an atomic bomb on Hiroshima. That event and the subsequent attack on Nagasaki ended hostilities with Japan.

With the defeat of Japan, the United Nations made the Marshalls, Marianas, and the Carolines a United States Trust Territory, and they came under the paternalistic sway of the Department of the Interior. This new master did not have the missionary zeal of the Spaniards, the stern discipline of the Germans or the Japanese, and no real policy. But it did succeed in bringing a huge bureaucracy and an attendant welfare state to life.

People in Washington tended to the idea that, since there were only a handful of people in the Trust Territory, they could be kept quietly occupied with handouts. And it was to Micronesia that the inhabitants of Bikini, an atoll near Eniwetok, were relocated in order for the first hydrogen bomb to be tested. That was in 1952 and, because of nuclear contamination, the Bikinians still can't return to their island.

Happily though, trustee status was never intended to be permanent and, now that it's over, there are signs that the US and these new states are beginning to work together productively.

How to Get There by Air

From San Francisco to Guam—Northwest Airlines flies SF—Tokyo—Guam daily. Round-trip excursion: $943.

From Honolulu—On Tuesdays and Saturdays, Continental's Air Micronesia, sets out on a "Stepping Stone Flight" from Honolulu to Guam. In order of appearance, the plane puts down at Johnston Island (off limits for military reasons), Majuro, Kwajelein (off limits too), Ponape, Truk, and finally Guam. The one-way fare for this most entertaining flight is $450.

From Guam, the flight continues south to Yap, Palau, and Manila.

Going north to Guam, "Air Mike" serves Rota, Tinian, and Saipan.

The "Stepping Stone Flight" can also be made in reverse, from Guam back to Honolulu. Our advice to visitors is to fly this run one way, then take the non-stop flight in the other direction.

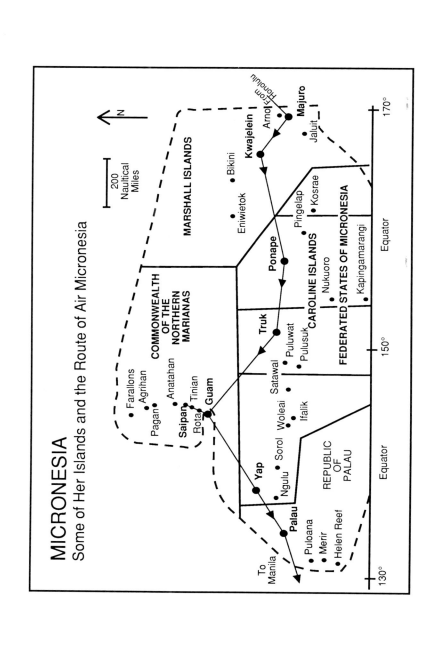

MICRONESIA
Some of Her Islands and the Route of Air Micronesia

At the present time the direct one-way Honolulu—Guam fare is $325. Continental makes this flight on Tuesdays and Thursdays.

Hawaiian Airlines makes the direct Honolulu—Guam trip every day except Monday and Friday.

From the South Pacific—Contact Air Nauru. One flight a week approaches Guam from Honiara (the Solomons) via Nauru Island and another goes into Majuro in the Marshall Islands.

From Japan—Japan Airlines has frequent services from Osaka and Tokyo to Guam.

From Manila, Philippines—Air Micronesia (Continental) flies to Guam via Palau and Yap twice a week.

By Sea

I'm sorry to report that the *Enna G.* of the Nauru Pacific Line no longer makes her epic run from San Francisco to Honolulu, then Majuro, Ponape, Truk, and Saipan. She was a jewel.

But for exotic freighter voyaging, consider the *Muskingum* which sails every two months from Japan and weaves her way through Indonesia, then goes to Palau and Yap. The 60-day round-trip voyage comes to a modest $600. Contact: Caroline-ship, Palau Shipping Co., Koror, Palau, Caroline Islands.

Be aware also of the *Herkimer* of Tiger Lines. She sails from Yokohama every two months and goes to Yap, Saipan, Truk, Ponape, and Ebeye. The round-trip fare is about $600. Contact: Tiger Lines, United Micronesian Development Assn., PO Box 238, Saipan, Marianas Islands.

Immigration

As an American, all you need to visit Micronesia is proof of citizenship. Most other nationalities will need passports.

Health

Micronesia is considered a healthy area. There is no malaria, yellow fever or cholera. Water is generally safe to drink from taps, and there are good health care facilities in all district centers.

Currency

United States currency is used throughout Micronesia. Banks are located in each District Center.

Newspapers, Radio and Telephone

Everywhere you go you will hear radio broadcasts in English, complete with local and American news. In Guam, the *Pacific Daily News* is published every day complete with the comics. Overseas phone calls are easily made from nearly everywhere.

Power

110 volts AC—the same as in the US.

Time Zone

Micronesia is so large that it has many different time zones, ranging from one hour earlier than Honolulu to the following day in Guam.

Climate

Tropical is the common climate word, but the islands also vary in temperature and rainfall. To escape the most rain, come between November and May.

There are typhoons in Micronesia, and nearly every year a storm of some kind occurs. Usually they're the "coconut variety"—winds just strong enough to blow down a few nuts. But once in a while the real thing comes along with winds up to 190 miles per hour. Fortunately, forecasting is good and residents have plenty of time to get braced.

Clothes

Bring summer clothing—but not the brief variety, which would offend the locals in many areas.

Languages

There are local languages in each district, but English is spoken everywhere. Older folks on many islands speak some Japanese, and on Guam everything is spoken: Japanese, English, Korean, Chinese, Philippine Tagalog, and the native language, Chammorran.

Tipping

The custom of tipping varies from island to island. On Guam and Saipan, follow mainland US customs. On Yap, tipping is not necessary, but in most other areas it's catching on.

Holidays

Micronesia celebrates all the usual American holidays, plus a wide assortment of local holidays and fiestas too numerous to describe. You'll always be able to get services though.

MICRONESIA AND HOW TO DO IT

Our approach to Micronesia will be as if we're aboard air Mike's "Stepping Stone Flight" going west from Honolulu toward Guam. Following that, we'll move north from Guam into the Marianas, and then south from Guam to Yap and Palau.

This twice weekly half-passenger, half-cargo 727 flight boards early in the morning and carries a variety of passengers. There'll be government employees with a "going-back-to-work look" bound for Johnston or Kwajelein. There'll be golden-hued men and women in island dress, island children with exotic heads of hair, a clutch of missionaries, and several businessmen bearing attache cases. Chances are, only a few will be traveling out of curiosity.

JOHNSTON ISLAND

Tiny Johnston Island 800 miles southwest of Honolulu is the first stop, a brief and disappointing halt on a drab almost treeless atoll. Here at this US Government off-limits island you won't be allowed to leave the plane and can only peer out at a golf course and numbers of square buildings said to store chemical weapons.

I landed at Johnston during the war, an equally brief stop, and I recall a sign nailed to the only palm tree in sight. The sign proclaimed this the "Johnston Island National Forest."

MAJURO, THE MARSHALL ISLANDS

Majuro atoll with a population of 18,000 is a slender palm-clad necklace of islands surrounding an immense lagoon. It's 800 miles beyond Johnston.

Majuro is the capital of the Marshall Islands, a collection of 34 low coral islands with 700 square miles of land scattered over half a million square miles of ocean. These are the smallest of the "tiny islands," among which are atolls with such remembered names as Eniwetok, Bikini, and Kwajelein.

On arrival, the slight amount of dry land separating sea from lagoon will startle you. And on the beaches near the town of Rita several miles north of the airport, you'll see debris that dates from the present back to World War II.

Rita, a town which sprawls along this narrow strip of land, wins few prizes for urban beauty and is inhabited by people who, while congenial, reflect little island culture.

Where to Stay

The four hotels are all good and have restaurant-bars.
The New Marshall Sun Hotel—now under construction.
The Hotel Ajidrik—$29 a double.
The Eastern Gateway—$32 a double and right on a good beach.
The Hotel Majuro—$32 a double and in the center of town.
The RRE Hotel—$55 a double, downtown.
At this writing, credit cards are not accepted in these hotels or anywhere else in Majuro.

Dining

Other than the hotels, there are a number of small mama-papa restaurants in Rita that serve a not-bad mixture of inex-

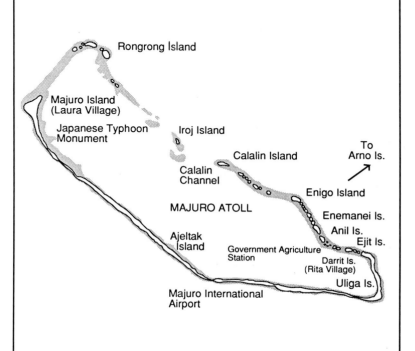

MAJURO
Marshall Islands

Rongrong Island

Majuro Island
(Laura Village)

Japanese Typhoon
Monument

Iroj Island

Calalin Island

To
Arno Is.

Calalin
Channel

Enigo Island

MAJURO ATOLL

Enemanei Is.

Ajeltak
Island

Anil Is.

Ejit Is.

Government Agriculture
Station

Darrit Is.
(Rita Village)

Majuro International
Airport

Uliga Is.

15 MILES

pensive Japanese and American food. The Japanese influence on food is a holdover from pre-war days. To get to these places, take one of the swarms of tiny taxis, which will cost 50¢. *The Yacht Club Restaurant* at the north end of Rita has good pizza. For Chinese food try *Formosa* in central Rita. Also in Rita, *The Skyline* serves a respectable selection of continental food.

Evening Entertainment

There are always video movies at the hotels or activities in the bar. The other night spots in town tend to be frequented mostly by men and are noisy places featuring American country-western music. Drinks are inexpensive.

Shopping

The most popular purchases in Majuro are the seagoing stick charts. These were and, some say, still are used for navigation. The roughly square configuration of interlaced sticks indicate currents, and the several shells indicate islands. They're inexpensive, good conversation pieces, and look good hanging on a wall. Other purchases are woven handbags and exotic shells. To buy local handicrafts, such as plaited pandanas floor mats, fans, baskets, and shell necklaces, visit the *Busy Hands Club* at the south end of Rita or *The Marshall Islands Handicraft Co-op* in the center of town.

What to Do

Away from Rita matters improve. If you set out by car down the longest straight stretch of paved road in all Micronesia, 30 miles from Rita to Laura, you'll find yourself driving among palms, alongside white beaches in settings of unforgettable beauty.

At Laura, a tiny village, life is more genuine and the beaches nearly perfect. A picnic lunch packed at your hotel will be ideal. Taxi fare round trip to Laura from Rita is $20. Buses run from Rita to Laura every day from 7 AM to 7 PM except Sunday. One-way fare is $1. Cars, mostly small Japa-

Stick charts, used for navigation in the Marshall Islands

nese models, can be rented from one of seven agencies, all competitive. Your hotel can arrange this, and your current driver's license will be acceptable.

The very best part of Majuro is the lagoon. Fishing, snorkeling and shelling are excellent, but the best activities involve camping trips to any one of the dozen of tiny islets that make up Majuro. There you'll have your own palm trees to gather coconuts from, and your own beach for shelling, swimming and fishing. Several organizations in Rita will provide transport to such an island and also supply the camping gear. Count on $40 a day for such a venture.

To get entirely away from the somewhat modernized influence of Majuro, consider a short trip across the open sea 25 miles to a more genuine Marshall Island, Arno. Spend a day on good beaches, have a picnic lunch, and return the same day. Cost per person is $40. Contact the Marshall Sun Hotel for this trip.

On Arno's satellite island, Enirik, visit Dado Ghaschino. He is beginning to harvest black pearls, some of which may be for sale.

For diving, contact Matt Holly, the resident dive instructor. Phone 3669. For deep sea fishing, the RRE and Marshall Sun hotels operate their own boats. There is good marlin, tuna, wahoo, and dolphin fishing in the open sea.

A.M.I., a small airline of Majuro, flies to 23 nearby Marshall Islands. Their flight to Arno is 10 minutes. All are remote atolls without amenities, but where Marshallese life can be seen largely unchanged.

As for ships to distant outer islands, if a ship's available, consider it. But we'd recommend saving seagoing energies for other parts of Micronesia, as the best is yet to come.

KWAJELEIN, THE MARSHALLS

Kwajelein, less than 300 miles from Majuro is another coral atoll, and like Majuro has a huge lagoon. It is, however, another off-limits island and in-transit passengers aren't allowed off the plane. What you see from the plane looks trim, well-landscaped, and abounds in US Government architecture, including a golf course. This is the home of Bucholz Air Base, a missile station.

Most of the local Marshallese live on other islands in the lagoon and commute to Kwaj, where many of them work.

PONAPE (POHNPEI),
THE EASTERN CAROLINES

Seen from the air an hour and 25 minutes after Kwajelein, the high island of Ponape will take your breath away. Below, within a many-hued fringing reef, lies a mountainous jungle island, rugged and laced with waterfalls.

Some call Ponape the most beautiful island in the world. And by Micronesian standards, its 117 square miles make it a big island. Ponape gets more than 300 inches of rain a year.

About 13,000 people live here, handsome golden-colored folks. Their capital, Kolonia, is a compact, utilitarian town within walking distance from the airport.

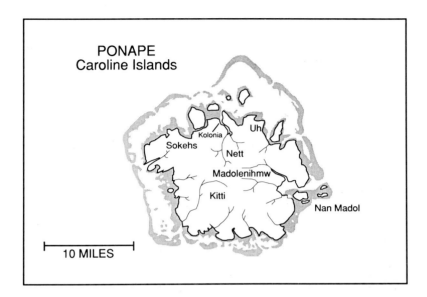

PONAPE
Caroline Islands

Kolonia
Uh
Sokehs
Nett
Madolenihmw
Kitti
Nan Madol

10 MILES

Where to Stay

There are a number of hotels in and around Kolonia.

The Cliff Rainbow—It has a bar-restaurant, is in town, has good views and car and boat rental facilities. About $45 a double.

Hotel Nan Madol—Just out of town, it has a good view of the harbor. $25 a double.

South Park Hotel—It has a bar-restaurant, is in town, and is nicely landscaped. $25 to $45 a double.

The Pohnpei Hotel—In town, $38 a double.

Village Hotel—Five verdant, but unpaved, miles from town. We stayed there and were enthusiastic, so a few words about this hotel are in order. Run by Patti and Bob Arthur, the Village is a series of thatched cottages built into the side of a jungled hill exposed to the tradewinds. It overlooks an impressive arc of lagoon. There is no air conditioning, nor is it required, since the trades blow through open, but screened, windows and guests nod off at night on immense waterbeds.

Meals in the bar-dining room are excellent, and include local specialties such as broiled tuna steaks, lobster, and mangrove

Dancers on Ponape Island

crab. Rates at the Village are $65 a double. We recommend it highly.

Dining in Town

Try the Palm Terrace or the PCR, both moderately priced and very good.

What to Do

Ponape is not a place to lie about on beaches, since there aren't many, but a day spent with a boat and guide will provide good diving and snorkeling on some extremely good reefs. The Village Hotel can make arrangements for about $40 a day. Perhaps you can find cheaper boats in town. Try Bernards Store, or the Kaselehlia Inn.

Nan Madol Ruins—These ruins constructed at least 700 years ago lie deep in a mangrove swamp, 25 miles southeast of Kolonia. They're reached only by small boat, canoe, or on foot.

Going by boat is the simplest, an all-day venture that will include pauses in the lagoon for snorkeling and a hike through the jungle to a refreshing waterfall. Then, when the tide is just right, the boatman will pole the boat the final distance to the ruins. Count on $25 per person for the trip.

Nan Madol is the remnant of an ancient canal city, similar to Venice. It was built by a dynasty of Ponapean rulers called the Saudeleurs. There, among man-made islands, these people constructed out of huge basalt rock logs a complex of royal houses, ceremonial buildings, tombs, temples, bath houses and pools for fish.

Saudeleur rule lasted for 16 generations and was followed by the Nahnmwarkis. The last of that dynasty now live on nearby Temwen Island and carry considerable authority.

Nan Madol is a quiet, eerie, not fully understood connection with the past. It is still considered sacred by Ponapeans and for outsiders respectful conduct is suggested.

Nan Madol ruins on Ponape

Hiking and Camping—The interior of Ponape is mountainous, covered with jungle, and the frequent cloud cover produces a mossy carpeted forest floor. Here you'll find deer, some huge lizards, and a colorful variety of birds. There are few roads into the interior, but there are trails, good hard walks to numerous waterfalls with pools good for swimming. There aren't many villages, as most people live scattered along valley floors or on the coast. They're friendly and hospitable but, for visitors approaching a remote habitation, the rules of courtesy apply.

One outstanding adventure would be to circle the island—at least a two-day boat camping trip. This trip, done entirely within the reef, would cost between $80 and $100 for boat, guide, food and camping gear. Check with the Village Hotel or the Kaselehlia Inn for this activity.

The Cultural Center—Plan a few hours at the Cultural Center in the village of Nett, just a short distance from town. There you'll see local, crafts, perhaps some island dancing and, if inclined, taste the local kava called sakau.

The Polynesians of Kapingamarangi—If you can't take the Field Service ship to distant Kapingamarangi, visit their village in Porakiet near Kolonia. There under breadfruit and palm trees these Polynesians have established a community. They still live in thatched houses, wear lava lavas, and the men continue to fish from sailing canoes.

Evenings Out in Kolonia—There are a number of lively places to drink in town, at least eight shabby but friendly bars with jukeboxes. You'll hear them before you see them. For starters try the Downtown Bar, the Seamen's Club, Airport Lounge, and the Nan Madol.

Going to Sea from Ponape—Two of the best Micronesian destinations are the Polynesian islands of Kapingamarangi and Nukuoro. Nukuoro is 250 miles southwest of Ponape; Kapingamarangi is an additional 150 miles. The only way to these complete unspoiled islands is by Field Service vessels which leave every five weeks for a voyage to Mokil, Pingelap, Kosrae, Ngatik, Nukuoro, and Kapingamarangi. The trip takes 10–20 days.

For cabin passengers, fares including meals are 7¢ a mile, plus $7 a day. Deck passage fare excluding meals is 3¢ a mile.

The only way to obtain passage on these ships is to be on Ponape at the time of sailing. Be aware that these voyages are not set up for tourists. The purpose of the trip is to load copra, sell trade goods, check births and deaths, pull teeth, or respond to a medical crisis. You can, however, always expect to be greeted at an island with song, flowers, food and palm liquor.

For ships sailing from Ponape, contact: Ponape Transfer and Storage Inc., PO Box 340, Kolonia, Ponape, 96941.

Shopping

Shells, carvings, model canoes, and Ponape black and white pepper in small bags are popular purchases. The pepper is the most pungent in the world. You can buy it at the airport.

KOSRAE ISLAND

Kosrae, 300 miles southeast of Ponape, looks in profile like a woman lying on her back, hair spreading out behind her head.

Kosrae is nearly as beautiful as Ponape, but certainly more remote. In the main village of Lelu there's an inn or two. But the main attraction is the ruins. They're practically in town and easy to find.

From Pohnpei or Majuro visitors get there by twice-weekly scheduled Air Micronesia flights.

TRUK, EASTERN CAROLINES

Truk Island, an hour by air beyond Ponape, is a collection of semi-high islands set in a huge lagoon. The lagoon, and what lies below its surface, is Truk's main attraction.

Before World War II Truk was the main Japanese base in the Pacific, and the island of Dublon, eight miles from the present district center of Moen, was Japan's Gibraltar. There in 1944 a sustained US bombing sent more than 60 ships to the bottom of the lagoon. If the weather is good when Air Mike makes its final approach to Moen, you can see these submerged hulks in the water below.

Fortunately for divers, the Truk Legislature has designated the crystal clear lagoon a protected district monument. The lagoon is shared by exotic fish, brilliant coral, and maritime hardware. Everything associated with diving is plentiful on Truk—equipment, boats, guides, even a decompression center.

For full diving information contact: Truk Tourist Commission, Moen, Truk, 96942.

Where to Stay

In Moen, where you'll land, there are four hotels.

The Truk Continental—It's the shiniest, with restaurant and pool, $72 a double.

The Miramar—On the rustic side, it has a restaurant, about $30 a double.

The Christopher Inn—With a restaurant, $36 a double.

Kristy's Hotel—Rates on request but for the budget-minded.

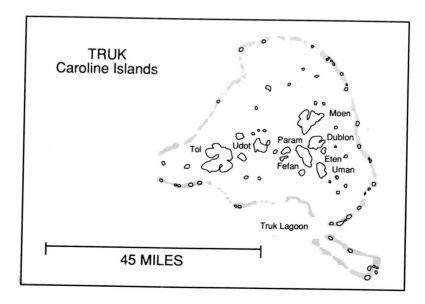

A Reminder about Truk

The island of Moen is "dry." Theoretically you cannot get a drink there. But drinking laws are bent and within reasonably convenient hours the bar at the Truk Continental happily provides drinks. Elsewhere on Moen beer is available.

What to Do

Other than the sprawling Truk department store which has everything an islander might want, Moen is of little interest.

Be sure to visit the other islands in the lagoon, especially Dublon. Boats for transport, including a large 44-foot trimaran, are available easily and cheaply. Dublon, the old Naval Base, contains ruins of Japan's naval might and there are isolated beaches for picnicking and swimming.

But for physical beauty, Truk does not compare with Ponape or other islands yet to come. Nor are the 33,000 Trukese widely noted for friendliness. Truk is mainly a mecca for divers.

For Going to Sea

Field Service ships from Truk provide monthly service to a number of sparsely settled low islands, Losap, Lukunor, Etal, Puluwat, Murilo. Contact: Truk Shipping, PO Box 669, Moen, Truk.

Shopping

Buy a love stick. The love stick was the traditional calling card of the Trukese male. He would push the stick through the thatched wall of his sweetheart's hut. Recognizing the individualized carving on the stick, she would either pull it, meaning he should come in, or push it, meaning he should leave.

GUAM

Guam, 3,300 miles west of Honolulu, is Air Mike's sixth stop on that "stepping stone" flight. According to her Chamber of

Commerce, Guam is where "America's Day Begins." It's an accurate description, for arrival on Guam is a return to the familiar, to a palm-clad extension of the USA where 130,000 patriotic full citizens of the USA live.

Agana, located about midway on the west coast of the island, is the main town. With its shopping centers, office buildings, parks, used car lots, and commuter traffic of sea-rusted cars, it could be Any Town, USA.

Guam's 8 by 32 miles make it the largest island in Micronesia. There are green mountains, jungle, palm trees but, other than at Tumon Bay and Tarague, there are few good beaches. Taragi Beach is probably the best, but unfortunately it's on the northern part of the island within the perimeter of Andersen Air Force Base. If you're not military, that area is forbidden.

There are no palm-thatched villages on the island. Only Umatac and Merizo in the south resemble an earlier Chamorran culture, but a closer look reveals that these villages are now fully Americanized. And, as you drive around the island on paved roads, you'll see a countryside orderly, clean and without litter—Middle America, only tropical.

In Agana you'll find Shakey's Pizza, Kentucky Fried Chicken, a Sizzler, and one of the biggest McDonald's in the world. You can eat Chinese, Korean, German, Japanese, Italian, or Mexican foods. If you buy at duty free stores, you can bring home $800 worth of non-USA-made merchandise duty free. There are glittering massage parlors too. We noticed that one of them, a new one, bore a sign put up during the night by a local wag which said "Gland Opening."

And on the beach at Tumon Bay, ten minutes by car from Agana, lies Guam's answer to Waikiki. There's a Hilton, a Dai Ichi, a Fujita, a Reef, a Pacific Islands Beach Club, all the domain of Japanese tour groups and honeymooners.

Recently we spent six months on Guam. Socially we've rarely been busier or had a better time. As a result we feel qualified to say that you can have fun on Guam, but it won't be because it's a tropical paradise. What you'll find is a tropical bit of Americana with an economy based on Uncle Sam's support, the military, and Japanese tourists.

GUAM

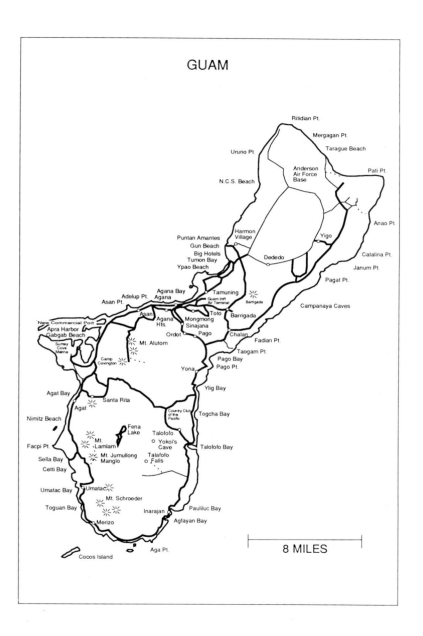

Ritidian Pt.

Mergagan Pt.

Uruno Pt.

Taraque Beach

Anderson
Air Force
Base

Pati Pt.

N.C.S. Beach

Anao Pt.

Puntan Amantes

Harmon
Village

Yigo

Gun Beach

Big Hotels

Dededo

Catalina Pt.

Tumon Bay

Ypao Beach

Janum Pt.

Pagat Pt.

Agana Bay

Tamuning

Adelup Pt.

Agana

Guam Int'l
Air Terminal

Barrigada

Campanaya Caves

Asan Pt.

Asan

Toto

Agana
Hts.

Mongmong
Sinajana

Barrigada

New Commercial Port

Ordot

Pago

Chalan

Apra Harbor

Gabgab Beach

Mt. Alutom

Fadian Pt.

Sumay
Cove
Marina

Taogam Pt.

Camp
Covington

Pago Bay

Yona

Pago Pt.

Ylig Bay

Agat Bay

Santa Rita

Agat

Country Club
of the
Pacific

Togcha Bay

Nimitz Beach

Fena
Lake

Talofofo

Mt.
Lamlam

Yokoi's
Cave

Facpi Pt.

Talofofo Bay

Mt. Jumullong
Manglo

Talafofo
Falls

Sella Bay

Cetti Bay

Umatac Bay

Umatac

Mt. Schroeder

Toguan Bay

Inarajan

Pauliluc Bay

Merizo

Agfayan Bay

8 MILES

Cocos Island

Aga Pt.

The People

Like Hawaii, Guam today has an exotic racial mixture. Modern Guamanians are the true "golden people," a blend of Philippine, Chamorro, Micronesian, Korean, Japanese, Chinese, Spanish, and American. And, while all these languages are spoken, English is the common tongue.

But the original Guamanians were Chamorros, brown-skinned handsome folks whose forebears go back to the Malays. For more than three centuries, until the Spanish American War, Spain controlled Guam, and today Spain's presence remains in their food, religion, customs, and names.

Where to Stay

Tumon Bay, a mile-long arc of palm-bordered beach, is home for the island's plushest resort hotels, restaurants, and night clubs.

Welcoming girls on Guam

Guam Hilton—On the best part of the beach, with all possible amenities. $94 to $135 a double.
Dai Ichi—A luxurious bit of Japan. $80 to $100 a double.
Guam Reef Hotel—All beach activities are available here too. $103 to $125 a double.
Pacific Islands Resort—It has all activities with a Club Med flair. $80 to $100 a double.
Fujita Tumon Beach Hotel—$55 a double.
Guam Hotel Okura—$90 a double.
Terrazo Tumo Villa—$55 a double.

Just five to ten minutes away from the beach area, rates are more modest and facilities almost as good. Here are a few.
Hotel Mai'ona—Near the airport. $78 a double.
Hotel Joinus—Near the beach. $77 a double.
Guam ITC Hotel—In downtown Agana. $33 a double.
Micronesian Village—$25 a double.
Island Garden Guest House—Modest. Rates on request.

Dining on Guam

Approach dining on Guam exactly as you would in the States, and in fact prices are about the same. All of the beach hotels have coffee shops, continental-style restaurants and, needless to say, nearly all provide excellent Japanese cuisine.
For formal dining in the beach area try:
La Londes—On Marine Drive. Continental food, moderate!
Chuck's Steak House—Steaks, seafood dishes, and extensive salad bar. Moderately priced.
Le Bistro—In the Pacific Islands Club. Continental-Western food. Moderate-to-expensive.
King's Restaurant—In the Gibson Shopping Center, open 24 hours, it has omelettes, steaks, seafood, and sandwiches. Inexpensive.

Good Chinese restaurants abound, try:
Shanghai Restaurant—In downtown Agana, it has an excellent variety of dishes.

Ting Hao—In east Agana. Locals are enthusiastic about this one. Moderately expensive.
Cuisine of China—In Tamuning near the beach, it's good too. Moderate.

Japanese dining, formal and otherwise, abounds. Try any of the hotels or step into one of many Japanese restaurants almost anywhere.

For American fast foods done unusually well, try: *Kentucky Fried Chicken*, the huge *McDonald's*, the *Sizzler* in Agana, *Taco Bell*, or *Shakey's Pizza*.

Fiesta Food—Do not leave Guam until you've attended a table-groaning fiesta. These events held in honor of village patron saints, weddings, christenings, and other special occasions, are something to behold. The assortment of food put on outdoor tables includes spicy chicken, seafood, noodles, taro, rice, lumpia (Philippine spring roll), and local fruit. Check *The Pacific Daily News*, Guam's newspaper, for announcements. Some fiestas are free, others charge a token amount, but you are welcome at all of them.

What To Do

There is a sort of public transport on Guam, but the best way to see the island is by rental car. A taxi all the way around the island, about 55 miles, will cost roughly $55. But rental cars are available for a flat rate of about $30 (including insurance), and driving is the same as in the US. Cars can be rented at the hotels, but the best deal is at the airport.

Pack a lunch and drive south. Pause in downtown Agana to see the Latte Stones in the park. They are the bases that supported the houses of ancient Guam. Wander through the Plaza de Espana Park, and look up at Government House on the hill overlooking Agana. The nearby museum is also worth a visit.

At Agat Bay nine miles south of Agana stop briefly to examine the scene of the US landing in 1944. Continue on past

"Fiesta food"

historic Spanish Bridge another six miles to lovely Cetti Bay. There, if a vigorous trek appeals to you, park well off the road and follow the path down through patches of jungle and groves of coconut palms to Cetti Bay. Allow three hours for the round trip. In the same area hikers can climb to the top of Guam's highest peak, Mt. Lam Lam. This mountain only 1,400 feet above sea level has its base 37,500 feet below the sea, which makes it the world's highest mountain.

Next, set in a pretty cove is the village of Umatac. Food is available and it's pleasant to stroll about in this village, the site of Magellan's landing in 1521.

Merizo, five miles beyond, has charm too. You can get boats from there to Cocos Island. The fare is free if you're staying at the Cocos Island Resort Hotel.

At Inarajan, a village at the southern tip, there are natural seawater pools for swimming, making it a good picnic spot. Then as you move north towards Talafofo Bay beauty abounds and, because there is no protective reef in the area, surfing is excellent. Good too is the hiking trail to Talafofo Falls, a respectable trek. Carry drinking water and allow several hours.

Nearby is the area where a Japanese soldier, who did not know that World War II had ended, hid in the jungle for more than 25 years. During that time his Imperial Army uniform wore out completely, and he made clothes from jungle materials. After Sgt. Yokoi was captured in the early '70s, he returned as a hero to Japan. There he was married, then came back to Guam for his honeymoon. Some of his survival gear is in the museum downtown.

Leaving Talafofo you've nearly completed the circle. There's more island to the north, but this part is under Anderson Air Force Base control and you're not welcome there.

There are two excellent golf courses on Guam, and any number of tennis courts, some of which are at the Hilton.

Spend a day walking locally around Tumon Bay, north of the big hotels. Picnic at nearby Gun Beach and continue on to Lovers' Leap. This is a point high over the sea where a pair of legendary star-crossed lovers leapt to their deaths.

ROTA ISLAND (NORTHERN MARIANAS)

Tiny Rota, only 45 miles from Guam, is a jewel. It's green, lovely, flanked by good beaches, and inhabited by friendly people who live in a village appropriately named Songsong. There are two hotels—*The Blue Lagoon* ($30 a double) and the large Japanese *Pau Pau Hotel* that is more pricey and favored mostly by Japanese. We enjoyed the Blue Lagoon and its food.

People come to Rota to escape the clamor of Guam. They come for their fiestas, for the beaches, and some come solely to gather wild fruit in Rota's jungle. The jungle is benevolent, with no snakes, no poisonous plants, nor marauding animals.

There is daily air service to Rota from Guam.

TINIAN (NORTHERN MARIANAS)

Tinian, with a population of about 800, has an economy based on agriculture. Farms there supply most of the other Marianas with dairy products.

But Tinian is not a choice destination, unless the crumbling airstrip where the *Enola Gay* took off to bomb Hiroshima is of particular interest. We recommend moving on.

There are three hotels on Tinian, all in or near San Jose village and all with food.

Where to Stay

Fleming Hotel—$35 to $70 a double.

Orinesia Hotel—$17 a double.

Tinian Center—$18 a double.

There is daily air service to Tinian from Guam.

SAIPAN (NORTHERN MARIANAS)

Saipan, 15 miles long and 5 miles wide, with a population of 13,000, is the capital of the Northern Marianas Commonwealth. The inhabitants of this island are similar in background and ancestry to the Guamanians.

Saipan is tropically dramatic, has excellent beaches and, for Japanese and American World War II buffs, the island is filled with reminders of that war. Rusting remnants of Japan's military past are much in evidence—field pieces, tanks, the old Japanese hospital, the sugar cane railway engine. And in Garapan, once a major Japanese town of 15,000, you'll see the letters "A.E." scratched on a cell wall. Amelia Earhart may well have died there.

At the northern end of the island you can visit the 800-foot sea cliff where hundreds of Japanese leapt to their death rather than be captured by the Americans.

Because Saipan has a sizable sheltering reef along its western shore, there are numbers of excellent sandy beaches that gently slope to snorkeling depth. To get to them, drive north or south along Beach Road. The island's not big and they're easy to find.

Where to Stay

Hafadai Beach Hotel—On a good beach, with restaurant, bar, pool. $70 a double.

Hyatt Regency—It's the most prestigious hotel on the island, and has all amenities. $100 to $125.

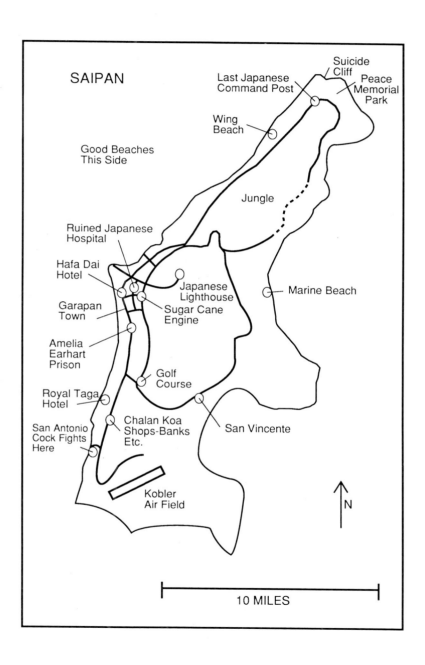

SAIPAN

Suicide
Cliff
Last Japanese
Command Post
Peace
Memorial
Park

Wing
Beach

Good Beaches
This Side

Jungle

Ruined Japanese
Hospital

Hafa Dai
Hotel

Japanese
Lighthouse

Marine Beach

Garapan
Town

Sugar Cane
Engine

Amelia
Earhart
Prison

Golf
Course

Royal Taga
Hotel

San Vincente

San Antonio
Cock Fights
Here

Chalan Koa
Shops-Banks
Etc.

Kobler
Air Field

N

10 MILES

Saipan Beach Hotel—Restaurant, bar and pool. $86 double.
Saipan Grand Hotel—Restaurant, pool and bar. $80 double.
Royal Taga—A comfortable old hotel on a good beach, with all amenities. $32 double.
Mariana Hotel—Comfortable; a friendly staff. $25 double.

What to Do

Car Rentals—About the same services and costs as on Guam. It's the best way to do the island.

Wander about at will, you can't get lost. Play golf at San Jose Village, swim, hire a boat and go fishing. And, for something unusual on Sunday nights, drive south to the village of San Antonio where they have "money betting" cock fights.

Night Life—It's not profound on Saipan. And what little there is happens in the bars and lounges of the hotels.

From Guam to Saipan there's daily air transport. The distance is about 112 miles.

YAP (WESTERN CAROLINES)

Twice a week Air Micronesia flies the 600 miles south to Yap, and then on another 300 miles to Palau. Both are choice destinations and, other than Ponape, may be the best in Micronesia.

Yap, 600 miles and an hour and a half southwest of Guam by Air Mike, has the most interesting cultural environment of these islands. Six thousand proud but warm and gentle people live on this 62-square-mile cluster of four islands and, clinging to traditional ways, they keep the 20th century at bay.

Colonia, the district center (not to be confused with Ponape's Kolonia), is the only town considered even partially modern, but the pavement and the 20th century end at the edge of town. Beyond, in the villages, islanders live by fishing or raising yams, taro, betel nut, breadfruit, and coconuts.

Then there is what visitors refer to as the "Trinity of Yap"— stone money, betel nut, and topless women. There's more to Yap than that, but those are its most distinctive features. The sign at the primitive airport reads "Welcome to Yap, the

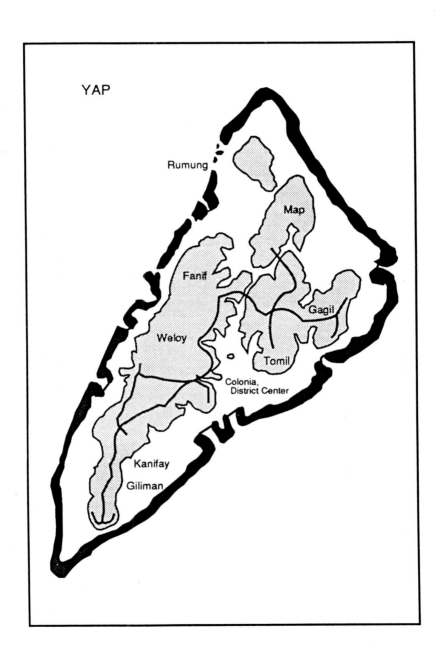

YAP

Rumung

Map

Fanif

Gagil

Weloy

Tomil

Colonia,
District Center

Kanifay
Giliman

Island of Stone Money." The customs official who checks your bags will probably have a lump of betel nut behind red-stained teeth. Then, on the way into Colonia, you'll no doubt see a number of eminently bare-breasted girls, their skirts aswing.

When we arrived Sylbestor Alonso, before delivering us to his E.S.A. Hotel, detoured down a side road where huge slabs of doughnut-shaped stone money lined the palm-bordered lane. This he called the "Bank." We'd done the whole "Trinity" in less than an hour.

Where to Stay

The E.S.A. Hotel—There's nothing resort-style about Sylbestor Alonso's small hotel. The initials I think refer to his mother's name, but for $35 a double it provides spotless, fully plumbed, air conditioned rooms, good food and unusual measures of hospitality. But no alcohol is served there. Sylbestor says this inconvenience keeps the local imbibers away.

People and stone money on Yap

The Rai View Hotel—This is the only other hotel in Colonia. It does have a bar and that's where the action is after dark. $36 double.

From either hotel you can walk into Colonia, a short walk under the palms along a betel-stained main street (spitting is a function of betel chewing.) Along the way, peer into some of the mama-papa stores that have shelves laden with Spam, kerosene, pots and pans, clothing, sea biscuits, and beer. Notice the school, wave back to the students, look at the several modest municipal buildings, and wander into the incredible market that's filled with produce, fresh fish, and handicrafts.

If ships and the even more primitive islands of the Western Carolines are of interest, continue through town to the docks. Perhaps one of the Field Service vessels that sails every five weeks will be ready to leave for Ulithi, Fais, Faraulep, Woleai, Ifalik, and Ngulu, atolls all within 400 miles of Yap. They are remote, genuine, completely off tourist routes, and without accommodations. Visitors generally sleep aboard ship, or put up with a local. Fare as on other Field Service Ships in Micronesia is 7¢ a mile, plus $7 a day for cabin passengers. Contact: Waab Transportation Co., Box 177, Colonia, Yap 96943.

If a Field Service vessel isn't available, try to catch one of the fishing boats that go to Ngulu Atoll, 100 miles away. These are two formerly Taiwanese fishing boats which were seized by local authorities for illegal fishing and, if you don't object to sleeping on deck and eating fish for a few days, this is an adventure which would cost next to nothing.

Walking about town we found was thirsty work so we climbed the hill behind town to the Rai View Hotel. There, with cold beer and a verdant view of town below, we pronounced Colonia a happy town, but one developed with utility in mind, not tourists. The term "laid back" came briefly to mind, but a local administrator we'd fallen in with disagreed. "Yap is quiet, but it's conservative, not laid back. It's no place for modern beach combers or the counterculture. The Yapese would not tolerate that."

What to Do

Unless you're deeply into anthropology, three or four days on

Yap should be enough, and the best way to see this quiet never-never land is to hire a car from Sylbestor Alonso at the E.S.A. for about $25 a day, or from Cliff Car Rentals in Colonia where rates are about the same.

Then pack a lunch and set off. But, before leaving town, stop at the Cultural Center for some orientation. It has a fine men's meeting house (a falluw), plenty of stone money, and some fair artifacts for sale.

When you leave town it doesn't really matter which direction you go, since any of the roads will fetch you to a beach, several villages, and lots of stone money.

Terang Island (O'Keefe's Island)—Just about a mile north of town you can get a boat to take you the short distance across to O'Keefe Island. There isn't much there except the ruins of his home, but you should be aware of his story.

In 1872 this Irishman with dollar signs for eyes realized that, by quarrying additional stone money on Palau 300 miles away, he could exchange it on Yap for Trepang (sea slugs, a delicacy in the Orient) and copra. In the venture he was entirely successful, and for nearly 30 years he with his beautiful half-caste wife reigned as near emperor of Yap. His end was poetically mysterious for in 1901 he disappeared at sea.

Stone Money—As to the original stone money, pre-O'Keefe, no one knows its age, but it was there when the island was discovered in the 16th century. Now it's all over the island, some of it as much as eight feet in diameter. A lot of it lies flat, nearly covered with vines, and you can see it leaning against schools, the traditional men's houses, along lanes, and in every village. Its location and size indicate prestige and wealth. We were told that stone money can be used as collateral for bank loans.

Etiquette—Nothing on Yap is developed for tourists and almost everywhere you'll be on private property. Simply ask permission to enter a village and carry a sprig of greenery, as it indicates peaceful intentions. And *never* photograph bare-breasted women.

Beaches—The best beaches are at Gagil to the north of Colonia, Map a few miles further north, Fanif on the western side of the island, and Gilman at the southern end. They're easy to find. A map will come with the car and, while distances are

A "failu" or traditional men's meeting house on Yap, with stone money

short, they seem long because the roads are so narrow and rough.

Japanese Zeros—Near the airport, behind the weather station, are a few well preserved Japanese fighter planes which were caught on the ground when the Americans bombed Yap.

Diving—Diving could be good here, but equipment is limited so divers should bring their own. For more information, contact: Yap Fishing Authority, PO Box 338, Colonia, Yap, FSM 96943.

Island Dancing—Rather uninspired dance celebrations are held about twice a year. If you insist, either of the hotels can arrange a performance.

Final Note—You'll find beauty on Yap. Some of the beaches are so magnificent that they look like Hollywood planned them. And you'll find handsome people in attractive villages. Thoughtful visitors to the villages will get the comfortable feeling of being surrounded by protective layers of tradition.

PALAU (THE WESTERN CAROLINES)

Palau is a composite of all Pacific Islands, and within its reef-fringed 80-mile length there are jungle-clad mountains with lacy waterfalls, and picture-perfect atolls. Best of all, set in crystalline water are the 200-odd clusters of verdant rock islands. The handsome, animated Palauans are difficult to describe. To say they resemble a mixture of Polynesian, Malaysian, and Filipino, is the best I can do.

Unfortunately there have been problems in this magnificent setting. Differences of opinion have come up over whether the new republic will accept an American military base and nuclear weapons. Several times the electorate of Palau has refused to allow such a compact, but in a recent election it was approved. Opponents say the election was illegal since it was carried out in a threatening atmosphere.

The father of a lawyer who challenged the vote was recently shot to death and bullets were fired into the house of another politician who opposed the compact.

According to pro-military Palauans, they cannot afford to lose the $15,000,000 of economic assistance provided by the US. The US considers the last election, in which 73% of the voters approved a military-nuclear presence, legally binding. The US also says that the millions in aid will continue, compact or not, and if we have reverses in the Philippines, Palau could be an alternative.

Koror, Palau's capital, is on an island just across the bridge from the airport. It's a busy community, and along its main street there are substantial stores, restaurants, schools, government buildings, and a number of interesting after-dark watering spots. Even so, Koror with its 8,000 residents is only a fraction of its pre-war size. The Japanese were in attendance then, and Palau was a military fortress, a fortress that fell violently to US forces in 1944. Remnants of those Japanese days remain, and you can touch the past, even walk up pre-war flights of steps going nowhere, or wander about the rubble of old Shinto shrines. There are field pieces, tanks in the jungle,

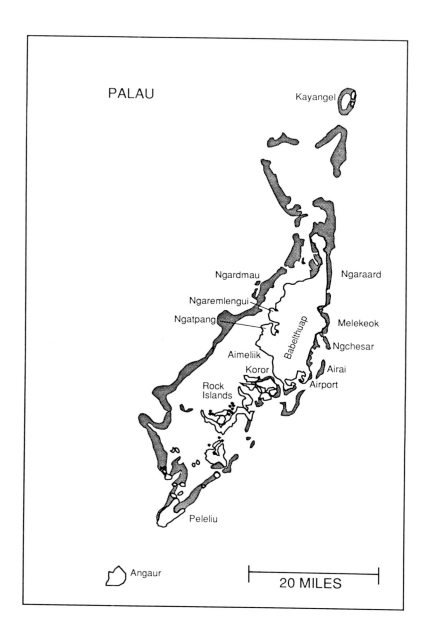

PALAU

Kayangel

Ngardmau

Ngaraard

Ngaremlengui

Ngatpang

Babelthuap

Melekeok

Ngchesar

Aimeliik

Koror

Airai

Rock
Islands

Airport

Peleliu

Angaur

20 MILES

and submerged Zero aircraft. But now that war seems very distant.

Where to Stay

There are a number of hotels from austere to luxurious in Palau, among them the following.

Hotel Nikko Palau—Situated in tropical opulence overlooking some of the Rock Islands, it's not far from Koror and has every possible amenity. $90 a double.

Palau Pacific Resort—An even more impressive accommodation that offers not only ocean view and beach, but tennis, duty-free shopping, two restaurants, and a live band. Close to town. $110 to $120 a double.

Palau Hotel—In downtown Koror, handy to everything. It features Western, Japanese and Chinese dining. Comfortable. $60 a double.

New Koror Hotel—Small, simple and clean. In town. Rooms with bath, $30 a double.

Carp Island Resort—This Rock Island resort is about an hour by boat from Koror. It has cottages with indoor plumbing and features excellent seafood. Good for divers. $55 double.

Ngerchong Hotel—This is a budget inn geared to groups where sleeping mats are provided. It's on a remote islet in the Rock Islands. Good swimming, diving, and fishing. Food is available. A group of 10 can stay for about $50.

D. W. Motel—Comfortable, fully plumbed, and in downtown Koror. $30 a double.

West Motel—Has rooms with kitchens and is handy to Koror's dock. $35 a double.

Wenty Inn—Located at the far end of Palau about 30 miles away on the island of Peleliu. A simple place on a beautiful white sand beach. Food is provided and there are some kitchens. $15 a double.

Dining on Palau

Other than the hotel restaurants mentioned above, there are a number of small restaurants that lean heavily to Japanese and Korean food. In town try the *Carp Restaurant, Arirang's, and Furusato's.* At the *Olbukl* you can get Philippine and

Western food. For simple but good American cooking visit the *Yokohama Restaurant.* For rather expensive international dining the *Nikko Palau Hotel* and the *Palau Pacific Resort* are best.

What to Do

Where you can go by vehicle is limited to the Koror area and only part of Babelthuap, the big island to the north. The rest of Palau is accessible only by air and water. Rent a car if you like, but we think taxis are the simplest solution and there are plenty of them. Fares are negotiable, but expect to pay about $10 an hour for longer hauls.

Car Rentals—There are at least seven agencies in Koror, all competitive. Try *D. W. Car Rentals* (about $25 a day, unlimited mileage) or *King's U Drive* (no mileage charge, insurance included, $30 a day).

The attractions of Palau are considerable, all different, and should be taken in unhurried increments.

The Rock Islands—Just south of Koror there is a cluster of 200 green knobs of land. These tiny limestone islets covered with vegetation that comes down to the waterline are mostly uninhabited. Some have white beaches, others caves, and around all of them the water, which is often disturbed by schooling wahoo and skipjack, is transparent and filled with vibrant coral formations.

The best way to see these islands is with boat and guide. Don't forget the guide, for wending your way through the labyrinth of islands is confusing business.

To Get a Boat—Go to the fishing docks in town. Try Fish 'N Fins, the New Koror Travel Service, or Western Pacific Travel. With them you can join a tour, which will cost about $30 per person for several hours among the Rock Islands. or for about $80 you can hire the entire boat for the day, then economize by taking another couple or two along.

A day spent among these strange verdant mushroom islands is near perfection. You can picnic on your own island, snorkel and, for diving, Fish 'N Fins will provide equipment and charge $55 for a boat and two dives.

Palau's Rock Islands

BABELTHUAP ISLAND

This island, the largest land mass in Palau, is jungly, mountainous, and 27 miles long. At the southern end near the airport, drive or taxi out to Airai. Here you can visit one of Palau's links to the past—a traditional men's meeting house. Then by car, a little farther north, there's a passable waterfall with a swimming pool at its foot.

Ngardmau—The best waterfall, perhaps the finest in the Pacific, is at the northern end of Babelthuap. To get there, go by boat (the only way) to Ngardmau. Get a guide at the village and hike in four hours to this waterfall which drops from a 700-foot peak. Then it's four hours back again. Fish 'N Fins in Koror can organize this rugged trip, which begins with first light and ends at dusk.

Kayangel—At Palau's northern tip, 50 miles north of Koror, there's an exquisite coral atoll, a small one with perfect beaches and a quiet village where you can probably arrange housing.

It's rather difficult to get to, but there are boats and charter planes. Contact Huan Polloi in Koror. Telephone: 229.

SOUTH PALAU

Peleliu—About 28 miles south of Koror the limestone platform island of Peleliu is where 12,000 Japanese and Americans were killed in World War II. Now it's a quiet and pretty backwater island that has good beaches, good shelling, and friendly people. At *Wenty Inn* you can get a bed and a meal.

To Get There—Take the *Peleliu Princess* which sails Sundays, Mondays, Thursdays, and Fridays and takes three hours. The trip, mostly within the reef, is aboard a simple, safe, no-amenities boat. Fare is $1.50 one way.

Both Paradise Air and Emerald Air have six-passenger Cessna 207s that fly to Peleliu, and ten miles further to Angaur Island. Rates are about $30 round trip to Peleliu and $40 round trip to Angaur.

Angaur—This island 38 miles south of Koror is at the very end of Palau. It's another limestone platform island, and the site of considerable pre-war activity. There were phosphate mines and there is a Japanese lighthouse to be seen. Now the main attractions are the rugged beaches (with good surfing), World War II relics, and Micronesia's only monkeys.

BACK ON KOROR

A casual day can be spent doing Koror, having lunch in town, seeing the Botanical Gardens, and the Palau Museum. And, for something to take home, consider a painting by the dean of local painters, Reverend Charlie Gibbons, the "Grandma Moses" of Palau. His paintings can be found in a number of shops, but the Palau National Museum is the best outlet.

Story boards are interesting too. Of varying sizes, these wood carvings depict Palauan stories drawn from legend. Some teach social values, some are graphically earthy, and they're unique to Palau. Visit the informal jail in the center of town. The inmates make some of the best story boards.

An Evening Out in Town—Away from the big hotels, there are several self-evident bars. We sat in one, a combination bar and Chinese restaurant, filled with noise, ribaldry and fellowship. Local night life in Palau is rough and uninhabited.

Away from Palau by Sea

The distant islands of Sonsorol, Merir, Pulouana, Tobi, and Helen Reef, lonesome atolls, the refuge of turtles, wild birds, and seldom-visited islanders, are reached every three months by Field Service ship. Contact: Palau Shipping Co., PO Box 6000, Koror, Palau 96940.

You can leave by Air Micronesia to Manila twice weekly, or return to Guam via Yap twice a week.

12

TUVALU

Tuvalu, formerly the Ellice Group, gained independence from Great Britain in 1978. It consists of 9 narrow coral atolls, none of which is higher than 18 feet above sea level. This new country, a "micro state," is just below the equator, north of Fiji. There are 7,500 people of Polynesian stock who live here.

Funafuti (I like that name) is the capital. Everything except coconuts, bananas, yams, breadfruit and fish has to be imported. Because the land is so close to sea level, there are no wells or springs, and all potable water comes from collected rain. And, for what it's worth, Tuvalu is said to be the second most isolated state on earth. The first is Tristan de Cunha in the South Atlantic.

Aid from Britain, Australia, New Zealand, plus the export of copra keeps Tuvalu going, but only just.

Getting There by Air

Either Air Pacific or Fiji Air flies there once or twice a week from Suva, Fiji. Because of cargo commitments and traveling officials, these flights are usually fully booked.

By Sea

Check with the Port Captain in Suva. Ask about the sailings of the *Moana Raoi,* the *Sami,* and *Pacific Sky.* We once went aboard the *Moana Raoi* in Suva and were shown one of her cabins. It was small but clean, had its own bath, and the dining salon looked pleasant. This vessel's two-week voyage to both Tuvalu and Kiribati would be the very best way to see both island groups. Being aboard a comfortable ship removes all worries about hotels, flights and involuntary pauses. Round-trip fare on the *Moana Raoi* is about $500 per person.

In Funafuti ask about the *Nivanga.* She is a small, trim trading vessel that sails from Funafuti once every six weeks and goes to Tuvalu's outer islands. Cabin-class fare for the short voyage is $65.

Where to Stay

The 14-bedroom *Vaiaku Langi* in Funafuti is Tuvalu's only hotel and drinking establishment—a no-frills hotel.

According to an official Tuvaluan brochure, "tourism is virtually non-existent, probably 200 visitors a year. Tourists are encouraged to come, as long as they don't disrupt the traditional lifestyle."

13

KIRIBATI

The low islands of Kiribati, ranging north and south of the equator, are the former Gilbert Islands and are inhabited by Gilbertese people. They are part of Micronesia.

Betio, on Tarawa Island of World War II fame, is the capital, a not entirely tidy community and one with much exotica. There are, however, plenty of rusty remains of the war to examine.

Abemama, 200 miles south of Tarawa, is an atoll offering more genuine island attractions. Robert Louis Stevenson appeared there aboard the *Equator* in 1889 and described his entering the lagoon, which was teeming with fish, and meeting the crafty ruler, Tembinok. Stevenson seemed more impressed with the autocratic, cruel Tembinok than the island itself, which he described as "lonely."

To Get There by Air

Air Pacific flies in every two weeks from Fiji to Tarawa. Air Tungaru, when they're flying, has a weekly service from Honolulu to Tarawa via Canton and Christmas Island.

Air Nauru flies in from Nauru.

By Sea

Check with the Port Captain in Suva, Fiji, and in Apia, Western Samoa. Some of the same ships that serve Tuvalu come to Betio on Tarawa.

Where to Stay

On Tarawa Island stay at the *Otintai Hotel* in the village of Bikibeu. It has a dining room-bar and overlooks the lagoon. Rates are $40 a double.

On Abemama Island stay at the *Robert Louis Stevenson Hotel.* It has a bar-restaurant and facilities for deep sea fishing, snorkeling, and diving. At the hotel they also put on traditional dancing, for which the Gilbertese are famous. About $35 double.

Time Zone

Time in Tuvalu and Kiribati is 12 hours ahead of Greenwich Mean Time, 17 hours ahead of Eastern Standard Time, and 20 hours ahead of Pacific Standard Time.

Newspapers, Radio and Telephone

Radio telephone calls may be made from Tuvalu and Kiribati during certain periods of the day. Check with your hotel for the hours. Radio broadcasts in English are received from Fiji. Overseas papers are flown in.

Power

220 volts AC.

Hundreds of other specialized travel guides and maps are available from Hunter Publishing. Among those that may interest you:

NEW CALEDONIA (all color)	128 pp.	$11.95
TAHITI & ITS ISLANDS (all color)	128 pp.	$12.95
*BALI (all color)	104 pp.	$10.95
MOBIL NEW ZEALAND TRAVEL GUIDES		
NORTH ISLAND	327 pp.	$14.95
SOUTH ISLAND	423 pp.	$14.95
A TRAMPER'S GUIDE TO NEW ZEALAND	243 pp.	$12.95
HILDEBRAND GUIDES (pocket sized, all color, fold-out map)		
AUSTRALIA	336 pp.	$10.95
INDONESIA	333 pp.	$10.95
NEW ZEALAND	192 pp.	$10.95
INSIDER'S GUIDES (larger format, all color, full-sized fold-out map)		
*AUSTRALIA	224 pp.	$12.95
*BALI	224 pp.	$12.95
*HAWAII	224 pp.	$12.95
HOW TO GET LOST & FOUND IN . . .		
TAHITI	264 pp.	$ 9.95
OUR HAWAII	296 pp.	$ 9.95
AUSTRALIA	320 pp.	$ 9.95
NEW ZEALAND	320 pp.	$ 9.95
THE COOK ISLANDS	224 pp.	$ 9.95

These can be found at the best bookstores or you can order directly. Send your check (add $2.50 to cover postage and handling) to:

HUNTER PUBLISHING, INC.
300 RARITAN CENTER PARKWAY
EDISON NJ 08818

Write (or call 201 225 1900) for our free color catalog describing these travel books and many more.

*These titles are available in the UK from Moorland Publishing Co., Ltd.